THE END OF THE CHURCH

THE END
of
THE CHURCH

A Pneumatology of
Christian Division in the West

Ephraim Radner

WILLIAM B. EERDMANS PUBLISHING COMPANY
GRAND RAPIDS, MICHIGAN / CAMBRIDGE, U.K.

© 1998 Wm. B. Eerdmans Publishing Co.
255 Jefferson Ave. S.E., Grand Rapids, Michigan 49503 /
P.O. Box 163, Cambridge CB3 9PU U.K.

Printed in the United States of America

03 02 01 00 99 98   7 6 5 4 3 2 1

Library of Congress Cataloging-in-Publication Data

Radner, Ephraim, 1956-
The end of the church:
A pneumatology of Christian division in the West / Ephraim Radner.
p.   cm.
Includes bibliographical references and index.
ISBN 0-8028-4461-8 (pbk.: alk. paper)
1. Church. 2. Holy Spirit. 3. Schism. 4. Repentance.
5. Catholic Church — Relations — Protestant churches.
6. Protestant churches — Relations — Catholic Church.
I. Title.
BV600.5.R33 1988
280′.042 — dc21   98-11281
                                   CIP

Contents

v

Preface

No one has asked for a book like this, a book devoted to limiting the claims of divided churches and to muting false clamors in celebration of the Holy Spirit that such claims continue to engender. The pinched condition of the mainline churches, not only in America, seeks self-assertion; the assertive character of Evangelicalism seeks, from others, acquiescence; the assaulted hegemony of Catholicism in so many places seeks solace and direction; and individuals are swept up by or wander amid the shifting strengths of these varied ecclesial impulses.

And they shall run their course, persons and impulses together. They shall run on, with or without books like this. May God, at least and in the meantime, grant us the grace, at some loose moment or another, to be still, to weep for the Church of Christ Jesus, to ask forgiveness, and to pray for those we do not yet love unto death.

My thanks, in writing this volume under trying circumstances, to my wife Annette above all; to R. R. Reno for continued comments and advice; to Louis Dupré for the witness of spiritual intelligence; and to my publisher, William B. Eerdmans, for embodied support.

Biblical references and citations are, unless noted, from the RSV. Cited translations from other works are mine, unless noted. Misstatements and errors of any kind are due to my own negligence and ignorance.

I dedicate this book to the Christians and people of Burundi and Rwanda, among whom I have lived and worked: may the Spirit of Christ one day and at last unveil its light for them and for us together.

The Week of Prayer for Christian Unity   EPHRAIM RADNER
January 1998

vi

Chapter One

Pneumatic Abandonment and the Dulling of the Senses: Scripture and the Divided Church

Describing the Divided Church:
The Nature of the Historical Problem in Christian Perspective

The general topic of this book is the manner in which the life of the Holy Spirit in the Church reduces itself to mortal repentance within a state of ecclesial division, such as we are in. Within the divided Church, the hearing of Scripture, pneumatic existence, the guidance of the ministry, the taste of communion, even the savor of penitence itself — all this is reduced to the insensible shell of ecclesial mortality, whose presentation on the stage of history, borne listlessly by time as in the image of our Savior's deposition from the Cross, itself provides, by grace, a vehicle of inspired penance. This is our topic, one that focuses on how division, a contingent reality, informs the very nature of "church" as the providential "body of Christ."

In general, this topic has received little attention, the origins and evolution of the Western ecclesial partitions having been subsumed into socio-historical explanations whose primacy has now overwhelmed the theological interests even of contemporary ecumenists and denominational apologists. The terms "protestant" and "catholic" now define either sociological phenomena or religious "styles" that, though they may provide some indirect theological directives, are themselves without much significance for unveiling the Christian

1

condition, let alone the Christian vocation. It may well seem that sidestepping — as we shall deliberately do here — the sociohistorical outlook on the Protestant-Catholic (or Protestant-Protestant) divisions carries with it some theological risks; for the linkage of historical contingencies within the life of the Church to the discernment of divine truths may seem to threaten the independence, and hence the seeming integrity, of the theological enterprise itself. Our chosen topic, however, assumes this risk, and in this opening chapter describes the extent of just what may be involved in asking the question of the divided Church's nature.

There is nothing particularly novel, of course, about linking church division, the mission of the Holy Spirit, and repentance. But if one were to argue, as we shall do, that, on the intellectual plane anyway, this linkage implies a reduction of pneumatology proper to the limited description of penitential reality, such a restrictive conclusion about one branch of theological endeavor might seem more than a little narrow. Further, if one were to consign *all* branches of theological endeavor, because of their intrinsic dependence on pneumatic direction, to such a penitential description, this might seem more absurd than narrow. And if, finally, one were to suggest that the very life of the Church, understood in its integrity, ought therefore to reflect the range of theology's pneumatic vocation, and thus must also be explicated according to the same narrow focus, that is, become the exhaustive subject of the penitential practice the reflective Christian mind discloses, absurdity might seem to give way to scandal. For how could we survive such a willful impoverishment of the living Gospel?

No doubt these implied reactions help to explain why it is that the original observation that would link together the Spirit's life, the Church's division, and the penitential calling has, for the most part, remained only an observation, noted ruefully perhaps, or expressed hortatively, but rarely explored fully to the distant extent of its reference. Were such a journey taken, one might well discover the voracious power of ingestion such a linkage wields with respect to the vast collection of Christian realities from which we forge our redeemed identities. Such voraciousness derives in part from the very character of repentance itself, which, if we presuppose its pertinence to the temporal phenomenon of Christian division as well as to the divine proddings of the Spirit, unveils an object of inquiry that has joined together inclusively the materials of experienced existence and the character and acts of an ordering God. In short, the examination of repentance, whether on an individual or on the communal level involved in any discussion of Christian division, implies the scrutiny of a providential history, whose descriptive limits depend only on the breadth or contraction of human capacity.

The theological and historical reach of repentance, in this regard, should not surprise us, and deserves a moment's reflection. In *general,* what are the theological implications of approaching some Christian reality penitentially? Historical research, in its secular and critical modes, has as one of its many ancillary goals the knowledge of self insofar as the self emerges from the past. Within the scriptural tradition, knowledge of self is also linked with the disclosing of a history, but usually with a particular and encompassing goal. We look at our pasts, in this scriptural context, with a view to clarifying the relation of a dependent self or people upon a magnificent and gloriously creative and purposeful God, whether that history be one of directive ordering and molding, as in the Pentateuch; or of judgment, as in the chronicled writings of the Prophets; or of redemption, as elsewhere in the Prophets; or of a combination of all of these, as in the Gospels. In each case, however, the knowledge of self that emerges from such "history" is one that humbles the proud and displays the glory of God, an outcome epitomized in the Psalms as a genre and demonstrative of the vast temporal insinuations of such articulations of repentance they provide: we are who we are because of what we have done as it stands in relation to what God has done and who he is in such doing. And so the truth of who God is, is captured clearly in this place wherein our penitence comes into being as a life accepted, and where the moments of the individual grow out of the times of the nation (cf. Psalm 106).

Ought one to go so far as to affirm that such "penitential history" is the very ground out of which all other aspects of Christian historical perspective arise? Whatever the case, the repentance that informs at least one broad area of Christian historical scrutiny must actually demand a descriptive hold upon the shape of God's own providential sway and upon the pneumatic character such a movement within time implies. For to repent we must somewhere ask and in some way determine how God disposes of our times; such that we might see that what we have done and who we have become can be named in conjunction with the sovereign will of God; such that what we have done and who we have become and what we might yet be are made possible by the grace of God's creation of this world where choices, conditions, and hopes are still subject to his reign. So, to speak of "repentance" and to speak of "Christian division" in tandem is, from the start, to imply a form a historical inquiry, and a very peculiar form at that. For the repentance to which Christian division may give rise will necessarily force the description of temporal experience, of events and thoughts, actions and choices; yet all the while, such a description will, in its very enunciation, seek to discern the shape and force of judgment and of mercy, by which the character of penitential knowing, the marks and notes of God's own Spirit in the Church of his Son, might assume its form.

Since the pneumatic history unveiled by such repentance is the subject of this volume, so will the shapes disclosed, in their insistent influence, inevitably seem, by turns, narrow, absurd, and scandalous to the degree, simply, that they remain the fruit of penitence itself. Among Christian inquirers such fruit offends because, at a radical level, the divisive tree from which it grows is itself a source of intractable disquiet. Here we must state baldly one of the realities any student of Christian division will confront *ab initio:* it is profoundly troubling to question the very shape of that ecclesial existence — a divided existence — out of which our questions arise in the first place, because such questions touch upon epistemologically and devotionally foundational realities. Early ecumenical pioneers discerned the offense of divisions, of course, but they also recognized the danger that the very depth of repugnance Christian division elicited for its own existence threatened the continued willingness Christians might have to confront its terror. In one of the most incisive descriptions of the condition and vocation of divided Christianity ever written, the Reformed theologian Jean-Jacques von Allmen noted in 1950 that there were at least three common temptations at work on those who at least recognized the "difficulty" posed by Christian division.[1] The first temptation leads to the conclusion that ecclesial unity is a kind of "edenic" state imaged in the first apostolic community, but abandoned almost just as quickly as the Church began to engage in the struggles, and compromises, of the real world. Such a vision of ecclesial "falling" from

1. Jean-Jacques von Allmen, "Pour une restauration de l'unité chrétienne," in *Verbum Caro* 4:13-16 (1950): pp. 49-73. This article, as fresh as when it was first written, and as challenging, could appropriately stand as a manifesto for ecumenical endeavor, and at least the motives and goals expressed were not uncommon among the ecumenical leaders of von Allmen's generation. The article itself, however, was written in response to already developing trends in the fields of ecumenical and ecclesiological theology, trends that have since come to dominate reflection in these areas. The notions that "visible, organic unity" was in fact a New Testament reality and normative bequest, that the divisions of the sixteenth-century Western church are *not* analogous to previous heretical movements and schisms but represent instead a true and established "dismemberment" of the Church, and that, therefore, the post-Reformation Church lies in distinct ecclesial *dis*continuity with the pre-Reformation Church, that the ecclesiological *character* of the modern Western Church (and those non-Western churches that derive from their mission) stands in a pneumatic contrast of some kind to both the New Testament and pre-Reformation Church, and that, finally, the historical parsing of these comparative conditions is one that requires the full application of forms of scriptural discernment, judgment, and prophecy — all these fundamental theses, which were also (however unarticulated) presuppositions of many leaders of the early ecumenical movement, have largely been abandoned by contemporary theologians, church leaders, and even ecumenical apologists and strategists, who have reverted to a description of the Church's historical experience that does not include the death of self as an act of God in the spaces of time.

4

visible catholicity may lead to a second temptation, which is to view the fulfillment of Christian unity as something to be accomplished by God's grace at the end times, when "all" things are restored — a view von Allman labels as a form of "ecclesiological docetism" that defers the Christian life in community to a kind of "faith" without "vision" that determines even the practice of love. Finally, and where both these two first temptations lead in terms of attitude, there is the sense of "fatalism" that simply recognizes the intractability of our present Christian distinctions and differences, leaving their ultimate sense to God's inscrutable working. And all of these temptations, of course, represent particular readings of the shape of the Church's historical experience, and of the way historical experience, in Christian terms and *in se,* must be read. But read, deliberatively, so as to obscure another possibly more real set of circumstances that describe the very nature of the Christian life as God's own being shapes it. For, in von Allmen's judgment, the "real" history of the Church in division is a history of "death"; a death, first, that is required as the outcome of the conscious dismemberment of the Church, and a death that is already assumed by the redeeming form of God's love taken flesh in Christ. Or, put in terms of the Church's integrated destiny, the real "history" of the Church — its *"opus proprium"* — as it takes form within the providence of God, is the history of "repentance," by which churches, "confessions," and denominations "die" to the "death of disunity" by "dying" to themselves, thereby living into the life-giving, uniting death of their Lord and his apostolic missionaries.[2]

---

2. Cf. von Allmen, pp. 72f.: "The confessions [i.e., denominations] will perhaps respond that they are very much interested in unity, and that they sincerely desire it, and that they are even ready to devote a portion of their resources, that is, of their money, to this end; but that it is out of the question that one expect them to engage in a self-renunciation, a full gift of the self, in order to restore unity. The search for unity, in effect, is really the work of their left hand; it cannot be allowed to compromise their *opus proprium,* their essential mission, which is evangelism, or prophetic ministry to the world, or intercession, or adoration, or exegesis, or ethics. Now if [denominations] were tempted to respond in this way to their vocation for, and duty to, unity, they should remember that Jesus, at Gethsemane, could well have fled the Cross in order to pursue his ministry as prophet and wonder-worker. He did not do this, because his *opus proprium* was to die for unity, 'in order to gather together into one body all of God's scattered children' (John 11:52; cf. Eph. 2:14-16). They should remember too how Paul, for whom missionary projects were so plentiful, might well have fled to Miletus, to Tyre, to Caesarea (cf. Acts 20:22–21:14 — note the parallel here between the apostle's life and the triple announcement of Jesus' death as he goes up to Jerusalem, or to the triple prayer at Gethsemane), and how he might not have gone up to Jerusalem, carrying the collection, the 'riches of the nations' (cf. Is. 60 and Rev. 21:26, and how the apostle's life stands in parallel with the account of the Palms), but might instead have gone off to Rome and then Spain, in order there to pass through

Contemporary ecumenical theology has, in fact, avoided the question of the potential sins or "deficiencies" or even "mortal wounds" of divided churches, a subject that had been popular fodder for post-Reformation controversy (if always directed only at the opponent). Modern ecumenical discussion has rather focused on the charitable discernment of positive commonalities among churches, and has sought ways to promote the mutual "recognition" of integrity within divided bodies. This method has been premised on the notion that visible reconciliation largely provides a symbolic stamp to an already existent, though ideal, unity, or at least to a unity whose fullness cannot be expected in this world and whose reality, therefore, lies present in some "proleptic" and/or symbolic expression. Such a premise, deriving at least from seventeenth-century, and later from nineteenth-century, conceptions of limited Protestant reunion,[3] has thrived within a context for which the kinds of "deaths" von Allmen discerned have been expunged from history.

Whether a nonpenitential history of the Church must prove incapable of addressing more basic Protestant-Catholic-Orthodox divisions, as well as the larger twentieth-century fragmentation of the international Church, is a question the present book will address. But there is no doubt that such a penitential history is a different *kind* of history from one from which the whole category of ecclesial sin, deficiency, or death has generally disappeared, replaced by socio-historical analyses of Western Christendom's evolution into ecclesial "diversity." Such analyses, especially when pursued by confessionally committed scholars, are not, of course, without pneumatological implications, which reflect an awareness and appreciation of the possibly "providential" character of, say, the sixteenth century. They may even go so far as to claim as the outcome of sixteenth-century division of the Church certain currents of social or intellectual or even theological development whose positive character implies the blessing of a benevolent orderer. But to the degree that they are not penitential histories, their theological repudiation of repentance merges easily with the commitment to canons of critical exactitude and detail whose data are, in themselves, mercifully independent of any demand that they be

---

in preaching the Kingdom. He did not do this, because his *opus proprium* was one of self-renunciation for the sake of the abiding unity of the Church, of which the collection he carried was the symbolic guarantee. So it was, in effect, for the unity of the Church rather than for the evangelization of the pagans that St. Paul died. And if the Christ and the apostle to the Gentiles accepted the abrupt ending of their lives for the founding and the manifesting of Christian unity, it ought to be possible to ask as much from church denominations."

3. Notice of proponents of these views, like the seventeenth-century Congregationalist John Owen and the nineteenth-century American Reformed theologian Charles Hodge, will be made later in this volume.

treated as the necessary signs of God's disposition of his Church.[4] If "modernity" represents something problematic to such historians, especially in the realm of religion, the problems are ones to be treated in terms of an adjustment to historical detail exterior to the actual character of the inhabited realm of a pneumatic or providential existence that might otherwise depict the present as more than the past's victim, but as its legitimately condemned coconspirator.

A penitential history, of the sixteenth-century divisions of the Western

4. The relation between the "confessional" history and the "critical" history of the Western Church's divisions will be discussed in Chapters 2 and 5 below. In general, "confessional" histories have tended to be self-justifying with respect to the separation of one Christian group from another. The elaboration of the critical apparatus used to study history was initially harnessed to such self-justifying schemes, and only later became useful to those who were set on rising above the spectacle of religious conflict and who used "critical" history as a tool to neutralize the competing claims of divided Christianity. The point here is that the "critical" character of historical study, as growing out of and as applied to the sixteenth-century divisions of the Church, has never been embodied as a "neutral" method with respect to the discernment of *providential* reality. The modern apogee of Protestant self-justificatory history is surely Hegel's analysis of the Reformation in his *Phenomenology of History* (IV:3) and elsewhere, a discussion replete with incisive critical observations that remain valid for many working historians today, but that are used to explicate a providential movement in time wherein the triumph of bourgeois "freedom" is given definitive expression in the emergence of German Protestantism. While writers like Voltaire and Condorcet are rarely ranked highly in their "critical" historical skills, only a little earlier than Hegel they nonetheless attempted a contrastive argument *against* the sixteenth century as a whole, on the basis of this defense of "enlightened" religious tolerance. In our own day, these kinds of differences recur among historians, whose objects range from social to cultural to intellectual products of the sixteenth century. There are those (e.g., Ozment) whose careful examination of quotidian detail still reveals an almost Hegelian vision of radical (and generally positive) novelty at work in the rise and expansion of Protestantism; or whose tracings of social organization and thought attribute contrary outcomes to the Protestant heritage (e.g., Horkheimer); or whose cautious sifting of intellectual strands from the late medieval period on (e.g., Oberman and McGrath) nevertheless discover in a Luther or a Calvin an epitomic evangelical insight whose normative validity, despite the relativizations of historical complexity and diversity, provides a definitive standard by which to judge modern Christianity; or whose attempt at deciphering popular devotion and attitude through the statistical study of local data or of alternative media (e.g., Febvre, Delumeau, or Thomas) uncovers in the sixteenth century a drastic unleashing of a noninstitutional religious piety through the demise of monolithic church regimentation, whose diversity and malleability both opened modernity onto its semi-pagan past and allowed for its organization into a semi-Christian civil religion, whose liberal tolerance can be variously judged. Finally, one might mention those especially intellectual historians whose reaction against the bequest of the post-Reformation's seventeenth- and eighteenth-century attitudes posits a culture-shattering "wrong turn" in modernity's development that, by implication, maintains the sixteenth century as a kind of prelapsarian norm, in general continuity with its ancestors on at least the major scores of epistemology, ethics, and hermeneutics (e.g., MacIntyre, Frei, Gunton, Newbigin, and other recent orthodox apologists).

Church as much as of anything, is in any case less a critical analysis of some set of ecclesial data than it is a kind of "theory" about the shape of the data itself, in both the scientific and the spiritual senses of the term. It is a kind of scientific theory in that it attempts to account for experienced data in its present order, to predict the ordering of future phenomena under defined conditions, and to incorporate the plausible details of alternate theories. A penitential history does this when it draws into some kind of general coherence, bounded by what can be known of God's truth, the ecclesial phenomena of past, present, and future as they pertain to faithfulness and unfaithfulness, and examines how this coherence reveals the humiliation of pride in the face of God's love and glory, even given, and precisely because there are given, the subterfuges provided by manifold Christian claims to the contrary. Penitential history is also a spiritual "theory" — according to the patristic usage of *theoria* — insofar as it is an act of "discernment" into the pneumatic character of God's design, through which the shape of the world, the form of our actions, and the order of our destiny cohere in the unveiling of divine truth. That is, as a theory, penitential history is also an experienced discipline, whose exact contours are neither defined in advance nor precise in their articulation, because they are granted by the grace of God whose condescension in the Word and (sometimes paradoxical) direction by the Spirit determine both the progress and the object of the history's practice.

In the penitential history of Christian division that follows, then, a peculiar relation to critical history and its responsible standards will obtain. As a theory about a specific historical experience and about how that experience might best be described in terms of the Christian destiny, this study will confine itself only to certain limited historical details, whose explication is designed to be experientially tested. And these details are those that pertain to particular Christian judgments about events, for example, faithfulness, epiphanic vigor, holiness, theological enunciation, whose character derives from the shape of God's own purposes for the Christian Church. For this reason, the historical elements that we will examine appear as broad theological and devotional trends, rather than as details of specific episodes, the latter of which ought, in some future investigations, to be used as tests for the theory itself. In place of such necessary testing, we will, as an ad hoc expedient, use observations of contemporary ecumenical practice as evidences confirming the trends that we will identify. This ecumenical practice, which adopts a prima facie favorable attitude toward the overcoming of the sixteenth-century divisions, might reasonably be expected to have escaped the fundamental deformities of division's violence, unless of course such violence, as the trends identified will indicate, has engulfed even the best intentions of the imperfectly penitent.

As a result of this approach, however, careful readers of our study will probably confront a number of obstacles. It is likely, for instance, that many of the particulars that are examined here will stand, as interpreted, in some tension, or even in seeming contradiction to the variety of critical-historical judgments scholars have properly and rightfully amassed over the past centuries with respect to aspects of sixteenth- and seventeenth-century Christian life and thought. The question the reader must ask, in this case, is how these particulars might fit into alternative theories that have as their object the discernment of God's phenomenal ordering of events in the context of ecclesial sin. A penitential history, after all, posits such an ordering and such a shaping of events that must claim a perspectival privilege of interpreted significance over other possible meanings for phenomena that are construed independently of its object. Because a penitential history talks about the Church in its full theological substance, and thus of the Church's "time" as a divinely constricted time, the phenomena of its study are given over to a privileged sphere of interpretation that must, inevitably, appear odd to the critical historian. For such a penitential history cannot *explain* the larger cultural phenomena in relation to which the Church stands — for example, the rise of atheism or secularism or civil religion or the trajectories of modern Western philosophy; it can only explain why these phenomena, when viewed as religious "problems," have no effective solution within the Church as it is given over to the suffering of its penance. Even misdescriptions of these problems, which no doubt appear in what follows, do not necessarily undermine the "theory" of the history itself, as long as their more accurately designated shape still falls within the order of the Church's penitential suffering.

It is likely, too, that an ecclesially devoted reader may wonder how it is that such a history seems so reticent about, indeed eschews, the articulation of a strategy for the renovation of the present Church in its divisions, some road by which the pneumatic life of the Christian community in the West can be reinvigorated. But a penitential history, in its theoretical aspect, is not a strategy but a discerned description, a kind of wisdom drawn from the discipline of a purgative contemplation — unless tears and restitution be a strategy for future building. In any case, with respect to Christian division itself, ecumenical programs already in place or already being put together have their own compulsions and impetus, and most are ordered to the realities of political change and engagement in such a way as to deserve, in the present context anyway, a genuine deference. To be sure, the character of the ecumenical judgment that a penitential history such as the present one will provide may well raise the issue of whether the theory's critical tools have anything to contribute to an assessment of current ecumenical programs or, more likely,

9

to an evaluation of the relationship that may exist between such programs and the congregational life of the churches that remain mired in divisional attitudes. But, despite the critical attitude taken by this book toward the logic of much contemporary ecumenical discussion, we should harbor no illusions that such discussions could be anything other than they are, and we should not hesitate to affirm that the noble and courageous intentions that inform them are, in themselves, flames of grace to be cherished and fanned. Even here, however, we must perhaps be willing to allow the failure of their light.

And even if this seems clear, the wider-visioned ecumenical reader will rightly question whether a penitential history of division that is not somehow essentially attached to the reality of the Eastern-Western schism can have theoretical integrity at all. To which one must reply that the theory's validity will indeed be given some measure of confirmation to the degree that its application to the larger schism is coherent, even granting to the two a different initial character and propagation. But that application need not first be carried out in order to observe the general lines of providential ordering that the Western divisions manifest. The more limited regional scope of the latter may actually offer a more useful arena in which to pry and to wonder.

More than anything else, however, the reader may take pause before the actual historical judgments that this penitential theory offers, shying away, when all is said and done, from two in particular, whose affirmation has in the past been acceptable only as these judgments are kept separate one from another: the judgment, first, that the Holy Spirit has taken leave of the divided Church, and, second, that we must yet stay loyal to the Church's empty precincts. "The glory of the LORD went up from the midst of the city" (Ezekiel 11:23), yet "her servants love her very rubble and are moved to pity even for her dust" (Psalm 102:14). These are historical affirmations, to be sure; though to grasp them willfully is itself a gift we must be patient in obtaining. Let the reader only stand respectfully before the question of God's will and grace, God's justice and mercy, in the face of those followers of his Anointed who pray separated from each other, and the obstacles that arise will appear less onerous than the weight of staring at this vision.

The Reformation Crisis: Scriptural Perspicuity and the Church

What then has Christian division wrought? Among the different answers that can be given to this question, a penitential history will demand that at least the shape of the Church's heart be laid bare in any useful response. How does the Church now think? How does it act? What are its intentions and its dispositions that flow from its condition, however we evaluate its central character? Let us begin on the ground of the Reformation's own asserted gifts, the recovery of Holy Scripture. We shall then see where this leads, but at least we are assured of moving from the center of a real concern, not a fabricated anachronism. And what then is the relation between Word and rending? How well does the Church, figured as the many churches, now *hear?*

The question has not escaped secular historians of intellectual culture. To take one example, Richard Popkin has, over the past few decades, forcefully explored the role of the Reformation division of the Church in instigating a range of theological and philosophical responses to the epistemological question of criteria that lie behind so much of modern Western philosophy.[5] Specifically, Popkin has argued that the burning problem of how Scripture ought to be interpreted in a divided Church helped to ignite a skeptical crisis regarding the source and context for our knowledge in general that has remained with us since the sixteenth century. With the Reformers' denial of the authority of the institutional Church in defining the right interpretation of Scripture in favor of various forms of individual pneumatic illumination, Protestants and Catholics were set against each other in a dizzying and always fruitless effort to justify their canons of interpretive criteria. One of the few ways of escaping this impossible argument lay in the adoption of now exposed skeptical postures toward the possibility of justified criteria at all. In the wake of the Reformation, the Christian claim to scriptural authority lay seemingly

---

5. Cf. Richard H. Popkin's now classic *The History of Scepticism from Erasmus to Spinoza* (Berkeley: University of California Press, 1979), ch. 1. See also "The Role of Scepticism in Modern Philosophy Reconsidered," in *Journal of the History of Philosophy* 31 (Oct. 1993): pp. 501-17. Cf. the adapted theory, though with less appreciation for the specifically religious issues involved, but with greater emphasis on the social dislocations brought on by the violence of religious division, in the broad argument of Stephen Toulmin, *Cosmopolis: The Hidden Agenda of Modernity* (Chicago: University of Chicago Press, 1990), esp. pp. 45ff. and 71ff. For a very different sociological confirmation of much that follows in this, as in other chapters, on authority and institutions, as well as on the "secularization" of religious practice and knowledge, in the wake of and genetically dependent upon the Reformation division of the Western Church, see Steve Bruce, *A House Divided: Protestantism, Schism, and Secularization* (London/New York: Routledge, 1990). Bruce's book, which uses some particular case studies from Scotland and Ireland, among others, offers good evidence that a penitential history's conclusions concerning divided Christianity, for all of their express religious categories, need not suffer implausibility in comparison with nonreligious critical analyses. His thesis can be seen as an unintended sociological extension of the seventeenth-century theological-historical argument of Bossuet, who saw the "variety" of Protestantism as a providential sign of its error — a perspective that worked out of just the concerns Popkin identifies in the wake of the sixteenth-century disintegration of Catholic unity.

mortally assailed, and along with it the claim to scriptural integrity and meaning.

From the perspective of history, I think Popkin's thesis is unassailable, and the confirming of this history can await the exposition of material to follow in not just this, but subsequent, chapters. All we need to do here is to remind ourselves of at least two of the well-known series of theological oppositions that have been drawn on by the evolving fractured Church on the matters, first, of Scripture's perspicuity, and second, of the authorizing locus of scriptural interpretation.

With respect to perspicuity, Popkin uses the Luther-Erasmus debate over free will as the foundational exposition of the skeptical crisis over Scripture that would fuel the exhausting quest of modern philosophy.[6] While Luther's own mature understanding of the relation of Scripture to Church is perhaps misleadingly gleaned from this encounter, the contrast between him and Erasmus nonetheless accurately establishes the developed polemical set of the post-Reformation controversy over Scripture between Protestant and Catholic. The positions therefore deserve to be restated.

Erasmus prefaces his argument with some straightforward affirmations: first, the Scriptures are filled with obscurities that are not designed by God to be uniformly clarified; if this were otherwise, people would not be arguing over such texts; second, whatever is necessary for a Christian life is made clear enough in Scripture, and all the rest is not worth fighting over; third, it is best to maintain a skeptical attitude toward controverted (and ancillary) points in Scripture; finally, though one can never be sure in such matters, if one is going to believe anybody's interpretation of these obscure passages, one ought to follow the official teachings of the Church, since this, at least, furthers peace and harmony.[7]

Luther responds by laying out what will become the classical parameters of the Protestant dogma of Scripture's perspicuity. Christians are not skeptics, he argues, and with regard to matters concerning God and God's will, only the "assertion" of "certainties" will do, "for what is more miserable than uncertainty"?[8] And Scripture itself is perfectly clear as regards its "subject

---

6. Erasmus, "De Libero Arbitrio," and Luther, "De Servo Arbitrio." A convenient edition of the two works is contained in E. Gordon Rupp and Philip S. Watson, eds., *Luther and Erasmus: Free Will and Salvation* (Philadelphia: The Westminster Press, 1969).

7. Rupp and Watson, pp. 38-47.

8. Rupp and Watson, pp. 105ff. For Luther's demand for absolute epistemological certitude in questions of hermeneutics — which was something of a novelty — see Marjorie O'Rourke Boyle, "The Chimera and the Spirit: Luther's Grammar of the Will," in Gerhard Dünnhaupt, ed. *The Martin Luther Quincentennial* (Detroit: Wayne State University Press for *Michigan Germanic Studies,* 1985), pp. 17-31.

matter," namely Christ and the truths associated with him (e.g., the Incarnation, the Trinity, and Redemption). "Are not these things known and sung even in the highways and byways?" If there are minor obscurities, they are due to purely linguistic ambiguities, and are negligible. If there are *disagreements* among people regarding the truths taught in Scripture, however, these are due not to Scripture's intrinsic obscurity, but to the spiritual blindness of the ungodly. "Let miserable men, therefore, stop imputing with blasphemous perversity the darkness and obscurity of their own hearts to the wholly clear Scriptures of God."[9]

Second, it was Luther who firmly set the authority residing in an intrinsically perspicuous Scripture rightly apprehended by the individual over and against the authority of the Church's official teaching offices. Luther argued robustly for the evident failures of the Church's leadership over time, to the point where he could boldly wonder, "What are we to do? The Church is hidden, the saints are unknown. What and whom are we to believe? . . . or who gives us certainty?"[10] If it is certainty we want — and we must in matters that touch our salvation — then only the Scriptures can provide it, and they do so efficaciously. In themselves, of course, the Scriptures are utterly clear and plain in their meaning, so that, "if Satan were not at work, the whole world of men would be converted by a single word of God once heard, and there would be no need of more." But to have a people freed from Satan to apprehend Scripture's intrinsic clarity, the Holy Spirit must provide them a special gift of "enlightenment."[11]

As is well known, of course, Luther did not mean somehow to subjectivize the interpretation of Scripture. Especially as he developed his expressions in the ongoing debate with the Anabaptists and "enthusiasts," he came to stress more clearly the pneumatic character of the Word as given through the "means" not only of Scripture's language, but of Scripture's public exposition, through

---

9. Rupp and Watson, p. 111.

10. Rupp and Watson, p. 158. This becomes a standard Protestant platform of attack against the Catholics: how can we be sure who are the saints and what constitutes the true Church over time and space? Since we cannot — that is, since the true Church is, on the basis of historical incertitude regarding its visible integrity, invisible — we must rely on the direct and concrete interpretive action of pneumatically assisted *individuals,* divorced from the fog of time. This is an attack on the knowledge conferred by a (providential) historical experience. See William Whitaker, *A Disputation on Holy Scripture Against the Papists, Especially Bellarmine and Stapleton* [1588], trans. and ed. W. Fitzgerald (Cambridge: The University Press for The Parker Society, 1849), pp. 403, 414, 448f, 455. The obscurity of holiness as a Protestant axiom, and its relation to scriptural interpretation, will be discussed at length below in Chapter 2.

11. Rupp and Watson, p. 167.

THE END OF THE CHURCH

the formal ministry of preaching, which clearly involves a range of external *communal* restraints.[12] Still, as modern Lutheran theologians have been careful to elaborate, this "exterior means" by which the Word speaks in Scripture has more to do with an event of existential presence than of historical tradition. With the theory of Scripture's perspicuous meaning effected through the Spirit's anointing in the Christian believer, Luther had — in theory, if not in practice — cleanly disposed of the historical teaching tradition of the Church as an authoritative guide.[13]

12. Cf. the famous text in the "Smalcald Articles," 3.8.3.

13. "All the fathers who interpret Scripture in their own way are refuted, and their interpretation is invalidated. It is forbidden to rely on such interpretation. If Jerome or Augustine or any one of the fathers has given his own interpretation, we want none of it. . . . The Holy Spirit Himself must expound Scripture." (Luther's "Commentary on 2 Peter 1:21," in *Luther's Works*, ed. Jaroslav Pelikan and Walter Hansen [St. Louis: Concordia Publishing House, 1967], vol. 30, p. 166.) Obviously, the promotion of teaching guides like the Smaller and Larger Catechisms, not to mention other authoritative documents, shifts the emphasis away from such sweeping disavowals of tradition and has given rise to a firm Protestant upholding of the *regula fidei* as a grid for scriptural exegesis. Further, as is well known, Luther's own attitude to, for instance, the "tradition" of the Fathers was subject to nuance and development. Still, the theory for such disavowals is firmly in place, and the direction Luther himself takes it, as well as the direction taken by his followers, conforms to the crude pneumatological distinction outlined above. (Cf. the clear exposition of the pneumatological issue in Luther given by John M. Headley in his "The Reformation as Crisis in the Understanding of Tradition," *Archiv für Reformationsgeschichte* 78 [1987]: pp. 5-22; also his earlier *Luther's View of Church History* [New Haven: Yale University Press, 1963], ch. 2 esp.) And despite the fact that there was a diversity of opinion and practice with respect to the authority of ecclesial "tradition" and the Fathers, for instance, among Lutheran and other Reformed theologians (cf. Alister McGrath's *The Intellectual Origins of the European Reformation* [Oxford: Basil Blackwell, 1987], chs. 5 and 7), the logical outcome of the initial set of the early-sixteenth-century debate was generally accepted, on the Protestant side, as being consistent with the thoroughgoing relativizing of ecclesial tradition, epitomized in Jean Daillé's 1631 *Du Vrai Emploi des Pères* (available in an 1841 edited version of the seventeenth-century English translation as *A Treatise on the Right Use of the Fathers in the Decision of Controversies Existing at This Day in Religion* [London: William White]). Daillé's popular work was an open repudiation of patristic authority on the basis of a primitive, but relentless, form of historical-critical skepticism: we cannot know what the Fathers really believed, and what they believed was so diverse and messy that "certainty" over their opinions could not possibly provide a basis for "certain" authority, even if one wished to grant them such a status (which one should not and which, given the perspicacity of Scripture, is in any case unnecessary). Daillé's clear exposition of this position, in fact, aided the formation of an articulated "antiquarian" reaction on the part of certain Anglican theologians (e.g., Pearson and Beveridge); but the reaction constituted a logical novelty within, not an evolution of, reformed thinking, which (as nineteenth-century events in Anglicanism proved) could not be easily sustained. The original Lutheran affirmation, then, will hold sway in post-Reformation Protestant generalizing about the relation of Scripture and ecclesial magisterium.

When, a generation later, another celebrated controversy took place, this time between John Calvin and the Catholic bishop Jacopo Sadoleto, who had addressed a letter to the Genevan citizenry appealing for their return to the Roman Church, the terms of the debate had solidified into a more dogmatic form, without, however, changing much of the substance.[14] Sadoleto had firmed up Erasmus's tepid skepticism with a strong argument for the divinely authoritative character of the undivided Catholic Church, defined according to the Vincentian canon — *quod ubique, quod semper, quod ab omnibus creditum est* — as the interpretive locus of Scripture. The Church "brought" the Gospel of salvation to the world and suffered for it, and the Church's common faith is now the standard by which the Gospel has any saving significance.[15] But what if the Church is unfaithful? Calvin, pressing for a more concrete ecclesiology than the early Luther, answered Sadoleto with a redefinition of the Church, now seen as a body of faithful people bound by a true scriptural doctrine, that is, as a community subjected, by the Spirit, to the Word of Scripture understood in a uniform manner.[16] But who decides what is the proper exposition of Scripture's Word? What is important to note here is how, on the basis of an argument over the interpretation of Scripture, the issue had been quickly recast into the question, "Where is the true Church?" Each side sought to found its positions on a criterion internal to its own argument: we know the true meaning of Scripture from Scripture itself, or we know that our interpretation of Scripture is Spirit-taught from the Spirit's own testimony; or we know the Church's authority over Scripture's interpretation from the Church itself or from our need for such an authority. (That the articulated argument over the "true church" arose within the context of a debate about Scripture in particular does not, however, define the causal relationship between these two issues, something that we will attempt to explore further.)

That two portions of a divided Church could never, in the face of their critics or antagonists, persuasively extricate themselves from the circularity of their criteriology was a realization quickly made by both controversialists and religious scoffers. As Popkin has shown, the very project of Christian arguing against separated Christian almost inevitably became enmeshed in methods of discourse that, all sides agreed, reeked of skepticism, but which no one was

---

14. See "Letter by Cardinal Sadoleto to the Senate and People of Geneva" and Calvin's "Reply to Cardinal Sadoleto's Letter" in John Calvin, *Tracts and Treatises on the Reformation of the Church,* trans. Henry Beveridge, intro. and notes by T. F. Torrance (Grand Rapids: Wm. B. Eerdmans, 1958), vol. 1.

15. Calvin, "Reply to Cardinal Sadoleto's Letter," *Tracts and Treatises,* p. 10.

16. Calvin, "Reply to Cardinal Sadoleto's Letter," *Tracts and Treatises,* pp. 36ff.

willing to forgo as long as it was aimed at the opposition. The most celebrated example of this development is the early seventeenth-century French Jesuit François Veron, whose success at debating his Reformed brethren gained him widespread publication and translation.[17] Veron's most famous "method" (he had many) involved the logical and practical demonstration that no Protestant actually read Scripture without applying to the words *ab initio* some interpretive frame of conceptualization. Even the bare Protestant effort to derive the meaning of biblical texts only from other biblical texts — interpreting "Scripture by Scripture" — demanded the application of a complex system of inductive and deductive logic that is by no means envisioned or implied by Scripture itself, and is rather a cultural construct imported to the text by the reader. This seemingly postmodern axiom Veron insisted upon for all readers of Scripture, and the issue for him lay in exposing the challenge that *any* Christian must face in finding a trustworthy communal context for interpretation.[18]

While Veron himself was aware that simply exposing the challenge did nothing to resolve it — he brought to bear other arguments to show the Roman Church's superior interpretive credibility[19] — this kind of approach tended to foster a relativistic assessment concerning the authority of *all* religious communities, let alone of individuals. For some, this situation only besmeared the force of Christian religion and its Gospel into weakened unrecognizability, while for others, still driven by a religious conscience, it gave rise to agonies of bewilderment. John Donne, like many others of the

17. See Popkin, ch. 4, pp. 66ff.

18. Cf. Veron's own epitome of his extended "methods," in his *Abregé des Methodes de Traicter des Controverses de Religion. Enseignées et prattiquées par S. Augustin & les autres SS. Peres; Reduites en art & preceptes* (Paris: Louys Boulanger, 1630), pp. 1-48. Veron himself insists that this method cannot be turned on the Roman Church, since they have never made the claims of Protestants as to the authority of *sola scriptura* divorced from the historical "tradition, authority of the Church, antiquity, miracles, etc." (p. 48). But, as he knew well, the possibility of being roasted on one's own fire was not so easily brushed aside — why is the Roman tradition of interpretation more authoritative than the Reformed? — and Veron elaborated at great length an alternative "method" of disputing Protestants on the exact basis of *sola scriptura!* On other Roman Catholic attempts at meeting Protestant attacks on the same playing field of the "sole" and "literal" Word of God, cf. Georges Tavard, *La Tradition au XVIIe Siècle en France et en Angleterre* (Paris: Les Éditions du Cerf, 1969), esp. pp. 325ff.

19. Cf. Veron, pp. 49-59, where Veron describes one of his "positive" methods for upholding the Roman Church's claims to interpretive authority, the method of "conjunction," by which Scripture, patristic exposition, conciliar decision, and the present teaching of the Church are shown to be mutually consistent. The criterion of "continuity" in teaching was obviously not self-evident, but Veron felt that Protestants at least bore the onus of disproving its weight given the initiative they took in breaking that continuity.

post-Reformation era, ran the gamut. He was able at once to counsel bemusedly the prospective Christian convert to "doubt wisely" in the face of five major Christian denominations in competition for his soul ("Third Satyre") and to lament wrenchingly "Shee, shee's dead; shee's dead" when taking note of the Church's general healing mission within a broken world all "out of joynt" ("First Anniversary").

If Popkin is right about the ongoing and unresolved character of the Reformation "crisis" over scriptural interpretation brought on by the divided Church, then contemporary manifestations of the same set of dilemmas should not surprise us. And, in fact, one of the more publicized recent debates over these matters took place, not unexpectedly, in the very context of the discussion over the reunion of Protestant and Roman Catholic churches. Shortly before his death in 1984, Karl Rahner, along with Heinrich Fries, made a proposal for "uniting" the separated churches into a federation of independent bodies that would mutually recognize each other, look to the "Petrine office" as some kind of "guarantor of the unity of the Church in truth and love," and eventually follow a broadly common form of ordination.[20] The main justification for conceiving such an arrangement as possible even now lay in the authors' conviction that "the fundamental truths of Christianity," expressed in Scripture and the Creeds, were accepted by most major denominations. "Beyond that," as Thesis II of the proposal affirmed, "a realistic principle of faith should apply," that would oblige each "partner" church neither to reject a "dogma" of another nor to impose their "dogma" on another.

It was Rahner's commentary on Thesis II that caused the most controversy. For in it, Rahner outlined a historical theory of knowledge that painted the modern era (implicitly identified with the post-Reformation) as one of increasingly fractured and multiplied fields of knowing, which, in their sheer number, now preclude any individual or group from being able to absorb the information necessary to form a "synthesis" of the material at issue. In short, we simply cannot "know" what is what, let alone what another person or group truly thinks is the case; we cannot understand each other, let alone the world, in any common or full sense. Rahner thinks this is a peculiarly pressing problem derived from modernity's pluralistic explosion of information. And given this "intellectual-political situation," Rahner argues that Christians should engage in a form of "epistemetological tolerance," which works on the basis of certain accepted fundamentals (i.e., the Creeds and some

---

20. Heinrich Fries and Karl Rahner, *Unity of the Churches: An Actual Possibility* (1983), trans. Ruth C. L. Gritsch and Eric W. Gritsch (Philadelphia: Fortress Press and New York: Paulist Press, 1985).

"minimal" common structures of practice), and which lets all other issues "slide" in the face of the Gospel promise of an eschatological unity of knowledge (this being the only kind we can ever expect).[21]

No less than in the seventeenth century, this kind of reasoning, now at the service of unity, gave immediate rise to charges of "skepticism." And those, from both the Protestant and Roman Catholic sides, who viewed the issue of truth as somehow distinct from the issue of the unity of churches — however much they may have been supportive of ecumenical movement toward future unity — denounced the Rahner-Fries proposal just at this point.[22] This, of course, is the question that the historical demonstration of the Popkin thesis thrusts upon us: is it possible to speak of the Gospel's truth apart from the actual unity of the Church itself? Does the truth of the Gospel become obscured outside of the unity of the Church? The question, posed this way, is obviously fraught with enormous implications, and not only for those who make the study of the truth their business — including scholarly enterprises like scriptural studies and theology. The question clearly touches on the very nature of the Gospel and of the Church that proclaims it. It may be possible, on an abstract level, to construe the arguments of the Protestant-Catholic split over Scripture and the Church in terms of a "dialectic," as a biblical theologian like Brevard Childs himself has done.[23] But such a dialectic

21. "The basic thesis is: in today's intellectual-political situation, no greater unity of faith is possible than the one proposed, and therefore it must be legitimate if the unity of the churches in faith is not to be abandoned despite all solemn declarations to the contrary. . . . In the light of a pluralism of thinking which can in no way be integrated into a higher synthesis, it would be totally unrealistic — at least at present and in future — to demand a larger and more tangible unity of faith" (Fries and Rahner, pp. 39-41).

22. Cf. Cardinal Joseph Ratzinger's discussion of this matter in the "Postscript" to his reprinted interview "Luther and the Unity of the Churches," in his anthology *Church, Ecumenism and Politics: New Essays in Ecclesiology* (New York: Crossroad, 1988), pp. 122-34: "If this [i.e., Rahner's assessment in Thesis ll] is how things are, if in the general fog nobody can see the other and no one sees the truth, then the 'epistemological tolerance' is displayed by the fact that no one contradicts anyone any more. The only thing that is clearly visible in the darkness of the tendencies of our civilization to diminish differences is Christ's command of unity which then becomes fundamentally the only at all clear component. The 'authorities' are now there to bring this unity to realization, and since anyway nobody can judge his or her own thinking, let alone anybody else's, obedience to this instruction should not be too difficult. But what kind of unity is it really? A formal unity without any clear content is fundamentally no unity at all, and a mere linking together of institutions is no value in itself. Unity conceived of in this way is based on common scepticism, not on common knowledge" (p. 131). Ratzinger, however, never evaluates his own rhetorically aimed presuppositions here: what if Rahner *is* correct about the "way things are"?

23. Cf. Childs, *Biblical Theology of the Old and New Testaments* (Philadelphia: Fortress Press, 1992), pp. 66ff.

will itself be "unified" only to the degree that its progress is seen as independent of concrete and concretely divided Christian communities, only as it is idealized according to some ahistorical scheme. In terms of concrete churches, the question of scriptural clarity and ecclesial division remains glaringly unresolved.

The Pneumatological Contradiction Inherent in the Post-Reformation Debate over Scripture

The same question is posed, furthermore, by the logical quandary embedded within the historical oppositions taken up in the Reformation debate (if not before), a dilemma involving the work of the Holy Spirit in the interpretation of Scripture in its relation to the Church. The actual Protestant-Catholic antitheses on the question of Scripture and the Church referred to above may or may not be more or less true in their respective assertions; that has always been the fuel of their argument. But they do give rise to a pneumatological contradiction that, from any confessional side, cannot be resolved into some particular position taken by one or another church.

The notion that Scripture is properly understood through the work of the Spirit enlightening the heart and mind was never in itself doubted by either side of the debate. But in what way or in what context did the Spirit illuminate Scripture? The Protestant-Catholic opposition on this matter took the form of contrasting emphases on individuals and communities respectively. In the classic late-sixteenth-century debate between the Puritan William Whitaker and the Jesuit Robert Bellarmine among others, Whitaker, for instance, reasserts that *if* Scripture is properly interpreted through the Spirit, then this Spirit must work individually, through each separate member of the Church without mediation. Did not the Apostle write in 1 John 2:20, "Ye have an unction from the Holy One"?[24] The theological problem of Scripture then turns on the methods the individual might use, either to assure him- or herself of the Spirit's guidance (e.g., prayer) or to master the linguistic and conceptual characteristics of Scripture.[25] For Roman Catholics, instead, the Spirit works within the "general" community of the faithful, and only thence speaks to

24. Whitaker, pp. 451f. Bellarmine kept a portrait of Whitaker hanging in his library, commenting to astonished visitors that "although he was a heretic and his adversary, yet he was a learned adversary." See James Brodrick, S.J., *Robert Bellarmine: Saint and Scholar* (London: Burns & Oates, 1961), p. 84.

25. Cf. Whitaker, pp. 466ff.

individuals.[26] The communal discernment of the Spirit, with respect to Scripture, then becomes the focus of theological interest, and this leads not only to orderings of authoritative pronouncement — *sensus fidelium,* theologians, Fathers, councils, Pope, in some such order — but also to the assessment of holiness in history, in saints and times, which confirm such authorities.[27]

As Puritanism, for instance, developed, theological emphases for many Protestants shifted to the subjective, rather than the literary, aspect (in Whitaker's scheme) of pneumatic assurance in the reading of Scripture. Introspective concerns regarding the experiential elements of the Spirit's inspiration took on increasing weight, and the interior shape of *illuminatio* became a major topic.[28] On the Catholic side, this kind of individualism was avoided in favor of a deliberately objective communitarianism, which sought to examine, historically, the characteristics of corporate experience, given in terms of the theorized ecclesial marks of "perpetuity," "continuity," "unity," "apostolicity," and so on, all of which, of course, are bound up with the identifiable "visibility" of the church as a social phenomenon.[29] Sadoleto had early on located the Catholic opposition to the Reformers in the former's understanding of *caritas* as central to the work of salvation (including justification). So central was *caritas's* effec-

26. Cf. St. Francis de Sales: "In a word, it is to the general Church to whom the Spirit immediately addresses its inspirations and persuasions for the common good of Christians; and next, through the preaching of the Church, the Spirit communicates to particular persons. The milk is produced in the Bride, and then the children suckle at her breasts." In Discourse 20 of his *Controverses,* in *Oeuvres Complètes de Saint François de Sales* (Paris: Louis Vivès, 1859), vol. 8, p. 321.

27. Cf. de Sales, pp. 449-519.

28. Cf. John Owen, "Pneumatologia," VI:2:7, in *The Works of John Owen, D.D.,* ed. W. H. Goold (London and Edinburgh: Johnstone and Hunter, 1852), vol. 4, pp. 202ff. Cf. also John Wilson's *The Scripture's Genuine Interpreter Asserted, or, A Discourse Concerning the Right Interpretation of Scripture* (London, 1678), which although occasioned by a philosophically skeptical account of Scripture's (lack of) perspicuity, by Lodewijk Meijer, is basically a typical anti-Catholic controversial work on the topic, happy to rely on Whitaker's standard categories. By the end of it, however, Wilson feels it necessary to provide an extended and elaborate outline of criteria for subjective pneumatic apprehension.

29. Thus, Bellarmine's definition, that "the Church is an assembly of persons as visible and as palpable as is the assembly of the Roman people or the kingdom of France or the Republic of Venice," which roused Protestant attack because of what today we would call its alleged "sociological " (and thus too purely human) conceptualization of a divine reality. Cf. Jean Claude's single-minded barrage against the whole idea of the Church's visible (and hence "perpetual," "continuous," etc.) character in his ongoing debate with Bossuet, for example, the *Réponse au livre de Monsieur l'Evesque de Meaux, intitulé Conference avec M. Claude* (Charenton: Veuve d'Olivier de Varennes, 1683), esp. the long preface. Bossuet, for his part, staked much of his vast anti-Protestant writing on just Bellarmine's kind of definition.

tive force in historical redemption that "communion," love's greatest work, was made the defining criterion, according to Roman Catholics, for any subsequent theological claim. Associating love with the actual Person of the Holy Spirit, as Sadoleto did (along with the side tradition he represented), he thereby pointed out as axiomatic the way that all positive pneumatic action was tied to the visible Christian community *qua* communion.[30]

How deep were these contrasts? Historically speaking, they have been irresolvable. And that may be because each aspect to the confrontation implies a pneumatology that cannot sustain at once the existence of both sides to the debate, without at the same time denying both in some fundamental manner. Protestants had stressed the perspicuity of Scripture, the rules for whose interpretation were made possible by an affirmation of Scripture's unified scope and method. They also linked this conviction, in a logical way, with ecclesiologies of diverse individualities or histories bound together in invisible unities.[31] This set of affirmations implied a particular pneumatology, according to which the Holy Spirit's work is diversely determined in history and embodied concretely only in the acts of proper scriptural interpretation, wherever they may take place. If unity exists concretely among Christians, it can be located, according to the Protestant paradigm, only in common ways of reading the Bible. Conversely, with ecclesiologies of effective unity so prominent on the Roman Catholic side, corresponding pneumatologies were implied by which the Holy Spirit was seen as working in a uniformly determined history, embodied immediately in ecclesial communion. According to this Catholic pneumatology, true scriptural interpretation is given only in the living, and hence pneumatic, practice of such unity.

But according to *both* accounts, the genuine existence of the *other* as a truly Christian church constitutes a pneumatological contradiction. From the

---

30. Cf. Sadoleto, in Calvin, *Tracts and Treatises,* pp. 9-10, 20. On this "caritative" notion of pneumatic oversight, which was tied to visible unity, see our discussion of the ministry below, in Chapter 3, as well as our discussion of the Eucharist in Chapter 4.

31. Cf. John Owen's "A Vindication of the Animadversions on 'Fiat Lux'" [1663], in his *Works,* vol. 14, esp. pp. 257-318. Owen's congregationalism flowed easily from his conviction that the Spirit worked, including and especially in the hearing of the Gospel in the Scriptures, primarily through individuals. His notion of the "unity" of the Church was necessarily informed by a theology of historical diversity, and Christian unity could therefore have as its only meaningful referent something historically "invisible." His remarks on what "Protestant unity" implies, versus the Roman notion of visible communion, are classic expositions of the unifying force common attitudes to the Bible are seen to wield. They also show in what way this kind of ecclesiology tends toward distorted historical judgments made in the interest of demonstrating an often fictitious minimum standard of agreement between separated Protestant denominations.

Protestant point of view, either Catholic interpretation of Scripture is unspiritual or the principle of pneumatic *illuminatio* is itself invalid, along with the Christian communities formed by the aggregates of its objects. Similarly, from the Catholic side, either Protestants are not members of the true Church, and hence are defective in their teaching about Scripture, or the principle of the pneumatic unity of concrete *caritas* is likewise mistaken. In each case, respective pneumatologies can be sustained only by ruling out the other as objects of pneumatic operation.[32]

The intransigence of the post-Reformation debate depended in part on this pneumatological contradiction. And as, with the rise of modern tolerance, the churches have proved more and more unwilling to maintain this rejection of the other party, the longstanding contradiction that has invigorated continued

---

32. Despite minor concessions here and there as to God's possible saving action within other Christian communities, until quite recently Protestants and Catholics have indeed viewed each other as, in different degrees, somehow not truly "Church." Cf. Luther's categorical denial of the Roman Church's pneumatic character, due to its lack of proper teaching concerning Christ, a pneumatic absence that rendered that "church" no true Church at all: "Where [the Holy Spirit] does not cause the Word to be preached and does not awaken understanding in the heart, all is lost. This was the case under the papacy, where faith was entirely shoved under the bench and no one recognized Christ as the Lord, or the Holy Spirit as the Sanctifier. That is, no one believed that Christ is our Lord in the sense that he won for us this treasure without our works and merits and made us acceptable to the Father. What was lacking here? There was no Holy Spirit present to reveal this truth and have it preached. Men and evil spirits there were, teaching us to obtain grace and be saved by our works. Therefore there was no Christian church. For where Christ is not preached, there is no Holy Spirit to create, call, and gather the Christian church, and outside it no one can come to the Lord Christ" ("Large Catechism," pt. 2, 43-46, in *The Book of Concord*, trans. and ed. Theodore G. Tappert [Philadelphia: Fortress Press, 1959], p. 416). This kind of exclusion on pneumatological grounds was perhaps more evident among Roman Catholics in recent years than among liberal Protestants. But even among liberal Protestants who participated in the rise of pan-Protestant ecumenical efforts in the nineteenth century, a pneumatology was at work that saw unity in terms of some basic uniformity of scriptural interpretation in such a way as contradicts the notion of a visibly pneumatic church altogether. It was the same pneumatology as could have been found two centuries earlier among Puritan congregationalists like John Owen. Further, the rise of historical criticism from Strauss on can be seen as an odd expression of this Protestant pneumatological paradigm as well, according to which unity in the faith can be achieved through the historically demonstrable, and hence uniform, reconstruction not of scriptural texts alone, but of scriptural contexts, from which can be pressed, as juice from a lemon, a common moral orientation by which to unite Christian people. On the relationship between the rise of "historical consciousness" and Christian disunity, see especially the discussion below in Chapter 5; see also remarks in Chapter 2 below on the way that scriptural texts became intertwined with an attempt to reconstruct a unitary history of either doctrine or ecclesial continuity, among Protestants and Catholics respectively.

separation has become only more difficult to bear. For if we are not to rule out the other, what are we to make of our presupposed pneumatologies? If the Spirit works preeminently neither to guide our hearing of Scripture nor to forge the common space for that hearing, what are we to say about the Spirit at all in its relation to Scripture and the Church? Are we faced, to use Bruce Marshall's term for the relation between Gospel credibility and the disunity of the churches, with a "genuine *aporia*," that is, with a conceptual problem for which there is no conceptual solution"?[33] Or are the basic pneumatologies in question simply inadequate to the truth, yet capable of reformulation?

The pressure to refashion the traditional Protestant and Catholic pneumatologies has in fact proved to be a major project in contemporary theology. But it has also led to a kind of impasse that has only further accentuated the original problem over the hearing of Scripture and Scripture's Gospel. The 1968 WCC Assembly at Uppsala, for instance, produced a report entitled "The Holy Spirit and the Catholicity of the Church," which attempted what some might think a typical ecumenical task, that is, bringing together two sides of an argument as if no tension between the two properly ever existed.[34] The report finessed the distinction between community and individual, visible and invisible, present and eschatological aspects of pneumatic existence in relation to the Church, by simply affirming at the same time elements of all of them, and lifting up a specific aspect of the Spirit's work that could conceptually hold all together: the Holy Spirit as "leader."[35] In speaking of the Church primarily in terms of being "led," all the Church's traditional marks are trans-

33. Bruce Marshall, "The Disunity of the Church and the Credibility of the Gospel," *Theology Today* 50 (April 1993): p. 86. Marshall states his *aporia* this way: "Four propositions create the *aporia:* (a) the gospel is true; (b) the gospel cannot be true if the church is eucharistically divided [this is a modern version of the mark of visible unity in the faith]; (c) there are eucharistic communities that are divided from one another (do not share the eucharist); (d) each of these communities is genuinely church (even if in some cases they recognize each other as such with some reservations)." Point (d) is obviously the new contemporary factor that creates the dilemma, since for much of the post-Reformation period, the dilemma was avoided simply by denying that other "churches" were truly "Church." Marshall himself responds to the *aporia* by pointing out that its only resolution is not conceptual at all, but practical: making (c) "false," by "reuniting now divided eucharistic communities." I am here outlining a pneumatological reality only related to the situation the *aporia* describes. And I shall be proposing not so much a means to do away with the *aporia,* but a way to make sense of it within the larger meaning of the Gospel. Which may well be the same as saying that, if looked at in its pneumatological context, it may not be a genuine *aporia* at all.

34. See the version in Norman Goodall, ed., *The Uppsala Report 1968* (Geneva: World Council of Churches, 1968), pp. 11-19.

35. Cf. secs. 1, 3-8, 12, etc.

ferred into the arena of historical process, which precludes firm judgments of pneumatic presence or absence. Unity, for instance, becomes something that is present to the Church in a diversity of ways over time, but by the Spirit remains something to be continually sought after in the future.[36] That this kind of formulation might really hide a lurking pan-Protestant version of the pneumatic Church — historically and spatially diverse individualities, reconciled inchoately through some shared fundamental commitment, but now extended to all Christian bodies — was something the Orthodox delegates evidently noted. Has the Church existed fully in unity continuously since the times of the Apostles or not, they wanted to know.[37] In any case, the direction taken by Uppsala's response was toward a celebration of pneumatic diversity wherein the significance of particularities — whether held in common or in opposition — became increasingly blurred.

The evolution of the WCC's Study Conferences on the Bible manifests this development.[38] The Wadham Conference of 1949 had nothing to say about the Holy Spirit, Scripture, and the Church. It stuck to historical-critical issues. The 1963 Montreal paper adopted a rather Catholic-sounding scheme whereby Scripture was said to "testify" to the "Tradition" of the Gospel, to which the "traditions" of preaching, sacraments, and teaching within the churches then bore witness. The Holy Spirit's work lay in "guarding" and "guiding" the Tradition's multilayered witness in Scripture and in the traditions of the Church.[39] But Montreal also shifted emphasis toward the pneumatic rendering of the plural "traditions," which pressed toward "diversity" of scriptural interpretation according to time and place.[40] "The Church," in the course of the document, became "the churches," held together by a common commitment to the singular Tradition mediated by the Spirit. The Bristol Report of 1967, dealing with hermeneutical issues, had little to say about the Spirit specifically; but the conference now extended the reality of diversity to the Scriptures themselves, explicitly drawing the parallel, in section III, between the diversity of churches and the variety of texts and

36. Secs. 5, 17ff.

37. Cf. Goodall, p. 9.

38. See Ellen Flesseman-van Leer, ed., *The Bible: Its Authority and Interpretation in the Ecumenical Movement*, Faith and Order Paper No. 99 (Geneva: World Council of Churches, 1980).

39. Flesseman-van Leer, par. 45.

40. Flesseman-van Leer, pars. 47, 52, 56, 57, 65. For a pungent analysis of this kind of move in the context of specific dialogues, see Cardinal Joseph Ratzinger's comments on the Anglican-Roman Catholic International Commission first summary report, in "Anglican-Catholic Dialogue: Its Problems and Hopes," in *Church, Ecumenism and Politics,* pp. 79ff.

meanings to be found in the Bible. If there was a unity in either sphere, it was to be found (and with difficulty and caution) only under the cover of diversity. This was a significant move. Finally, the 1971 Louvain paper brought all this together, by openly tying the Holy Spirit's reality to the granting of authority to diverse Scriptures within diverse communities (section II). At this point, the work of the Spirit was made almost synonymous with scriptural and ecclesial disintegration.

Taken as a whole, then, the ecumenical path for resolving the post-Reformation pneumatological contradiction was to redefine the Holy Spirit's office into that of mediating visible disunity into an invisible unity. Or, to put it in the terms of the confessional debate, ecumenical theologians and biblical scholars determined to give up both the Protestant demand for scriptural uniformity (a premise upon which perspicuity was based) and Catholic visible unity (a premise upon which scriptural authority was based). And the search for an embodied resolution to this pneumatological problem has thus led to an attempt at cutting its Gordian knot completely, by saying, in effect, that there *is no* problem in the first place. Incoherence — with respect to the doctrine of the Spirit, or of the Church, or of Scripture's use — in this approach herein becomes itself a pneumatic virtue. The official ecumenical certification of scriptural diversity as a reflection of the Spirit's own creation of variety only leads to a novel Christian affirmation: that is, that Christian unity — whether visible, or defined in terms of some concrete and identifiable attribute of communion — is not a fundamental evangelical imperative, and is mistakenly seen to be so. At the least, lack of such unity or communion is not an efficacious defect. By upholding this position, the activities of ecumenical relationship, the theological understanding that undergirds these activities, and, of course, the practice of the churches themselves who are part of such relationships have adopted the patent task, in J.-M.-R. Tillard's phrase, of "managing division." And the character of such management is said to derive from the Holy Spirit's action.[41]

41. Those looking for a succinct summary of this attitude, as it touches upon pneumatology and ecclesiology (although only implicitly on Scripture), an attitude that is "liberal" in both the moral and ideological senses, can peruse the vigorous 1950 essay of Russell Henry Stafford, then president of Hartford Seminary, entitled "The Body of Christ" (in *Religion in Life* 19, no. 3 [1950]: pp. 389-99). Stafford takes as his theme the "dangerous" trend, as he sees it developing among "neo-orthodox" and "Anglo-Catholic" "sacramentarians," and now driving the ecumenical movement itself, to press for the reintegration of Christian "churches" and "societies" into a single, visible community. "Unless we are on our guard, we shall be entangled again in a yoke of bondage" (p. 391), a bondage that contradicts "Protestant revolutionary freedom" through its insistence upon the congruence of a "true church" and "visibility," which

The Figuralist Alternative: Pneumatic Absence from the Church

Self-consciously orthodox scholars and exegetes have, of late, vigorously opposed this kind of pneumatological maneuver within the discipline of biblical theology, in particular.[42] But such attempts have also tended to leave the historically epistemological issue of Christian division largely unaddressed. In any case, another alternative also exists. To those who refuse to accept the management of division (or incoherence) as a pneumatic vocation, one might also wonder, in surveying theologically the condition of the churches' division today, whether, in fact, the Holy Spirit is *absent*.[43]

---

must be a condition for apprehending the Kingdom. Far from seeing this danger from the eyes of dogmatic Protestant sectarianism, however, Stafford upholds a view of the churches that has literally reduced ecclesiology to the discernment of a "fellowship kindness" among Christians of all types, that is "inaugurated" by the Holy Spirit. "There was no uniformity save the spirit among the primitive churches" (p. 397), he claims. Such pneumatic coherence takes form only in the sense that Christians felt impelled to a mutual openness and good feeling for one another, given through their being joined "in Christ." Ecclesial diversity, whether it be among organized institutional churches or voluntary associations like the Salvation Army or Alcoholics Anonymous (p. 396), is simply "a matter of taste, like the houses we choose to live in" (p. 397), whose individualities "emphasize one element in the total symphony of witness to the faith, without which the symphony would not be complete, while [these notes] might not be sounded if there were not a special instrument to bring [them] out" (p. 398). All of this represents what is now an engrained outlook among most leaders, and even members, of mainline churches and probably informs, on a more unconscious level, the major approach to Christianity taken by the Western religious consumer, of whatever denominational (or nondenominational) stripe. What is surprising is the way that it has come to characterize the practical efforts of even many ecumenical enthusiasts who were once (as Stafford noted of his own era, p. 390) driven by a "neo-catholic" perspective that sought after the *Una Sancta*.

42. Cf. Brevard Childs's attempt to reappropriate patristic and reformed notions of the unifying *scopus* of Scripture, as well as his reaffirmation of Scripture's "subject matter" of the One Lord as that unifying character. This kind of judgment about the way to approach Scripture stands in explicit contrast to the kinds of textual "diversifications" upon which many ecumenical theorists have based their reflections. See Childs, pp. 83ff. and 719ff.

43. So Tillard wonders about the WCC Assembly at Canberra earlier this decade, ironically given over to the theme of the Holy Spirit. Was the Holy Spirit even present at the assembly? Tillard cannot quite bring himself to answer in the negative. But if the Spirit was indeed present — and it certainly was not in the "sermons" and other proclamatory actions of the Council, he claims — it was only in offering (to some few) the "grace of clarity which led to the discovery that the ecumenical movement is beginning to go adrift," without "rudder or anchor." Pneumatic presence was thus fleetingly grasped as the sobering knowledge of a dissipated vocation. Cf. J.-M.-R. Tillard, "Was the Holy Spirit at Canberra?," *One in Christ*, 1993, no. 1, p. 62. The remark on "managing division" is made on p. 57 in the midst of a discussion of the way the original thrust of the WCC's foundational vision for the reestablishment of unity among the churches has increasingly been pushed to the periphery of the Council's concern.

If we are to grasp what is at stake, pneumatologically, in the existence of separated Christian bodies, this question is among the most important to raise. For to "invoke" the Spirit in a situation of theological and ecclesial incoherence — as the WCC has done in its gatherings, and, indeed, as individuals and churches continue to do in their own daily life — is to call down a voice that bespeaks a confusion, a confusion that involves, in a central fashion, our grasp of Scripture itself. This, I think, is the only path to follow here as we try to assess how the Scripture can speak the Gospel to hearers bound in a condition of division: the answer being that it *cannot,* except insofar as it unveils our deaf incomprehension.

Is such an answer defeatist about the power of Gospel? Only if we believe that it is not consistent with a proper evangelical understanding of the Holy Spirit itself, consistent, that is, with how the Holy Spirit does indeed create among us the new life of Christ Jesus. But such consistency, I believe, can be persuasively discerned. If the post-Reformation Protestant and Catholic construals of the relationship between Spirit, Scripture, and Church do in fact result in the positing of some basic pneumatological obstacle, then we can confirm the truth of the Christian Gospel only by subsuming such obstacles into our very confession of the Holy Spirit's life and perhaps even positive mission. We must confess, in short, that the "absence of the Paraclete" from within the Church ought to be constitutive of historical pneumatology (our understanding of the Holy Spirit's life in time) and that Christian division and scriptural obscurity are themselves pneumatic realities of the historical present. How we do this coherently is what we will now begin to explore, even as we lay the groundwork for a broader consideration, in the chapters that follow, of the experiential shape and theological articulation of such a condition.

A clue to how we might use Scripture itself[44] to bring into relief a proper

44. It may seem paradoxical to assert that only a particular understanding of Scripture can help explain our inability to understand it. But this, I think, is the case: a certain way of receiving Scripture's elucidation of our history — our history as a broken church — allows us to perceive as well our intrinsic alienation from Scripture's saving significance at the same time. Only by claiming such a continuing role for scriptural speech can we still link Scripture and Gospel together, much as Paul insisted that a law whose life-giving purpose had turned to death was still a "spiritual" entity given by God (cf. Rom. 7). In this case, the logical paradox, in any absolute sense, is averted, insofar as we assign to the historical reality of divine grace the coherent use of definable entities — in this case, Scripture — for a purpose that reflects the complex character of God. This, after all, is the way traditional Christian theology has almost always attempted to articulate the reality of Jesus' Crucifixion, which even Scripture itself transferred into a transtemporal symbol — the "Cross" — that was tied to an expressive aspect of God's providential and ordering will for history. Thus, Scripture can be seen as being *used* by God for the integrated purposes of temporally expressing "mercy and judgment" simultaneously — a

27

pneumatology of absence is given by Joseph Ratzinger in the course of a rather negative assessment of the Anglican–Roman Catholic dialogue in the form of the ARCIC I Reports. Ratzinger writes: "perhaps institutional separation has some share in the significance of salvation history which St. Paul attributes to the division between Israel and the Gentiles — namely that they should make 'each other envious', vying with each other in coming closer to the Lord (Rom. 11:11)."[45] Several things about this comment, made in passing, deserve to be noted. First, the separation of the churches may properly be seen in terms of "the significance of salvation history": that is, it may be caught up in the sovereign shaping of history by God in a way that must point, intrinsically, to the heart of the Gospel of Christ. Second, Ratzinger suggests that the division of the churches in this respect might be related to the division of "Israel and the Gentiles." Related, but how? It is precisely through each reality's sharing in the same divinely "disposed" significance that they are related, that is, brought together in the one Gospel of Christ.[46] Each set of divisions plays a part in and reflects the salvation wrought in Christ in some mysterious fashion. Each set of historical episodes refers to the other — intra-Christian division and Jewish-Gentile division — through the mediating and effecting reality of Christ Jesus, to whom, in fact, each refers in a primary way. In the terms of classical hermeneutics, then, Ratzinger suggests we adopt a "figuralist" approach to assessing the significance of Christian division.

Such a figuralist approach to Christian division is a fruitful one to pursue.

---

venerable observation made acute within the modern era by Pascal — and we need not be befuddled by the fact that the gracious instrument of mercy that the Scriptures are, and that we can indeed perceive them to be even in very particular ways, is at the same time revealing to us an obscured condition that is reflected in our own misuse of its forms.

45. Cardinal Joseph Ratzinger, "Anglican-Catholic Dialogue: Its Problems and Hopes," in *Church, Ecumenism and Politics*, p. 87.

46. In a later essay in the volume, on "The Progress of Ecumenism," Ratzinger explores the same point on the basis of Paul's remark in 1 Cor. 11:19 that "there must be factions" (*Church, Ecumenism and Politics*, pp. 138ff.). Moving from comments on this text by Augustine and H. Schlier, Ratzinger suggests that it be taken in terms of "an eschatological and dogmatic proposition," and that "schisms," however originated in human sin, be confronted as part of a "dimension that corresponds to God's disposing." Ratzinger has no interest here in the pneumatological implications of such an assertion, in large measure because, for all his sensitivities and indeed openness to Christ's salvific work among Protestant churches — indeed, *because* of such sensitivities — he remains a firm Roman Catholic chauvinist: the Spirit's concrete operative mission in the churches, however divided and necessarily including his own, is assumed. This is why he can favor a position on ecumenical relations that counsels "patience" in the midst of division and argues against attempts to effect communion *in sacris* before communion in doctrine.

Nor is it at all novel, although rarely practiced in our day. Although, for instance, Yves Congar outlined in 1948 the basic shape of, as well as the basic questions raised by, a figuralist construal of the divided Christian Church after the type of divided Israel, he did not (nor did anyone else) elaborate his suggestion.[47] At the time of the Reformation, however, theologians were quick to turn to a figural interpretation of Scripture to shed light on the astonishing prospect of a disintegrating Christian Church laid out before their eyes.[48] To

47. Yves M.-J. Congar, "Reflections on the Schism of Israel in the Perspective of Christian Divisions," orig. in *Proche-Orient chrétien,* 1951, no. 1, and trans. and reprinted with additional notes in *Dialogue Between Christians* (London: Geoffrey Chapman, 1966), pp. 160-83. This important article assumes, without defending, the figuralist reading of the Church elaborated upon below, and then applies it to the situation of the divided Church in particular. Congar spends a good deal of time — perhaps too much, considering the unstable character of such identifications — tracing the specifically *socio*historical parallels between Israel's national union and disintegration and the Christian Church's. From his Roman Catholic perspective, he also lays great stress on the "privileged" character of the Roman Church vis-à-vis Protestantism, in parallel with the Southern Kingdom's maintenance of the site of Israel's true worship, vis-à-vis Samaria's idolatrous shrines (Calvin himself applied the same distinction, although he reversed the referents between Protestants and Catholics). Finally, he only hints at the nature of Christian reunion suggested by the type of Israel's destruction and exile, and has nothing to say about the pneumatological implications of his figuralist scheme. Still, Congar's overall suggestions are in line with the basic thrust of the present argument. Jean-Jacques von Allmen, in the article discussed at the opening of this chapter, also made use of the divided Israel figure, quite pertinently and vigorously, although only in passing (cf. von Allmen, pp. 65, 71).

48. In later chapters, especially Chapter 2 below, we shall be considering whether or not the Reformation and post-Reformation controversialist appeal to scriptural figure in fact represents the classical "figuralism" of the pre-Reformation period. The conclusion I shall draw is that it does *not.* That being the case, a distinction can, and will usually be, made (although not in the immediate argument) between "figural" and "figuralist" interpretation of Scripture. "Figural" exegesis, as I shall use the term, will stand as a general designation for *any* exegetical denotation that relies upon the intersignificatory coherence between diverse biblical texts and their referents, which may also extend their reach to nonbiblical events within history, especially the history of the Church. Thus, typology, reiterated and reapplied metaphor, allegory, and so on all fall into the category of "figural" reading. In contrast to such a general, catch-all category, however, we shall use the term "figuralist" exegesis as a designation for a particular (and ultimately theologically distinct) form of figural reading, one that perceives the intersignificating character of the scriptural text in a consistent and integrated (rather than merely occasional and/or limited) fashion and that, in particular, insists that the context for such intersignification lies primarily in the temporal realm of God's "economy," which links Israel to the Church via the central "figurating" form of Jesus Christ (see below, in the present discussion). The distinction between "figural" and "figuralist" exegesis, clumsy as it is, is an attempt to capture some of the contrasts between the broad "spiritual" readings of post-Reformation Roman Catholic exegetes (however limited) and the intentional theological hermeneutic practiced by Jansenist exegetes of the seventeenth and eighteenth centuries, to which was later applied the specific term *figurisme* and

be sure, such methods tended to serve polemical ends, but they were serious nonetheless. Calvin, for instance, already in the *Reply* to Sadoleto, attempts to explain the apparent "schism" of the Reformers in terms of the figure of the faithful "remnant" of Israelite prophets and their followers who set themselves "against" the corruption of the rulers and priests of the nation. He further characterizes the Roman church as being figured in the Israel of kings Zedekiah and Jehoiakim, far fallen from the purity of David and Solomon's rule, and prophetically destined for dismemberment and destruction at the hands of God's avenging agents.[49] Catholics, for their part, could also make use of divided and assaulted Israel, but in their case to cast the Roman Church in the figure of a chosen people victimized by their own children.[50]

---

which attempted a self-conscious and theologically defended reappropriation of the (less consciously explicated) standard and encompassing interpretive practice of the early Fathers and Western monastic exegetes especially. Such "figuralism" relied, ecclesiologically and pneumatologically, on a specific and normative understanding of the nature of the Church in its historical existence, an understanding generally contradicted by the divisions of the Church and (except for rare cases and movements, like the Jansenists) gradually discarded in the Reformation and post-Reformation churches, both Protestant and Catholic.

49. Calvin, "Reply to Sadoleto's Letter," *Tracts and Treatises,* pp. 60 and 38. Cf. the later Puritan John Owen's long description of the Roman Church's "falling" in terms of her conformance to the figure of sinful Israel, against whom the prophets spoke (the "prophets were Protestants — God protested against [Israel] by his prophets") in his "Vindication," in *Works,* vol. 14, pp. 212ff. Owen later provides the following summary of Roman Catholic institutions: "She hath fallen by *idolatry* and corruption of life; as did the church of the Jews before captivity. She hath fallen by her *relinquishment* of the written word as the only rule of faith and worship, and by adhering to the uncertain traditions of men; as did the church of the Jews after their return from captivity. . . . She hath fallen by *schism* in herself, — as the Judaical church did when divided into Essenes, Sadducees, and Pharisees, — setting up pope against pope, and council against council, continuing in her intestine broils for some ages together" (p. 224).

50. Cf. below on the ways in which Bellarmine and the Jansenist Jean Hamon described the figure of "lamenting Israel" in terms of the tears of sorrow engendered by the Protestant agonies: Robert Bellarmine, "De Gemitu Columbae," II:4, and *passim;* Jean Hamon, *Commentaire sur les Lamentations de Jérémie* (Paris: 1790), p. 3. Bossuet was among the first Catholics to take strong exception to the limited way in which the Reformers made use of the Israel figure to justify their separation from Rome. Cf. his *Seconde Instruction sur les promesses de Jésus-Christ à son Église* (1701), chs. 53-79, in *Oeuvres Complètes,* ed. Guillaume (Paris: Berche et Tralin, 1887), vol. 4, pp. 129-34. Bossuet argues, against an unnamed Protestant antagonist (probably Jacques Basnage), that the Old Testament figures of "schism," for example, of Jeroboam or the prophets Elijah and Elisha, however applicable to the present time, can only be so under the form of judgment, since Scripture itself evaluates these separations negatively. Certainly Bossuet's exegesis is by far the better in this exchange; but, no less than his Catholic *confrères,* he remains unwilling to transfer the negative aspect of the schismatic figure to the Church itself, confining its referent to the Church's (Protestant) enemies. This reluctance ultimately derives from an

This figural construal of the divided Church was appropriated by the post-Reformation debate from the early exegesis of the Fathers.[51] Most commentators from the first centuries of the Church worked from a common, though by no means universal, assumption that the Israel of the Old Testament and the Christian Church were continuous, even identical, bodies, if living under distinct dispensations of the divine economy. Such figural identification of Israel and the Church did lean towards supersessionist interpretations, according to which the apostolic Church took the place of a now wholly rejected Jewish Israel.[52] On this reading, the figure of divided Israel and its divinely ordered condition in this state was applied narrowly to the "unfaithful," and not to the "true" Church.[53] This tended to be the tack, as just noted, of later Protestant controversialists like Calvin. But the primary assertion of figural identity by the early Church was more fundamental even than its

---

articulated and deliberate ecclesiology constricted by the events of the Reformation and reliant, in consequence, upon a peculiar interpretation of the relation between the historical experience of the Church and pneumatic reality.

51. This seems more likely than the possibility that medieval uses of the figure were followed. In any case, such uses were rare, and were generally adapted to the Western-Eastern schism. Cf. Congar, "Reflections on the Schism of Israel," pp. 160, 182f., who mentions the twelfth-century John of Santa Maria, Joachim of Fiore, Gregory IX, Bonaventure, Humbert of Romans, and Nicholas of Clemanges as authors who compare the Greek "schism" to the rebellion of Jeroboam.

52. Cf. the material richly referred to in Marcel Simon's *Verus Israel: A Study of the Relations between Christians and Jews in the Roman Empire (135–425)* (Oxford: The Littman Library by Oxford University Press, 1986), passim and, e.g., pp. 76ff. and 169ff.

53. Cf. Jerome's commentary on Jeremiah, on vv. 3:18 and 4:5; or Ephraem's commentary on Isaiah, 44:1ff. However regrettable, from the standpoint of modern Jewish and Christian history, was the patristic supersessionist construal of the relation of Jewish Israel and the Church, it should be noted that one motivation for this construal lay in the seriousness with which the historical integrity of prophecy was taken, something that today is simply out of our ken. A general criterion applied to the referential interpretation of an Old Testament text acting as a "figure" was whether this prophecy could rightly be called "fulfilled" for the Jews since the Captivity. If not, it was best to assume that the Christian Church was the "proper" *(proprie)* referent for the figure. While there are limits to this kind of criterion, it is clear that if it were applied today, given the condition of the Christian Church, our figural evaluations would necessarily have to take a different slant. Finally, holding the two — patristic and contemporary — uses of the criterion together, one might arrive at the kind of fuller interpretation here being suggested. In addition to the mainstream patristic use of the divided Israel figure, we should also note the way the figure was used, in anticipation of Protestant-Catholic polemical usage, by the Donatists. They claimed the "southern," or Judah-based, privilege of being the true Church (cf. Congar, "Reflections on the Schism of Israel," p. 182), much as Calvin would repeatedly do in identifying Rome with Jeroboam's "idolatry," even while the revealed worship of the Temple remained intact within the confines of Jerusalem.

supersessionist temptations, as is proved by the equally pervasive insistence by many patristic commentators that Jewish and Christian Israel be seen as figurally continuous in a scripturally integrated fashion, and therefore that the figure of divided Israel be applied directly to the Christian Church as a whole.[54]

In our day, George Lindbeck has been eloquent in calling for a retrieval of the basic hermeneutical presuppositions lying behind this patristic figural identification of the Old Testament's Israel and the Christian Church.[55] In suggesting an explicit ecclesiology that takes the Christian Church's character as essentially explicated in and through the figure of Israel, Lindbeck has proposed a "narrative" theology of the church that takes the story of Israel as "prior" to any distillation of distinguishing "marks" or "images"; a theology that insists, therefore, on the ecclesial referent of scriptural figure as concrete and "visible" (versus one prominent trend of Reformed theology); and one, finally, that appropriates or applies the "whole" of the figural story to the church, and not just the "favorable" parts divorced from narrative elements of judgment and disease. Significantly, Lindbeck locates the possible working of these elements of a narrative ecclesiology in the mediating reality — the figurating reality, if you will — of Christ himself:

> Thus, despite most later exegesis, the relation of Israel's history to that of the church in the New Testament is not one of shadow to reality, or promise to fulfillment, or type to antitype. Rather, the kingdom already present in Christ alone is the antitype, and both Israel and the church are types. The

---

54. Cf. Origen's Homily IV on Jeremiah, 3:6-11, which provides one of the few explicit attempts before the seventeenth century to connect figurally the division of Israel's kingdoms and the relation of Jew and Gentile as given by Paul in Romans 9–11. Cf. also Theodoret's commentary on Isaiah, c. 49, where Christ himself is made the main figural referent of Israel's distorted life, and only through him, is the Church linked to Israel as well. On the importance of this kind of interpretive move, see below. With respect to the application of the specific figure of *divided* Israel to the Christian Church, there was, however, lack of consensus. Cyprian, for instance, was explicitly clear that the divisions of the Kingdom, symbolized in the figure of the prophet Ahijah's torn cloak, could not possibly bear figural transference to the Church, whose indefectible "unity" was symbolized in the seamless and undivided garment of Jesus at the Cross; cf. his *De ecclesiae catholize unitate,* c. 7. But just these kinds of distinctions in application pointed to the need for a more rigorous consistency, as did subsequent historical realities, which pressed against Cyprian's discriminations.

55. Cf. George Lindbeck, "The Story-Shaped Church: Critical Exegesis and Theological Interpretation," in Garrett Green, ed., *Scriptural Authority and Narrative Interpretation* (Philadelphia: Fortress Press, 1987), esp. pp. 165-70; and "The Church," in Geoffrey Wainwright, ed., *Keeping the Faith: Essays to Mark the Centenary of Lux Mundi* (London: SPCK, 1989). The latter essay appropriates quite closely much of the constructive material of the former and extends its meaning to some specific ecumenical questions.

people of God existing in both the old and the new ages are typologically related to Jesus Christ, and through Christ, Israel is prototypical for the church in much the same way that the exodus story, for example, is seen as prototypical for all later Israelite history by such prophets as Ezekiel.[56]

It is just this insistence upon the central mediating figure of Christ to the relating of the Church and Israel that allows for the "whole story" of Israel to touch the Church's life in a salvific fashion, whatever the punishing elements of its specific contours. For if Christ lies as the central referent of both Israel's life in the Old Testament and the Christian Church's life, then the drawing of one to the other into a single Israel whose narrative shapes inform each other mutually can be affirmed as manifesting, in whatever mode, the figure of the Gospel itself.[57]

56. Lindbeck, "The Story-Shaped Church," p. 166.

57. This Christocentric figural claim on Lindbeck's part ought to lessen somewhat the fears of many conservatives and evangelicals especially, like Brevard Childs, that Lindbeck's "narrative" approach has somehow excluded a concern with the "reality outside the text," namely God, in Christ Jesus. Cf. Childs's brief comments in *The New Testament as Canon* (Philadelphia: Fortress Press, 1984), pp. 544-46, and in *Biblical Theology of the Old and New Testaments* (Philadelphia: Fortress Press, 1992), pp. 21f. It is true that in his discussion of the narrative basis for understanding the Church, Lindbeck makes use of critically descriptive categories based on the apparent use of Scripture by the early Church and that this involves the deployment of both literary-critical and sociological tropes that, in themselves, have little reference to "truth-claims." This can result in the use of ambiguous judgments such as the Church's narrative character being "Israel-like." But at the same time, he claims a primacy for the "narrative" of Jesus in construing the figural relationship of Old and New Testament Israel that itself subverts a casual conception of narrative altogether: the positing of a figural center in the "story" of Jesus — "the uniquely privileged *sensus literalis* of the whole of scripture" — that somehow grants the Christian Church access to the "narrative" identity of Israel, back and forth over time in history, is a religious insight, however much it is buttressed by New Testament "exegesis." To claim, as Lindbeck does more consistently, that the Church *is* Israel and not simply "Israel-like" derives from reading the Scriptures from a particular standpoint of faith that places the entire discussion in the realm of a Christian discourse whose truth-claims are not only necessarily presupposed, but decidedly rooted in historical "factuality" (cf. "The Story-Shaped Church," pp. 164, 170). Ecclesiologically, the very notion of a Scripture in which the central "story" of Christ mediates figurally the whole range of specific references to the Old and the new Israel raises into relief the way that, for instance, the figure of the "Body of Christ" operates less as an ancillary "image" of the Church (cf. "The Story-Shaped Church," p. 165), and more properly as a historical reality whose *res* must escape altogether the scope of literary-critical conceptualization. For a discussion of some of these more general concerns about historical reference, as they touch upon the kind of "narrative" theology promoted by someone like Lindbeck — for example, Hans Frei — see George Hunsinger, "What Can Evangelicals and Postliberals Learn from Each Other?" in *Pro Ecclesia* 4, no. 2 (1996): pp. 161-82. Hunsinger wants to distinguish Lindbeck from Frei (cf. Hunsinger, p. 174, n. 59), on the basis of the former's allegedly more comprehensive "perfor-

This proves an important point if we wish to find a place within that Gospel for the reality of the Church's division and for the implications that this reality embodies regarding the life of the Holy Spirit in our midst. Lindbeck himself has not pursued this question, although he notes that the relation of the Holy Spirit to Israel is consistent through both Testaments — that the Spirit is present and working in Old Testament Israel as in New, and that "it departs from the faithless in the present as it did in the past." Pneumatic fullness, in other words, is a "relational attribute referring to what God is making and will make of [the church], not . . . an inherent property."[58]

If it is not an inherent property, and rather is a "relational attribute," the vagaries of the Holy Spirit's operation in the Church ought to be traceable according to the figure of Israel. This is the main point I would stress here. And it *is* the case that the figural appropriation of Israel and the Christian Church remains one of the few, if not the only, means of rooting the present situation of the divided Church in Scripture in such a way that Scripture's own place in this "relation" can be more clearly specified. For apart from such a figural location of the problem — one that opens up for "instruction" the "type" of Israel (cf. 1 Cor. 10:11) — the Church's division finds little place within the explicit ecclesial referents of the New Testament. In nonfigural terms, the New Testament simply does not envision the entrenched division of the Church; it merely points in passing to the eschatological distresses to be suffered by the Christian community at the hands of Satan, only one of which will include factions and schisms (e.g., 1 John 2:18ff.; Jude 17–19). How one understands the Church as itself a divided entity is not a topic the New Testament openly broaches.

Small wonder, then, that Reformers and Catholics alike struggled to find alternative scriptural resources for their embattled situation, turning, however imperfectly and limitedly, as we have seen, toward the Old Testament discussion of divided Israel, for example, for help. Yet without grasping the central figuring character of Christ in this process, joining Jewish Israel and the Christian Church together as one body narrationally, the kind of truncated

---

matory" (versus "propositionalist") view of doctrine and the scriptural texts that inform it. Hunsinger himself, although generally sympathetic to Lindbeck's "post-liberalism," I think misreads the fundamental seriousness with which Lindbeck must take the "historical factuality" of scriptural referents if they are to function in the ecclesiologically figural way he has argued they do. In this sense, Lindbeck's hermeneutics may be more historically grounded, in terms of its views of scriptural reference, than was Frei's, who never (to my knowledge) used the figural strategies he had identified among the Reformers for applying Scripture to the life of the historical (and contemporary) Church.

58. Lindbeck, "The Story-Shaped Church," p. 168.

attributions of "faithful" and "unfaithful," remnant and sectaries, to one party or the other that we have indicated was inevitable.[59]

In reflecting on the positive meaning of Christian "unity," it is true, it was always possible in the Reformation debate to see the way in which a figural relation of the Church to Christ implied some kind of transhistorical constant in signification, that, logically anyway, ought to have tied the Christian community's character to Israel in a more consistent historical fashion. Calvin, for instance, in commenting on John 17:21, in which Jesus prays "that all may be one," is careful to show how intimately tied is the Son's eternal oneness with the Father to our union in him as historical Mediator. He speaks abstractly here — "in order to prevent the *unity* of the Son with the Father from being fruitless and unavailing, the power of that *unity* must be diffused through the whole body of believers."[60] But he at least proposes that the historical shapes of the Christian community's life are properly bound, as fruit on its tree, to a divine reality that reaches over time and therefore, in theory, ought to produce consistently in the history of the faithful, including Israel, concrete forms of its fecundity. The shape of unity, on this account, and its significance in time ought to be visible in the whole history of Israel.

However muddled, the theological tools for grasping the significance of the divided Church in terms of the shape of Jewish Israel have been available to the church for some time. But their lack of full deployment has contributed to our stunted ability to comprehend our ecclesial situation. That said, let me now sketch how it might look if we proceeded to apply the approach I have been proposing to the question of pneumatology and the pneumatic appropriation of Scripture.

The Scriptural Figure of the Pneumatically Abandoned Church

As some controversialists of the Reformation saw, the figure of divided Israel itself provided the locus for confronting the reality of the divided Church. Likewise, as they saw, the figure of divided Israel, according to the Old Testament, was embedded in a narrative of divine judgment and cascading

59. For a brief discussion of the theological rationale for applying the figure of the divided Israel to the contemporary Church, see Ephraim Radner, "The Cost of Communion: A Meditation on Israel and the Divided Church," in Ephraim Radner and R. R. Reno, eds., *Inhabiting Unity: Theological Perspectives on the Proposed Lutheran-Episcopal Concordat* (Grand Rapids: Wm. B. Eerdmans, 1995).

60. John Calvin, *Commentary on the Gospel According to John,* trans. William Pringle (Grand Rapids: Baker Book House, repr. 1979), p. 184.

disaster. From the time of Jeroboam's rebellion and the rending of Israel into northern and southern kingdoms (1 Kings 12), the people of Israel were dragged down into a steady decline marked by internal apostasy and external victimization. Although there were respites and brief reversals to this pattern — for example, Hezekiah's or Josiah's reigns — both kingdoms eventually succumbed to almost total annihilation at the hands of Assyria and Babylon, and the people were taken into exile and scattered.

But while the polemicists of Christian division have tended to apply this story one-sidedly, choosing to identify their particular communities with various righteous "remnants" alluded to in the course of the narrative, it should be stressed that the narrative as a whole forbids such distinguishing of actors within the history. Both kingdoms are ultimately destroyed; the peoples of both are murdered and enslaved; and only the reunion of both as having come through this common ordeal embodies the restoration of Israel in the public arena of time (cf. Jer. 50:2-4). That there was to be a "remnant" for whom this restoration was ordered is not in question (cf. Isa. 10:20ff., or 37:34). But to give this remnant some definable status as "the true church," granted some continuous character over time as the "elect," literally separated out from the fate of Israel as a whole, is to misconstrue the theology of the "remainder" altogether. For in the destruction of divided Israel, both the righteous and unrighteous suffer together, true prophets and false prophets. The "remnant" — survivors, literally — are thrown by God into the same cauldron and share the same burdens of destruction and enslavement (cf. 2 Kings 17:19f.; Ezek. 5:10). The restoration of the remnant is not the unveiling, let alone the vindication, of the "true church" from amid its travails, but rather the gracious action of recreating a united people out of the dust of their past obliteration (cf. Ezek. 11:14-21).[61]

We are dealing, then, with the character and fate of the whole people of Israel; and whatever distinctions are given to members of that people on the basis of their division are not such as to remove them from that general character and fate in which their division lies. It is not the case, of course, that the Old Testament narrative relates the division of Israel to this character and fate as a cause to its effect. Indeed, the partition of Israel at the time of Jeroboam is itself seen as the punishing effect of earlier and deeper apostasies, leading back to the time of the Exodus itself, and certainly given relief at the time

---

61. Cf. Congar, "Reflections on the Schism of Israel," p. 181: "One is tempted to ask what trials or deportations will perhaps be necessary before Christians find themselves united once more . . . one begins to wonder what price we shall perhaps have to pay for the grace of reunion."

36

when Israel clamored for a king (1 Samuel 8). This needs to be stressed lest, in all that follows — in this chapter and in the volume as a whole — the impression be given that disunity *in itself* is the sufficient and necessary cause of the whole breadth of the Church's modern life. Such an assertion is clearly untenable, if in fact such disunity, within the context of Israel's own experience, draws its providential burden out of the sack of some more primordial sin, or at least stands in some mutually informing relationship to such sin. The assertion is untenable as well on even purely sociohistorical grounds. The intellectual and experiential contours of the modern Church are variously related to various kinds of causes, which are properly assigned to the tools of modern historical-critical examination. But division as a divine judgment whose realities are implicated in those variously identifiable intellectual and experiential contours of the Church, as it stands in continuous identity with Israel through the incarnated life of Jesus, must properly imply as well a consistent and comprehensive effect, in a peculiar fashion that will necessarily "shape" — figurate — the Church in specific historical forms. Thus, given that the restoration of Israel is to be a patent expression of renewed unity, we must evaluate the previous divisions as being intimately bound to the causal nexus of the people's sinfulness, which brings upon itself only a deepening embroil-ment in further unfaithfulness. Not only is the whole people bound to the effects of division, then, but these effects are properly seen in terms of the whole range of judgments visited upon the people. In terms of scriptural figure, then, ecclesial division is an appropriate and essential heuristic lens for histori-cal description.

And what does such description reveal? By viewing the division of Israel within the integral history of the people's sin and punishment, we can see that the condition of disunity itself is characterized by the *increase* of sin, by the accelerating inability of the nation to right itself, to perceive the truth of God's will and call, to heed his warnings, repent, and seek forgiveness. Just as the sin of the monarchy was given as a punishment for the desire for a king, so too the deadening confusion of competing and self-deceiving claims to truth that mark the evolution of the prophetic and priestly offices is given as a festering of the disease of national fragmentation. According to the scriptural pattern of divine "abandonment" in sin, divided Israel was left to encounter its shat-tered life on its own.[62]

This fact determines how we are to view the topic at hand: partitioned Israel is "abandoned" Israel; and this Israel, separated among its members, is separated too from the Holy Spirit. This equation between sinfulness, abandonment, and

---

62. Cf. our concluding discussion of ecclesial repentance, in Chapter 5.

"resistance" to the Spirit is the burden of Stephen's speech in Acts 7 (cf. vv. 42 and 51), and it stands as an explicator to the large number of texts from the prophets where the condition of divided Israel is described in the explicit terms of pneumatic absence or antagonism. Isaiah, in particular, offers us a number of examples. Verses 63:10ff., for instance, are part of a prayer for the nation that has much in common with beleaguered rehearsals of Israel's history such as Psalm 106. After extolling God's love in the past, the prophet declares that the people still "rebelled and grieved his holy Spirit; therefore [God] turned to be their enemy, and himself fought against them." Although, in the course of the people's history, repeated forgiveness is forthcoming, the present condition of the nation brings the lament, "O LORD, why dost thou make us err from thy ways and harden our heart, so that we fear thee not?" (v. 17).

The sense that opposing the Spirit of God (cf. again Ps. 106:33) carries as one of its effective aspects a divine hardening, or a positive dislocation of expected pneumatic assistance, is a common feature of these kinds of texts. In Isaiah 6:10, 28:7ff., and 29:9ff., the normal prophetic efficacy of vision and teaching is described as obscured, and the people become like drunkards and the blind, unable to perceive and hear what God is telling them or might tell them. Yet it is God himself who authors this darkness, and so the Spirit's power is made to reveal itself in its own inefficacy: "Stupefy yourselves and be in a stupor, blind yourselves and be blind! . . . For the LORD has poured out upon you a spirit of deep sleep, and has closed your eyes, the prophets, and covered your heads, the seers. And the vision of all this has become to you like the words of a book that is sealed. When men give it to one who can read, saying 'Read this,' he says, 'I cannot, for it is sealed'" (29:9-11).

Two things at least need to be said about these kinds of texts. First, they are in general set within larger discussions that treat of Israel's punishment and restoration. Thus, the themes of pneumatic antagonisms or abandonment and communal blindness to God's Word are explicitly tied, through contrast, to the specific elements of Israel's sinful condition. There will come a time when "the deaf shall hear the words of a book, and out of their gloom and darkness the eyes of the blind shall see" (29:18), but such is precisely the time when God will choose to overturn the present shape of the people, to restore to the nation a single and coherent worship. In Ezekiel's terms, the restoration of the Holy Spirit upon the divinely abandoned people of Israel must coincide with their return as a united body (Ezek. 39:25-29). In this way, the prophets make clear that a firm connection exists between the condition of division and the experience of pneumatic deprivation (even if that connection, however comprehensive, does not exhaust all that can be said about the character of redemption).

Secondly, we must note that several of these texts from the Old Testament have found a place in the New: Isaiah 6:10 in Matthew 13:13-15 and John 12:40, and Isaiah 29:9f. in Romans 11:8-10. Here, the judgment of pneumatic deprivation is linked to Jewish Israel in particular over against the Christian Church. And while the circumstances of Paul's and the evangelists' time make that contrast concrete, we must, as Ratzinger also suggested, recognize that the contrast itself is figurally prophetic of Christian Israel too, just because its participation in the larger Christic form allows for the initial figural transposition through the two Testaments. And given this fact, we are enabled to see how the pneumatic deprivation described by the prophets of beleaguered Israel stands within the entire history of redemption, and how, with the disunity that is its partner, they represent central Christological truths. The bitterness of Paul's own struggle with Jewish Israel's "blindness" and "stupor" has manifested in his body, he says, "the marks of Jesus" (Gal. 6:17; cf. 2 Cor. 4:10); yet in this very engagement in opposition were contained a universal "mercy" (Rom. 11:32) and new "life" (2 Cor. 4:12).

Taken together, these two points underscore how the particular aspects of Christian division and pneumatic deprivation — deafness, blindness, visionary failure, the deadness of the letter — all these stand as figural realities that themselves, in their conjunction and historical context, indicate the grace of Christ's own Cross and Resurrection. And we can see, therefore, that to affirm these experiential elements as constitutive of Christian division, and hence, in some sense, as inescapable parameters to our present Christian existence, is not somehow to give up the Gospel, let alone to void it.

The Pneumatic Vocation of Sensibility's Demise

Precisely the fact that pneumatic deprivation reveals itself through the constriction or dulling of the "senses" by which God's life is known and joyfully received by the Church points to the area of the tradition — asceticism — in which this negative reality has, in the past, at least been assimilated into the affirmation of the Gospel's salvific power and historical manifestation. Indeed, the ascetic tradition of the Church especially, has described this precisely, albeit usually in individualistic terms, in the following way: when we suffer the conjunction of these besieged senses, we receive both pneumatic judgment and the pneumatic means by which a conformity with Christ Jesus is not only attained but actually expressed. Among the early Fathers, for instance, this conjunction was less explicit and tended to emphasize more narrowly, and in a generalized Neoplatonic perspective, the need for the Christian to discipline and finally abandon a reliance upon, and subjugation to, the corporeal senses.[63] But there was also an early recognition that such a "death" to and of the senses stood in a relationship of configured union with the incarnate Jesus of the Passion. What Ambrose first called the "mystical death" *(mors mystica)* was, in all of its ascetic and antimaterialist implications, nonetheless firmly explicated in terms of the scriptural (especially Pauline) texts that touched upon "dying" with Christ (e.g., Gal. 5:24; 6:14; Col. 3:5, etc.).[64] In Paulinus of Nola's phrase, "our heritage is the death of Christ; we cannot participate in the glory of His resurrection, except on condition that we imitate His death on the Cross, putting to death the body and the senses of the flesh" (Epistle 45); such a death he hortatively designates as "evangelical."[65] The "death" of the senses, in their linkage to terrestrial concerns whose character is sin, is also the meeting place of Christ's embracing form, which, in the negative transfiguration common to this traditional discourse, provides new spiritual "sight" to organs that must first be rendered blind, new hearing to what must be made deaf, and so on.[66]

This tradition, elaborated and rooted in the monastic spirituality of the Middle Ages, blossomed anew in the sixteenth and seventeenth centuries. (Although the relation between this development and the particular religious exigencies of the Catholic reformation are complex enough to defy insertion into the present scheme, they are certainly worth considering.)[67] In a seminal figure like John of the Cross, to take a well-known example, the mortifying vocation of Christian sensibility was given a new intensity, but also raised to

---

63. Cf. Origen, *Contra Celsum,* I:48 and VII:39.

64. Cf. *De fuga saeculi,* 9:57; the phrase *mors mystica* is found in a discussion of "three kinds" of death in *De bono mortis,* 2:3.

65. In *Saint Paulin de Nole, Poèmes, Lettres et sermons,* ed. and trans. Charles Pietri (Naumur, 1964), p. 164.

66. Cf. Gregory of Nyssa, *On the Song of Songs,* 10.

67. The notion that early modern (or "postmedieval") Catholic spirituality was somehow decisively informed by the Roman Church's struggle with Protestantism, in a self-disciplined and activist direction, is now a commonplace. Cf. the remarks of H. Outram Evennett in his now classic 1951 Birkbeck Lectures, later published as *The Spirit of the Counter-Reformation,* ed. John Bossy (Cambridge: Cambridge University Press, 1968), pp. 30ff. Aside from a perspective determined by the search for causal genealogies, whether historical-theological or social-economic, one might also wonder how certain devotional interests of the period, including the contemplative, are actually expressive of divinely rendered pneumatic possibilities for the time. The relation between, for instance, the "modern" Catholic contemplative's reparative perfectionism and the experience of Protestant assault demands further study. Cf., for example, the opening chapters of Teresa of Avila's *The Way of Perfection,* for an indication of one such publicly articulated causal linkage.

a level of palpable pneumatic paradox and ambiguity. For John, the exercise of the corporeal senses offered a positive avenue to the still struggling contemplative through which, and via the creative and self-humbling grace of God, the soul might be prodded toward a budding knowledge of divine being and attraction. The intrinsic limitedness in this sensible function, however, gives rise, according to John, to a fundamental recognition of divine *absence,* expressed in an insistent longing after God's presence.[68] At this stage, the senses themselves must be left behind, a process that John likens to a "death" that is fueled by a holy desire for what is beyond reach. In an odd coincidence, holy desire takes form along with the desire to die, and this suspension in "death" now extends beyond a narrow ascetic corporal discipline, but enters the soul with a defining evangelical force: the fullness of the *mors mystica* still lies beyond reach, producing a condition of sensible death that envelops the soul's contemplative ministry.[69] "I am dying because I do not die" *(muero porque no muero),* he writes in a beautiful poem, expressing the work of divine grace that permits such a dilation of longing and love for the beauty and intimacy of God's glory that, though glimpsed, is achingly distant.[70] This "wound of love," as John came to express it, then founded the entry into a new stage of prayer, wherein the devil takes direct charge of the senses with a new ferocity, and engages in a battle with holy suffering itself, whose outcome, finally, is death's full opening of the space wherein the Holy Spirit enters to distribute its gifts of divine intimacy's delight and joy.[71]

In terms of pneumatology, the ambiguous status of the senses here is tied, in large measure, to their occasional relation with the Spirit's advent and absence. The deployment of the senses prods toward God, through grace, but these senses also dissolve into obstacles of sin. In this tension arises the experience of their own death, within which promise and discipline the entries and exits of the Spirit are embodied in an afflicted "love." The pneumatic character of this unstable place of service is, if only fleetingly, described by John through the forms of the incarnated passion, wherein the "wound" of the "lover" is now transferred to the "beloved," who stoops to embrace in his own person the suffering of the outstretched soul.[72] This was, in any case, the traditional

---

68. Cf. John of the Cross, *Spiritual Canticle,* 4-6.

69. Cf. John of the Cross, 1.

70. "Coplas del alma que pena por ver a Dios" ("Stanzas of the soul that suffers with longing to see God"), in Kieran Kavanaugh and Otilio Rodriguez, trans. and eds., *The Collected Works of St. John of the Cross* (Washington, D.C.: Institute of Carmelite Studies Publications, 1964), p. 720.

71. *Spiritual Canticle,* 15-19.

72. This is represented by the "wounded stag" in *Spiritual Canticle,* 13.

scriptural context in which to explicate the pneumatic character of the experience of the *mors sensorum,* which was given its figural context in the scriptural-liturgical event of baptism. Along with all of its narrational implications for the life and Passion of Jesus, baptism also pointed in its outcome to the Spirit's refashioning of the Christian, "dead" with Christ, and only then raised to a new existence that included a transformation of the senses themselves.[73]

In contrast to the sixteenth- and seventeenth-century ordering of this contemplative structure according to the shape of the individual Christian vocation, the figurally communal character of its pursuit was generally presupposed, in almost providential terms, in the Middle Ages. It is with this in mind, finally, that we can grasp in what way the ecclesial reality of pneumatic deprivation emerges, in its coherent explication, from the figural reality itself of the Church living temporally within the forms of Christ's own history. The prevalence of a related set of iconographic themes, dating at least from the twelfth century, points to this presupposition. In one image, the Crucifixion is rendered in terms of a woman — *Ecclesia* — wielding the lance that pierces Christ's side, from which, sometimes, a stream of blood flows to be caught by a cup. In another, the blood from the side is itself caught by *Ecclesia,* as Jesus is nailed to the Cross by figures representing the Virtues. In still others, elements of these scenes are combined with a contrast between *Ecclesia* and another woman, who represents the Synagogue of the Jews, forced to give way to her Christian counterpart. The notable element in these common allegories, at least for our purposes, is the manner in which the "wounding," even the "killing," of Jesus is enacted by the Church, or by her (personified) evangelical character. According to the pervasive "spousal" spiritual theology underlying this iconography, these pictures displayed the manner in which Love itself perpetrates the "wound" through which redemption flows, a love that, in both its initiating and its passive postures, is embodied not only in the figure of Jesus, but in the receptive figure of the Church, whose own life both causes and benefits from, as well as participates in, the affliction of her Savior. It is the temporal display of this intimate figural relation that marks the Church's ascendance and the Synagogue's displacement.[74] But it is also one that allows for the elaboration of a symbology of the afflicted Church that would even-

73. Cf. Diadochus, *Capita Gnostica,* 25 (available, with French translation, in the edition of the *Sources Chrétiennes,* V (1955). Cyril of Jerusalem, in his *Catechetical Lectures* 20 and 21, on Baptism and Chrism, brings together the elements of mortifying participation in the Cross and subsequent pneumatic sensory transfiguration. John of the Cross too looked to the "spiritualizing" of the senses; cf. his *Ascent of Mount Carmel,* 11 and 17, and the *Dark Night,* I:24.

74. For an overview, cf. Gertrud Schiller, *Ikonographie der christlichen kunst* (Gütersloh: Gerd Mohn, 1966-90), vol. 2, pp. 149ff., and vol. 4:1, pp. 104ff.

tually support the provocative application, many centuries later, of the Five Wounds of Christ to the ecclesial Body itself, in the notorious tract on the Church's disorder by the nineteenth-century Catholic philosopher and theologian Antonio Rosmini-Serbati.[75]

The fact that this iconographical complex of images for the Church disappeared almost completely in the sixteenth century and after, in itself raises some interesting questions about the reconceived character of ecclesial participation in Christ's life that, in the wake of the Reformation divisions, may have rendered the thematic experience incoherent. It may also indicate the way in which the descent into the figure itself, historically enacted, transformed the sensible apprehension of its meaning through the obscuring process of its own participatory depth. The issue of the "hearing" of Scripture and its pneumatic contradiction, and the nature of the deployment of the other "senses" of the Church that may be distinguished beside it, does not, in any case, demand an explanation outside the broad boundaries of this intuited vision of the ecclesial *mors mystica*. It may well demand, however, a sober engagement with a historical impasse that, however bounded by the Gospel's promise of the efficacy of divine love, or perhaps because so bounded, unveils the Spirit only as if presented on Salome's platter.

Ecclesial Implications of Pneumatic Deprivation

Were we to remain within these bounds and turn more specifically to the question raised by the Christian people's controverted hearing of the Scriptures — if, that is, we were to ask, for instance, "Where is the True Church, in which the Gospel is truly preached?" (a question that both a Luther and a Ratzinger would press with varying emphases) — it is true that we would now have to prescind from a direct answer. For we would now have to say that the True Church — even if present and visible — subsists in a relationship to the Holy Spirit and is constituted by the Holy Spirit, not in the form only of division, but of division tied — in its relation to Scripture in particular — to an inevitable deafness. Ecumenists of diversity cannot run from this

---

75. The notion of the "suffering" as well as "groaning" Church, in both its positive yearnings and its negative degradations, appears in a number of well-known writers like Alvaro Pelayo, Catherine of Siena, Ruysbroeck, and Bellarmine (see below). Rosmini's notorious *Delle cinque piaghe della Santa Chiesa* (1848), which related five categories of necessary reform for the Italian Church to each of the five wounds of Jesus on the Cross, was translated into English, in a slightly abridged form, by H. Liddon (London: Rivingtons, 1883).

judgment.[76] This is the Church's negative visage; but it is inescapably the Church's. Positively, we would say that this ecclesial constitution by the Spirit is ordered toward the manifestation of Christ, figurally in the form of his Passion, anagogically only in the disclosure of his Resurrection.

Nor are we without scriptural support for this suggestion. The pneumatological aspect of this positive visage of the divided and deafened Church is perhaps alluded to in Jesus' discussion of the Spirit in John 16. Traditionally, when engaging the topic of Church and Scripture, attention has been focused on verses 12-15 of the chapter, in which Jesus speaks of the "Spirit of truth," come to "guide" the Church in all things concerning the Son. But the previous verses (7-11) set the operational context for this promise of pneumatic leading. They speak of the Spirit's work in "convincing" the world of "sin," "righteousness," and "judgment," which are linked to the disclosure of "unbelief," the departure of the Son, and the sentence of Satan, the "ruler of this world." There seems little doubt that Jesus here is pointing to his death and ascension, in their confrontation with sin, as the acts through which the Spirit performs its mission. And he speaks of these acts of suffering and departure as themselves the manifested embodiments of pneumatic grace, not only in their discrete historical accomplishment, but as the ongoing figure through which the evolving history of the Church will live, under and with the Truth of the Son's Gospel.[77] Though Jesus speaks of the

---

76. Cf. G. R. Evans, *Problems of Authority in the Reformation Debates* (Cambridge: Cambridge University Press, 1992), who argues that the main stumbling block in the post-Reformation debates and confrontations lay in the inability of the various parties to grasp "the notion of a diversity arising from complementary perceptions of a single and immutable truth" (p. 281; cf. this same notion expressed by Russell Henry Stafford, n. 41 above, in his polemic *against* structural ecumenical *rapprochement* and, more generally, against any "catholic" notion of visible unity; it is revealing to see the same appeal to diversity-in-complementarity for the sake of practically opposing ecclesial agendas). Certainly, this was a problem. But if, as Evans seems to think, we are all wiser about this notion than in the past, it is a wisdom that yet resides in a context of pneumatically ordered incomprehension that still does not know what to do with this notion, let alone with the truth upon which it hangs. Realizing that our differences are not really divisive at all, but rather interesting points of view, does not speak to our real condition, which remains one of deafness.

77. Cf. the remarkable discussion of this text by Pope John Paul II in his Encyclical letter of May 18, 1986, on the Holy Spirit (Section II). Linking this text to Hebrews 9:14, which speaks of the self-offering of Christ upon the Cross "through the eternal Spirit," John Paul speaks of the manner in which the Holy Spirit "descends into the depths of the sacrifice" in order to "consummate" it by the "fire of love" (II:41); and through this act, carried to a universal scope, the "manifestation" or "conviction" of sin, of which Jesus speaks in John 16, is given the efficacy of conversionary redemption. The Spirit works by manifesting the eternal sacrifice of Christ in time. John Paul, however, is less interested in the strict ecclesiological implications of this line of thought than in its ability to illumine something of the Church's mission within the world.

"world" here, it is of a world confronted by the Spirit of the Church. And redemption thus takes place through the form of the Cross's pneumatic display, even in the Church.

Within the constraints of their era, some earlier Catholic thinkers have adopted a similar pneumatology, even to the point of (implicitly anyway) eschewing the chauvinist figural readings of the Church used by most of their coreligionists. Bellarmine, for instance, in a somewhat odd work entitled *De Gemitu Colombae* ("On the lament of the dove"), structured an entire treatise around the notion that the Church, as the place of the Spirit, is a body called to mourning and tears.[78] Divided into three sections, the book first gives a detailed look at the scriptural precedents for such a vocation of sorrow, drawing the Christian community into a figural identity with a wide range of Old Testament prophets and saints. The second section of the volume treats the array of motivations for such sorrowing, the Church's disunity being only one of many ills afflicting the Body of Christ. Finally, twelve *fructus lacrymarum* — "fruits of tears" — are advanced that demonstrate the manner in which the Church fulfills its calling to the Gospel's new life precisely in dwelling patiently amid its brokenness. Bellarmine, of course, is not questioning the Roman Catholic Church's status as the authoritative locus of the Gospel. But in literally identifying that church with the *columba gemens* of Romans 8:26, he links her to the very infirmity under which the whole of creation labors (v. 22), now taken up, through grace, by a *Deus patiens*.

More marginalized Catholics like the Jansenists took this kind of thinking further in concretizing the historical realm in which the Church takes form. In the late seventeenth century, Jean Hamon, the humble doctor of Port-Royal, wrote for the beleaguered nuns of the convent a commentary on Lamentations, in which he embraced the Israel-figure of the Church rigorously, here in the

---

78. Robert Bellarmine, "De Gemitu Columbae, sive De Bono Lacrymarum," in his *Opera Omnia*, ed. J. Fèvre (Paris: 1873, repr. Frankfurt: Minerva GMBH, 1965), vol. 8, pp. 397-484. The title, pregnant with scriptural allusions, may be taken directly from Song of Songs 2:14 and/or Isaiah 59:11. Bellarmine follows in the tradition of the fourteenth-century Franciscan theologian and later bishop, Alvaro Pelayo, whose profound reflection upon the Avignon papal schism gave rise to a remarkable ecclesiological volume, *De statu et planctu ecclesiae*, whose printed editions of 1517 and 1560 fed a demand for Catholic reform in the period. Alvaro took as his figural basis the book of Lamentations (see below and Chapter 5); and in Book II of his work, he examines with great detail the various ills of the Church, according to the various stations and offices of its members. His own positive ecclesiology is based on a ripe understanding of the "Mystical Body," its intertestamental figural reality, and the character of penitential abandonment upon which its integrity depends. For a limited discussion of this significant, but widely overlooked, author, cf. Nicolas Iung, *Un franciscain, théologien du pouvoir pontifical au XIVe siècle, Alvaro Pelayo, évêque et pénitencier de Jean XXII* (Paris: J. Vrin, 1931).

form of the destroyed city of Jerusalem. Starting from the historical point of the Church's interior corruptions and divisions, Hamon turns each of the prophet's sorrows into a description of the Catholic Church, the ultimate integrity of which he can maintain only by recasting its character in the form of its crucified Savior, the "spouse" to the lamenting bride.[79] When, then, he comes to the famous verse 1:16, in which the "absence of the Comforter" is asserted, he speaks of the Church's necessary figural conformance with its Lord, abandoned in the grip of sin by God upon the Cross.[80]

Hamon here points to the direction that Jansenist thinking will later take with respect to the reality of ecclesial division, when, commenting on 1:5, he describes the proper attitude in which the Church, and her members, is to suffer her afflictions:

> We must imitate the spirit of the Church, for it is the spirit of her Spouse; and we must never stray from his moderation. She does not oppose those who mistreat her, since she understands that the true cause of her mistreatment are her sins. They are her sins because they are our own. We have nothing else to do but to humble ourselves in the face of all these disorders, to silence ourselves and to groan.[81]

By the end of the seventeenth century, Jansenists and especially those associated with Port-Royal were already aware of their precarious status within the Roman Church. The notion of the Church — Christ's Bride and hence his Body — suffering her own internal attack at the hands of her members seemed an evident reality. Hamon's counsel of suffering moderation, then, became axiomatic for the party. And it was extended to an entire theory

79. Hardly an idiosyncratic insistence, Hamon follows the interpretive line drawn by the seventeenth-century French liturgical elaboration of the *Tenebrae* services, at which portions of Lamentations were methodically sung as figures of the Passion through the repentant voice of the Church. For all that, Lamentations was not frequently commented upon, perhaps because the figural implications so patent in the Church's continued use of this text were evidently disturbing. Calvin, who no longer had the liturgical framework as a guide, was free to read Lamentations in a purely "historical" sense, useful for its moral warnings but with little ongoing prophetic center (see his brief commentary on the book). Other Protestants, like the Irish Anglican John Hull, used the book as a basis for elaborate displays of encyclopedic erudition, drawing on Kabalah, Midrash, Joachimism, the Fathers, and medieval mystical exegesis in order to provide a cosmic hermeneutic of divine sovereignty, in contrast to which his few attempts to locate the Churches of Ireland and England within the text fall rather flat. Cf. John Hull, *An Exposition upon a Part of the Lamentations of Ieremie* [1617] (London: 1718). Lamentations, in its figural role as an explicator of the Church, is discussed below in Chapter 5.
80. Hamon, pp. 59f.
81. Hamon, pp. 21f.

regarding the character of dissent within the Church that included within it, logically, an evaluation of the Protestant separation as well. Pierre Nicole, for instance, in his celebrated attack on French Calvinists, had contemporaneously put forward the claim that no supposed sin on the part of the Church justified the establishment of a new alternative Christian society and ministry. The most that a Christian could ever be pressed, by conscience, to allow was a "simple and negative separation, which consists in the refusal of certain acts of communion, without however involving positive acts of separation against the community from which one separates."[82] It is best, under such circumstances, that the disaffected remain "without pastors and without an exterior cult, as they wait for God to provide for them in some extraordinary fashion," than that they should erect a distinct ministry.[83] By the eighteenth century, when many Jansenists were deprived of sacraments for their opposition to the Bull *Unigenitus,* this "negative" separation became a fulfilled practice. But *as a practice,* it was possible only because, *contra* Calvin and the Roman Catholic triumphalists together, it was nourished by a vision of the Church as a Body whose pneumatic indefectibility was informed by the reality of the Passion's pneumatic abandonment. No other perspective allowed for the simple suffering of, and hence repentant redemption through, the Church's disarray.[84]

82. Pierre Nicole, *Prejugez legitimes contre les Calvinistes,* nouvelle ed. (Paris: 1725), p. 137.

83. Nicole, p. 145.

84. Nicole's argument was in fact quite traditional from a Catholic perspective. It informed most sensible Romanist responses to Protestant separation from the time of people like Erasmus: one might well admit to abuses, indeed horrendous corruption, within the Church; but such illnesses were to be borne and opposed from within the Church's structures, not from without. Erasmus's weary remark that "there will always be some things good men must endure" points to the sense of a profound suffering of the Body, even in the face of its manifold evils. Cf. the selections of Erasmus on disputes and divisions in the Church in *Erasmus and the Seamless Coat of Jesus,* trans. and intro. Raymond Himelick (Lafayette, Ind.: Purdue University Studies, 1971), p. 82 and passim. By Nicole's time, this argument was a commonplace. Bossuet, for instance, bases a large part of his famously effective 1655 attack against Paul Ferry's Protestant "Catechism" on just this attitude: only the patent inability of a person to be saved within the Church could possibly justify separation from it. If, as Ferry and most mainstream Protestants allowed, salvation was still to be had in the Roman Church at least up to 1543, prior to the Council of Trent's decisions, then the whole Reformed separation is condemned from the start, since a basic definition of the true Church is that it be a place in which salvation is engendered through Christ. In any situation short of the Church's losing that status, Christians must be willing to endure its failures. Cf. Bossuet's *Réfutation du Catéchisme du Sieur Paul Ferry,* in *Oeuvres Complètes,* vol. 4, pp. 184ff. "Enduring" the fallen Church, however, remained a largely theoretical proposal for most Catholic controversialists (certainly for people like Bossuet). And not until the Jansenists demonstrated what it might mean (and, by extension, what it might have meant for the Reformers of the previous century) did the proposal manifest the depth of its ecclesiological rationale.

Pneumatic Deprivation and the Church's "Hearing" of Scripture

Applied to our present era, then, this kind of vision asserts that the pnuematic deprivation implied in the Church's division does *not* falsify the truth of the Gospel, or its power for salvation. But it nonetheless still leaves unanswered the whole issue of scriptural comprehension within the Church, of how we can *hear* God's Word spoken to us. If the hermeneutic incoherence observed earlier is indeed regnant, let alone celebrated, and if it is intrinsically so because of the negative relation existing between Holy Spirit and divided Church, then what divine role is Scripture in particular to play in the Church, and how are we to receive it?

Theologians from all sides of the confessional divides have always affirmed the pre-Reformation principle — whether we see it as Pauline or Augustinian — that true "understanding" of the Bible is embodied, somehow, in obedience; otherwise Scripture functions not as a living Word, but as a "dead letter." It is a simple matter of description to observe, on the basis of this principle, that within the divided Church Scripture is not, by definition, understood *in general (generaliter)*, because the general character of the Church, whether or not one subscribes to an ecclesiologically unified structure, clearly does not represent the scriptural descriptions of its normative faithfulness as Church. That *in particular (in partes)* Scripture is still understood, that specific aspects of Scripture are still evident and still open to accurate apprehension, no one would doubt. But in all the debates between Reformers and Romanists, this was *never* in doubt, and the Erasmian hermeneutic of erudition, even when leveled to its most basic plane of commonsense reading, was never questioned as a universal possibility among the reprobate or the apostate.[85] The issue turned not on particular understandings, but on the general understanding of Scripture as the Gospel of Christ manifest and perceived, on "true hearing." And this possibility, both Protestant and Catholic affirmed together, was tied strictly to the integrity of pneumatic operation. So we must ask if the Scripture is not generally understood, how is it that the Spirit is working through it?

One way of getting at an answer to this question is to examine how Christians have construed more limited examples of the Spirit's absence with respect to the hearing of the Gospel. In Catholic spiritual theology, there are

---

85. Cf. Owen, "Pneumatologia," in *Works*, vol. 4, VI:8 (pp. 209-26), on the various means of parsing scriptural discourse clearly, available to all, which yet demand the special work of the Holy Spirit to "perceive the mind of God and Christ therein," available only to "good" and "holy believers."

the many analyses of pneumatic "aridity." Puritans, for their part, worried about this issue on an individualist basis, as they analyzed situations in which a Christian might no longer receive the proper fruit from, among other things, the reading of Scripture. To take but one example from this wide literature, we can look at the seventeenth-century New England pastor Nehemiah Hobart's attempt to describe the shape of the Holy Spirit's self-distancing from the Christian. It must be admitted that Hobart's firmly Puritan discourse on the *Absence of the Comforter* hardly shared the ecclesiology we have been suggesting is necessary if we are accurately to place divided Church and Spirit in relation to one another. For although he apparently believed that the churches of Connecticut were in a bad way, spiritually — a fact that motivated his reflections in the first place — he affirmed that the Gospel (as against the Law) was still being preached within them and that there was sufficient unity among them so as to preclude a complete "withdrawing" of the Spirit.[86] Further, as he wrote within the tradition of Congregationalist pneumatology established by John Owen, Hobart's interests were basically focused on the individual Christian. Elements of individual Christian behavior alone seemed to him to signal the possibility of pneumatic deprivation.[87] Nonetheless, the very fact that Hobart chose to provide a kind of dark counterpoint, however unconsciously, to someone like Owen's vast subjectivist pneumatology is worthy of notice; and his remarks on the topic, if projected ecclesially, are pertinent to our argument.[88]

Near the opening of his treatise, Hobart outlines some of the main ways in which the Holy Spirit fulfills its mission as "Comforter." These include, in paradigmatic Puritan fashion, the work of "convicting" a person of sin, conversion, and sanctification. Within this triad, Hobart lays special stress on the role of the Comforter in enacting a right and saving relationship between Scripture and Christian: the Spirit comforts by "opening the heart to the truth" of Scripture; by "applying" God's "Promises" to the contexts of Scripture, the Gospel, Christ, the future, and the individual heart; and by "reminding" us

---

86. Nehemiah Hobart, *The Absence of the Comforter, Described and Lamented* (New London [Conn.]: Timothy Green, 1717), pp. 124ff. Hobart's book was published posthumously, under the circumstances described in the Preface by Eliphalet Adams. As a Congregationalist, furthermore, Hobart (like Owen) saw "unity" as residing in perceived fundamental common doctrines, irrespective of visible differences and antagonisms.

87. Hobart, pp. 134ff.

88. Hobart's project was not, in itself, extraordinary in the context of Puritan introspective analyses, which attempted to delineate the shape of interior spiritual health. But the systematic way in which he tried to forge a pneumatological basis for this unveiling of the soul's disease ("soul misery") was, as far as I know, exceptional.

of God's actions, as given in Scripture. All this constitutes the central pneumatic work of "instruction," on the basis of Nehemiah 9:20 ("Thou gavest thy good Spirit to instruct them . . .").[89]

The possible and in fact frequent "absence of the Comforter," in contrast, Hobart takes to be axiomatic of much human experience. Such absence, noted literally in Lamentations 1:16, is a real fear for the Psalmist in 51:11, and a real fate for many others in Scripture (e.g., Saul, in Sam. 28:15). So obvious and common is this possibility that Hobart does not even bother to describe in any detail its "cause." Instead, having explained the Comforter's mission positively, he spends most of the treatise detailing in what forms the deprivation of that mission will affect either the ungodly[90] or, more importantly and extensively, the godly. Yes, he notes, there is a sense in which the Holy Spirit is never "absent" from either group, working with both in their creation and natural preservation, speaking through "conscience," providing continuously a "carnal offer" of the Gospel, and "grieving" over sin. For the godly (i.e., the elect), in particular, the Spirit is, in some sense, always present in providing the grace of perseverance and, in a kind of negative fashion, in rendering them "sensibly dissatisfied" by pneumatic withdrawal.

But although Hobart explicitly affirms the promise made in Isaiah 59:21 — "my spirit which is upon you, and my words which I have put in your mouth, shall not depart . . . from this time forth for evermore" — he describes its fulfillment as given in only a hidden fashion under the circumstances of the Comforter's absence. The Isaiah text, of course, offers a clear assertion of the promised relation between Spirit and Word. Yet given that this relation is established in the Spirit's work as "Comforter" in particular, the absence of the Comforter must logically alter the embodied form such a relation can take for the Christian. And so Hobart insists that one of the clearest "signs" of the Spirit's "withdrawing" does indeed touch upon the manner in which Scripture is able to speak to the Christian; that is, it results in "dullness in learning or coming to the distinct understanding of the truth."[91] This is the sum of the matter: when the Spirit withdraws, as it often does, we are dulled to the truth of the Scriptures. There are, to be sure, other signs of the Spirit's absence. But for Hobart the reversal of the basic role of the Comforter in "instruction" is linked, as their fundamental source, to the whole range of more particular signs of pneumatic deprivation that manifest themselves in discrete forms of ungodly behavior.[92]

89. Hobart, pp. 34-53.
90. Hobart, pp. 62ff.
91. Hobart, pp. 143ff.
92. On the latter, cf. Hobart, pp. 87ff.

All this is in line with prophetic texts that, as we have seen, speak of pneumatic deprivation and antagonism in terms of "deafness" or "stupor," although now made explicit in their application to the Gospel's obscurity within the Scriptures. But does Hobart have some constructive purpose in proposing this analysis? Curiously, the book seems to have little interest in providing directives for "retrieving" the Spirit. There is no attempt to offer the Christian a means of "fixing" the "soul-misery" of the Comforter's absence. Rather, Hobart wishes only to alert the Christian to the shape and meaning of this particular pneumatic condition. And the fruit of such awareness will be twofold. First, there will be a knowledge that the absence of the Comforter is consistent with the Gospel itself. It is promised in the Gospel (understood as underlying the whole of Scripture), and it embodies that Gospel insofar as it drives the godly to a new humility and dependence upon God. Much of this talk by Hobart sounds themes commonly found in Puritan discussions about the "profitable" aspects of scriptural obscurity.[93] Awareness of the Comforter's absence offers a second fruit: that a faithful response to such consistency between the Gospel and the Spirit's withdrawal is the difficult and patient suffering of it in repentance. All that is left to the pneumatically deprived Christian is an unadorned "listening" to Scripture, unconcerned with any "disputation" of its significance; all that remains is a dogged waiting before the Word, excruciating though its ostensible silence may be.[94]

Projecting Hobart's vision from the individual to the ecclesial spheres, we can say that, in a situation of the Spirit's deprivation, Scripture works, even in and because of its pneumatically rendered obscurity, for the manifestation of a promised condition of spiritual poverty. In a particularized manner parallel to the Spirit's own mission within such a situation, the silence of Scripture in the churches somehow testifies, in a negative fashion, to the reality of Christ, *sub contrario,* in the form of his Passion. The Reformers themselves understood something of this aspect of Scripture's universally effective power, whatever the circumstances of its apprehension. They tended to cast this negative role, however, in terms of bringing into relief the unbelief of the reprobate, thereby "damning" them in the act of their refusal to hear

---

93. Cf. Whitaker, pp. 365ff.; John Owen, "Pneumatologia," in *Works,* vol. 4, pp. 190f. and 197.

94. "Disputation" over Scripture leads to "disunity" in the Christian community. This is one of the few places where Hobart actually links together — if unreflectively — the realities of pneumatic withdrawal, the hearing of Scripture, and Christian *division* in particular. In this case, however, division is a secondary consequence of the former elements, not a primary locus of pneumatic deprivation. But, as we noted, Hobart has no real concern with the possibility of Christian division. Cf. Hobart, pp. 284ff.

Scripture's truth.[95] From our perspective, however, we can say more properly that the Church in which the Scripture is pneumatically rendered obscurely silent is the Church in which the Word of God reveals the judgment upon sin made manifest in the death of Christ. In doing so, according to John's image, Christ is still and perhaps especially "glorified," even as the Church itself stands astounded in the face of such an open act wrought upon it. The Gospel proclaimed in such a Church is still the Gospel, though in a way that escapes the Church's explicit testimony. For that the Church is formed and lives by grace can be nowhere more evident than here.

Far from contradicting the promise made by Jesus concerning the Holy Spirit's "counsel" in "teaching the truth" to the Church, for example, in John 14, this kind of construal of pneumatic deprivation in the voice of Scripture allows for the continuing fulfillment of that promise amid a community of Christ's followers who have egregiously opposed the fundamental element of the promise's context, "love one another as I have loved you" (John 15:12). By revealing the power of God's justice exercised in the divided Church, yet first provided in Christ's self-giving, such justice is made congruent with God's mercy; and despite the Church's own practical contradiction of Jesus' exhortation, the Spirit is shown, through its own withdrawal, yet to "bring to remembrance" all that the Lord had spoken (John 14:26).

What then does the Scripture mean to us in the divided Church, or what is it destined by God to mean? There is some parallel to this pneumatically deprived functioning of Scripture in Paul's discussion of the nature of the "old covenant"'s and the Gospel's significance to the non-Christian Jews (2 Cor. 3:7–4:6). In each case, some scripture or message, "spiritual" in itself (cf. Rom. 7:14), fulfills its purpose in a negative way through the Spirit's particular ordering toward its obscurement. And even while Paul clearly does not have in mind in this text the relation of Gospel to Christian Church, he notes that that relation, even at its most positive, is one borne in an "earthen vessel" designed to make visible the "death of Jesus" in the Christian's body (2 Cor. 4:7-12). Applied to the Church as a *divided* whole or in its scattered parts, which is a deliberately "figuralist" application, we can say that the Christian community manifests the death of Christ in its body now to the degree that it becomes as the Jews standing before the veiled Gospel. In being confronted by this Gospel, there is revealed to the Church a limited "splendor"; but what the Gospel's full splendor might be, the splendor of the unobscured Word,

---

95. Cf. Calvin's remarks on Hebrews 4:12, in his commentary on that Letter: God never speaks "in vain," bringing, through the proclamation of his Word, some to salvation and driving others to perdition.

spoken in a, by and large, pneumatically unobstructed Church, cannot yet be imagined. In this way, Christian Israel has indeed been thrust back, through the weight of its present history, upon its unity with Jewish Israel. What I am suggesting, quite bluntly, is that we consider Paul's warning in Romans 11:21 as a prophecy fulfilled: "For if God did not spare the natural branches, neither will he spare you."

Thus, the figural parallel tentatively drawn by Ratzinger between Christian division and the division of Christian and Jewish Israel in Romans 9–11 appears to be more than simile. It is a connection rendered organic — fulfilled — in Christ. We do not, because of our condition of pneumatic deprivation, either cease to read the Scriptures or cease to preach upon them. We can still apprehend and proclaim the Gospel such as, for instance, Paul describes it in 1 Corinthians 15:1-11 — elements of factual detail whose significance, in a broad way, is fundamental for the outcome to human destiny and is still perceivable as such. Christ's death for our sins according to Scripture, and his Resurrection and living appearances to his followers are not historically obviated by the Church's division. Yet our method of reading and applying this Gospel and Scripture as a whole must now surely demand a shift from a mode of scriptural authorization (by which we use biblical texts as positive explicators or imperatives) to a mode of "sifting" or "searching," much as the Jewish community in Beroea did (Acts 17), seeking to dwell more knowingly in the realm of listening that explores again the fundamental relationship between "Jewish" and "Christian" Testaments, the "scriptures" "according" to which the Gospel has any significance. We must learn to read the Scriptures in a manner parallel to that of the first-century Jewish believers. And though we consider the New Testament's apostolic witness as a now integrated portion of that Scripture, it is still one that stands, in relation to the Old Testament, in a position requiring exegetical testing by the Old.

In doing this, then, Christians will read Scripture not from a posture of skepticism, but from the conviction that the revelation of God in Christ Jesus takes its meaning from the character of Israel, its promises, and their fulfillment. Thus, if, as Bruce Marshall has potently suggested, the "credibility of the Gospel" is tied to the unity of the Church, then in our given situation we are called to test not *whether* Jesus is Lord, for example, but *how* this conviction is credibly explicated in the context of the Scripture's promises, given the state of the Church. Much as with the first Jewish Christians, the Scriptures will here function as a grid by which to render coherent an accepted claim about God's work in the world, although in this case in the face and in the midst of an incoherence that the Christian Church has itself incarnated. Just as we reappropriate our identity as Israel, witnessed to in Scripture, we are called to use that Scripture, its opacity speaking against us in the form of the Passion, as the basis for a "Christodicy": by means of Scripture we must ask, how are the ways of Christ shown to be righteous in the life of the Church as it is now constituted?[96] Therefore, although the Gospel can still be proclaimed, it will speak only to the degree that it is put to the test in describing God's dealing with the Church, and in this description revealing the form of Christ.

There are indications that some theologians of Scripture have at least glimpsed this possible demand pressed by the historical situation of the Church (however variously analyzed — and division rarely functions in such analysis).[97] Yet such testing of the Gospel itself, trying its voice and meaning on the hard surfaces of the Church's actual experience of disarray, is not something that has ever been easily assimilated to the scholarly task, within either the biblical or the theological disciplines. (The Reformers and their opponents were perhaps among the last scholars to have done this, albeit with a negative outcome!) And it is to be wondered if in fact these are the contexts where such testing can take place at all to any real degree.

96. This question — and hence the central role that only Scripture can play in answering it — cannot be resolved simply by applying to the Church the character of *simul justus et peccator,* as if the Church's failings in, among other things, maintaining unity is to be expected given its human constitution. Cf. Marshall, p. 85: if, as even Calvin supposed, the Church's unity instantiates the unity of the Trinity, and indeed the Church is "Church" because of this, then its disunity can have nothing to do with the categorically different relationship of human sinfulness to divine grace. Of course, if we wish to understand this latter relationship in figural concert with the sacrifice of Christ, who became sin even though he knew no sin, we might be able to speak in terms of the Church as simultaneously sinner and justified. But even in this case, the compatibility of the Church's disunity with its status as "Church" would be clear only in terms of the credible ways in which Christ's sacrificial life might be shared with the Church through its self-denials. This remains the crucial issue that is avoided in attempts to describe the divisions of the Christian Church solely in terms of *inevitable* human frailty. The early Fathers had no trouble denoting the Church as sinner, even as "whore"; yet they could do so because they saw its condition as one of integral union with the "One who became sin" in the act of redeeming his people from sin; the Church's sinfulness, then, did not, in their eyes, undermine its integrity as a people among whom and with whom Christ was to be found; and "separation" from sin could never, contrary to a Puritan view, justify separation from the Church. Cf. Y.-M.-J. Congar, *Vraie et Fausse réforme dans l'Église* (Paris: Éditions du Cerf, 1969), pp. 78-83, for a discussion of this material, with bibliography.

97. With respect to the practice of biblical theology, the kinds of topics and approaches given by this inescapable role of Scripture in the Church are only indirectly suggested in the remarks above. Certainly Brevard Childs has courageously and carefully ordered his own study according to the reality of the Christian Church's convoluted obduracy in the face of Scripture's pure speech, an ordering that must remain foundational to the challenge of testing the Gospel. And Childs has further begun to speak in terms of a larger vocation the Church has to "search for the Christian Bible," in a way that is perhaps analogous to the present suggestion. Cf. Childs, p. 67.

For the testing of Christodicy, by which the scriptural promises of Christ are justified in the life of the Church, must ultimately proceed to the sensible embrace of the Spirit's own power at work in the contradiction under question.[98] This has been rather the province of holiness than of learning, of saints than of savants. In such people, on whom the weight of the Spirit is let down, in presence or in flight, brusquely and forcibly, unexpected paths are pursued, barriers are thrown down, and the Scriptures opened up to the clarity of apprehended hearing. Were there not popes, monks, seminary professors, even tinkers or cobblers — individuals who in the past proved servants of our ecclesial rending, of our spiritual deprivation, and of our blindness to the Word? Who knows? It is perhaps time for these offices to be visibly redeemed from their legacies through their use by unexpected individuals of grace. Few today would perhaps care what a Protestant of sanctity did. But were the Pope to walk to Wittenberg or Canterbury on his knees in pursuit of the form of Christ, the greatest beneficiary might be the Scriptures, a vessel of grace from which would pour the host of theological and, more importantly, ecclesial blessings that now seem so parsimoniously distributed. Because of men and women, the Church quietly fractured over centuries and then exploded into fragments. Is it too much to expect that the same power that used these limited vessels — individuals of power — to such destruction might not turn them again to another end? For is not this the power "who has torn us to pieces that he might heal us" (Hos. 6:1)?

But, then, the restoration of ecclesial unity may not really be a "goal" in the normal sense of a practical agenda, for the sake of which practical (if also necessarily courageous, even holy) people pursue well-ordered strategies. To the degree that disunity does, in fact, reflect something yet more profound and mysterious, involving the destiny of God's redemption of human sin as it takes historical form, even the form of a divinely incarnate servant whose figure now confronts the groaning for redemption among traitorous Christians, it cannot properly be viewed as a broken structure awaiting its repair at the hands

---

98. Cf. Ratzinger's remark that "today unity is not to be created through doctrine and discussion alone but only through religious power" ("Luther and the Unity of the Churches," p. 105). This is to be contrasted, in Ratzinger's mind, with a "forced march" approach to ecumenism (allegedly commended by Rahner-Fries) by which church leaders will simply forge reunions not based on real communion of faith, but on hierarchical fiats, expecting flocks to follow. But if the "force" is the bonding example of holiness, how is the freedom of the Spirit thereby contradicted? The "fiat" of ecclesial leadership, in any case, is hardly to be expected, under the present circumstances, to risk such radical departures from denominational self-preservation. This is probably not because of cowardice, but because of the constricted ecclesiological options that division itself bequeaths.

of the most skillful. Ecclesial disunity conforms to a "body," a given body shaped by the details of experience described in the terms of the Scriptures (however reticent those terms may now be to theological analysis). Bodies, especially bodies laid out with the pallor of insensibility, bodies of the dead, await not medical specialists, but Creators. Their quieted subjugation within the realm of benumbed feeling receives the facets of their history as a temporally unmeasured openness to the Coming of God. Hearing awaits the forming and the offer of its primordial noise. So too, one would imagine, must rest the complement of corporeal receptors that engage the Church's form in its enforced divestiture of apprehension. It is to these other senses that we now turn, aware, perhaps, that penitence will require the recognition of their stunted usefulness.

Chapter Two

Contesting the Visible:
Miracle and Holiness
in the Divided Church

The Ecumenical Appeal to Holiness

To say that the Word may await its true hearing only by "saints," by the unattended vessels of God's Spirit in the Church, whose radiant sanctity proves itself through the overturning of imprisoning expectation, is not to say that somehow the Church can compensate for the loss of hearing through elevated guidance by the holy — as if all that were at issue was the relocation of the seat of power from the scholar to the charismatic, and so the Church could simply reconstitute its faithfulness through some adjustment of regard. Affirming the kind of servants God will use for the Church's restoration, even awaiting them with expectation, cannot result in a structure for their encouragement and identification. For the morass of misunderstanding into which the Word is thrust within the divided Church extends to include even the brilliance of the Spirit's human instruments. After all, can the basis for their recognition come independently from the ear of faith?

This question arises in the face of contemporary assertions that it might — that if we cannot agree on the meaning of the Scriptures and their rule, at least we can be drawn close in the Spirit's human rustling and force. Most recently, Pope John Paul II forcefully reaffirmed this characteristically current hope that, if the doctrinal path to unity be blocked, there is an alternative

57

route by way of holiness, given ultimate expression in the phenomenon of martyrdom, among both Catholics and Protestants:

> All Christian communities know that, thanks to the power given by the Spirit, obeying [the Father's] will and overcoming those obstacles [to unity] are not beyond their reach. All of them in fact have martyrs for the Christian faith. Despite the tragedy of our divisions, these brothers and sisters have preserved an attachment to Christ and to the Father so radical and absolute as to lead even to the shedding of blood. . . . The fact that one can die for the faith shows that other demands of the faith can also be met. . . . While for all Christian communities the martyrs are the proof of the power of grace, they are not the only ones to bear witness to that power. Albeit in an invisible way, the communion between our communities, even if still incomplete, is truly and solidly grounded in the full communion of saints. . . . When we speak of a common heritage, we must acknowledge as part of it not only the institutions, rites, means of salvation and the traditions which all the communities have preserved and by which they have been shaped, but first and foremost this reality of holiness. . . . This universal presence of the saints is in fact a proof of the transcendent power of the Spirit. It is the sign and proof of God's victory over the forces of evil which divide humanity. . . . Since God in his infinite mercy can always bring good even out of situations which are an offense to his plan, we can discover that the Spirit has allowed conflicts to serve in some circumstances to make explicit certain aspects of the Christian vocation, as happens in the lives of the saints. In spite of fragmentation, which is an evil from which we need to be healed, there has resulted a kind of rich bestowal of grace which is meant to embellish the *koinonia*.[1]

The import of the Pope's comments here, near the end of his encyclical on ecumenism, is clear: "obstacles" to ecclesial unity not only *can* be overcome, but *are being* overcome even now in the lives of holiness formed in the Spirit by individuals from all Christian denominations. And such holiness is a "sign" and "proof," a phenomenal evidence, not only of what God is doing, but of how we are to follow in his plan for the healing of his Church. This is a sentiment already stated elsewhere in particular ecumenical dialogues.[2]

---

1. John Paul II, *Ut Unum Sint* (1995), par. 83-85.
2. Cf. the remarkable Methodist–Roman Catholic statement on the Holy Spirit (the "Honolulu Report") of 1981, especially section II, where pneumatic holiness, as valued by both Methodists and Roman Catholics, is tied to the present "signs" of the Spirit's work in the world, and is linked also to the visible authority of the Church (II:B). The topic of this report was itself unique in the ecumenical movement up to this time, and provides a striking contrast with

This ecumenical commonality of sanctified witness is, however, only obliquely demonstrated by John Paul, in a footnote where he refers to the Catholic affirmation of the grace of martyrdom given in the experience of the Protestant victims of persecution in nineteenth-century Uganda.[3] The affirmation, accepted by earlier commentators on the Uganda Martyrs, is based on solid scholastic arguments concerning the nature of martyrdom itself, as it may apply among "heretics" and "schismatics."[4] But within these parameters, the demonstration is a historically limited one upon which to base a sweeping pneumatological claim applicable to the breadth of the divided Church.[5] Most Protestant "martyrs," according to these very arguments, would not qualify for Catholic recognition because their witness was tied to an explicit support for "heretical" or "schismatic" structures, to which their understanding of the Gospel was attached. It is by no means easy, within the limits posed by the Catholic Church's traditional teaching on the matter, to disentangle "dying for the faith" from dying for a "faith" that is founded in heretical commitments. Yet the Pope himself seems to imply that the very divisions that ground such

---

other dialogues in its approach to discussing the Church. Yet at the same time, the entire report (as with earlier reports of this working dialogue) is premised on the consistent working of the Holy Spirit among all Christians throughout the Church's history, and the resulting eeriness of the contradiction between subject matter and its *historical occasion* is all the more evident: what does it mean for churches to "agree" about pneumatic holiness when the framework for their discussion is one of Christian separation? What is the living witness to the Spirit within the Church that grounds their affirmations? The assumption, of course, is that sanctification and the "experience" of the Spirit are uniform even within division. But then, how understand division's wound, except in an extra-pneumatic fashion? We have seen that this path is probably a dead end.

3. Footnote 137 (and later 139), where he cites Vatican II's *Unitatis redintegratio* 4, presumably the phrase "it is right and salutary to recognize the riches of Christ and virtuous works in the lives of others who are bearing witness to Christ, sometimes even to the shedding of their blood" (echoed in the main text of his encyclical), which is given concretization through citations of Pope Paul VI's addresses at the canonization of the Uganda Martyrs and later at their shrine in Uganda.

4. Cf. J. P. Thoonen, *Black Martyrs* (New York: Sheed & Ward, 1941), pp. 290ff., with references; and also James Edward Sherman, *The Nature of Martyrdom: A Dogmatic and Moral Analysis According to the Teaching of St. Thomas Aquinas* (Paterson [N.J.]: St. Anthony Guild Press, 1942), pp. 74-78.

5. In general, Catholic theologians have argued that the Protestant Ugandan martyrs were "ignorant" of the specifically heretical character of the church in which they had received the Gospel, because of their ignorance of ecclesial division itself and of its significance; thus, their death for the sake of the Gospel was, in their own mind, purely focused on Christ, untainted by the defect in faith otherwise attendant upon Protestant "testimony." It is not at all clear how many other Protestant "martyrs" — according to Protestant acclaim — could actually meet this standard.

structures might be instruments of the Spirit's "making explicit" its power of sanctification, by providing divided Christians the opportunity to demonstrate faith even unto death. While unity among Christians remains only "invisibly" sustained by such cross-denominational witness, the witness itself, he seems to argue, is clear evidence of such unity.

Does this kind of statement about pneumatic clarity in holiness make sense? What can be the logical relation between the obscurity of unity and the "explicitness" of the Spirit's grace across the boundaries of divided churches, which still somehow gives "proof" of such (albeit "incomplete") unity that most Christians have refused to accept? One need not invalidate John Paul's basic assertions by posing such a question, since, in the end, the assertion's truth turns on the meaning of "proof" and the scope of its accessibility. Just as in our more general discussion of the character of pneumatic deprivation it is possible to assert the Spirit's absence even while affirming that absence as somehow bound to its larger mission of figural exposition, so it may well also be possible to claim the lucidity of pneumatic *martyria* within the divided Church as an element of Christ's own ostensively redemptive form. But in either case, the intimate relation between clarity and obscurity is necessarily paradoxical, and can hardly bear the commonsense connotations of "evidence."

The question itself points to the significance of the Church's phenomenal history, wherein division seems less to emphasize, even by contrast or perverse provocation, the eruption of sanctity into view than to envelop it within the clouds of its own internal contentious combustion. Despite the kinds of theoretical convergences on the matter of holiness and the Spirit's "signs" the Methodist–Roman Catholic dialogues may envisage, to the present day most Protestants, including these same Methodists (and many Catholics raised within a common civil culture), would probably reiterate, in a more subtle way, the judgments still made "explicit" on the subject of Catholic saints and their luminous wonders, well into the nineteenth century and beyond, by one of Newman's notorious controversialist partners, the Scottish theologian John Cumming:

> Now, there is not a Roman Catholic saint who does not positively weep and perspire miracles. He seems like an electric jar, for they burst from him in brilliant coruscations at every pore. A Romish saint unsurrounded by miracles would be a nonentity, an absurdity.
>
> . . . Those miracles. . . are, some so ludicrously grotesque, some so palpably absurd, others so meaningless, pointless, and objectless, and others so anile, that not to laugh at, or deplore, and certainly scout them as the proofs of lunacy, or fanaticism, or wild delusion, is to do injustice and discredit to the sublime and solemn miracles of Christianity. There is such

a similarity, almost identity, between heathen and Romish miracles, — both about equally authenticated, — that one cannot help thinking that Satan is doing for the Popedom what he did for heathendom, and no more.[6]

If sanctity brings evidence or proof of anything beyond perversion at the bar of disputing Christians, then it must first be sifted and distilled before the eyes of the world by some process the violence of which few would today wish to lift up as a standard means of ecumenical judgment. Even John Paul's "supreme" distinction, the testimony of the blood shed for the faith, drains into a contested well, where blood challenges blood by the brightness of some color undetected, and where, in the end, what is seen can no longer be believed, since the senses have been apprenticed to the Devil, and one church's martyr is the other's satanic minion:

> We [Protestants] have a real unity: We only need to develop it. Rome has a false unity, and the more it is known the less it will be seen to be real. And let us all have a strong pull . . . together; and by God's blessing, a thousand promises will converge, and unite their echoes in that anthem in which angels and martyrs around the throne will join, "Babylon the great is fallen, is fallen!" And if there should be anyone in this assembly so ill informed as to sympathize with her in the day of her destruction, such sympathies will rush back to Bartholemew, to Smithfield, to the Marian martyrs and they will return armed with indignation, and rejoice to join the cry, "Reward her as she has rewarded you. Hallelujah!"[7]

If the true Church, at unity with itself, is known by the gleam of its sanctity and the blood of its martyrs, each shouting for vindication at the Lamb's throne, one against another, is it any wonder that even a Pope would toy with "invisible" evidences? Or that, at least, the Spirit might seem to delight in disguisement?

---

6. John Cumming, "Review of Dr. Newman's Lectures" and "Romish Miracles," in his *Lectures on Romanism* (Boston: John P. Jewett and Co., 1854), pp. 580f., and 692f.

7. Cumming, "Review of Dr. Newman's Lectures," pp. 591f. Cumming can scathingly apply the Protestant argument, common since the sixteenth century, that Romanism is a satanic tool of skepticism, since, by demanding the acquiescence of faith to alleged "miracles" that the senses cannot truly corroborate, it ends by tainting all of religion with the charge of "superstition"; and so "do not be startled if I say, that Voltaire, and Diderot, and D'Alembaert, and other of the infidels of the last century, were the creations of the Roman Catholic religion" (p. 590). But who shall guarantee the sense that discerns the blood of deepest hue as that flowing from the wounds of Protestants, dying at the hands of Catholics, rather than Catholics at the hands of Protestants?

The Adjudicatory Character of Pneumatic Visibility

The contrast between the hearing of the word and the visibility of the church is one that is today usually associated with the contrast between Protestant and Catholic theological mentalities. To the degree that the contrast refers more narrowly to popular liturgical and devotional forms — for example, the place of the sermon and the role of Scripture in individual piety among Protestants vs. the ecclesially centered worship and imagistic devotion of Catholics — the commonplace comparison may have some merit.[8] But the relationship between hearing and seeing within the Christian life and Church is far more ambiguous and complex, in a fundamental way, than the evolution of practical denominational styles, nor is it properly located in strict theological attitudes. The theology of the Word was for post-Reformation Catholics as determinative of Christian truth as for Protestants, though the instrument or means of hearing was differently construed by each group.[9] But it was a difference, as we saw, that derived from a pneumatic confusion, and because hearing and seeing relate to each other, theologically, in the same pneumatological arena as hearing alone, the confusion moves to envelop Christian sight in its own right. The

8. David Yeago provides a nuanced and, as far as it goes, appropriate delineation of the contrast of "complementarity" between hearing and seeing under the rubric of "theological ethos" (in this case, between Lutherans and Anglicans) in his "Theological Renewal in Communion: What Anglicans and Lutherans Can Learn from One Another," in Ephraim Radner and R. R. Reno, eds., *Inhabiting Unity: Theological Perspectives on the Proposed Lutheran-Episcopal Concordat* (Grand Rapids: William B. Eerdmans, 1995). The theoretical *possibility* of a complementarity, however, is not the same thing as its historical realizability ; and the latter depends on the more essential pneumatic character of the churches held in comparison.

9. Even within the specific realm of the sermon, the contrast between Protestant and Catholic practice cannot be located in the hearing/seeing difference. By the seventeenth century, the great homiletic expositors in both sets of churches were often equally centered on Scripture and equally luxuriant within the still predominantly verbal, and even oral, culture. It can be argued, further, that each camp was fully participant in the shift within that culture toward the word as "written" — and hence visually located — and away from the word as aurally signed and passionally derived (although I think this bit of folk wisdom about the influence of Ramist and Cartesian "idealism" is far overplayed). But where shall we locate, theologically, the sensible difference between Puritan visual schematism and Catholic visual classicism? Certainly not in the crude contrast between hearing and seeing itself. For seminal discussions of the general shift, in early modern rhetoric, toward a "visualistic" rhetoric, spatialized and diagrammatic in Ramist (and later Puritan) hands, and more classically idealized in the hands of Port-Royalists, see Walter J. Ong, *Ramus — Method, and the Decay of Dialogue* (Harvard: Cambridge University Press, 1958); on the relation of Port-Royal "rhetoric" to more traditionally "classical" practice, cf. Hugh M. Davidson, *Audience, Words, and Art. Studies in Seventeenth-Century French Rhetoric* (Columbus, OH: Ohio State University Press, 1965).

very Lutheran emphasis upon the expanded significance of Paul's phrase that "faith come from what is heard, and what is heard comes by preaching" (Rom. 10:17) may well indicate something about the peculiar shape of the doctrine of justification *sola fide* — a Protestant construction — but it does not mark some kind of boundary between Protestant and Catholic sensibilities.[10] And therefore, even if the contrast is now lifted up irenically as a complementarity of ecclesial styles in need of each other, pieces of the ecumenical jigsaw that require a refitting, the question of their viability as Christian senses is still left unaddressed. It may or may not be the case that distinct denominational bodies have specific theological or devotional attitudes from which others have much to learn. But it is not theologically coherent to claim, for instance, that there are various deaf churches, various blind ones, and so on, according to the senses of their lives, whose conglomeration would provide a fully sensitive Body. The senses of the Body of Christ are not analogous to the diversity of the Body's individual gifts; rather, each "sense," as it functions, represents the historical expression of the Spirit's integral indwelling. For the visible stands tied to the audible, as organs of a single sensibility, synonymous with the pneumatic life of the Church; and only a firm common basis in the Spirit allows for their subjective distinction in the first place.

In the scriptural tradition, to speak of Christian "visibility" is to lay out a contrast, less between styles of theological understanding or expression than between understanding and expressing the life of Christ and not understanding and expressing it at all. Visibility refers to the factuality, or phenomenality, of Christ's life in the world, affirmed in contrast to its denial, deliberate or otherwise. The sense of "sight," then, comes into play not as an alternative

---

10. The *Apology for the Augsburg Confession* itself uses the verse to uphold both *sola fide* justification through the preaching of the Word (Art. IV) *and* the "visible" effects of the sacraments for changing hearts: "as the Word enters through the ears to strike the heart, so the rite itself enters through the eyes to move the heart; the Word and the rite have the same effect, as Augustine said so well when he called the sacrament 'the visible Word', for the rite is received by the eyes and is a sort of picture of the Word, signifying the same thing as the Word" (Art. XIII, in *The Book of Concord,* ed. T. G. Tappert [Philadelphia: Fortress Press, 1959], pp. 211f.). But the contrast, given in terms of theological and devotional styles, however important in implication, continues to reappear, and is taken for granted in many ecumenical discussions. Cf. the Anglican-Orthodox dialogues, where a distinction is made between Orthodox under-standings of the redemption of "visible" matter — embodied in the veneration of icons — and "Reformed" spiritualizing attitudes, deriving from the nonmediatory *solo Deo* principle of Protestantism; it is a distinction that the dialogue itself is designed to overcome, in this case in favor of Orthodox "visibility," especially as a means of applying a distinctive theological/devotional style to a secular cultural *ethos* where "visual imagery plays an important part in people's lives" (*The Dublin Agreed Statement* [1984], par. 79-87).

mode of apprehending the truth, but as the historical instantiation of the truth. The constellation of terms the New Testament uses to refer to the visible, in both the Gospels and the Epistles,[11] clusters around the reality of Jesus' life and ministry — his historical being, including the resurrection "appearances" — as it confronts the world with its demand for acknowledgment and its risk of rejection. Particularly in John, Jesus makes visible, or "shows outright," who he is, through his working of "signs" and "wonders."[12] This occurs through his "appearance" in the flesh, given literally to the "eyes" and the "hands" and through his works of "love."[13] The contrastive impetus of this visibility is given in its insertion into a history of opposition: Jesus shows himself in his flesh and works in order to counter unbelief and to overcome the works of the Devil.[14] If "sight" is posed in opposition to "hearing," it is hearing as vain and powerless, as metaphor for the superficial and the forgetful, the "word *alone*," which is without fruit or power.[15] The "light" who is Christ Jesus is light most fully as it shines in the "darkness."[16] The Christian "visible," then, pertains to a set of phenomenal realities — works, deeds, signs, fleshly enactments — by which the person of Christ stands over and against that which denies the truth and purpose of his mission.

The pneumatic character of this set of visibilities is basic, and becomes fundamental in the tradition of the Church. Not only do "signs and wonders" tend to be brought within the sphere of the Spirit's working,[17] but that working itself, its phenomenal "power," generally moves in the oppositional direction of Jesus' own contrastive reality with respect to the "world," or "sin," or the Devil. The miracles of the redeemed flesh represent, above all, the *adjudicative* power of the Spirit, to bring to light the truth of who Christ is in the midst of a context of unbelief. Both Paul and John give rich testimony to this basic pneumatological premise. In John's Gospel, Jesus describes the future mission of the Spirit as one of "convicting" the world concerning "sin and righteousness and judgment," by exposing the world's unbelief, revealing Jesus' resurrection and ascension, and condemning the "ruler of this world" (John 16:8-11). This mission of adjudication is connected with the "works" that Jesus has done in the face of the world (15:24), and it is given its future expression in the "fruit" of Jesus' followers. Whatever they ask in Jesus' name will be granted them,

11. Words like *phanizo* or *phaneroo* or *deiknumi*, etc.
12. Cf. John 2:18; 5:20; 10:32.
13. Cf. 1 John 1:2; 3:5, 8; 4:9; John 14:21.
14. John 10:32; 1 John 3:8.
15. Cf. 1 Thess. 1:5; 1 Cor. 2:4; 4:10; notoriously in James 1:22ff.
16. John 1:5ff.; 3:19ff.
17. Cf. Luke 4:14, 36; 9:1; 10:19; Acts 14:22; Rom. 15:19.

including the doing of works greater than Jesus' own, works whose possibility springs from the sending of the Spirit (cf. 14:12ff.). The works of the Spirit, then, are themselves acts of adjudication on behalf of Christ within the world.

For Paul, the truth of God in Christ Jesus is "demonstrated" (literally, "shown forth") as a sign to the unbelieving "rulers of this age" (1 Cor. 2:8), through the working of the Spirit in "power" *(dynamis),* that is, in signs and wonders (cf. Rom. 15:19). This visible demonstration of power draws the line, in its reception, between faith and disbelief within the world, by demarcating the distinction between those who receive and those who reject the phenomenal "witness" of the Spirit's acts. "Witness" becomes the significant denominator of the Spirit's historical mission, embodying in its visibility the decisive actions of Christ's life by which God's truth is made manifest in the face of unbelief. And so both John and Paul speak of the Spirit's phenomenal existence within the life of the Church as its "martyrial" ministry (cf. John 15:26f. and 1 Cor. 2:1[18] [according to a major manuscript tradition]), a ministry embedded in what would become the term's traditional connotation, "testimony" as "suffering" or "martyrdom" (cf. John 15:18–16:4 and 1 Cor. 2:2f.).[19]

The adjudicative character of Christian visibility, its pneumatic center, and its martyrial outcome are important to grasp if one is to pursue the question of the *fate* of visibility within the Church as it succumbs to division. Even in John, the environment for the Spirit's adjudicative witness in manifest clarity is explicitly described in terms of the Church's faithfulness in mutual affection, in the love for one another rooted in Jesus' and the Father's love and left to his disciples as a "command" (John 15:8-17). And Paul uses his articulation of the pneumatic demonstration of power within the Cross as a basis for addressing the contradiction posed to such power by "jealousy and strife" within the Christian community (1 Cor. 3:3ff.). It is not only the case that the Church's visible existence in the Spirit is properly governed by its "powerful works" of adjudication, given in martyrdom, but that such witness must emerge from the Church's unity. The Spirit, in short, unveils itself as "clarity" — this is its power of judgment — as it takes the form of charity.

The historical conditions for this adjudicatory display are rightly emphasized, since the display itself is given in the midst of opposing "signs" and phenomenal claims. Much of the framework of visibility that is attached to the Spirit is also linked in the New Testament to the embodied work of unbelief,

18. So, at least according to the major manuscript tradition that reads *martyrion* instead of *mysterion.*

19. Cf. 1 Cor. 4:9ff., where the suffering of the apostles in their ministry is described in terms of their visible "showing forth."

expressive of the opposing force of Satan, that is pursued finally to the pitch of actual "alternative" displays made by the temporal servants of spiritual evil — by men and women, or even demonic figures appearing in the flesh, who do the bidding of the Devil. This achieves historical culmination, according to someone like Paul, in the literal "unveiling" to sight of the "son of perdition," a personage later linked with the Antichrist of 1 and 2 John, who makes use of "signs and wonders" in a manner that mimics the pneumatic gifts of Christian saints, or even of Jesus himself (cf. 2 Thess. 2:1-12). At issue here is the way that this satanic opposition works by "deception," flooding the world with counterfeit radiance, to the point even, in Paul's language of 2 Thessalonians, of "displaying" itself as God and enveloping people in the palpable apparatus of seductively striking deeds. There is a specific context into which the Holy Spirit's adjudicative "power" is unfolded, and that is the context of the "lie," where truth and falsehood stand side by side, requiring an acute and discerning judgment.

The fact that Paul echoes the language of, for example, 1 Kings 22:23f., Ezekiel 14:9, and even Isaiah 29 on God's "sending" of a "spirit of stupor," as the form of "delusion" worked by Satan, locates the entire discussion of eschatological deception within the boundaries of pneumatology proper, a pneumatology shaped by the adjudicatory concerns of visibility.[20] The antidote to palpable deceptions lies in the application of genuine pneumatic gifts, such as those for "discerning spirits" (1 Cor. 12:10) or "testing" them (1 John 4:1). Even more so, however, they lie in the visible display of the "form" of Christ within the life of his servants: for Paul, the distinction between "deceptive" apostles, whose own appearance bears the tinctures of "light" to the same degree as Satan's angelic "disguise," lies in the exhibition of "weakness," suffering as Christ suffered for the love of the world (2 Cor. 11–12); for John, the distinction between the false spirits of the "antichrists" and the "anointing" Spirit of the true Christ is given proof in the mutual subjection in love of members of the church, literally, in the maintenance of unity, which figures the palpable incarnation of the Son (1 John 2:18-24; 2 John 6-7). The *martyrion* of the pneumatic Christian, then, joins suffering or death to the contrastive reality of the church's unity, thereby exposing the deceptions of otherwise radiant, seemingly pneumatic, phenomena.

The fact that the clarity of charity embodies the luminously adjudicatory character of the Spirit may well stand as a kind of axiom in scriptural hagiology. But charity and adjudication need not — cannot? — maintain their pneumatic "power" precisely when their historical context alters the nature of their bond-

---

20. The tradition of "deception" is given evangelical foundation in Mark 13 or Matthew 24, and recurs throughout the Pauline and Johannine corpus.

ing. The hagiological problem posed by the historical experience of Christian division is how pneumatic clarity can logically function within a context in which potential agents of deception operate out of a mutually excluded charity. Given accepted division, one might suspect that, negatively, *locating* the seat of deception, in its satanic form, would become for Christians an activity devoid of martyrial tools; and that positively, the phenomenon of the Spirit's self-enunciation would become shrouded. For the visible character and meaning of Christian *pneumatica* would seem to demand that, within a context of Christian division, both the search for Satan, or for his deceiving servants like Antichrist, will become a consuming task and that the task will prove irresolvable, because unattended by the determining judgments of apprehended sanctity. A glance at how the experience of deception in fact migrated into the center of the Church's self-apprehension, in tandem with ecclesial division's constraint upon pneumatic possibility, confirms this suspicion.

Two Types of Ecclesial Deception: Exterior and Interior

Who is the deceiver of humankind? The traditional answer has always been the Devil, the "father of lies" (John 8:44). But the actual relation of the Devil's deceiving activity to the integrity of the Church's phenomenal experience has admitted of various possible conceptions, of which two major types have been demarcated by the Reformation split. In the first and "catholic" type, associated generally with unaccepted division (whatever the actual experience of schism or contestability), satanic deception comes to the Church from the outside, *ab extra;* in the second type, associated with deliberated division and separation, deception arises from *within* the Church itself. The theological migration — to take a principal instance of this contrast — of the Antichrist from the exterior to the interior of the Church marks the shift from (theoretically) unacceptable to acceptable division. And this migration itself is both logically and experientially linked with the increasing obscurement, within the Christian community, of pneumatic sanctity as a "power," capable of disclosing the truth of God.[21] The existence of this contrast points to an underlying principle

21. This broad ecclesiological issue of the conceptual evolution of the relationship between satanic deception and the Church, tied as it is to practical capacities for ways of experiencing the Christian life, should be clearly distinguished from other sociohistorical perspectives on the actual application of developing Christian demonologies or diabologies in Church history. It is possible to trace a range of social applications or, conversely, to trace a range of theological articulations that derive from social experiences in the demonological realm, that provide compelling evidence of more general psychosocial movements for which the Church has been but a vehicle, albeit a

governing the life of good and evil "spirits" in relation to Christians: the unity of the church, in both cases, stands as a condition for pneumatic disclosure.

The distinction between these two types is not always clear in particular cases, but shows itself rather in a general contrast between epochs of ecclesial division.[22] Even so, from its initial New Testament expression, satanic deception was clearly understood as an exterior force, the very "resistance" to which

---

formative one. And within these movements, the sixteenth-century divisions themselves serve as secondary occasions, rather than as primary causes, a perception that is proper, with more or less greater degrees of accuracy, within the perspective of critical history. The ecclesiological question of satanic deception and sanctity, however, assumes, as a matter of Christian logic, that possibilities of theological conception on these matters disclose the shape of the Church, and vice versa, as it actually holds significance in God's eyes. And this significance, which overlaps with the findings of critical history, but is to be sharply distinguished from them in the way it is apprehended, contributes to what usually falls under the Christian doctrine of Providence. Hence, in what follows briefly on the question of heresy, deception, and the Church, both the sociohistorical and psychosocial concerns with the whole issue of "demonization" — of opponents, marginal groups, and the like — as well as its conceptual supports within Christian discourse itself, will be left aside as ancillary to our basic ecclesiological purpose. This purpose is focused on the theological and providential significance of actual Christian division itself, not on how the dynamics of diversity and division have reflected a range of (quite real) human motives. The literature on the latter is vast. Among more well-known reflections and references, see Elaine Pagels, *The Origin of Satan* (New York: Random House, 1995); Jeffrey Burton Russell, *Satan: The Early Christian Tradition* (Ithaca: Cornell University Press, 1981); Jeffrey Burton Russell, *Lucifer: The Devil in the Middle Ages* (Ithaca: Cornell University Press, 1984); Jeffrey Burton Russell, *Dissent and Order in the Middle Ages* (New York: Twayne Publishers, 1992); R. I. Moore, *The Formation of a Persecuting Society* (Oxford: Oxford University Press, 1987); Valerie Flint, *Religion and the Rise of Magic in Early Medieval Europe* (Princeton: Princeton University Press, 1990); Richard Kieckefer, *European Witch Trials: Their Foundation in Popular and Learned Culture 1300–1500* (Berkeley: University of California Press, 1976); Norman Cohn, *Europe's Inner Demons* (St. Alban's: Granada Publishing, 1976); Norman Cohn, *The Pursuit of the Millennium* (Oxford: Oxford University Press, 1970); Richard Kenneth Emmerson, *Antichrist in the Middle Ages: A Study of Medieval Apocalypticism, Art, and Literature* (Seattle: University of Washington Press, 1981).

22. In proposing these two types, I am engaged in some broad generalizations that may appear contradicted by a host of particular cases, especially with regard to the question of continuity between Reformation and late-medieval perspectives on the relation of satanic deception and the institutional Church, not to mention precedents from even earlier periods. I hope, however, that with reflection on the logic behind the divisional characteristics of demonization, it will become apparent, in contrast to the many particular cases of the pre-Reformation, in what way whole swathes of Christian experience were constrained by the established ecclesial fragmentation of the sixteenth century and thereafter. A helpful overview of some of these particularities, glossed over in our account, can be found in Bernard McGinn, *Antichrist: Two Thousand Years of the Human Fascination with Evil* (San Francisco: HarperSanFrancisco, 1994); but the sense of these explications, divided as they are along a periodized line of conceptualization, in the tradition of the "history of ideas," is quite other than the providential ecclesiology we are attempting to expose.

in fact marked the martyrial demonstration of sanctity. The classic depiction of this is in 1 Peter 5:8-9, where the Devil is given the image of a "roaring lion" whom one faces across a free space as an external "adversary" and whose overcoming is marked by a "suffering" common to the Christian body as a whole.[23] When identified with the power of sin, of course, Satan's work could be described in interiorizing terms, as a force at work from the "inside," but always "inside" in a personalist, not an ecclesial sense; and sin's defeat was still publicly marked by the demonstration of martyrial suffering (cf. Heb. 12:4). In their very notions of visibly agonistic victory, both the early Church's understanding of martyrdom as "struggle" against Satan and the parallel development of an ascetic demonology early associated with Jewish conceptions of interior "instincts" to good and bad nonetheless maintained this sharply *ab extra* sense of deception's origins, even when manifested interiorly.[24]

With respect to the corporate Church, the same general sense holds true, even though, by definition, deception "in" the Church is something that cannot be easily externalized. When 1 John (2:18-19) speaks of the many "antichrists" among the brethren in the "last hour," he describes them as "coming out" of the Church, though never being part of the Church. But this lack of original identity is proved by the separation itself, and to this degree the work of the antichrists does not carry its force until it is demonstrated through division itself, and the externalizing opposition among groups such division entails. The association of "heresy" and "heretics" with the Devil, then, remains an association proven, largely, through the final corporate distinction created by heretical schism in particular;[25] Antichrist remains an antagonist whom one can confront across a line of distance. Hence, he can be opposed through the visible and public confrontation of virtue and truth, by which deception is exposed.

Where this kind of "demonization" of opponents eventually led the Church, in its attitudes toward dissent in general, is another story; but it is important to note that satanic deception was deemed exposable precisely because it could be visibly sifted through the unveiling of its exteriorized character, in ecclesial terms. Although heresy became consistently identified with satanic

23. Cf. also James 4:7.

24. On the "struggle" against Satan that martyrdom embodies, see early on Ignatius, e.g., Trallians 4:2; Romans 5:3, 7:1, or *The Martyrdom of Polycarp* 3 and 17. On the interior struggle within the heart, cf. Hermas, *Shepherd,* Mandates 6:1 and 2.

25. Heresy is always factionalizing and finally divisive. Thus, when Ignatius identifies with the Devil those who oppose the episcopacy, he does so on the basis of such opposition's ultimate unveiling of separation (cf. Smyrneans 9:1 and Eph. 13:1); satanic deception embodies its externalizing origin by returning to its ecclesially exterior point of departure.

deception,[26] such deception was never seen as corrupting the visible integrity of the Church, even when it took power within its midst, as in the periods of the great Trinitarian and Christological controversies, during which the demarcation of truth was always, in theory, possible because of visible confrontations of holiness between distinct parties.[27] While the Church, in various ways, was consistently understood as being "sinful," this acknowledgment did not go so far as thinking the Church, as it were, "possessed" (a view of sin in general that was eventually denied in the condemnation of the "messalian" heresy).[28]

26. Moving from 1 John and other Epistles, through Ignatius, and achieving clear definition in Irenaeus (cf. *Against the Heresies*, 1:25, 27; 4:41; 5:26, etc.), the identification of heresy with the Devil has been a classic Christian teaching. But *where* are the heretics?

27. Athanasius's *Letter to the Bishops of Egypt* (356) offers a good place to examine the nuances of this model. The opening sections (1-5) provide a detailed exposition of the link between Satan and heresy and in particular of the need, since his defeat by Christ, that drives the Devil to work by increasingly devious and deceptive methods to entice Christians from the truth, manipulating Christian discourse and concepts to nefarious purposes. By the end of the letter (21, 23), Athanasius is outlining the kinds of suffering, even death, at the hands of the Arians that true Christians must be willing to engage in "struggling" against heresy. From one aspect, the reality of deception *within* the Church is patent, and the kinds of oppositional realignment such ecclesially interior deception will demand are parallel with later Protestant strategies and their justifications. At the same time, however, Athanasius operates on the assumption that the difference between truth and deception is easily grasped and will be clearly demonstrated (4), through the pneumatic blessing of discernment granted the followers of Christ; and this clarity and ease finds its embodiment in the object of his final exhortation to suffering and martyrdom. There is never any doubt in Athanasius's mind that the Church's integrity is anything but temporarily placed in visible doubt (and only for the ignorant) by the presence of heretical leaders in its midst and that the oppositional set of the Church's present life is only a brief interlude. While he counsels a kind of refusal of communion with the Arians, it is one that has as its context the maintenance of the Church's claim to its visible structures and community, even if inhabited by deception briefly (cf. the fragment from the later Letter 29, on the use of church buildings by the Arians). And although Athanasius uses Antichrist language on many occasions to refer to his opponents, nowhere does Athanasius imply that the visible Church has been fundamentally corrupted: the struggle is not over where the Church is to be found — among Arians or among the orthodox — but over who shall control the Church, a question whose visible resolution is never in doubt precisely because Satan is a weak interloper in comparison with the consistent pneumatic existence of Christian people. Christians do not "go out" from the Arian-controlled Church; rather, they await their sure vindication through the historical adjudication of the Spirit. The contrast with later Protestant understandings of ecclesial deception is, as we shall see, sharp; so is the contrast in pneumatic confidence with both post-Reformation Protestantism and Catholicism.

28. Cf. Y.-M.-J. Congar's *Vraie et Fausse réforme dans l'Église* (Paris: Editions du Cerf, 1969), pp. 78-83, for some detailed references to patristic discussions of the Church as "sinner." The point in these discussions, however, is not the Church's inherent corruption by Satan, but its relation to Christ as "penitent," that is, as ever joined to his gracious presence as Redeemer.

Furthermore, it was never clear whether heretics or persecutors were actually the Devil's progeny or slaves, in the sense of somehow "belonging" to him, or whether they were his ignorant (though still responsible) instruments. The latter possibility, which is enunciated through the prayers that are often offered by Christians on behalf of persecutors, only underscored the kind of ecclesially external character of deception as it was perceived. And although there gradually evolved a notion of a kind of mystical "body of Satan" that parallels the Body of Christ as the Church,[29] this obvious manner of linking satanic tools with actual genetic relation in evil rarely turns into an irreformable association between internal ecclesial opposition and infernal infiltration. Indeed, the consistent interpretation of the Antichrist (including its identification with 2 Thessalonians' deluding "man of perdition") as someone who assaults the Church from outside and whose deceptions are always ones that visibly lead people *away* from the Church to some other place, reinforces this externally oppositional character maintained by deception in the Church.

Of all the Fathers, Augustine's framework of the historically intertwining bodies of the earthly and divine "cities" would seem most conducive to a picture of internal deception. Yet he too, perhaps more than most, is careful to extricate satanic deception from any substantive influence over the Church's visible projection, in large part because of his fundamental apprehension of the Church's visible unity as a pneumatic ground, whatever its internally mixed character. The two cities are likened to two "bodies," and therefore their intermingling on earth would seem to open the possibility that within the Church the "body" of the Devil might dwell; and so it does, but not in its deceptive force. In fact, it is the holiness of the Church — in suffering, in charity, in forbearance, in justice — as it patiently tolerates within its midst those who are not ultimately "of it," that demonstrates the Church's heavenly truth, visibly established in its unity. Heresy, in the traditional pattern, is demonstrated in its separation from the Church — its "going out" — and until that point it exists within the bosom of the Church as a kind of providential means for the exercise of visible virtue. Deception per se acts from without the Church, drawing people away from it, only from the moment that heresy becomes manifest in its divisiveness.

> Those, therefore, in the Church of Christ who savour anything morbid and depraved, and, on being corrected that they may savour what is wholesome and

29. Cf. Origen's *Contra Celsum* 5:9; 6:44-45. The late Donatist use of this image is well known, as is Augustine's occasional appropriation of the idea (cf. its presence in his listing of the Donatist Tychonius's "rules" for interpreting scriptural figures, in the *De Doctrina Christiana* III:55).

71

right, contumaciously resist, and will not amend their pestiferous and deadly dogmas, but persist in defending them, become heretics, and, going without, are to be reckoned as enemies who serve for her discipline.

. . . For all the enemies of the Church, whatever error blinds or malice depraves them, exercise her patience if they receive the power to afflict her corporally; and if they only oppose her by wicked thought, they exercise her wisdom: but at the same time, if these enemies are loved, they exercise her benevolence, or even her beneficence, whether she deals with them by persuasive doctrine or by terrible discipline. And thus the devil, the prince of the impious city, when he stirs up his own vessels against the city of God that sojourns in this world, is permitted to do her no harm.

. . . The heretics themselves also, since they are thought to have the Christian name and sacraments, Scriptures, and profession, cause great grief in the hearts of the pious, both because many who wish to be Christians are compelled by their dissensions to hesitate, and many evil-speakers also find in them matter for blaspheming the Christian name, because they too are at any rate *called* Christians. . . . But that grief which arises in the hearts of the pious, who are persecuted by the manners of bad or false Christians, is profitable to the sufferers, because it proceeds from the charity in which they do not wish them either to perish or to hinder the salvation of others.[30]

The presence of Satan's servants within the Church — and elsewhere Augustine goes so far as to call them present "antichrists" in the manner of 1 John — does not indicate an obscurement of the truth as it is experientially apprehended by Christians, nor a corruption of the Church's visible integrity, but rather forms the occasion for the unencumbered display of the Church's sanctity.[31] And when Augustine comes to a discussion of the Antichrist (e.g., *City of God* 20:8, 13, 14, 19), even with this being's full powers of deception deployed, he carefully surveys a range of interpretative assessments that emphasize not the insurgence of lying within the mixed body of the Church, but the way the members of the earthly body are now simply exposed in their real allegiance, through finally taking leave of their true Christian brethren. In the

---

30. Augustine, *City of God* 18:51, trans. George Wilson (New York: Random House, 1950).

31. Cf. his sermons on 1 John (3:9). On this Emmerson (pp. 65f.) makes too great a distinction between two strands of Augustine's thinking on the Antichrist, as if there were a tension in exegetical reference between the historical figure of the end times and the "bad Christians" and heretics within the Church. It is because the Antichrist is a discrete historical figure external to the Church that his "figures" — in the sense of prefigurements — within the Church's fold and history pose so little substantive threat to its integrity and can be overcome so decisively (if continuously) through the exercise of faithfulness and sanctity.

end, the very possibility of Augustine's conception of the *corpus permixtum,* the mixed body of the visible Church, depends on his confidence in the clarity with which deceptive powers are in fact kept distinct from the phenomenal identity of the Catholic *ecclesia.* The Antichrist is a historical figure who arises outside the Church, his deluding works are discretely "sent" into the world, and his figure stands manifestly as a contrasting shadow to the form of the Christ embodied in the Church.

Augustine's ecclesial attitudes to the Antichrist remained standard for the Western Church through most of the Middle Ages; and, in their elaboration, they provided for a variegated perspective on the nature of history and its scriptural form. The exteriorized character of the final agent of deception, although tied to a particular moment at the end of the history, did not crudely dissociate the Church from an ongoing temporal life of pneumatic adjudication. The "end," after all, was related to the Church's integral life through time by the continuous revelation of scriptural form within the Church's experience, the encounter with "figures" that consistently typified the Antichrist even before his final appearance. And in this figural encounter, embodied in actual events and characters from the two Testaments as well as ongoing ecclesial history, the Church exercised its discernment and martyrial disclosures in a manner that prefigured the last battle with Antichrist, even as that battle had already found its completed summation in the life of Christ. The generally accepted Augustinian schema of history that placed the Church's current life in the "Sixth Age" of the world's seven epochs, the very "millennium" announced in the book of Revelation, before the last conflict with Satan, framed the Church's life between the Incarnation of Jesus and the coming of the Antichrist. Within this period, then, the figurally rehearsed experiences of deception and its defeat were brought together as a reiterated crescendo of the single Church's conformation to Christ's own form of suffering victory over an alien enemy.[32] As with Augustine, even a concentration on the "delusive" aspects of satanic deception, associated with Antichrist or the equivalent "son of perdition" and identified with the continuous efforts of heretics and schismatics, never moved so far as to infect the character of the Church itself: the actual history of the Antichrist was a specific one, yet to be revealed, yet quite particular in details whose real shape consigned them to the future; while the

---

32. On the Sixth Age, cf. Augustine's *City of God* 20:33, carried through in the tradition in, e.g., Isidore of Seville's *Etymologia* 5:39; Bede's and later Richard of Saint Victor's, and later still, Nicholas of Lyra's commentaries on the Apocalypse. On the "age of the Church" as a period of ecclesial conformation to Christ's own suffering "witness," cf. Honorius of Autun's *Gemma Animae* 3:134.

deceptive ravages of the heretics in the present, however interior to the life of the Church, were only passing figures of this end, and not somehow definitive of the Church's substantive status in time.

The advent of the second descriptive type for ecclesial deception is marginal to this main medieval and Augustinian outlook. The decoupling of the Antichrist from the historical end of the Church's life — its exterior location — and the projection of this end into the present experience of the church — the interiorizing of the Antichrist into the Church's own life — was a theological and devotional phenomenon of the late Middle Ages. It represents the merging of two distinct elements in the medieval theology of deception, the presence of "multiple antichrists" (in the form of, e.g., heretics, à la 1 John) with the determination that the end of the Sixth Age was already upon the Church and hence that the "historical" Antichrist was already doing his work within the world. In the wake of someone like the late twelfth-century Joachim of Fiora identifying the present age with the era of Antichrist, preceding some further historical developments, polemical identification of alleged heretical opponents with "antichristian" ministries took on a decisive aspect: now it was possible to accuse members within the Church not only of instrumental participation in satanic deception, but of incarnating that deception itself. In the course of the debates among Franciscan Spirituals, among agents of competing papal claims at Avignon and elsewhere, and other internal conflicts, Antichrist entered, through the discourse of hostile polemics, into the very sanctuary of the church's authoritative seat.[33] Even before the well-known accusations of Hus and Wycliffe, popes like John XXII were reviled as being the "mystical Antichrist," set up within the precincts of the Temple, and, from within the Body, perverting the faithful through lies and falsehoods.

This is all well-known material.[34] And it forms one topic whose similarity with Reformation polemics has been drawn into the line of continuity that is seen by many as connecting Protestant and late-medieval conceptions of dissent and Church order. Three aspects of this seeming continuity need to be stressed, however. The first is that the interiorizing of the Antichrist into the Church's midst — including the decoupling of Antichrist from a future end and his insertion into the present — was, in the later Middle Ages, made possible by the formulation of a separatist *logic* that could be disengaged from actual social experiences and reapplied elsewhere (i.e., to the varied perspectives of the

33. Cf. Emmerson, pp. 60-71; McGinn, chs. 5-7.
34. Much useful primary source material can be found in translation in Walter L. Wakefield and Autin P. Evans, eds., *Heresies of the High Middle Ages, Records of Civilization: Sources and Studies,* 82 (New York: Columbia University Press, 1969).

Reformation). The shape of the relation between deception and Church had reversed itself from the earlier periods: with Antichrist *within* the (visible) Church, the vocation of the true Christian was to leave it, to "go out." Heresy was no longer seen as manifested through its own separation, but as requiring a faithful separation on the part of heresy's opponents. Secondly, this late-medieval (as opposed to Reformation) reversal of relations was exclusively dependent, usually, upon a specific historical judgment about the moment, not about the nature of the Church per se. Since the End was now, Antichrist too had assumed a new position with respect to the Church. Initially, the late-medieval internalizing of Antichrist was linked to a specific person — a given pope, for instance; later, it is true, it was linked less with a specific person than with a generalized office, like "papacy." But in both cases, the linkage was based on the particular and time-limited prophetic disclosure of Antichrist within the "end" of the Church's history. This is distinguished from what became of the Protestant vision of the Antichrist's history, wherein person and office were together generalized into a perpetual feature of the Church's internal history as a principle of interpretation (even when punctuated by the imminent or present End, as Luther, many of his followers, and particularly English Protestants believed). Finally, whatever continuities in conception exist between the late Middle Ages and the Reformation on this score, the actualization of conception differs starkly: the Reformation division *applied* the logic of interiorization to the ongoing character of the Christian life as a whole, and to this extent marks an experientially deliberative theological reconstruction of ecclesiology and pneumatology that before had been merely ad hoc.

Luther typifies the way Protestantism took over the marginal late-medieval view. Maintaining, against certain radical chiliasts, the traditional Augustinian view that the millennium of the Sixth Age coincides with the temporal life of the Church as a whole, he brings it to conclusion in the temporal past as well, placing the start of Antichrist's historical work in a period sometime before the present. Already by 1520 he had proclaimed the clear identification of the papacy as an office, associated with its supporters, with the Antichrist; and he located its activity within the Church already for "many generations."[35] At this stage, there is a kind of conditional evaluation of the

---

35. Cf. *The Babylonian Captivity of the Church.* The relation between Luther's "diabology" in general — his sensibilities concerning the activity of the Devil and their late-medieval Germanic context — and his notions regarding anti-Christian deception within the Church are not obviously causal. The former question has much interested Luther scholars and social historians of the period (cf. Heiko Oberman's biography, *Luther: Man Between God and the Devil* [New Haven: Yale University Press, 1989]). At issue here, to repeat, is the application of a particular kind of logic regarding the church and deception; and this logic was adapted by Luther, and

Roman Church that is tied to its doctrinal and disciplinary activity, and that decidedly mutes the personalistic identification: "if" or "as long as" they persist" in false doctrine, "then" they are the Antichrist. With his excommunication of that year, Luther was quite clear that the "see of Rome" was "held" by Satan and formed the throne of the Antichrist.[36] And by the end of his life the demonizing of the papacy and Rome had become extravagant, extensive, and historically rooted.[37] But it was the early association of Antichrist with the history of doctrine within the Church that, while less personalistic, in fact marked the formative impetus to the Protestant shift into the ecclesial interiorizing of Antichrist.[38] For as the Reformation confrontations took their mature form in the controversy over doctrine and doctrine's historical foundations, inevitably the Antichrist and his deceptive mission followed the scholarly trail further and further back into the uncovered origins of ecclesial life. Romish corruptions, to the degree that they could be traced in their evolution through the early life of the Church, became synonymous with the history of Satan's anti-church, parading as Catholicism.

The kind of historical work on the part of Protestants who made this move began early with Lutheran researchers and polemicists, finding an initial summation in the famous *Magdeburg Centuries,* which traced the course of ecclesial corruption, according to standard Reformed criteria, from the foundation of the Church through each successive "century."[39] More pertinently,

---

later Reformers, for the purposes of ecclesial conflict *tout court,* the implications of which brought logic and experience together in a novel set of constraints that profoundly differed from the pre-Reformation period.

36. Cf. *On the Execrable Bull of Antichrist* (1520).

37. E.g., the late and notorious *Against the Papacy of Rome Founded by the Devil.*

38. Luther's broader theological and perhaps devotional orientation can also be seen as receptive to this perspective. The *solus Christus* focus, from which justification by faith alone was doctrinally explicated, carried with it a concomitant denigration of human natural powers. One implication of this, which Luther himself draws out, is that the distinguishing between divine and satanic action within the Church is an act of pure grace (which, of course, includes the application of the Word of God in Scripture). Within this framework, the Church becomes itself the historical arena where, to sinful persons, God and the Devil are continually confused. This ties in, logically, with Luther's convictions concerning the "hidden church" and, similarly, with his denigration of ostensive pneumatic phenomena like miracles (see below).

39. See below, Chapter 5. However "anticritical" much Lutheran historiography may appear, especially given its impetus in a kind of apocalyptic expectation of history's imminent "end" — which, in turn, provoked a search for signs, portents, and the means to decipher them that verged on the magical and expressed an almost "gnostic" distaste for the temporal altogether — I would maintain that the search to elucidate a "history" of deception, according to a uniform principle of doctrine, actually encouraged, if not coincided, with the promotion of an historical-critical practice. In this, I would differ in my interpretations of the conceptual forces at work

the theological rationale for this kind of investigation lay in the formulation of an ecclesiology of deception by degrees, which was tied to the interiorization of the Antichrist within the Church's midst. Calvin, as an important example, set out a classic description of this ecclesiology in the *Institutes* that, along with other Reformed versions (e.g., Bullinger's) was to have lasting influence on all subsequent Protestant historical thinking.[40] In both IV:2 and 7, Calvin deals with the history of Rome's perverted and perverting claims to supremacy (specific discussions of Roman Catholic doctrines are dealt with elsewhere). These corruptions point, in Calvin's argument, to the conclusive judgment that the Antichrist controls the papacy and has done so for some time. Calvin provides a remarkably learned account of the origins of the papal claims that stretches back to apostolic times and passes through patristic and medieval periods. While he sees a gradual increase in false claims through the first few centuries, it is not until the Carolingian concordat of Empire and Roman Church that he definitively identifies the "great apostasy" as taking place. All this is relatively nuanced. Yet the underlying historical truth of this temporal development, in Calvin's eyes, is the *perpetual* working of the Antichrist within the Church, from the apostolic period, secretly deceiving Christians in the form of Paul's "mystery of iniquity" "already" active (according to 2 Thess. 2:7), only the open disclosure of which awaited a later century.[41] And in order to formulate an ecclesiology of perpetual interior deception, Calvin has recourse to the Augustinian historical bifurcation of the Two Cities, now thoroughly recast into the categories of "Two Churches," the "true" and the "false." Eschewing the integral figuralism of the tradition, by which Israel of the Old Testament typified the Church in its wholeness, Calvin reaches for scriptural types that can justify a perpetually unfaithful and visible people existing as a cover for a separate, if invisible, faithful remnant within it —

---

from, for example, Robin Bruce Barnes in his brilliant work *Prophecy and Gnosis: Apocalypticism in the Wake of the Lutheran Reformation* (Stanford: Stanford University Press, 1988), who sees the mid-seventeenth-century collapse of hope in the end of time as the real period of transition into a more secularized critical history among German Lutherans. I would rather see the latter period's historiographical outlook as a logical development of the sixteenth century's, despite differences in the historical scaffolding of the projects involved: it was not the "end" that defined Protestant historiography, but the character of the ecclesial time — experienced "history" that precedes the end — and here there is a continuity in perspectives.

40. Bullinger's *The Old Faith,* both on the Continent and in its 1547 translation by Coverdale, also exerted a defining authority on the topic. Equally important, especially in its English translation (cf. *The Thre Bokes of Chronicles,* with additions by John Funcke [1550]), was Melanchthon's edition of Johannes Carion's *Chronicle,* 1st ed. (1531), whose preface laid out a similar historical ecclesiology.

41. *Institutes,* 4:7:25.

deception as a husk covering a kernel of truth. He turns to the Northern Kingdom of Israel, then, after its separation from Judah, and compares its condition in the grip of satanic delusion with the Roman Church coexisting, over the centuries, with a small group of faithful Christians (parallel to the Prophets). Although he cannot find a scriptural figure that justifies actual separation, he underlines the radical historical nature of the distinction between true and false churches by comparing it to Paul's allegory in Galatians of the free and enslaved children, or of the two covenant mountains — the false church, like the Jews, was allowed to exist over time in conjunction with the true Church of the free woman, until a point when their decisive separation must take place and the false church's reality must be repudiated (the present time of the Reformation, in parallel with the separation of Christians from Mosaic Judaism).[42] Although Calvin himself does not make the precise prophetic link here, the apocalyptic moment of the last conflict is evoked, when the true Church is called to "come out" of "Babylon" (Rev. 18:4) for God's last sifting. The present division of the churches represents simply a disclosure of a permanent division that has existed within the boundaries of the visible church from the beginning, heretofore obscured to the natural eye and heart by the perpetual working of satanic delusion.

Implications of the Separative Logic of Interiorized Deception: Deceptive Histories, Veiled Appearances, Doctrinal Adjudications, Decontextualization of Scriptural Holiness

This classic expression of the second, interiorizing "type" relating deception to the Church points to several conceptual implications. These elements govern a number of evolving religious attitudes tied to the experience of division, but also together end by constraining in particular the experience of pneumatic disclosure in the life of the Church. These elements deserve to be explored each in its own right, but for our purposes can be generally noted now as defining parameters for the obscurement of pneumatic phenomena that we shall be indicating in the rest of the chapter. All of these elements of the type derive logically from the justification of ecclesial separation and cannot stand apart from it. What Calvin and other Reformers needed was a way of adapting the division in which they found themselves engaged, or which they found themselves heirs to, to some scripturally justificatory model that could maintain both the long history of Catholicism and its subsequent fragmentation. The

42. *Institutes,* 4:2, passim, esp. 3, 7-9.

image of a temporally extended interior corruption within the Church upheld Catholicism's longevity, while the possibility of identifying two primordially discrete and conflicting parties within that history upheld an eventual distinction and separation within the Church's history (whether at the End or sometime before the End makes little difference). Scripturally, an adjusted apocalypticism involving the deceptive, and therefore to some extent "secretive" and interior, workings of Satan, through his parodic Antichrist, proved most effective. And in the hands of the Reformers, the late-medieval adaptations of this traditional material moved from the margins of polemical and sectarian theology into the center of an integral ecclesiology. The first, and major, element of the classic Reformation type, then, is the conviction that deception in the Church is a phenomenon endemic to its history. To be sure, a final separation has taken place or is yet taking place; but these are the Last Days of the true Church in history, and the controversy between Catholic and Protestant is, in large measure, the ongoing outworking of the contestation over deception, still left unresolved. To the degree that the Church is enmeshed in time, it is covered and so manifests itself historically in the garb of deceptive ambiguities.

This leads to the second element of the classic divisive type: ostensive phenomena within the Church are, in their historicalness, veiled, because wrapped in the shrouds of those competing deceptive phenomena that define the internally corrupted body. If there is such a thing as pneumatic disclosure, adjudicating Christ in the midst of the world and convicting the world of its separation from God, such disclosure cannot come in the form of ostensive phenomena. Thus, even in the sections of the *Institutes* just mentioned, Calvin disassociates the true Church from the visible manifestations of ecclesial self-expression — from worship, buildings, sacrifice; and elsewhere, along with the entire early Protestant tradition, from miracles, wonders, signs, or visibly affective sanctity. If there is pneumatic "holiness" that somehow "marks" the Church, it is a "hidden" holiness, very much in line with Luther's own early articulation, in something like the Heidelberg Disputation, of the paradoxical "manifestation" of the Cross — which is, historically, a kind of veiling — in contrast with the false Christianity of "glory."

Thirdly, since Protestants could not surrender altogether the accessible possibility of adjudication, especially given their eschatological vocation of final separation from the false church, some form of disclosive standard needed elevation. But it had to be one that was, in a fundamental sense, independent of particular historical phenomena whose origins and endings could be precisely linked with individuals and moments. As is well known, the adjudicative criterion to which the Reformers quickly turned was that of "doctrine," a category supremely equipped to provide a dehistoricized plumb line of distinction, since its identification lay more in tracing the expression of principles through broad periods of the Church's life and within the abstracted character of written documents than in scrutinizing the shape of particular lives. Here is one area where the Reformed adaptation of late medieval paradigms concerning the Antichrist proved a major mutation, since the earlier sectarian interpretations of, for instance, the Papacy as satanic had focused on particular persons and individualized practices even within the office as a whole; and the "morals" of the corrupt church leaders formed the base upon which accusations of anti-Christianity were founded. Protestants, although originally driven by the exposure of "abuses," generally made use of the argument from morals only peripherally in their accusations against the Papists, speaking from a position of condescension in addressing a topic they knew their opponents valued, even if in itself it cannot bear major weight in pressing the charge of anti-Christianity.[43] Where true and pure doctrine is discernible, there is the true Church — and the shift away from historical personages and their actions, the traditional vessels of pneumatic disclosure, has been made in favor of the formulation of a host of doctrinal templates against which to measure this or that epoch of the Church's life for distant signs of pneumatic integrity. Like astrophysicists who measure and even identify invisibly distant cosmic formations through the analysis of secondary phenomena, the doctrinal adjudication performed by Protestant *historians* proved a way of discerning the truth about pneumatic phenomena that were otherwise inaccessible because of the very nature of ecclesial history.

Finally, mention must be made of a purely hermeneutical element introduced into the experience of pneumatic reality by the interiorizing of deception within the Church, an element that is logically tied to the pneumatic obscurement of Scripture we have examined earlier and to its historical link with the demise of Scripture's figural coherence. This element is the transformation of Scripture's purpose from its pre-Reformation role of being the *context* of adjudication to being the adjudicator itself. What is involved here is a particular instance of Hans Frei's notion that early modern hermeneutics saw a shift away from figuralist narrative interpretations of scriptural unity to an understanding of Scripture's meaning as "ostensive reference," a book whose meaning was subsumed by its factual accounting of particular events and persons.[44] With

43. Calvin, for instance, in the sections of the *Institutes* just mentioned, waits until the very end of his long historical and theological disquisition to bring up the matter of the popes' "morals" (IV:7:29), as a brief fillip of rhetorical degradation.

44. Cf. Frei's *Eclipse of Biblical Narrative* (New Haven: Yale University Press, 1974), pp. 11f., for a summary of his argument.

the pneumatic adjudication removed from the historical sphere of contemporary ecclesial experience, due to endemic ecclesial deception, and transferred into the realm of ascertained doctrinal conformity, Scripture itself became the basic means by which the doctrinal template was applied. In the pre-Reformation period, pneumatic clarity, in the form of a holy life or of wondrous works, was gauged and celebrated in its refiguring of the holy lives and deeds of scriptural characters, especially of Jesus himself, and pneumatic phenomena were thus formed within the figurating context of Scripture. But if such phenomena were intrinsically deceptive, as the Reformers affirmed, and if adjudication must take place instead by the evaluation of expressed doctrinal purity by an individual's or a party's formal communications — for example, writings — then Scripture's relation to pneumatic clarity is no longer one of formative context, but of criterial source.

Scripture performs this role for the Reformers in at least two major ways: first, by supplying the fundamental doctrinal principles by which contemporary theological formulation is measured (in, e.g., Lutheran terms, the "Gospel"); and second, by providing historically exemplary proof of the primacy and power of such principles (e.g., in furnishing a history of the Gospel's ultimately victorious fate). This second use of Scripture is especially relevant to the discussion of pneumatic phenomena, for it makes of the scriptural history a record of events that somehow "prove" the truth of particular doctrines in a way that stands independent of contemporary experience altogether. The bite to Frei's observation concerning modern hermeneutics' understanding of Scripture's meaning as "ostensive reference" derives from this peculiar criteriological role Scripture was now to play in adjudicating between the true and false churches: since Scripture was now seen as the record of true doctrine's shape and of its vindicated history, the meaning of Scripture's historical character lay in its reference to probative events. The shift can be seen clearly in the way that the meaning of the term *figura* in Scripture became almost exclusively tied to "prophecy," and hence in the way that "figural" interpretation became subservient to the practice of outlining the "fulfillment of prophecies," a species of evidentialist reasoning that still holds scriptural interpretation in its grip, on the part of "fundamentalist" proponents and their historical-critical antagonists.[45]

---

45. The restriction of *figura* to prophecy maintained itself through much of the eighteenth century, when the term was broadened to include especially "poetical" significances that were distinct from historical reference. This, however, did not really constitute a broadening of figural interpretation as much as a concession to the constraints of prophetical interpretation, whose rational limitations demanded some method of dealing with "hard cases." See below on eigthteenth-century British figuralism.

Each of these four elements, in their conjunction, received obvious expression in what became a classically "Calvinistic" Reformed theology (however accurately labeled), typified in something like the Westminster Confession. The element of endemic deception lies embedded in the Confession's stress on double predestination and the distinction it makes between "effectual" and ineffectual calling within the Church (cc. III; V; X). These are topics that easily and inevitably support the continued language of "two churches," the "true" and the "satanic" (i.e., "synagogues of Satan," always explicitly including the Roman Church as the seat of Antichrist — cf. XXV:4-6). Further, the dehistoricization of pneumatic adjudication into doctrinal forms finds its expression in the clearly enunciated "federal theology" that stresses the continuous "Covenant of Grace" from fallen Adam to the present, which embodies even through the Old Testament a particular doctrine of faith in Christ (VII; VIII:6, 9). And, finally, the scripturally probative, referentially based understanding of this process of pneumatic adjudication, exclusive of any other form of clear disclosure, is laid out as the foundational method behind the Confession's understanding of the articulated Christian faith within history. This is apparent from the Confession's opening principle that the "supreme judge" *(supremus judex)* in all "religious controversies," of any kind and in any place, remains "none other than the Holy Spirit speaking in Scripture" (*nullus alius esse potest, praeter Spiritum Sanctum in Scriptura pronunciantem* — I:10).

1. Endemic Ecclesial Deception

This conjunction of elements, here manifested by the mid-seventeenth century, not only is fortuitously linked to the separative character of Reformation and post-Reformation denominational self-justification, but it derives logically from experience and is sustained by that character's maintenance, however particularistically one might identify each element's conceptual genealogy.[46]

46. This point bears emphasis. For, just as in the case of the doctrine of the Antichrist, what is crucial for determining the significance of the doctrine itself in the Reformation era is not its demonstrable medieval antecedents, but the manner in which the doctrine was adapted to a particular ecclesial experience. Similarly, one might legitimately trace a line, or number of lines, of theological origin in late scholastic thinking for sixteenth-century discussions of predestination or "covenant" theology; one might further uncover a history to their formulation in intratopical debate, that is, in its historical conceptuality, independent of the issue of ecclesial division and its justification (and clearly, a major topic like predestination in Protestant and Roman Catholic theology was carried forward by a theological impetus far more wide-ranging than ecclesiology!). But as with the particular issue of the Antichrist, one cannot escape the

Already in the mid-1520s, Luther had tied several of these elements together, in what would prove a consistent fashion, in his reply to Erasmus over the role of free will.[47] In trying to refute Erasmus's appeal to the tradition of saintly teachers who had upheld the existence and exercise of human free will in obtaining eternal life, Luther had recourse to the ecclesiology of deception and hiddenness to which we have referred earlier. Here, however, he casts it in an implied antagonistic framework that is identical to God's predestined will for the elect and reprobate and that, in the end, is adjudicable only by the application of scriptural doctrine. The "true Church" cannot, in a doctrinal dispute, be appealed to through its visible representatives, because the true Church is always hidden as a "remnant" within the "midst" of a larger "erring" body — this is God's "way" of ordering his salvific will "from the beginning." To appeal to the visible Church's teachings, given through individual "saints," is inevitably to enter into a web of deception. Instead, like Abel, the "elect" are actually those who are visibly vanquished and who therefore cannot manifest themselves as guides. Only Scripture is left, through its coherent doctrine, to provide clear judgment. The need, then, to extricate adjudication from a visible ecclesial unity — embodied in the historical persons of individuals tied to the already demonized papacy — pressed Luther, from the start, to adapt particular theological constructions, such as we have already identified, that together were able to buttress what became a separative logic fueled by the conviction of ecclesially endemic delusion.

This adaptation took place across the theological board in the wake of the Reformation division. The model, for instance, of the perpetual struggle between the two churches, given in the figures of Abel (the true) and Cain (the false), was a popular one from the time of the early Fathers. Augustine, of course, is its most notable exponent, and he joins the model to his evolving elaboration of the Two Cities image, which itself is tied to his thinking on predestination in its historical outworkings.[48] But what was traditionally a

---

question of how particular theological concerns and the answers given them coalesced, one with another, and themselves maintained a vitalizing origin, without confronting the logical service they offered to a continued form of ecclesial existence.

47. See the English edition of his "De Servo Arbitrio," in E. G. Rupp and P. S. Watson, eds., *Luther and Erasmus: Free Will and Salvation* (Philadelphia: Westminster Press, 1969), esp. pp. 154ff. On the churches of Abel and Cain displaying themselves in the conflict between reformer and papacy, see also Luther's "Lectures on Genesis" (English ed. of *Works*) (St. Louis: Concordia Publishing House, 1958), vol. 1, p. 252.

48. For example, most famously in the *City of God* (15:1, 17; 18:51); or in his commentaries on the Psalms (90:2:1; 118:29:9); without speaking explicitly of Abel and Cain, but already of the Two Cities in a mature historical fashion, cf. *De catechizandis rudibus* (cc. 19; 21).

figural ecclesiology designed to maintain the *spiritual* integrity of the *visible* Church in its unity across time and within the formative history of Scripture (inclusive of both Old and New Testaments) — a design to articulate the Christically participatory character of the scripturally denoted People of God — became, in the Reformation controversy, a tool both to justify distinctive separation between two putative "churches" and to explain their failure to separate until the present. The figure of Abel was in fact used by both Protestants and Catholics in this fashion, the former seizing on the perpetual hiddenness of Abel in the face of his evil "older" brother (the "alleged" church of the devil), the latter stressing the continuous distinction of the visible Church from false heretics.[49]

This separative adaption of the model is brought into relief, furthermore, by the way its traditional pre-Reformation meanings reassert themselves, anachronistically, in the hands of deliberately nonseparative theologians, like the Jansenists, whose intentions (at least within the Catholic fold) were aimed at the maintenance of a unity-despite-doctrinal-disagreement. For contrary to the whole prevailing trend of post-Reformation interpretation of the figure in terms of permanent ecclesial distinctiveness, seventeenth-century Port-Royalists and eighteenth-century Jansenist Appellants turned to Abel as a figure of "sanctity" *tout court,* whose typification of Jesus grounded his own distinctive holiness as a person of faith and hope, self-denial, gratitude, and martyrdom. No longer a cipher for an historical argument about the locus and topic of adjudication, the Jansenist Abel assumes his Augustinian role as founder of the "heavenly city" defined in terms of love of God, distinctive in the radiance of his actions over and against the vast, yet identifiably vague, "city of the world," which is given no necessary ecclesial mask.[50]

49. On this topic, see Yves Congar's article "Ecclesia ab Abel," in Marcel Reding, ed., *Abhandlungen über theologie und kirche. Festschrift für Karl Adam* (Düsseldorf: Patmos-Verlag, 1952), pp. 79-108. Congar notes only in passing the Protestant use of the theme (pp. 93f.), but points out the way in which post-Tridentine Catholicism itself shifted the import of the model away from a positive mystical participation in Christ to one of almost exclusive juridical significance: the "Church of Abel" was to be identified with the historically continuous people existing under legitimate authority, presently constituted in the episcopal succession under Rome (pp. 94ff.).

50. The Jansenist interpretation here was, to be sure, formally defined by the movement's strict adherence to patristic exemplars, like Ambrose, Augustine, Chrysostom, and some of the Cappadocians, and not ostensibly by an ecclesiological thrust, which often worked only tacitly. One can see some of this in De Sacy's late seventeenth-century commentary on Genesis. More impressive still is a production like Nicholas Cabrisseau's enormous seven-volume *Discours sur les vies des saints de l'Ancien Testament* (Paris, 1732), which is wholly conceived on the basis of the theological principle of the *ecclesia ab Abel*. In its lengthy consideration of a full sweep of

But the Two Churches opposition was, in fact, supported by the ancillary development of strong predestinarianism. Whatever the scholastic background to the way this topic came to be framed among Continental and English Reformed theologians, the popularity that its most schematic expositions enjoyed derived in part from their ability to give permanent establishment to the separative ecclesial distinction, locating it directly in the deepest reaches of God's hidden will.[51] The famous *tabula predestinationis* of Theodore Beza, Calvin's successor in Geneva, was quickly disseminated, in one form or another (and despite misgivings by many theologians), through teaching manuals and woodcuts, as well as through the erudite advocacy of particular writers (e.g,. in England, William Perkins).[52] Beza's graph sets out on the top God's inscrutable will, from which proceeds his manifested decree for the election and reprobation of the members of the human race for his glory. The fall of Adam then provides the context out of which the schema draws two parallel lines, detailing the fates of each group of people, leading them each to God's final judgment and experienced sentence. In the course of these two lines, elements of the history of the elect and reprobate mirror each other contrastively: God "freely loves" the elect," he "justly hates" the reprobate; the elect receive an "effectual calling," the reprobate an "ineffectual calling" or "no calling" at all; the elect receive "conversion" and "faith," the reprobate "hardening" and "ignorance" or "contempt" of the Gospel; and so on. The formal beauty of the scheme, however, gains its force, in part, to the degree that it is viewed as explanatory of an *integrated* history of ecclesial

---

Old Testament figures, however, the work approaches their lives as "moral histories" (cf. Preface), punctuated by the account of their "miraculous deeds," whose purpose is to instill adoration and virtue and prove a vehicle for deepening fellowship with Christ. Cabrisseau's treatment of Abel, in particular (vol. 1, pp. 62-115), is distinctive in this regard and covers an array of pneumatic categories, including prayer, sacrifice, participation in the "states of Christ," almsgiving, the evangelical virtues, martyrdom, and the scripturally figural integrity of historical experience devoid, despite its ample citations of Augustine, of denominational pleading or ecclesially contrastive rhetoric.

51. For this background, as well as for thorough reviews of primary and secondary literature on the topic of predestination and covenant theology, cf. Stephen Strehle, *Calvinism, Federalism, and Scholasticism: A Study of the Reformed Doctrine of Covenant* (Bern/Frankfurt/New York/Paris: Peter Lang, 1988), and David Weir, *The Origins of the Federal Theology in Sixteenth-Century Reformation Thought* (Oxford: Oxford University Press, 1990).

52. Also known as the "Summa totius christianismi," it is found in Beza's *Tractationum Theologicarum* (Geneva, 1582), or the reprinted *Opera*, I:170. An accessible English version of the schema can be found in Heinrich Heppe, *Reformed Dogmatics,* trans. G. T. Thomson (Grand Rapids: Baker Book House, repr. 1978), pp. 147f. See also Johannes Dantine, "Les Tabelles sur la Doctrine de la Prédestination," in *Revue de Théologie et Philosophie,* 1966, pp. 365-77.

identity: the parallel lines of elect and reprobate, of Abel and Cain, mark the generally *hidden* currents of divine providence at work within the otherwise uniform historical experience of visible Christianity; or, to the degree that God's "manifest" decree erupts into visibility in history, it will be a visibility of antagonistic confrontation, appropriate to the separative dynamic of the end times.

The experienced temporal juncture of the divine decree's movement and its final temporal exposure in the last days was what, of course, put firm flesh upon the separative logic of division during the sixteenth and seventeenth centuries. Flourishing, for instance, in the soil of English ecclesial conflicts, an extraordinarily rich tradition of eschatological piety grew up around this scheme that, in the last analysis, acted as a historical explicator to the experience of a unified history of ecclesial delusion now giving way to an ultimate conflict.[53] The English reformer John Bale, notorious for the vitriol of his writings and personal comportment, provided early on what became a classic corpus of writings sustaining the Two Churches framework, which, in its explicit eschatological description, imprinted the delusive context of ecclesial experience firmly upon the interpretive conscience of many English Protestants for decades to come.[54] One of Bale's most successful books, an early commentary on the book of Revelation, was tellingly entitled *The Image of Both Churches.* In it, Bale ingeniously uses the Apocalypse as a field for exposing the present disclosure of an age-long conflict between the two streams of God's providential ordering of the Church, only now revealing its obscure outwork-

53. The secondary literature on English eschatological thought through the seventeenth century is large. I have found especially useful G. J. R. Parry's *A Protestant Vision: William Harrison and the Reformation of Elizabethan England* (Cambridge: Cambridge University Press, 1987), which studies a truly exemplary figure of the tradition of separative deception we are examining, and whose typical writings remain, largely, in manuscript. Cf. also the overviews of K. R. Firth, *The Apocalyptic Tradition in Reformation Britain 1530–1645* (Oxford: Oxford University Press, 1979); Richard Bauckham, *Tudor Apocalypse* (Oxford: Sutton Countenay Press, 1978); Paul Christianson, *Reformers and Babylon: English Apocalyptic Visions from the Reformation to the Eve of the Civil War* (Toronto: University of Toronto Press, 1978); Bryan W. Ball, *A Great Expectation: Eschatological Thought in English Protestantism to 1660* (Leiden: E. J. Brill, 1975). Christopher Hill's *Antichrist in Seventeenth Century England* (Oxford: Oxford University Press, 1965) is to be used cautiously with respect to its theological expositions.

54. Christianson, pp. 13ff., places the critical development of Bale's eschatology during his exile in Germany after 1540; and he attributes great originality to Bale's elaboration of the Two Churches schema, noting the way its historical analysis of endemic deception broke radically even with the marginal Antichrist tradition of the late Middle Ages. Bale's location within the mainstream of Continental reform, however, points to his thought less as an originating source than as an illustration of the inevitable articulation of a common and undergirding logic.

ings in the conflict between Reformers and Papists. There is a paradoxical character to this "coming into view" of a long-hidden battle, since even the true meaning of the Reformation can still be apprehended only through piercing the veil of scriptural obscurity encountered above all in the book of Revelation: the historical reality of Abel and Cain's parallel histories is both adjudicated and veiled by the scriptural record. Bale ends the work with an illustrative devotional exhortation:

> Here hast thou, good christian read, to thy soul's consolation, from the eternal Trinity, the Father, the Son, and the Holy Ghost, three distinct persons in one everlasting Godhead, the universal estate of the church from Christ's ascension to the end of the world, in wonderful mysteries described, and directed unto them of him by the most holy apostle and evangelist St. John: wherein it is fully by all due circumstances manifested of the said Holy Ghost, what the innocent christian church is, with all her justifications and blessings, to the singular comfort of the Lord's true elect; and what the proud synagogue of antichrist is, with her filthy superstitions and plagues, to their fore-warning also. This is specially done here of the said Holy Ghost, that no true believer should profess himself a citizen of this wretched world with Cain, Nimrod, and other reprobate vessels, at the execrable doctrine of men; but at the pure voice of God with Abel and Abraham to seek for that heavenly heritage, which is purchased for them in Christ's blood. Mark here the condition of John being in most painful exile; for he in mystery through all this book representeth every godly believer. By this shall ye well know in this revelation the one church from the other; for the one is maintained by the only preaching of God's pure word, the other by all kinds of Jewish ceremonies and heathenish superstitions. And by this they also differ, that Christ would have all of love, antichrist of tyrannous constraint, as evidently appeareth in Mahomet and the pope. For that only cause are many necessary things here written in mystery, that they should be hid from the worldly-wise hypocrites, and that the just or God's meek-spirited servants should ask them of their Lord in faith and prayer.[55]

Prying apart the two churches, in the life of an individual Christian, clearly demands a willingness to enter into an arena where "mystery" shrouds the obvious, even at this last stage of the world's history and most especially here, since now delusion becomes an identifiably principal actor.

---

55. In *Select Works of John Bale, D.D., Bishop of Ossory* (Cambridge: Cambridge University Press, for the Parker Society, 1849), p. 640.

2. and 3. The Historical Veiling of Pneumatic Phenomena in Favor of Doctrine's History

Within this tradition of Reformed theology, then, the problem of endemic deception, now given historical bite by the specific workings of the Antichrist in the last days, required some kind of alternative adjudicatory instrument, which, as we have noted, formed itself around the dehistoricized framework of abstracted doctrine. On the one hand, the continuity and uniformity of the true Church through all of time, explicated in predestinarian terms, and eventually dogmatized in terms of the coherent "covenant of grace" in existence from Adam to the present, made of ecclesial history even back through the Old Testament a delineation of the exhibition and discovery of particular doctrines that embodied the *sola gratia Christi*. Historical exegesis for many Protestants became a process of ad hoc sifting for such doctrine amid the records of ecclesial time and irrespective of coherent scriptural narrative or integrity. The Scottish Confession of 1560, for instance, speaks to the question of ecclesial adjudication within the otherwise confusing experiential mass of the purported "Church" by encouraging an investigation of ecclesial "marks" that are independent of the shape of ecclesial history itself:

> Since Satan has laboured from the beginning to adorn his pestilent synagogue with the title of the Kirk of God, and has incited cruel murderers to persecute, trouble, and molest the true Kirk and its members, as Cain did to Abel . . . So it is essential that the true Kirk be distinguished from the filthy synagogue by clear and perfect notes lest we, being deceived, receive and embrace, to our own condemnation, the one for the other. The notes, signs, and assured tokens whereby the spotless bride of Christ is known from the horrible harlot, the false Kirk, we state, are neither antiquity, usurped title, lineal succession, appointed place, nor the numbers of men approving an error. For Cain was before Abel and Seth in age and title . . . and greater numbers followed the scribes, pharisees, and priests than unfeignedly believed and followed Christ Jesus and His doctrine . . . The notes of the true Kirk, therefore, we believe, confess, and avow to be: first, the true preaching of the Word of God, in which God has revealed Himself to us, as the writings of the prophets and apostles declare; secondly, the right administration of the sacraments of Christ Jesus, with which must be associated the Word and promise of God to seal and confirm them in our hearts; and lastly, ecclesiastical discipline uprightly ministered, as God's Word prescribes. . . . When controversy arises about the right understanding of any passage or sentence of Scripture . . . we ought not to ask what men have said or done before us, as what the Holy Ghost uniformly speaks within the body of the Scrip-

tures. . . . For it is agreed by all that the Spirit of God, who is the Spirit of unity, cannot contradict Himself.[56]

A "note" here (*index* in the Latin) refers to a manifest sign; and within the stream of ecclesial history, otherwise indistinguishable in its twofold partition due to the deceits of Satan masking as the true Church, only the application of a set of doctrinal tests to this or that person, group, or period can possibly bring it into visibility. The "sign," thus, is intrinsically latent, hidden. Even "unity" itself ceases to be a visible pneumatic quality, but has migrated into the intratextual reality of scriptural interpretation.

History as it is doctrinally apprehended, then, is monochromatic. But the uniformity of the covenant of grace's significance and elected partners, as they are artificially identified (in the sense of not manifesting themselves automatically), allows for a subsequent and almost theoretical reformulation of the shape of history itself, according to the possible manners in which one might constellate visible events with what is otherwise the obscurity of the twofold uniform stream of the two churches. Periodizing history, of course, had a long tradition behind it within the Church.[57] And most such attempts were as artificial as sixteenth-century efforts, at least until they reached (as with Franciscan examples) the moment of contemporary concern. The difference in pre-Reformation periodizations lay, in general, in their more generally figural foundations, drawing from scriptural numerology (e.g., days of creation or gifts of the Spirit) and pulling the significance of these distinctions out from scriptural moral or ascetical forms. In the hands of the Reformers, however, periodization became an instrument for systematizing the uniformity of ecclesial history's bipartite significance through its otherwise inchoate details; there was little moralizing or ascetical bias to the framework, as in the past; and instead the distinctions of "ages" grew into an underlying dispensationalist order designed to rationalize the continuance of right doctrine and the true Church through seemingly contradictory times. The effect of such organization was to subordinate particularistic elements within history to a scheme that

56. Article 18 of the Confession, as translated in Arthur C. Cochrane, ed., *Reformed Confessions of the 16th Century* (Philadelphia: Westminster Press, 1966), pp. 176ff. The original English and Latin versions can be found in Philip and David S. Schaff's *The Creeds of Christendom* (repr. Grand Rapids: Baker Books, 1996), vol. 3, pp. 460ff.

57. For the early portion of this tradition, cf. the standard work by Auguste Luneau, *L'Histoire du salut chez les Pères de l'Église: la doctrine des âges du monde* (Paris: Beauchesnes, 1964); for an outline of some medieval developments, cf. Joseph Ratzinger, *The Theology of History in St. Bonaventure* (Chicago: Franciscan Herald Press, 1971). For some Lutheran versions, cf. Barnes, ch. 3.

could uphold uniformity of doctrine to time; indeed, temporal particularities came to be viewed as having existential integrity only to the degree that they might be signs of or might advance the succeeding maintenance of the underlying Gospel.

One finds this seeming paradox in the developing federal theology, to take the example of the seventeenth-century Dutch theologian Johannes Cocceius, whose *Summa Doctrinae de Foedere et Testamento Dei* became, despite objections from some Reformed quarters, a textbook for many Continental and English-speaking Reformed thinkers.[58] Cocceius could outline clearly the primacy of the covenant of grace, made in Christ with a view to Adam's fall (and in distinction from the prelapsarian "covenant of works"); and this covenant of grace, properly articulated in terms of *solus Christus* doctrines, overarches the whole of the Old and New Testaments, until the present day. Within this unity, however, Cocceius begins to identify a sequence of smaller dispensations, not only between the Old and New Testaments, but within the Old Testament itself and, later, within the history of the Christian Church to the present. Hans Frei has perceptively indicated the unstable way in which this scheme attempts to grasp some particular significance for individual events in time, all the while unable to free them from their subordinated, and finally indistinguishable, place upholding the uniform character of historical experience. Despite a penchant for "figural" interpretation of both the Old Testament and contemporary history, Cocceius ends by flattening out the scriptural narrative of its distinctive forms and emptying present events of any integral particularity.[59] With someone like Herman Witsius, working a generation later, dispensationalism had by now managed to iron out the problem of particular events within and outside Scripture, subsuming them wholly into the range of periods that described the single covenant of grace and allowing their details to work solely for the explication of the larger doctrinal theme.[60] And Witsius's example is important, not only because his systematic work was influential among English Puritans, but because his hermeneutic disquisitions became textbooks even for Anglicans in general as they attempted to find some way to apply the Old Testament figurally to contemporary exegesis. For, given the schema, figuration became a means of using Old Testament events and persons

58. Leyden, 1660. Cf. Charles McCoy, "Johannes Cocceius: Federal Theologian," *Scottish Journal of Theology*, December 1963, pp. 352-70.

59. Frei, pp. 46-50.

60. Witsius's *De Oeconomia Foederum Dei* (1685) achieved continued propagation in the English-speaking world and was still being translated in the second half of the eighteenth century (cf. his *The Oeconomy of the Covenants Between God and Man: Comprehending a Complete Body of Divinity* [London, 1763]). On the dispensations of the covenant of grace, see bk. 3, ch. 3.

(or perhaps New Testament events in connection with ecclesial history) as significant in their ahistorical manifestation of Christ. Or, as controversy shifted to the questions of the Deists, figuration was useful as offering probative examples in support of the authority of the underlying object of the Scripture as a whole, the doctrine of Jesus Christ, proven through the fulfillment of prophecy.

In any case, "dispensationalism," even when it came to embrace the practice normally associated with the modern use of this term, as in the seventeenth-century Anglican Calvinist John Edwards, served to rationalize the continuity of historical deception and obscurity within the Church, not to bring into relief the particularities of historical visibilities. Where these were undeniable, they were explicated in such a way as to relativize their importance with respect to the larger shape of the true Church's shrouded temporal existence within the vessel of a false Christianity that only the present times, if with difficulty (as Bale earlier believed), could attempt to separate. Edwards was one of the first to systematize explicitly what was already, as we shall see, an established view that the visibilities of the past, whatever their integrity as markers of pneumatic adjudication at a given time, could not stand as determinative of the present.[61] In particular, under the aegis of the covenant of grace's consistent ecclesial outworking in duality, he articulated dispensations within the history of the New Testament Church that allowed for the setting aside of ostensive pneumatic phenomena as essential to the integrity of the Church. Having divided the "Evangelical economy" itself into five dispensations on the model of the "ages of man,"[62] he reserved adulthood to the imminent eschaton, wherein the "destruction of the Antichrist" will be fully manifested, but before which the true Church must labor under a variety of obscuring imperfections, included among which are the pneumatic gifts and

---

61. John Edwards, *"Polypoikilos Sophia," a Compleat History or Survey of All the Dispensations and Methods of Religion, from the Beginning of the World to the Consummation of All Things, as Represented in the Old and New Testaments*, 2 vols. (London, 1699). Twentieth-century "premillennial dispensationalism," in the tradition of John Nelson Darby, has sometimes pointed to Edwards as a progenitor of the movement's ideas. But Edwards was drawing out a logic inherent in the separatist ecclesiology. Given this fact, it is tempting to see someone like Darby, with his notion of the "ruin of the Church" and its utter hiddenness in the ecclesial structures of the world — doctrines that shocked most of his denominational contemporaries in the nineteenth century — not as an idiosyncratic thinker, but as someone giving voice to the formal conclusions of a way of thinking that committed denominationalism, despite its allied genesis, could not bring itself to own up to. On American dispensationalism, see Clarence B. Bass, *Backgrounds to Dispensationalism: Its Historical Genesis and Ecclesiastical Implications* (Grand Rapids: Wm. B. Eerdmans, 1960).

62. Edwards, pp. 586ff.

miracles of the apostolic age, permitted only in condescension to the infantile character of the period. "This Dispensation of Christianity, under which the *Apostles* were, was not arrived to a very considerable Pitch. There were some relicks of the *Jewish Oeconomy* still remaining: they had not quite laid aside the *Ceremonial Law* and *Mosaick* Rites."[63] This period complete, the Church now suffers its tribulations at a more mature level, subjected to contradiction without the crutches of any form of visible adjudication: "This is the *Second subordinate Dispensation of the Gospel,* or the present Period we are now under. This began when all the Legal Ceremonies and Jewish Observances were laid aside, when the extraordinary Gifts of the Holy Ghost ceased, when immediate Inspirations were withdrawn, and when signs and Wonders, and working of Miracles were out of use."[64] Dispensationally, pneumatic visibility is equivalent to Jewish "ceremony" in its carnal crudeness.

This principled and fundamental denigration of the "miraculous" was, to be sure, not widely shared, nor openly admitted. But even a Calvinist apologist for an orthodox "enthusiasm," like Jonathan Edwards in America, managed to build a periodized framework that, if different in details and sensibility, embodied the same dualistic logic according to which ostensive *pneumatica* must lose their adjudicative role in the midst of a history of ostensive deception overruled, ultimately, only by the continuous, though hidden, power of evangelical doctrine. Edwards's *History of Redemption* (1739),[65] although it is systematically founded on a positive exposition of Christ's gracious work within the single stream of the Elect, in practice follows firmly in the tradition of providing "an image of two churches." In offering a summary of the progress or "improvement" made during the final "period" of the work of redemption, from Christ's Resurrection to the end of the world, Edwards notes how the history of the Church is itself a "proof" of the truth of its Scriptures and election, in that it constitutes a history of continuous "opposition" from Satan:

> So that the opposition which has been made to the church of God in all ages, has always been against the same religion and the same revelation, which is a strong argument of their truth. Contraries are well argued one from another. . . . That the church of God has always met with great

63. Edwards, p. 592.
64. Edwards, p. 603.
65. The work was originally given in the form of sermons, from whose manuscripts a continuous discourse was edited and published in 1774 by John Erskine. I have followed one of the many reprints of this version from what became the standard edition of his works in the nineteenth century, an 1838 edition put out by the American Tract Society.

opposition in the world, none can deny. This is plain by profane history as far as that reaches; and before that, divine history testifies the same. The church of God, its religion and worship, began to be opposed in the time of Cain and Abel.[66]

This primordial opposition, deriving from the continuous antagonism of the Devil, proves to be the antiphonal motif of Edwards's tale, and it reaches a resounding tenor when he comes to treat of this final period of the explicitly Christian Church, detailing the pre-Constantinian persecutions, and then culminating in the "age" or "rise of Antichrist" in the form of the papal Church. The whole scheme, even in its correlations with apocalyptic images, is familiar. What is notable in this developed example of Protestant history, however, is the way in which Edwards's version has now almost completely eliminated even documented historical particularities from his story of the Christian mission, in favor of a reiterated and unique activity that finally offers an adequate temporal mirror to the uniformity of the overarching pattern of redemptive antagonism: the true Church, embodying the "work of redemption" in time, is known only by its preaching of Scripture doctrine and by converting souls. Except for a brief mention of "an age of miracles" that lasted for one hundred years after Christ's ascension, to be done away with once the "New Testament" was established as "an infallible and perpetual rule of faith,"[67] the entire history of the Church, including the first four centuries, is depicted as a secret triumph over Satan through the often hidden preaching of conversion in a manner that resembles nothing so much as the habituated homiletic style of eighteenth-century Northampton. In this, the Apostles, Tertullian, Hus, and Edwards actually participate in the same pneumatic experience, whose commonality is not visibly demonstrable, but implied by a (purported) subjection to the same bounded doctrinal pronouncements.

4. Adjudicating Scripture versus the Scriptural Context for Holiness

The reduction of redemption history to a single embodied form of doctrinal pronouncement, of course, was a conception complementary to a similar reduction of scriptural narrative, and the two give equally little place to the formation and manifestation in their midst of distinctive pneumatic disclosures. In our previous chapter, we noted the Protestant reconceiving of Scripture's pneumatic

66. Edwards, pp. 358f.
67. Edwards, pp. 282ff.

meaning as uniform doctrine, which in turn became the foundation for an abstracted ecclesiology. Here we need to stress the way this reconceptualizing served to exclude the appearance of contemporary sanctity that itself might grow out of scriptural form. There was no room here for the kind of project the Jansenist Cabrisseau envisaged in his extensive *Discourse on the Lives of the Old Testament Saints* (see above), through which the particularities of scriptural personages were presented as formative figures, through the Incarnation, for contemporary Christian life. Cabrisseau was, in effect, ascribing to scriptural lives in their particularity the same vital role played by Christian saints in the Catholic tradition. But because they were scriptural figures, access to whom was through a bounded history overtly attached to the larger scriptural narrative, the effect was both to conform specific pneumatic manifestation, even in contemporary terms, to the contours of scriptural figuration and also to open up the Scriptures as the field in which contemporary pneumatic existence might flourish.[68] The logical possibility for this perspective and practice, however, was an anachronistic notion that the variegated wealth of the scriptural narrative was integrally applicable to the Church's life, because of the Church's unity with that narrative. It was just this presupposition that the interiorization of ecclesial deception no longer permitted, and with this disallowance, Scripture could no longer function as formative context for pneumatic existence, but could only act as the external adjudicator of an existence independently constructed according to the principles of the Christian Gospel, which, while derived from Scripture, could not be equated with it generally, but only with its "spirit."

The difficulties Protestants had with figural sanctity may seem odd, given their often welcoming embrace of typological figuration in general, especially in the Reformed tradition. But typology was, in their hands, primarily an instructional tool concerning the meaning of the Gospel, not a witness to or a locus of formative power. When William Whitaker addressed the issue of figural readings of Scripture, for instance, in his famous *Disputation,* he did so in the context of a discussion on interpretive authority.[69] Rejecting the tradition of "multiple senses" drawn from some of the Fathers and from

68. That this viewpoint may have been more or less peculiar to Jansenism at the time is pertinent, since it was their figural ecclesiology that distinguished them from their contemporaries among both Protestants and Catholics. The attitude, however, was classically founded. Cf. the discussion in David Brakke, *Athanasius and the Politics of Asceticism* (Oxford: Oxford University Press [The Clarendon Press], 1995), ch. 3 esp., and those sections dealing with imitation and Scripture.

69. William Whitaker, *A Disputation on Holy Scripture against the Papists, Especially Bellarmine and Stapelton* (1588), trans. and ed. W. Fitzgerald (Cambridge: Cambridge University Press for *The Parker Society,* 1849), Question Five, pp. 402-95; on figuration per se, pp. 403-10.

medieval exegetes, he ties appropriate "figurative" readings to the single "literal sense" of Scripture given it by the Holy Ghost, which may well at times involve metaphorical or prophetical meanings, but only as they are intrinsically established by the sense of the text. And where they are not, as when Hosea 11:1's "out of Egypt have I called my son" is applied to Jesus, they are clearly demanded by the Holy Spirit through their explicit application in the New Testament. However, Whitaker's strict limitation of scriptural figuration here is not an abstract judgment about the character of the Bible's language; it derives directly from his concern about ecclesially authoritative interpretation. Multiple senses are problematic, not because they are not all overtly embedded in the original text — neither are most Christological prophecies and types, as he himself acknowledges — but because they may require adjudicative support, in circumstances of controversy, from visible ecclesial authorities. And, as his argument takes off on this theme, he makes clear that such adjudication is impossible given the *deceitfulness* inherent in the "Church."

It is curious, though not surprising, then, to see the way that Protestants struggled negatively with making sense of the practical formative role of Scripture, which had heretofore found its usual devotional place in the liturgical context inherited from the Catholic tradition. The great Puritan revolt against the too "papistical" — that is, medieval — forms of the Elizabethan Prayer Book included a range of reasonings that brings together a number of the elements we have been examining. The "Second Admonition," presented to Parliament in 1572 by Puritan divines protesting what they saw as the abuses of the Church of England's ministerial and liturgical order, opens brazenly with a disquisition on the deceptive character of the Church's history, moving from the original antagonism of Cain and Abel: "It is as olde a custome as it is lamentable, to finde such as shuld be most frends, most foes. To leave the eldest times, when Abel found no worsse freende then Caine, his owne brother. . . ."[70] The authors go on to indicate at length why it is that a liturgical order established by the Church is in fact a tool of corruption, attached to the very satanic errors associated with "papisterie." The Puritan principle in this case, that only what is expressly allowed or prescribed in Scripture ought to find embodiment in church order, is well known. But that this principle in reality derives from the separative logic sustained by a distilled and uniform doctrine extracted from Scripture comes clear when the "Admonition" comes to discuss the use of Scripture in the Church of England's liturgy proper.

---

70. The "Admonition" can be found in W. H. Frere and C. E. Douglas, eds., *Puritan Manifestoes: A Study of the Origin of the Puritan Revolt, With a Reprint of the Admonition to Parliament and Kindred Documents, 1572* (London: SPCK, for the Church Historical Society, LXXII, 1907). The citation is from p. 87.

Why, they wonder, do the Psalms find a regular reading in course, or why do the New Testament canticles appear as a form of "prayer"?

> Againe, the Psalmes be all red in forme of prayer, they be not all prayers, the people seldome marke them, and sometime when they marke them, they thinke some of them straunge geare. . . . Are all the praiers that are used, agreeable to the scriptures? to let passe the benedictus, where I woulde knowe howe I might say in my prayer: for thou childe shalt be called the Prophet of the highest, and the Magnificat, where I woulde knowe howe any man, yea, or woman either might say the tenure of these very wordes: for he hathe regarded the low degree of his handmaide, for beholde from henceforthe all generations shall call me blessed? marke this well, and you can never answere it well, but that it is palpable follye and vaine praying.[71]

Clearly, this extreme kind of sentiment concerning the devotional application of the Bible's own descriptive language to contemporary life was not shared by most subsequent Puritans, let alone Protestants in general, especially Lutherans (not to mention Anglicans).[72] But the path by which a devotionally formative participation in Scripture's figural language, like that of the psalmist or Mary, could be excluded, was conceptually common, even if not pursued to the end. When Richard Hooker replied to this kind of argument about the Prayer Book, he did so by affirming its opposite premise, that is, the visibly integral continuity over time of the Church, whose palpable unity necessarily posited a scriptural unity of ostensive figuration, even in the life of the contemporary Christian. Referring to Hezekiah's commended use of the Psalter for public prayer, he writes:

> Ezechias was persuaded as we are that the praises of God in the mouths of his saints are not so restrained to their own particular, but that others may both conveniently and fruitfully use them: first, because the mystical communion of all faithful men is such as maketh every one to be interested in those precious blessings which any one of them receiveth at God's hands: secondly, because when any thing is spoken to extol the goodness of God whose mercy endureth for ever, albeit the very particular occasion whereupon it riseth to come no more, yet the fountain continuing the same, and yielding new effects which are but only in some sort proportionable, a small resem-

---

71. Frere and Douglas, p. 117.

72. A wonderful little book, which contains a good deal of discussion about European psalmody as well, is Hamilton C. Macdougall's *Early New England Psalmody: An Historical Appreciation 1620–1820* (Brattleboro: Stephen Dye Press, 1940). The writers of the "Admonition" were not, of course, opposed to the recitation of the Psalter in worship; the issue was its status as personal "prayer."

blance between the benefits which we and others have received, may serve to make the same words of praise and thanksgiving fit though not equally in all circumstances fit for both; a clear demonstration whereof we have in all the ancient Fathers' commentaries and meditations upon the Psalms: last of all because even when there is not as much as the show of any resemblance, nevertheless by often using their words in such manner, our minds are daily more and more inured with their affections.[73]

Against the Puritan notion that visible figural unity across history was patently absurd — because denied by the facts — Hooker appeals to a patristic notion of the Mystical Body, and its demand for *publicly* visible and demonstrable sanctification, in this case through the liturgy.[74]

Hooker himself had a perceptive grasp of the fact that Protestantism's *sola Scriptura* principle, as it was actually enunciated according to "evangelical doctrine" in the context of anti-Romanism, gave rise to a certain kind of denigration of the Old Testament that was in fact tied to a more fundamental, and dangerous, logic of division.[75] But even he, given that he could not simply appeal to the Catholic argument for integral ecclesial continuity between Israel and the unified Catholic Church over time, was forced to deal with the continuing significance of Old Testament particularism — figuration — in a purely functional manner, picking and choosing this or that element of Jewish "ceremonie" that might "reasonably" be retained in Christian worship for its edifying purposes.[76] In fact, Hooker was one of the few Protestants who could enunciate the integral figural vision that allowed for pneumatic disclosure in ostensive phenomena, even while, in practice, undercutting that vision by the denominationally necessitated piecemeal application of its force.

---

73. *Of the Laws of Ecclesiastical Polity* V:40:3 (London: J. M. Dent and Sons, Ltd., 1907 ed.), vol. 2, p. 156.

74. For a classic patristic treatment of the reading of Scripture, especially the Psalms, in this fashion, cf. Athanasius's *Letter to Marcellinus.*

75. Cf. Hooker, IV:8 and 11:1, on the equation of the logic of division as anti-Romanism with a kind of anti-Judaism.

76. Hooker struggles, for instance, to distinguish how Christians might, and ought, to "separate" themselves from "communion" with the "odious" Christ-hating Jews, while also retaining here and there some of their practices and "representative" symbols (IV:11:3). Ultimately, his only principles are historical expedience — if what one has received from the (Catholic) past can be given an edifying interpretation, it can therefore be retained so long as it is understood that this has nothing to do with upholding a Christian-Jewish commonality. But in adopting this ad hoc approach, Hooker also denies in practice for the Church any inherent *imperative* within Scripture to enter into its integral formative matrix, a denial that is tantamount to acknowledging the Church's essential independence from its manifest forms.

In any case, it is noteworthy that figural exegesis by and large disappeared in conforming Anglicanism until the eighteenth century, while Puritans and other Nonconformists adapted it in a wholly nonformative way, to the purpose of vindicating evangelical doctrine.[77] In neither case could Scripture act as the

77. In Reformed circles, especially during the seventeenth century, figural interpretation of Scripture, and of the Old Testament in particular, took the adjudicative form of identifying markers for doctrinal continuity through history. Once identified, such markers could also be applied moralistically, in the sense of serving as "examples" (though not participatory forms or figures) for the modern Christian. There was a great latitude among interpreters with respect to whether figural applications from Old to New Testaments, or even to the present day, must confine themselves to an explicit scripturally validated practice or whether "inferential analogy" might permit figural applications not actually found in Scripture. Whitaker provided the theological foundation for the former "restrictive" school, which reasserted itself vigorously in the early nineteenth century, now taking on the garb of historical criticism (the genealogy here is instructive), through the widely used textbook lectures of Herbert Marsh (cf. *A Course of Lectures, Containing a Description and Systematic Arrangement of the Several Branches of Divinity* [Cambridge: Cambridge University Press, 1809], esp. Lectures XIII through XVIII on scriptural interpretation and typology). Marsh had an inordinate influence upon Anglican hermeneutics during the following century, despite and in direct conflict with the revival of "spiritual reading" among the Tractarians. The latter, more expansive use of figural applications was encouraged through a number of Continental hermeneutical textbooks of the seventeenth century, by Glassius, Cocceius, Witsius, and others. In the English-speaking world, Samuel Mather's 1683 *Figures or Types of the Old Testament Opened and Explained* (based on a series of sermons in Dublin some years earlier) was among many popular manuals of typology, influential in America as well, that provided relatively profuse Old Testament applications to the New (although eschewing contemporary fulfillments). (A useful modern reprint of Mather's book is provided by Johnson Reprint Corporation [New York/London, 1968] with an introduction by Mason I. Lowance.) It is important to note that even with Mather, one of the impelling purposes to his treatise is a wholly negative one: to detail in what ways all the ceremonial baggage of popery (and Anglicanism to a lesser degree) derives from a mistaken retaining of Judaic ordinances in fact wholly *fulfilled* — and hence utterly abrogated — in Christ Jesus. These include miracles and other extraordinary pneumatic disclosures, which fall under the "Old Dispensation," brought to its final close with the destruction of the Temple by the Romans (hence their brief continuance among the Apostles). The more profuse the figural connections between Old and New Testaments, then, the less the Old impinges directly upon the present. For a "restrictive" overview of some of this material, see Patrick Fairbairn, *The Typology of Scripture: Viewed in Connection with the Entire Scheme of the Divine Dispensations* (1845–47), 3rd ed. (Philadelphia: James S. Claxton, 1867), vol. 1, pp. 2-45. Not everyone, obviously, will agree with this assessment; there are many scholars who continue to insist that Protestant "typology" is a species of a more general, and hence rooted, application of scriptural figures to the contemporary life that was inherited by the Reformation from the tradition and then applied with a new vitality to Protestant experience (cf. Deborah Shuger's *The Renaissance Bible: Scholarship, Sacrifice, and Subjectivity* [Berkeley: University of California, 1994]). The issue here is obviously the motive and character of the application, which, I would argue, was sufficiently novel in its self-justificatory mode as, eventually, to imply the actual destruction of figuralism altogether.

fertile ground in which distinctive pneumatic forms might emerge in contemporary Christian life, since the kind of transhistorical figural linkage between individual persons that Hooker had indicated was either shrouded or repudiated outright by the question of visible credibility posed because of ecclesial separation. It was not until the eighteenth century, within the enlarging debate with Deism, that figural interpretation came to be studied with any new vigor. And at this point, the dominance of Protestant logic reasserted itself, by confining virtually the entire discussion of the Old Testament's unity with the New to the terms set by the vision of doctrine's uniformity and Scripture's probative role in affirming that uniformity. When, in 1737, the freethinker Anthony Collins published his notorious *Discourse of the Grounds and Reasons of the Christian Religion,* the orthodox ground he wished to undermine was the argument for Christ from prophecy, which he did by mischievously reducing its effectiveness to "allegory" and "mystical" and "spiritual" readings. Frei seems to think that Collins did not rightly appreciate the integrity of typological interpretation, defining it aright, but mistaking its orthodox significance in literalistic, historically referential terms, which he had adopted as a disciple of John Locke.[78] It is more likely, however, that Collins was correctly reacting to the limited figuralistic vision of his Protestant culture, which had refined its principles of probative value to a point that was easily parodied by a skeptic like Collins: if the Old Testament record exists to "prove" the truth of Christ and his Gospel, then this evidentialist purpose must have some bite. Arrayed against outright unbelievers, however, the doctrinally probative value of the Old Testament figures, which had hitherto been pressed against Christian heretics (e.g., Roman Catholics) but was now explained in terms of "proof from prophecy" aimed at individuals who did not even accept a general Christian framework, carried little conviction. There was nothing convincing — as Collins well knew — with respect to Jesus being the Messiah, about a Jewish prophecy or event that, on its own terms, referred to a limited Jewish context. What is telling about Collins's book is the way that he contrasts such ineffective evidentialism with a vaguer "mystical" and "cabalistic" hermeneutics of Scripture, which alone, he mockingly claims, could ever have convinced first-century Jews seeped in such a spiritual method — a method entered into by prayer, study, holiness, and a conviction that "the whole Oeconomy of former Times, having always the CHRIST, as it were, in View, had form'd all Things to resemble him."[79] It was this latter "rabbinical" method — oddly enough upheld today by many historical critics as in fact being the

---

78. Frei, pp. 66-85.
79. Collins, p. 57. Collins's discussion of "mystical" interpretation is found on pp. 45ff.

interpretive method of someone like St. Paul — that Collins knew to be anathema to his orthodox interlocutors. And yet, it was just such a method that rested on an ecclesial experience that had logical space for pneumatic display as well as understanding. When a century later the Tractarian John Keble pressed for a reappropriation of the "mystical reading" of the Old Testament, he identified three other experiential features that made such reading possible, and even necessary, in the early Church: a belief in the extension of figuration to the breadth of the natural world, a strong belief in the divinely providential power to order both the spiritual and natural worlds figuratively according to a scriptural form, and a strong commitment to the ascetic values of holiness as expressive of such form.[80] Keble cites Bishop Van Mildert's 1814 Bampton Lectures and Thomas Horne's enormously popular *Introduction* to the Bible as well-known orthodox denigrators of patristic figurative reading, but he may just as well have cited Collins's good-humored "rabbinical" carica- ture of "allegorism."[81] Well into the twentieth century, such parody has re- mained a standard orthodox view of nonprobative figuralism, even within non-Calvinistic Anglicanism.[82]

Orthodox theologians responded to Collins, then, not with a more refined version of his caricatured "mysticism" — they were repelled by it as much as he — but with a reassertion of probative propheticism, whose eviden- tialism derived far less from new developments in empirical philosophy than from the intrinsic separative logic embedded in the ecclesiological vision out of which scriptural history was viewed in the wake of the Reformation.[83] The kind of hysterical "proof from prophecy" form of anti-Catholic polemics, filled

80. John Keble, *On the Mysticism Attributed to the Early Fathers of the Church,* Tracts for the Times no. 69 (Oxford/London: James Parker and Co., 1868), pp. 6ff.

81. Van Mildert's Lectures on hermeneutics, the seventh of which deals especially with "figurative and mystical" interpretation, can be found in his *Works* (Oxford: John Henry Parker and J. G. and F. Rivington) 1838), vol. 4. Horne's *An Introduction to the Critical Study and Knowledge of the Holy Scriptures* (1818) went through ten editions within two decades, and numerous others through the nineteenth century. Both adhered to the limiting perspectives of someone like Marsh, with Van Mildert providing a peculiar spin on its "moderate" Anglican features.

82. Cf. A. C. Headlam's popular handbook *Christian Theology* (Oxford: Oxford Univer- sity Press, 1934), pp. 73ff., which continued to attack the loose "allegory" of the Fathers and its (too Catholic) proponents, as being "erroneous and dangerous," capable of "justifying any superstition" and incapable of supporting the underlying doctrine of the Gospel.

83. Cf. what became a popular handbook, Thomas Newton's *Dissertation on the Prophecies, Which Have Been Remarkably Fulfilled, and Are at This Time Fulfilling in the World* (1754-58), whose ostensible presentation of a figuralized history is actually a narrowly evidentialist probative defense of orthodoxy in response to Collins and the Deists in general.

with revitalized concerns over the Antichrist and the end, and linked to the reaction of someone like Pierre Jurieu to the repeal of the Edict of Nantes in the late seventeenth century, is usually associated with a certain "sectarian" response to persecution or attack.[84] But Protestant orthodoxy, to a great degree and on this hermeneutical score at least, was bound by a "sectarian" — in the sense of ecclesially separative — logic writ large. One of Collins's most admired and successful opponents — at the remove of other Deists like Thomas Woolston and Charles Blount — and credited by many as a resuscitator of figural hermeneutics in later eighteenth-century Britain, was Richard Hurd, whose frequently reedited 1772 Warburtonian Lectures on prophecy aimed to display the reasonableness of founding the "truth of Christianity" upon the "evidences" of prophecy.[85] Hurd advances little of originality in his argument for the Old Testament prophecies' probative significance, not as individual predictions, but only within a single "scheme" of "mutual connection," "system," and "harmony" according to an overarching "divine wisdom."[86] He does, on the other hand, contribute to the growing literary-critical consideration of prophetic language.[87] But the eventual thrust of the whole argument, for all its incidental general insights, is the probative applicability of scriptural prophecy to an identification of Antichrist with the Roman Church, a project that takes up fully the second half of his lectures.[88] "Put, I say, all these correspondent marks together; and see if they do not furnish, if not an absolute demonstration, yet

84. Cf. his *L'Accomplissement des Prophéties de l'Eglise* (Rotterdam, 1686).

85. Richard Hurd, *An Introduction to the Study of the Prophecies Concerning the Christian Church, and, in Particular, Concerning the Church of Papal Rome* (delivered in 1768, 1st ed. 1772), 4th ed., 2 vols. (London: 1776).

86. Cf. Hurd, Sermon 3, pp. 56ff.

87. Hurd, Sermon 9. This kind of concern grew apace in the eighteenth century, generally in response to complaints by Deists about the "obscurity" of scriptural language, which made it therefore of poor probative value. Cf. Daniel Waterland's *Scripture Vindicated; In Answer to a Book Intituled, "Christianity as old as the Creation"* (London, 1730), whose "General Preface" on rules of figuration became a useful touchstone for the rest of the century. More well known today is the exegetical and critical work of Robert Lowth, whose studies of the "poetic" character of the Old Testament proved so groundbreaking. On the shift from probative prophecy to the "poetic" in especially English hermeneutics of the eighteenth and nineteenth centuries — although without much theological interest in its significance — cf. Stephen Prickett, *Words and "The Word": Language, Poetics and Biblical Interpretation* (Cambridge: Cambridge University Press, 1986), chs. 2 and 3, and his "Romantics and Victorians: from Typology to Symbolism," in Stephen Prickett, ed., *Reading the Text: Biblical Criticism and Literary Theory* (Oxford: Blackwell, 1991).

88. This argumentative purpose was in fact written into the chartered intentions of the Lectures, reflecting, as they did, the virulently anti-Roman sentiments of its founder (who was also Hurd's mentor and close colleague).

a high degree of probability, that apostate papal Rome is the very Antichrist foretold."[89] In fact, in his concluding summary, Hurd returns to the explicit and logical congruity in the Protestant vision of interiorized ecclesial deception, the doctrinal uniformity of scriptural narrative, and the separative impulse:

This conclusion, that THE POPE IS ANTI-CHRIST, and that other, that THE SCRIPTURE IS THE SOLE RULE OF CHRISTIAN FAITH, were the *two* great principles on which the Reformation was originally founded. . . . The Reformation will, then, be secured against the two invidious charges of SCHISM and HERESY (for *neither* of which is there any ground, if *the Pope be Antichrist,* and if *the sole Rule of faith to a Christian be the canonical scriptures*), and will, thus, stand immoveably on its antient and proper foundations.[90]

Over two centuries of consideration had done little to alter this fundamental orientation, even among the more liberal and erudite of a decadent church.[91]

89. Hurd, vol. 2, p. 195.
90. Hurd, pp. 212, 217f.
91. And beyond. In 1848, Christopher Wordsworth's Hulsean Lectures on the Apocalypse provided a new generation of moderate Anglicans with a trove of tools for discerning the papal Antichrist, buttressed by a critical apparatus anchored in patristic and Caroline exegesis. Obviously, not all shared this anti-Roman view, even when prone to eschatological thinking. Cf. F. C. Mather's remarks on Bishop Samuel Horsely, in his *High Church Prophet: Bishop Samuel Horsely (1733–1806) and the Caroline Tradition in the Later Georgian Church* (Oxford: Clarendon Press, 1992), pp. 260ff. The case of the eighteenth-century exegetes and theologians known as "Hutchinsonians" (after the seventeenth-century idiosyncratic Hebraicist John Hutchinson), most notably George Horne and William Jones of Nayland, deserves special treatment elsewhere. (For an accessible example of Hutchinson's hermeneutic, with all of its oddities and anti-Judaisms as well as its fundamental figuralist thrust, see his "Glory or Gravity Essential and Mechanical. Wherein the Objects and Articles of the Christian Faith, Are Exhibited; as They Were Originally and Successively Reveal'd, Hieroglyphically, by Representations in Figures," in his *Works* [London, 1749], vol. 6.) Horne's *Commentary on the Psalms,* with its lucid preface, is a model of a revived figuralism that self-consciously breaks out of the orthodox mode of probative propheticism, and harkens back to the paleo-Catholic views of Hooker. Jones's many writings on or based on this kind of figuralism (e.g., *Lectures on the Figurative Language of the Holy Scripture* and the children's catechism *The Book of Nature*) mark an even more deliberate reaction to the hermeneutics of the time. But the "reactionary" character of their work is prominent, and it remains for scholars to assess more deeply the theological stakes in that reaction. In part, this seems to involve an attempt to reassert the unity of the English church at a time of its legal and doctrinal fragmentation; and the grasp at figuralism was a response that was governed by the intuitive sense of the logical structures we have been observing, much in the way Hooker himself, under different circumstances, inchoately sensed that integral scriptural figuralism had some connection with ecclesial comprehension. Even more than with Hooker, however, writers like

The Post-Reformation Experience of Obscured Charismata

Within the cognitive arena limited by this general adoption, on the Protestant side, of a developing notion of entrenched dispensational deception, the actual fate of experienced pneumatic visibilities must seem obvious: such phenomena will be excluded, either as false (if alleged by Catholics) or as irrelevant and unnecessarily confusing (if sought after by Protestants). The actual assertion of this obscurement will now only need to be noted as a result. And if nothing has been said up to this point about post-Reformation Roman Catholic attitudes to pneumatic visibility, it is because the practical outcome to these attitudes was eventually determined simply by the emergence of dispensational deception as a prominent and immovable feature in ecclesial engagement across denominational lines, and this despite the retention among Catholics of traditional, pre-Reformation conceptions of ostensive *pneumatica*. On the one hand, these traditional conceptions were consistently reaffirmed; but on the other, the continual need to present the Roman Church always in contrast to a Protestantism whose entrenchment contradicted historical evanescence pressed Catholicism into a novel attitude: a non-evolving self-awareness that displaced the vitality of integral figuralism from central attention, in favor of

---

Horne and Jones (and the Tractarians afterward) were faced with the intrinsic limitation on their instincts represented by continued anti-Romanism. The literature on Hutchinsonianism is growing, although most of it concentrates on narrowly historical concerns to the side of theological substance. Cf. Nigel Aston, "Horne and Heterodoxy: The Defence of Anglican Beliefs in the Late Enlightenment," *English Historical Review,* October 1993, pp. 895-919; David Katz, "Hutchinsonians and Hebraic Fundamentalism in Eighteenth-Century England," in D. Katz and J. Israel, eds., *Sceptics, Millenarians and Jews* (Leiden: E. J. Brill, 1990), pp. 237-55; C. B. Wilde, "Hutchinsonianism, Natural Philosophy and Religious Controversy in Eighteenth Century Britain," *History of Science* 18 (1980): pp. 1-24; Albert Kuhn, "Glory or Gravity: Hutchinson vs. Newton," *Journal of the History of Ideas* 22, no. 3 (July–Sept. 1961): pp. 303-22. There is, it seems to me, a good case to be made (historically) for an apprehended logical link between integral figuralism, as a narrowly scriptural hermeneutic, and the experiential search after ecclesial unity: at those moments when unitive pressures are felt, such figuralist interpretive strategies often seem to resurface — although, when pursued within a (e.g., denominational) context that forbids any fundamental reordering of the divided churches, such interpretive modes will necessarily appear artificial and forced. Cf. the production, from the unstable period immediately preceding the Restoration, of Henry Vertue's *Christ and the Church: or Parallels, in Three Bookes* (London, 1659), which offers one of the few post-Reformation studies wholly devoted to ecclesiological typology, rendered with an express (and very Anglican) purpose of countering exclusivistic descriptions of the Church, yet all the while conveying an impression of woodenness, not least because it inveighs against "schism" in the same breath as it castigates Roman Catholic apostasy and paganism (e.g., pp. 388ff.). The chasm between a consistent hermeneutics and its consistent application has often subverted the coherence of either side.

a monolithic conflictual imagery that ended by surrendering the adjudicative power of pneumatic phenomena to the irresolvable contestations of intereccclesial hostility. Because of the contrastive demand for a consistent historical experience that could justify, for instance, the papacy's divine and *unchanging* shape and character over time, Scripture as a mode of contextual conformance (which Protestantism, as we have seen, also discarded) devolved into a form of occasional figural citation for the purposes of moral exemplarism. Unlike Protestantism, the obscurement of pneumatic phenomena in post-Reformation Catholicism derived less from the broad hermeneutical constraints of conceptual logic than from the experiential logic of an atrophied historical consciousness, demanded by an unremitting Christian separatism.

Apart from the peculiar case of the Jansenists,[92] then, we find that well into the eighteenth century, Roman Catholic consideration of apocalyptic scripture had taken on the form of monochromatic historical descriptions, almost mirroring in its ostensively undifferentiated temporal details the hidden unity of doctrine that Protestants had disguised under the proliferated dispensations of their own historical reconstructions: for unchanging Protestant doctrine, Catholics provided unchanging temporal experience. Taking up traditional delineations of ecclesial epochs, Catholics insisted that the "age of the Church" included a single and undifferentiated period, before those "end times" (not yet upon us) in which alone the tribulations of satanic deception would be met with any full force.[93] The Protestant Reformation, then, was

92. On some aspects of and background to Jansenist eschatology, cf. Catherine-Laurence Maire's *Les Convulsionnaires de Saint-Médard. Miracles, convulsions et prophéties à Paris au XVIIIe siècle* (Paris: Gallimard/Mulliard, 1985). The present author's unpublished dissertation, "A Pneumatological Investigation of the Miracles of Saint-Médard and Their Rejection" (Yale University, 1994) provides a somewhat wider documentation. On the Jansenist place in "contesting the miraculous," see below.

93. One of the most influential expositions of the matter was Bossuet's, who (following Augustine) tended to limit much of the prophetic material in the book of Revelation to the Roman Empire at the time of the early Church, while allowing also for a future fulfillment at the end times. The main history of the Church, then, was given over to a period of consistent experience, in which the sharp application of scriptural figure was not pertinent. Cf. especially his *L'Apocalypse Avec Une Explication* (1689), as well as other works relating to apocalyptic themes, directed especially against the Protestant millenarian Pierre Jurieu, for example, *Avertissement aux Protestants sur leur prétendu Accomplissement des prophéties* (1689) and *De excidio Babylonis apud S. Joannen* (published only in 1772). The counter to Jurieu's (and Protestantism's general) sectarianism lay, according to Bossuet's typically Catholic mind-set, in draining ecclesial history of much of its pre-Reformation figural tension. And this mind-set, well established by the end of the sixteenth century, grew out of the Catholic reaction's stagnating of ecclesial history in the face of the Reformers' more variegated dispensationalist claims. On some major (and unremarkable) post-Reformation Catholic views of the Antichrist in particular, cf. McGinn, pp. 226-30.

appropriated by Catholic historians to the single and consistent model of earlier limited and passing "heresies," an odd denial of experienced fact in the late sixteenth and early seventeenth centuries. The denial itself was a reflection of the Reformation's inescapable shadow, now cast over the historical vista of the Church's life.[94] And in this undifferentiated history of the Church, even pneumatic experiences remain constant.

But if constant, then also constantly adjudicating in their appearance. This, after all, was the obvious use pneumatic phenomena held out for Catholic controversialists. De Sales, in his popular controversial pamphlets and sermons against the Protestants, provided (following Bellarmine)[95] a vigorous defense of the explicitly miraculous that was based on just this consistent shape to ecclesial history: when Jesus promises that his disciples will be accompanied by miraculous "signs" (Mark 16:14), de Sales insists, the Lord speaks to the Church "absolutely, without limitation of time." The performance of miracles, then, is properly considered as being a perpetual "mark" of the Church, and in a period of controversy, that is, with the Protestants, the performance of miracles ought to be used to distinguish which is the party of the true Church.[96]

94. A popular example of this exegetical outlook — a kind of Catholic "History of Redemption" — is Charles Walmesley's late-eighteenth-century *A General History of the Christian Church: from Her Birth to Her Final Triumphant State in Heaven: Chiefly Deduced from the Apocalypse of St. John,* which went through several English editions in England and America and was translated into French. (I have examined only the 1777 French version, in 3 vols., as well as an American version [New York: Hopkins and Seymour, 1807, 4th ed.].) Walmesley outlines the history of the Church according to seven "ages," corresponding to the seven seals of Revelation 6 and 8. Although he divides the temporal history of the Church into different periods, placing the contemporary Church from the time of the Reformation to the present in the "Fifth Age," in fact the only distinctive difference in ecclesial experience is given by the still-to-come Sixth Age, which will mark the "Final Days" of satanic tribulation. Protestantism, in this scheme, remains no different, in kind, from the ephemeral Albigensian heresy (a fact also claimed, to very different purposes, by many Protestant historical apologists!). Reading Walmesley, one is impressed by the way this kind of popular Catholic dispensationalist history, tinged with a vaguely prophetic cast, is really nothing else than the seventeenth-century anti-Protestant tradition of the "perpetuity of the faith" given a vatic chronological garb.

95. Cf. Bellarmine's two discourses "De Gloria Miraculorum" and "De Miraculis Haereticorum" in his *Opera Omnia,* ed. Justin Fèvre (Paris, 1873), vol. 9, as well as his more extensive disputative writings on the notes of the Church.

96. Discours 53 of the "Controverses," in the (critically revised) English version of Henry Mackey, *The Catholic Controversy* (London: Burns and Oates, 1886), vol. 3, p. 178. On this line of reasoning in general, cf. Gustav Thils, *Les notes de l'église dans l'apologétique catholique depuis la Réforme* (Paris: Desclée de Brouwer, 1937). For the Protestant version (in France, at any rate), cf. René F. Voeltzel, *Vraie et fausse Eglise selon les théologiens protestants français du XVIIe s.* (Paris: Presses Universitaires de France, 1956).

De Sales's argument thus requires that he offer a historical account that demonstrates the Roman Catholic Church's consistent display of miracles over the centuries, something he attempts to do in a summary way, leading up to the assertion of contemporary miracles within the Catholic fold, in contrast to a Protestant dearth. The principle of historically experiential (as opposed to doctrinal) uniformity is broadly asserted: if Protestantism represents the true Church, it should resemble the church of St. Gregory the Great (given that even Protestants [i.e., Calvin] do not locate the Roman church's "fall" until after his pontificate). But Gregory's was a church that was patently filled with miracles. If Protestants cannot demonstrate such pneumatic continuity in their communal life, then the Reformers must admit to their own "novelty."[97]

De Sales meets Protestant arguments about the inherent deceptiveness of miracles by explicitly retaining, in contrast with his opponents, the traditional medieval delimitation of the Antichrist. In effect, he simply denies the possibility that deception can form an intrinsic part of the Church's ongoing life: the Antichrist's purported miracles will be brief in duration (three to five years), will be easily exposed by all but the most gullible, and, in any case, will be openly refuted by the identifiable advent of Elijah and Enoch (the "two witnesses" of Revelation 11), who will precede the last coming of Jesus. Since none of these discrete prophetic fulfillments can be said to have occurred — nor could they, on the explicit terms set by de Sales — all that is dependably left is the consistent miraculous witness of "centuries" of unchanging ecclesial life.[98]

But de Sales and his Counter-Reformation colleagues had already tied their notion of pneumatic appearance to an increasingly narrow range, something that can be seen from the way he initiates his discussion of miracles in the first place. It is only because "sanctity," which is the overarching character of the Church's "second" credal mark (i.e., holiness), is in fact invisible to the eye during a time of division that miracles must take its place as a *discrimen* of ecclesial authenticity. "The interior sanctity cannot be seen; the exterior cannot serve as a mark, because all the sects vaunt it."[99] With miracles bearing the full brunt of disclosing the true Church's pneumatic character, the blurred edges of its manifestation became liabilities to pneumatic presence. What would one do if particular miracles came to be dis-

97. Discours 54, in Mackey, pp. 179-87.

98. De Sales relies on traditional eschatological material, dating back to early Fathers like Hippolytus, some of which can be traced in Emmerson (cf. pp. 95-101 on the Enoch and Elijah prophecy). This material remained popular in Jansenist writing, especially in the eighteenth century.

99. De Sales, Discours 50, in Mackey, p. 177.

puted? Against the onslaught of critical investigation, Catholic miracles had now been so elevated as to be exposed to critical weapons that, in the context of their traditional performance and reception, they had never been designed to tolerate. Even de Sales must speak of the "circumstantial" character of a true miracle, which makes of an odd occurrence — for example, the wedding miracle at Cana — something genuine only when conjoined with evident divinity. This, however, was a line of defense that worked only with an indisputably "holy" person like Jesus; and, in any case, it easily became entangled in a circularity of confirmation that the appeal to miracles had been designed to obviate.[100]

Holiness and miracle, of course, not only as evidentiary marks of the Church but as celebratory and instructional tools for the reformation of Christian life and institutions, flourished within the Catholic Church of the late sixteenth century and onward. There had been, to be sure, a sixty-three-year cessation in canonizations during the most troubled antagonisms of the actual Reformation struggle (from 1523 to 1588), but popular devotions throughout this period carried on apace in the tradition of the late Middle Ages, and were promoted in many places by a growing erudite effort at encouragement and documentation.[101] By the early seventeenth century, wide areas of the Catholic world — in Italy, Spain, parts of France, and southern Germany — were readied receptors of post-Tridentine attitudes toward the deliberate promotion and control of pneumatic manifestations, whose conciliar strictures did less to constrain than to regularize, or at least organize, what was still a tradition of devotion and religious perception in broad continuity with the pre-Reformation past.[102]

100. Cf. Discours 51 and 52, in Mackey, pp. 312-16.

101. For an overview, as well as a focused study of northern Italy, cf. Simon Ditchfield, *Liturgy, Sanctity, and History in Tridentine Italy: Fietro Maria Campi and the Preservation of the Particular* (Cambridge: Cambridge University Press, 1995), esp. ch. 4 and the whole of Part II. The most prominent sixteenth-century writer in this field, preceding Trent's directives, was Laurentius Surius, whose *Commentarius brevis rerum in orbe gestarum ab a. 1500 ad a. 1564* (Cologne, 1566) was followed by the even more popular *De probatis sanctorum historiis*, 6 vols. (Cologne, 1570–1575), both of which detailed the intertwining support to the Catholic Church's continuous authenticity given by saints and their associated miracles in a time of ecclesial dispute.

102. Cf. Jean-Michel Sallmann, *Naples et ses saints à l'âge baroque (1540–1750)* (Paris: Presses universitaries de France, 1994); Philip M. Soergel, *Wondrous in His Saints: Counter-Reformation Propaganda in Bavaria* (Berkeley: University of California Press, 1993); William Christian, *Local Religion in Sixteenth-Century Spain* (Princeton: Princeton University Press, 1981). The major study of late-medieval sanctity is André Vauchez's *La sainteté en Occident aux dernier siècles du Moyen Âge d'après le procès de canonisation et les documents hagiographiques* (Rome: École Française de Rome, 1981).

But in areas where contact, and even confrontation, with Protestantism was pressing, the simple appeal to miracles became embroiled in questions that ended by inserting the phenomena of pneumatic manifestation more firmly into the web of deceptive antagonisms. Exorcisms, as a category of miracle, tended to have a higher profile, and the visibility of holiness was often linked, negatively, to the demonstration of diabolic presence.[103] From the Catholic side, this was almost inevitable, since the pre-Reformation tradition of external deception that it maintained had identified heresy with the Devil, and such externalized hostility was properly defeated by an open exposure of its presence, most notably in the course of a public miracle. But when Protestants argued that the miracles themselves, emerging from a satanically misled "church," were diabolical in nature, the *discrimen* of authenticity was logically cast into a murky confrontation of putative demonic powers. Pneumatic manifestation, within this realm of divided negative claims, easily shifted away from epiphanic disclosure into a shrouded arena where divine presence was marked rather by the Devil's struggle.

Given the Reformers' general structure of perception, as we have outlined it, their particular attitude to pneumatic visibilities, especially miracles, was inescapable. Both Luther and Calvin, and the traditions that followed them, came to a dispensational rejection of contemporary miracles, though each arrived at his conclusions from a different perspective. And both ended up by demonizing any claim to such pneumatic phenomena.[104] The severity and completeness of these judgments, representing as they did an astonishing break with a Catholic tradition whose roots were well grounded in and could not be gainsaid by the Scriptures, have too often been ignored outright or down-played by its subordination to more systematic theological descriptions concerning Protestant theology. Even the advent of "enthusiastic" movements in the early modern period, and more recently "charismatic" groups both at the margins and in the center of denominational Christianity — which have tended to be explained sociologically in terms of reactions against either authoritarianism or a developed rationalism — have done little to bring into focus the chasmic shift in Christian experience and affirmation asserted by the

---

103. Cf. Soergel's account of the shrine of Altötting, in Bavaria, and the polemics surrounding Peter Canisius's exorcistic prodigies there (Soergel, chs. 4 and 5).

104. For a brief overview, cf. Carlos Eire, *War against the Idols: The Reformation of Worship from Erasmus to Calvin* (Cambridge: Cambridge University Press, 1986), pp. 221ff. Reflections on the matter that wholly ignore the way the reality of ecclesial division determined the topic can be found in Peter Jensen, "Calvin, Charismatics and Miracles," *The Evangelical Quarterly* 51 (1979): pp. 131-44; and, even more impressionistically, Bernard Vogler's "La Réforme et le concept de miracle au XVIe siècle," *Revue d'Histoire de la Spiritualité* 48 (1972): pp. 145-50.

Protestant denial of contemporary miracle and its hagiological context. Within a generation or two, the actual pneumatic visage of the Church was wholly redescribed, and in a way that can only be admitted as being utterly novel. Why was the scope of this shift never felt in its breadth? Catholics, of course, harped upon it at length, as is obvious from the typical apologetic features we have just described. But even here, the arguments in defense of miracle, however important, are but one item in a long arsenal of controversial tools deployed against the Protestants. And if Protestants defend themselves against these arguments, it is usually in an ad hoc fashion. Both parties seem to realize that there is a framework more fundamental to their controversy, within which miracles become a natural — and hence far from shocking — casualty to contention. And that framework, as we have emphasized, is the logic of ecclesial separation that presses for the necessary and prior obscurement of pneumatic visibilities in their generality, thrusting their manifestation into the arena of demonic potential. If modern movements of religious enthusiasm have attempted to reclaim these manifestations, they have done so without questioning the framework of these phenomena's original contestability, a fact that must go far to explaining their continued irrelevance and marginalization in the life of the wider Church.[105]

We have already noted, in his discussion with Erasmus over the basis of doctrinal authority, Luther's stress on sanctity's "hiddenness" in the face of deception, and the concomitant and exclusive adjudicative primacy left to Scripture. His associated remarks on the inability to discern true miracles along with true saints are made, not surprisingly, in the same context as his discussion of the churches of Cain and Abel.[106] There is no question but that, in general, the positive elements of Luther's "theology of the Cross," independent of ecclesiological concerns, played an influential role in determining his elevation of "interior miracles" of faith over and against "exterior miracles" that were visible to the eye. But his final dispensational rejection of contemporary miracles derived, more fundamentally, from the historical demonization of

---

105. This is why the Pentecostal and Charismatic movements of the late twentieth century, however widespread, probably do not constitute a major pneumatic development in the life of the Christian Church. They have tended to be church-dividing according to the same logic as the separative ecclesiology out of which they have grown, however antagonistically; and most of the admittedly new and cross-denominational realignments these movements have encouraged are simply that, realignments, and not dismantlings of the structures of separation that still inform these kinds of pneumatic claims. It remains to be seen, of course, if the kinds of contests these new movements have instigated actually come to be used pneumatically in some greater way; it is proper to trust that they will.

106. Luther, "De servo abitrio," in Rupp and Watson, p. 158.

ecclesial experience his separative ecclesiology demanded. Ultimately, Luther asserted that "the day of miracles is past," having been confined to the life of Christ and his immediate disciples, in order to confirm the weak faith of the Gospel's original believers and to prepare the ground for the "greater miracles" of interior faith and the Church's teaching and devotion.[107] Subsequent to the apostolic age, visible miracles and purported holiness pertain to the world in which Satan works to seduce the true Church; and, in the case of the Roman Church, such phenomena are properly identified as the particular acts of the Antichrist, as predicted in Scripture:

> It is empty talk when the Romanists boast of possessing an authority such as cannot be contested. . . . St. Paul says to the Thessalonians [2 Thess. 2:9] that the Antichrist shall, through Satan, be mighty in false, miraculous signs. . . . Miracles and plagues prove nothing, especially in these latter days of evil, for specious miracles of this kind are foretold everywhere in Scripture. Therefore, we must hold to God's Word with firm faith. The devil will soon abandon his miracles.[108]

Calvin made the dispensationalist logic yet more explicit, in confining miracles to the first age for the initial confirmation of the Gospel, given form in the written Word of God, whose teachings replaced the ephemeral character of these first manifestations. Pneumatic activity, thenceforth, resides in the power of the Scripture to speak and be heard by the inner conscience. Calvin touches on this reality repeatedly, notably in his Commentary on Acts.[109] At one point in the *Institutes,* in defending the Reformed Church's right to dispense with the apostolic laying on of hands associated with episcopal confirmation, he directly addresses the issue:

> If this ministry [i.e., granting visible gifts of the Spirit] which the apostles then carried out still remained in the church, the laying on of hands would also have to be kept. But since that grace has ceased to be given, what purpose does the laying on of hands serve? . . . Those miraculous powers and manifest workings, which were dispensed by the laying on of hands, have ceased; and they have rightly lasted only for a time. For it was fitting that the new preaching of the gospel and the new Kingdom of Christ should be illumined

---

107. Luther, *Lectures on the Gospel of John,* ch. 14, vv. 10-12.

108. Luther, "An Appeal to the Ruling Class of German Nationality as to the Amelioration of the State of Christendom," in *Martin Luther: Selections from His Writings,* ed. John Dillenberger (Garden City: Doubleday & Co., 1961), pp. 416f.

109. E.g., on ch. 3, v. 9, and ch. 5, v. 12; cf. also his commentary on John 14:10-12, which is much like Luther's on this topic.

and magnified by unheard-of and extraordinary miracles. When the Lord ceased from these, he did not utterly forsake his church, but declared that the magnificence of his Kingdom and the dignity of his word had been excellently enough disclosed.[110]

Where postapostolic miracles are alleged, they are "papist abuses," used by the Devil in his delusional work upon the Church. In his "Letter to King Francis," written as a preface to the *Institutes,* Calvin addresses, head-on and at a certain length, the ecclesiological debate over miracles. Here his response to Catholic demands for Protestant miracles as a sign of the Reformed churches' authenticity is brushed aside by a pure appeal to the history of satanic anti-Christian deception, lodged in the bosom of the visible Church. Since the Reformers do not proclaim a "new" Gospel, they have no need of miracles to confirm it, as in the age of the apostles. Indeed, any "confirmatory" miracles after the apostolic age are by definition satanic, since there is no need for them. Roman "miracles," then, are prima facie tools of deception; and pneumatic visibility in general (except in the undefined sense of "glorifying" God) is rejected in favor of right "doctrine," presented purely and in its own right. "Those 'miracles' which our adversaries point to in their own support are sheer delusions of Satan, for they draw the people away from the true worship of their God to vanity."[111] So committed is the identification of the miraculous with Satan that one observes in the course of the (especially Calvinist) Protestant tradition's development the bizarre spectacle of theologians evacuating the natural world of divine epiphanic manifestation altogether and leaving the astonishment of "wonders" solely within the province of evil. Purported "miracles" soon became patent proofs of witchcraft.[112]

Catholics, of course, could simply oppose such categorical rejections of miracle with their own categorical affirmations, as indeed they did. But the Protestant rejection was not without persuasive tools besides vitriolic accusation. It was possible, through simple research — or even clever juxtaposition of documentation — to demonstrate the historical fictions that lay behind many Catholic claims to pneumatic visibility. Calvin himself contributed to the genre of hagiological *exposé* with his scathing tabulation of alleged holy relics scattered around Europe, whose existence in triplicate or more in various

110. Calvin, *Institutes* IV:19:6, trans. F. L. Battles (Philadelphia: Westminster Press, 1960), p. 1454.

111. Calvin, *Institutes,* pp. 17f.

112. Cf. John L. Teall's "Witchcraft and Calvinism in Elizabethan England: Divine Power and Human Agency," *Journal of the History of Ideas* 23 (1962): pp. 21-36.

locations easily disclosed their spurious origins.[113] In Calvin's mind, this kind of blatant fabrication was inevitable, since the concern with relics was itself a form of apostasy deserving of a double punishment of self-deception. The Devil had wanted Moses' body (cf. Jude) from the first, in order to replace the intangible truths of spiritual worship with carnal adoration, and had made do with the paltry remains of latter-day and little-known Christian corpses. Against this kind of debunking — already common enough in humanist circles — Catholics had to respond with an affirmation that was critically sophisticated if they were not to cede the popular rhetorical ground to a space devoid of the miraculous and wondrous altogether. It was in this critical sphere, originally indicated by the Protestant controversy, and officially delineated by Tridentine reforms with respect to the cult of saints, that Catholics ended by unconsciously succumbing, and only in pragmatic and unprincipled ways, to the same demonizing of the visibly pneumatic that was founded on Protestant presuppositions.

The story of the rise of Catholic critical-historical approaches to holiness is still not well understood, at least in its effect on larger ecclesial attitudes, and is best left for others to explore.[114] What is clear is that, however traditional the object such work was designed to attain — a lucid and indisputable account of the life and works of holy persons, their relics and their shrines, which might form the basis for official cults and even canonization — the practice itself altered the erudite consciousness of theologians within the Catholic Church. And this process, in turn, eventually altered the relationship between the miraculous and the Church's public life in general (however slow popular attitudes, in this or that region, were to follow suit). Already by the seventeenth century, critical attempts at reconstructing the lives of saints in a "responsible" manner had led some Catholic authors to provide a picture of pneumatic visibility that — in the minds of more traditional critics — was more "Calvinist" than Geneva.[115] Not only did these projects raise the critical awareness

113. Calvin, *Advertissment tresutile du grand proffit qui reveindront a la chrestienté s'il se faisoit inventoire de tous les corps sainctz et reliques qui sont tant in italie qu'en france, allemaigne, hespaigne, et autres royaumes et payes* (Geneva, 1543). Cf. the introduction and brief conclusion of this treatise.

114. Cf. Ditchfield, the last section, for a recent discussion. We shall touch on the question of "critical history" itself in our chapter on repentance. The work of the Jesuit "Bollandists" in producing a critically sound version of the "Acta Sanctorum" of the Church is well known. Cf. G. Du Gaiffier, *Études critiques d'hagiographie et d'iconologie*, Subsidia Hagiographica 43 (Brussels: 1967).

115. The Jansenist Adrien Baillet's voluminous *Les Vies des Saints*, one of the most radical of these versions, was nevertheless, for all of its historically skeptical character, highly popular. By the time Voltaire mocked the veneration of saints altogether, as in his "Canonisation de Saint

of the general reading public, and so spread abroad a general skepticism over immediate "accounts" of contemporary miracles and holiness, they thereby decoupled pneumatic astonishment from temporal encounter, and shifted its significance to the patient results of intellectual research. It was a process that drained the adjudicatory character of pneumatic event, by displacing its force from palpable context. It is not odd, then, to find amongst the most apocalyptically oriented elements of the Roman Catholic Church — the missionaries to the Americas — an already developed dispensationalist historical scheme that relegated miracles to the ignorant infancy of the Church's life, while the end times, led by a learned and powerful papacy, must convert the world through the moral force of human effort. Such, at any rate, was the argument of the Jesuit José de Acosta's *De temporibus novissimus* (1590). And it was an argument not without force: for despite the stories related of Far Eastern missionaries like Francis Xavier, the general experience of modern-day conversionary projects was noticeably lacking in visibly supernatural gifts.[116]

This evolving attitude, however, became conjoined with a more concrete fear that was directly related to concerns growing out of the Church's fragmenting life. Already by the late Middle Ages, worries began to arise about forms of spiritual life whose "affective" quality seemed open to delusional perversions. The Reformation divisions, however, went on to transform what were specific and localized questions about "mystical" states into broad and subsuming pressures to discriminate and adjudicate between competing claims to spiritual authority, even where direct ecclesial confrontations were not at issue.[117] A whole new range of concerns, all centered on the issue of distinguishing "true" from "false" sanctity,

---

Cucufin," "holy" individuals were easily grasped as normal, wine-swilling human beings, whose claim to pneumatic clarity was veiled in the obscurity of human folly and credulity and depended only upon institutional *fiat*.

116. Cf. Adriano Prospero, "America e Apocalisse. Note sulla 'conquista spirituale' del Nuovo Mondo," *Critica Storica* 13 (1976): pp. 1-61. Particularly galling to Catholics was the absence of the apostolic "gift of tongues," which now forced missionaries to endure years of usually imperfect linguistic study if they were to communicate with the newly discovered peoples of American and Asia.

117. The whole of the collection by Gabriella Zarri, ed., *Finzione e santità tra medioevo ed età moderna* (Turin: Rosenberg & Sellier, 1991), speaks fascinatingly to this less-studied reality of Catholic pneumatic adjudication in the post-Reformation. See especially the contributions of Zarri (" 'Vera' santità, 'simulata' santità: ipostesi e riscontri"), Andrè Vauchez ("La nascita del sospetto"), Peter Dinzelbacher ("Sante o streghe. Alcuni casi del tardo medioevo"), Adriano Prosperi ("L'elemento storico nelle polemiche sulla santità"), Gianvittorio Signorotto ("Gesuiti, carismatici e beate nella Milano del primo Seicento"), Andrea Tilatti ("Riscritture agiografiche: santi medievali nella cultura friulana dei secoli XVII e XVIII"), and Guiseppe Orlandi ("Vera e falsa santità in alcuni predicatori popolari e direttori di spirito del Sei e Settecento").

entered the realm of the Church's official and unofficial discriminating functions. It was an issue that gave rise to new inquisitorial, forensic, medical, and confessional methods and distinctions. And hovering over the entire range of concerns, and often forcefully entering them with explicitness, was the reality of deceit, especially satanic deceit, which used individuals and their lives as tools to mislead the Church's people.[118] The regional peculiarities behind the so-called witch craze of the late sixteenth and early seventeenth centuries, while they deserve special attention, cannot obscure the broader conditions of possibility for such forms of social frenzy offered on the Catholic, as much as on the Protestant, side by this embracing context of dispute, whose very range required that even Roman traditionalists, who did not overtly accept the Reformers' ecclesial internalizing of deception, acknowledge Satan's far-reaching infiltration of the Church.[119] Michel de Certeau's brilliant, if highly interpretive, reconstruction of

118. The well-known "Rules for the discernment of spirits" that forms part of Ignatius's *Spiritual Exercises* is a typical example within an obvious trend; cf. also the popular discussion in Teresa of Avila's *Life,* ch. 25, which deals with a similar set of concerns.

119. For a straightforward discussion of the way defenders of the Catholic faith, even at their most militant and confident, ended by granting the Devil a wide sphere of activity within their fold, cf. the chapter "Le juge Boguet et les démons de la contre-réforme," in Sophie Houdard, *Les sciences du diable. Quatre discours sur la sorcellerie* (Paris: Les Éditions du Cerf, 1992). Henry Boguet's descriptions of his own prosecution of witchcraft in the late sixteenth and early seventeenth centuries were openly aimed at manifesting the truth of the Roman Church in its fight with the Protestantism of the nearby Swiss cantons. Historians have drawn sociological distinctions between the rural/communal outbreaks of seventeenth-century witch hunting and the more "urban" and "individualized" phenomenon of demon possession, linked with an evolving laicization of mystical theology and more common in the seventeenth than in the sixteenth century. But causal bonds between these social matrices and the experience of ecclesial division have not been documented. What is clear, however, is that Protestant and Catholic shared a similar theological acceptance of demonic activity through individual human vassals; further, much of the persecution and accusation occurred in areas on the frontier between Catholic and Protestant separation, in areas where tensions and religious struggles continued to simmer for some time or where religious identity, in opposition to some other Christian party (even if distant) was a major social definer (e.g., Geneva, Scotland, or even America, especially during times of conflict with the French). It is not necessary to accept Hugh Trevor-Roper's thesis of witchcraft/possession accusations as an explicit tool used against confessional opponents — a now discredited theory — to nonetheless accept the fundamental role assigned to separative deceptionism as a developed cultural outlook accessible to a variety of less immediately religiously aggressive projects. For an overview of the literature, cf. Geoffrey Scarre, *Witchcraft and Magic in 16th and 17th Century Europe* (Atlantic Highlands [N.J.]: Humanities Press International, 1987). For some historiographical reflections, especially on demonic possession, cf. Michel Lagrée, "Le démoniaque et l'histoire," in *Figures du démoniaque, hier et aujourd'hui* (Brussels: Facultés universitaires Saint-Louis, 1992), pp. 13-29. A purely sociological, but detailed, study of neighboring Protestant and Catholic regions in France and Switzerland can be found in

the famous 1634 possessions at Loudun is clearly built around just this reality of socially experienced religious deception, to which the entire episode of possession, exorcism, trial, and final execution (of the directing priest accused of a satanic seduction of the nuns in question) gave a kind of embodied expression. Loudun, a confessionally divided city since the religious wars of the sixteenth century, when at last pushed by new political pressures, gave perverse voice to the religious *incapacity* to find adjudicatory resolution to the divine controversies that had first destroyed and then politically enchained its inhabitants. Sifting through the speech of the allegedly "possessed" provided a figure of the impossible, though inescapable, task of distinguishing a governing falsehood among the many only "apparent" truths the Devil had misleadingly "mixed" with his seductive discourse:

> In fact, the need for exorcists at Loudun derived from the current social situation. During a period that comes to an end in 1650 (although its currents will resurface by the end of the century), Christian truth disappears amid the boiling confusion of ideas, of stark divisions of all kinds. The experience of believers was that such truth had lost itself amid the lies. . . . To find the truth within a lie was a religious task symbolized by the work of discerning those truths mixed up among the words of the possessed.[120]

E. William Monter's *Witchcraft in France and Switzerland: The Borderlands during the Reformation* (Ithaca: Cornell University Press, 1976). Trevor-Roper's theory is given in his *The European Witch-Craze* (Harmondsworth: Penguin, 1969).

120. Michel de Certeau, *La possession de Loudun* (Paris: Julliard, 1970), p. 219. Cf. also Michel Carmona, *Les Diables de Loudun. Sorcellerie et politique sous Richelieu* (Paris: Arthème Fayard, 1988), ch. 3 and pp. 327ff. on the relationship of possession, exorcism, and confessional conflict. Bérulle's early *Traité des energumenes* provides an interesting general exposition on satanic possession within a larger theological context of divine providence, history, the Incarnation, and the Church's vocation. While Bérulle, who was at the time actively engaged in controversy with Protestants, does not in fact link possession to heresy, the bulk of his argument centers around the way the possession and exorcism at the hands of the Church offer a kind of adjudicatory "sensible" sign, in the midst of a confused world, pointing to God's existence, to His power over the world and Satan, and to the Church's own authority, given in participation with the incarnate Christ. Satan, in fact, continues to work deceptions, even on Christians, by disguising his presence, so that "possession" itself becomes something vague, which requires unveiling — an element clearly at odds with Bérulle's explication in terms of "clarification." Bérulle speaks of the confusions and doubts that beset "atheists," "libertines," new Christians — indeed, even the saints — in such a way that, by the end of the treatise, the claim for exorcism's adjudicatory clarity becomes more of a plea bespoken out of need than an outright affirmation. In any case, the work as a whole points to the spreading sense, within even militant Catholicism, that deception was a determining characteristic of historical experience, whose reality was somehow defining the Church's vocation. The treatise can be found in volume 1 of Bérulle's *Oeuvres Complètes* (1644).

Deceptive confusion, then, became a subtheme of the Catholic Church's otherwise categorical affirmation of its superiority in holiness. But as a consistent subtheme, it became subversive of the original affirmation itself. No extended episode demonstrates more clearly the force of this subversive drift than the French Catholic Church's spectacular encounter with miracle and allegedly miraculous sanctity in its own midst, in the course of its struggle with Jansenism. The first round of the encounter began as early as 1656, when Pascal's young niece, then a nun at the Paris convent of Port-Royal, was purportedly cured of a chronic eye ailment through grace associated with a relic of the Holy Thorn, then displayed in the convent. The "miracle" was much publicized by supporters of Port-Royal as a vindicating act of God on behalf of the persecuted nuns, already at the time embroiled in the initial conflict over Jansenist doctrine. The miracle also elicited some harsh rebuttal by opponents. The debate over Jansenist miracles did not truly enter into its own, however, until the next century, when, in the late 1720s, numerous miracles of healing were associated with the tomb of an otherwise obscure Jansenist deacon, François de Pâris, buried at the small neighborhood church of Saint-Médard on the edge of Paris. The commotion in this case was immense, and after continuing for several years, the miracles were brought to an end by the closing of the cemetery on the orders of the government. The episode took a less traditional turn, one that caused the Jansenist party embarrassment and division as well as increased persecution, when meetings of devotees were subsequently carried on in private homes, now accompanied by convulsionary agitations and prophetic utterances and dramatizations.[121]

The miracles of Saint-Médard, especially, drew from the French Church's theologians a vast controversial literature, which displays the complete reversal in lines of argumentation that had taken place among Catholic controversialists on the subject of pneumatic manifestations since the opening years of the Counter-Reformation. Already in the case of the miracle of the Holy Thorn, opponents of Port-Royal, in their attempt to discredit the traditionally probative claims of the Jansenists, had begun to offer arguments that negativized miracles in general, claiming, for instance, that miracles were generally worked punitively, as demonstrations of the "unbelief" of onlookers (in this case, the

---

121. On the miracle of the Holy Thorn, cf. Tetsuya Shiokawa, *Pascal et les miracles* (Paris: Librairie A.-G. Nizet, 1977), and Jean Orcibal, "La signification du miracle et sa place dans l'ecclésiologie pascalienne," *Chroniques de Port Royal* 21/22 (1972). The standard work on the eighteenth-century Jansenist miracles is B. Robert Kreiser's *Miracles, Convulsions, and Ecclesiastical Politics in Early Eighteenth-Century Paris* (Princeton: Princeton University Press, 1978). See also Radner, "A Pneumatological Investigation," esp. sec. II:2 and sec. III:3 and 4. Cf. also Maire.

nuns of Port-Royal).[122] But by the eighteenth century, the negativization had turned into an outright demonization of miracles in general, whereby leading theologians of the Catholic hierarchy seemed eager to apply the whole separative apparatus of Protestantism's assessment of *pneumatica* to the disputed phenomena. They did this, to be sure, in the course of developing a kind of Veronian skepticism that would vindicate the need for hierarchically authoritative decisions, independent of the pneumatic vindication. In doing so, however, they also embraced the most radical elements of their Protestant antagonists, as if, in encountering within their own midst a questionable movement, their only mode of response now excluded any unitive tools. It is an odd experience today to read the Catholic Bishop of Soissons, Languet de Gergy,[123] as he dismisses the significance of a Jansenist miracle, in this case officially certified by the Archdiocese of Paris, with a dispensationalist appeal to the cessation of adjudicatory miracles after the apostles — and for reasons identical to Calvin's! Since the early Church's confirmation of the true doctrine, according to Languet, the purposes of God's actions in the contemporary world properly remain inscrutable, capable of articulated purpose only when clearly explained by the Church's hierarchy. (Hence, though a miracle be "genuine," it has no meaning and is experientially irrelevant unless the hierarchy explicitly grants it significance.) As the Saint-Médard miracles proliferated, without official authentication, this line of reasoning became more radical still. Languet and others, notably the head of the Sorbonne, Jean-Baptiste-Noël Lerouge, now simply demonized the whole of postapostolic *history*, labeling it the end times of the Antichrist, whose delusional "miracles" must be supposed to reign unless otherwise distinguished by the hierarchy. Indeed, apart from the Church's express decisions, one must assume the activity of Satan, even in the Church's midst.[124] The traditional relationship of deception to ecclesial life had thus been abandoned, just as with the Protestants, although the authorities by which a pathway within the shadows could be determined differed between the two parties.[125] It was an astonishing evolution of judgment, according to

122. Cf. the main treatise attacking the miracle, *Rabat-joie des jansénistes ou Observations nécessaires sur ce qu'on dit être arrivé au Port-Royal au sujet de la sainte Epine par un Docteur de l'Eglise catholique* (1656?).

123. See Jacques-Joseph Languet de Gergy, *7e Lettre pastorale* (1726).

124. Cf. Languet de Gergy, *Instruction pastorale au sujet des prétendus miracles du diacre de Saint-Médard et des convulsions arrivées à son tombeau*, 2 vols. (Paris: 1734–35); Lerouge, *Traité dogmatique sur les faux miracles du temps, en reponses aux differens ecrits faits en leur faveur* (1737).

125. Note must be made of the attempts made by certain eighteenth-century Jansenists to forge another alternative that could somehow make sense of the reality of the Church's

which the world's experience, and the Church's experience too, was thrust into a realm of fundamental ambiguity and insensible meaning — a virtual de-divinization of ordinary experience, in the face of its frightening and even demonic confusions and silences — apart from the occasional and punctiliar pronouncements of the Church's authority. Contestation and division had pushed the Catholics into the same pneumatologically self-contradictory and mirrored opposition with the Protestants as it had on the issue of authority: a reified institution vs. an abstracted Scripture. In between, the pneumatic sense of the visible had vanished.[126]

What is to be noted, in closing this section, is simply the way this conclusion among French Catholics, in the exclusive breadth of its denial of *pneumatica,* parallels theological perceptions as they developed in wholly different social contexts, like that of England, related only in the common bequest of ecclesial division. By the end of the seventeenth century, for instance, we can observe the continuing Protestant-Catholic debate over miracles in Britain, making use of the same arguments as of a century earlier, but now extended, on the Protestant side, to a whole realm of religious experience that begins to engulf much of traditional Christianity, including prayer, meditation, and holy living.[127] The dispensationalist logic, the accusations of sorcery and diabolism

---

post-Reformation existence, without simply reasserting the traditional relation between deception and Church. If Satan's empire was not to be actually *identified* with the (Catholic) Church (versus the Protestants), but also not arbitrarily excluded from the Church's common life (versus hierarchical pronouncements), some way of expressing Satan's intimate conflict *within* the Church needed to be articulated that did not undermine the Church's general historical integrity. One of the clearest examples of such a Jansenist attempt is given by Jean-Baptiste-Raymond de Pavie de Fourquevaux, in his *Idée de la Babylone Spirituelle Prédite par les Saintes Écritures* (Utrecht, 1733), which worked out a figural reading of the Church's history by which the identity was given in the ongoing "interior" struggle the Church experienced with its own sin, informed by its temporal expression of Israel's own life and in conformity with Christ's redemptive suffering. More will be said about this notion in our concluding chapter.

126. What the Jansenists themselves did with the contestation of their miracles is another matter, and touches upon the question of the figural construal of the Church through time, an aspect of which will be touched upon in our concluding chapter.

127. The controversies engaged in during the 1670s by Edward Stillingfleet, later Bishop of Worcester, provide a typical and fulsome example of the ever-lively genre. Cf. his *A Discourse Concerning the Idolatry of the Church of Rome and the Hazard of Salvation in the Communion of It,* 2nd ed. (London, 1671); *An Answer to Mr. Cressy's Epistle Apologetical to a Person of Honour Touching His Vindication of Dr. Stillingfleet* (London, 1675); *A Second Discourse in Vindication of the Protestant Grounds of Faith, against the Pretence of Infallibility in the Roman Church,* and so on. Stillingfleet's opponents included Abraham Woodhead and his *The Roman Church's Devotions Vindicated from Doctor Stillingfleet's Mis-representation* (1672), and Edward Worseley in his *The Infallibility of the Roman Catholick Church and her Miracles* (Antwerp, 1674) and *A*

— all envelop the opposition. But the dedivinizing of the world this contraction of pneumatic clarity and particularization suggests begins to make itself felt with greater force than on the Continent. A "naturalized" space, from which the miraculous and authoritatively illuminated order of the Spirit had been evacuated, began to claim its own intrinsic significance, independent of "spiritual realities." And so "Nature" comes to assert itself as the primary context in which scriptural forms and their elaboration were to be parsed. No longer would Nature submit its own forms to the context of the scriptural history.

From this perspective, the emergence of Deism as a naturalistic product of the separative logic of ecclesial division seems inevitable. So too the constricted response of orthodoxy on the singular basis of evidential miraculism, bound exclusively to the scriptural dispensation, in the form of either prophetic fulfillment or the prodigies of Jesus.[128] Not a few commentators observed the difficulty into which Protestant apologetics had placed itself: denying miracles in the face of the Catholics and asserting them in the face of the freethinkers![129]

Discourse on Miracles Wrought in the Church (Antwerp, 1676). In this series of attacks and counterattacks, the stock arguments are drawn out anew, although now with greater detail and at greater length. Stillingfleet has by now focused Romanism's appeal to miracle in terms of its "bombast," "fanaticism," "flatulence," "distemper," and more — in short, in terms of "enthusiasm," much like the "Quakers." He can thus include in this foolishness the whole range of devotions, including affective prayer, "contemplation," counsels of perfection, and the rest, which somehow contradict the "plain intelligibility" of evangelical religion, given in the Scriptures. Only a people given to "melancholy" and susceptible to demonic influence would continue to press these kinds of outmoded beliefs, appropriate only to the first years of the Church, when an ignorant world greeted the initial preaching of the Gospel. As for Stillingfleet's respondents, they stick pretty much to the kind of confirmatory appeal to historical continuity sketched out by de Sales eighty years earlier. On Stillingfleet, see Robert Todd Carroll, *The Common-Sense Philosophy of Religion of Bishop Edward Stillingfleet, 1635–1699* (The Hague: Martinus Nijhoff, 1975), esp. ch. 3, which discusses his views on authority versus the Catholics and his dispensational view of miracles.

128. Cf. R. M. Burns, *The Great Debate on Miracles: From Joseph Glanvill to David Hume* (Lewburg [Penn.]: Bucknell University Press, 1981). See also Henry B. van Leeuwen, *The Problem of Certainty in English Thought, 1630–1690* (The Hague: Martinus Nijhoff, 1963), esp. ch. 2, on the search for certainty within the theological debates of confessionalism (e.g., Chillingworth).

129. Cf. William Weston's *An Enquiry into the Rejection of the Christian Miracles by the Heathens. Wherein Is Shewed, The Low Opinion Which They Had of MIRACLES in General; and This Accounted for from Their Situation and Circumstances* (Cambridge, 1746), esp. ch. 10, "A comparison between the situation of the Heathens in regard to the Christian Miracles, and the situation of the Protestants in regard to the Roman Catholic." Weston's ostensive purpose is to refute those Deists who question the authenticity of the New Testament miracles on the basis of their absence from the accounts of pagan historians. The ancient Greeks and Romans of the period, Weston argues with great erudition, simply didn't *believe* in miracles

The demonization of the opposition appeared less inconsistent if one could join, as became a custom, Deists and Catholics together, accusing the latter of fomenting the former in a Veronian plot to breed a general skepticism that would feel forced to find ultimate resolution in the naked authority of the Roman pontiff.[130] But, as with the eighteenth-century Catholic opponents of Jansenism, it became increasingly difficult to distinguish even the New Testament miracles from at least potential satanic origin, and the entire realm of *penumatica* was consigned to the same pit as "enthusiasm," a hole into which (as Luther had first noticed with respect to Catholics and Anabaptists) one could, according to a certain reasoning, drive both Papists and Methodists together (along with their crafty cousins, the Deists).[131] The intellectual effort

---

— their own were patently ridiculous — and so dismissed any claim whatsoever to the miraculous. But Weston also raises the ironic question of why Protestants, who come out of a tradition that *respected* miracles, should so cavalierly dismiss them *in toto* among Catholics: is it not more understandable why the heathen gave no credit to Christian miracles than why Protestants question the Catholics? It is unclear whether Weston, in the end, is actually reinforcing the Deist case. At any rate, the instability of Protestant apologetic on the topic is clearly exposed. Cf. also Weston's *Dissertation on Some of the Most Remarkable Wonders of Antiquity* (Cambridge, 1748), pp. 347ff.

130. Cf. P. Skelton, *Ophiomaches: or, Deism Revealed,* 2 vols. (London, 1749), vol. 2, pp. 261ff., 400ff. Skelton is none too consistent in his accusations: on the one hand Deism and Catholicism share a common reliance on human sufficiency; on the other, they press such sufficiency to the breaking point of requiring an external authority. The irrelevance of holiness in general is now openly stated; cf. vol. 2, pp. 240ff. All this kind of mud slinging seemed to ignore the way that the Deists themselves used the traditional Protestant disregard of Catholic miracles as a ploy to undermine even scriptural miracles. Cf. Conyers Middleton's *A Free Inquiry into the Miraculous Powers Which Are Supposed to Have Subsisted in the Christian Church, from the Earliest Ages through Several Successive Centuries* (London, 1749), preface. Holding the middle — rejecting Catholic miracles, but maintaining scriptural miracles — was a challenge. Dispensationalism proved the only useful scheme in this regard, although it had the effect, as we have said, of simply making the history of the Church an irrelevant pneumatic event. Cf. John Douglas' *The Criterion; or Rules by Which the True Miracles Recorded in the New Testament Are Distinguished from the Spurious Miracles of Pagans and Papists* (1752), new ed. (London, 1807), pp. 377ff.

131. The most famous of these mismatched and yoked demonizations is Bishop George Lavington's *The Enthusiasm of Methodists and Papists Compar'd* (London, 1749), which plays on what he perceives to be the traditional Catholic recognition of potential satanic "obscurities" in all spiritual prodigies — hence the consistent Catholic demand for "discernment of spirits"; and in a situation of inherent confusion, clarity demands (in good Anglican fashion) the prudential rejection of prodigies altogether. The fact that contemporary Catholics and Methodists, at least in their official dialogues, have decided to make a virtue of this common curse from the English Protestant establishment indicates, I think, a misguided denial of the separative framework that made the "commonality" plausible in the first place.

to redivinize the universe was so demanding, given the common logic in which one might work, that its few exemplars, like John Hutchinson, tended to be pressed into intellectual contortions that can only be judged as strange. The whole legacy of late seventeenth- and eighteenth-century British thought on the topic of pneumatic visibility proved so straightjacketed by the ecclesial context of justified division seeking to ground a uniform religious practice and outlook[132] that it is no wonder if one of England's most lasting bequests to modern ecclesial existence was the "invisible Kingdom" of Benjamin Hoadly, embodied in the mutually tolerated irrelevancies of a multidenominational society, embedded in a world characterized by the jaded assumption of perversion, and joined by a common hatred of "Roman" superstition.[133]

The Testimony of Hiddenness:
Post-Reformation Divided Martyrdoms

That British "common sense" should derive its compelling social features from a general pessimism about the world is plausible enough. But the banalization of the good that results from such an attitude is unsettling to the same extent that the corporate constraints upon evil such an attitude brings may appear salutary. When contemporary ecumenical dialogues appeal to the integrating witness of a "common" holiness, as among Methodists and Catholics, the discussion is framed in terms of a generic concept of "spirituality," whose concrete embodiments are rarely spelled out, except in terms of an "experience" of a number of abstractions — "mystery and clarity, feeling and reason, individual conscience and acknowledged authority" or "contemplation, community and compassion."[134] And parallel to these efforts at dealing with pneumatic life ecumenically within at least traditional categories, one might interpret the much larger ecumenical concern with issues of

132. On Hutchinson, see references above.

133. Hoadly's famous 1717 sermon, instigating the "Bangorian controversy," on "The Nature of the Kingdom, or Church, of Christ" (*Works* [London, 1773] vol. 2) depicted the Church as an invisible reality "not of this world," and hence open to disestablishment and toleration of other sects in general. Except, of course, Roman Catholics. Cf. the 1715 sermon "The Present Delusion of Many Protestants Considered" (*Works,* vol. 3), whose political topic is buttressed by a typical foundation in the Protestant logic of the Antichrist. Cf. Henry D. Rack, " 'Christ's Kingdom Not of This World': The case of Benjamin Hoadly versus William Law Reconsidered," in Derek Baker, ed., *Church, Society and Politics* (Oxford: Basil Blackwell for The Ecclesiastical History Society, 1975), pp. 275-91.

134. Cf. the sections on "spirituality" in the Denver (1971) and Honolulu (1981) reports.

"justice" as an even more direct response to the area of pneumatic visibility within the constraints of modern division — a response that has sought after common features of pneumatic existence that, in fact, lie outside of ecclesial, and ultimately Christian, grammar altogether, in that they (rightly or wrongly) identify the contours of their commonalities in terms almost wholly appropriatable by non-Christian perspectives. In each case, the distinctive holiness of immediate pneumatic encounter has tended to be thrust aside — for example, Lourdes, which, for all its continued promotion, can hardly be called vigorous in its contemporary appeal or, even more obviously suspect, traditional ascetic discipline — in favor of commonalities of holiness that are based on assessed structures of practice measured by abstract principles. This takes the form of the psychological principles of much contemporary spirituality, for example, or even the political discipline, to the point of martyrdom, of much "justice ministry."

The question of martyrdom poses the ultimate test for pneumatic visibility in division. Certainly the religious commonwealth of British commonsense toleration is a far cry from the ecclesial society marked out within the world by the luminous outline of the Spirit's handiwork. At the time of the Reformation and after, both Protestants and Catholics had still thought, within the province of contested deceit, that the truth, and with it the Church itself, could be witnessed to with the clarity necessary for a demonstration of divine glory before the eyes of men and women. Was not the fact of martyrdom itself the last wall upon which the pneumatic standard could be raised in full view of the world? Initially, this was the case, and there is something in this hope expressed during the first century of the post-Reformation that is common to John Paul II's appeal to the ecumenically unifying witness of "blood" spilled for the faith, across denominational lines: if the Spirit does nothing else clear, surely this can be jointly acknowledged?

The feature especially characteristic of Reformation and post-Reformation martyrdom, however, is that it was both denied by competing Christian parties and usually deliberately directed *against* other Christians, both in its perpetration and in its possession. This simple reality — that sixteenth- and seventeenth-century martyrdoms were most often at the hands of other "Christians" and were celebrated as signs *against* other Christians — renders their significance as pneumatic acts highly problematic. In Edward Gibbon's eighteenth-century voice of sobriety gone sour in the face of contemporary Christian claims to persuasive visible holiness, the problem was obvious, if deflating:

> We shall conclude our chapter [on Roman persecution of the early Christians] by a melancholy truth which obtrudes itself on the reluctant mind;

that even admitting, without hesitation or inquiry, all that history has recorded, or devotion has feigned, on the subject of martyrdoms, it must still be acknowledged that the Christians, in the course of their intestine dissensions, have inflicted far greater severities on each other than they had experienced from the zeal of infidels.[135]

It is worth reminding ourselves, in this regard, about the way that pneumatic clarity was perceived in the deaths of Christians by the early Church — a fact to which even Gibbon, in his own way, accedes — as described in the paradigmatic Acts of the Martyrs. For theirs was a form of perception logically obscured when martyrdom became an intra-Christian phenomenon. If we take as an example the account of the Martyrs of Lyons,[136] for instance, we can see the typical adjudicatory opposition between the Spirit and Satan. It is an opposition, however, that is given open assertion in the contrast between confessing Christ, quite simply, and denying him on the part of the pagans. The whole episode, in fact, is suffused with this agonistic theme, and every act of torture and oppression is assigned to the "Adversary," "Satan," the "Beast," the "Devil," the "Tyrant," the "Evil One," and so on; while, in contrast, the Christians are supported and speak openly and faithfully through the power and presence of the "Advocate," and the "Spirit." And while the human authors of the persecution are tied to Satan, in this account, as his "minions," "wild and barbarous people once stirred up by the wild Beast," the narrative has little to say about these subordinates, and focuses instead on the action itself of Satan (though not on his person). The focal deed is confession of Christ's name: will a Christian remain firm in this public affirmation, or will he or she recant? The story speaks of both possibilities. Finally, the demeanor of the confessing martyrs becomes the confirming evidence of their sincerity: they are filled with gentleness and love, even toward their persecutors, who, we learn, by the end must be judged less as satanic servants than as ignorant tools of a greater power, and still capable of transformation. The conclusion of the narrative speaks of the martyrs' prayers on behalf of their enemies, in the manner of Stephen saying, "Lord, do not blame them for this sin." Through the sustained act of charity thus displayed, "the throttled Beast might be forced to disgorge alive all those whom he at first thought he had devoured," and so, the final victory over Satan, and the supreme pneumatic witness of the Christian truth, would be evident.

135. Edward Gibbon, *The Decline and Fall of the Roman Empire* (J. B. Bury edition), ch. 16.

136. The Greek text and translation are given in Herbert Musurillo, *The Acts of the Christian Martyrs* (Oxford: Oxford University Press, 1972), pp. 62-85.

The externalization of deception and the determined enactment of charity toward the opposition both constitute the conditions for pneumatic clarity within these traditional narratives.[137] Sixteenth- and seventeenth-century Roman Catholic accounts of martyrdom at the hands of Protestants more or less retain these features.[138] But there is now a new dimension explored, not always explicit in the accounts themselves: the persecutors, being Christian heretics, are liable to some greater kind of punishment than would be a pagan executioner. Robert Southwell's justly admired *An Epistle of Comfort* (1587), written (by a future martyr himself) to persecuted Catholics in England facing possible martyrdom, while filled with a mellifluous recital of traditional themes of sanctity associated with death for the faith, now gives over significant space to an explication of the historically peculiar character of the Protestant persecutors.[139] It is obvious that Southwell recognizes the difficulty faced in simply contrasting Christian faith to an inimical force, when that force sincerely carries with it the name of "Christian" too. There is a confusion on the loose that the author valiantly tries to overcome. In one unusual chapter, Southwell provides a microcosm of anti-Protestant apologetic, within the sphere of pneumatic sanctity.[140] He stresses the argument from continuity for the Catholics, in the realm of martyrdom, holiness, and miracle; he also uses the minimizing argument of ephemeral heresy by contrast, in which "Luther's novelties" are linked to those many movements of the past whose "memory is quite abolished, [whose] names commonly unknown, [whose] books perished and no more mention of them than the condemnation and disproof of their errors recorded by Catholic writers."[141] Yet Southwell also acknowledges that the present era is different from the past, and that, though all heretics be members of the

---

137. There are exceptions, of course. The conviction that persecutors deserve divine vengeance and that the proven certainty of such vengeance is a vindicating sign was expressed on more than one occasion. Cf. "Martyrdom of Saints Marian and James," Musurillo, p. 211; or, more formally, a literary production like Lactantius's *On the Deaths of Persecutors*.

138. Cf. *The Life and Death of Mr. Edmund Geninges Priest, Crowned with Martyrdome at London, the 10 day of November, in the Yeare M.D. XCI* (1614, reprinted, Menston: Scolar's Press, 1971, in the series English Recusant Literature 1558–1640, vol. 69), whose final account of the torture and death of Geninges (ch. 9) is singularly devoid of reference to Satan or even to the character of the opposition, and focuses rather on the inherent dignity of holiness in patience, and the charity of the martyr toward all, including his captors.

139. Robert Southwell, *An Epistle of Comfort to the Reverend Priests, and to the Honourable, Worshipful, and Other of the Lay Sort, Restrained in Durance for the Catholic Faith*, ed. Margaret Waugh (Chicago: Loyola University Press, 1966).

140. Southwell, ch. 6, "The sixth cause of Comfort in Tribulation is that the cause we suffer for is the true Catholic Faith."

141. Southwell, p. 95.

"synagogue of Satan, the Antichrist," the Protestant heretics represent a culminating epoch of satanic rage, refiguring the whole history of deceit and now ranged against the triumphant Church of what can only be the final days:

> But if comparison with saints be not presumption, this, for our great comfort, may we say: that though the cause of religion were always honourable, yet it is in us more worthily defended than of any martyrs of former ages. For they defended either against epicures and heathens, or against the Jews and rabbis, or against some one heretic and his offspring. But we are now in a battle not only against men of our times, who are epicures in conditions, Jews in malice, and heretics in proud and obstinate spirit, but against the whole rabble and generation of all heretics that since Christ's time have been in league with Satan, the father of lying, and his whole army; who, albeit they be fast chained in hell and there reap the fruit of their blasphemies, yet have these companions of theirs borrowed all their weapons and revived some of all their heresies. So that in combating them we challenge all the old heretics into the field. We must in one age sustain a multitude of enemies, jointly assaulting us, every one of whom hath, in times past, made work enough for divers doctors in several ages, according as they did rise one after another.[142]

With this admission, however, Southwell also opens the window onto a new spectacle, in which the evidences of holiness must somehow be more powerful if they are to overcome the weighty force of an accumulated lie. Martyrdom is something that must squeeze its blood through the thin cracks of "this foggy night of heresy, and the confusion of tongues which it hath procured."[143] For which reason now Southwell seeks to overwhelm his reader with the kind of adversarial images of threat and warning that, in the past, were rare in martyrial literature. The hell that awaits the persecutor, while it is ostensibly offered for his conversion, acquires a kind of independent assertion.[144] Finally, Southwell must devote an entire chapter to the most troubling outcome of martyrdom through ecclesial division: what is one to say of the courageous deaths of opponent Christians? Thus, in the thirteenth chapter, "That heretics cannot be Martyrs," Southwell confronts the obvious reality of Protestant death for the sake of a Gospel sincerely believed, with the simple answer of the tradition: quoting Cyprian, "he can be no martyr,

---

142. Southwell, p. 98.
143. Southwell, p. 3.
144. Cf. Southwell, ch. 12, "The unhappiness of the schismatics and lapsed, and comfort against their example."

that is not in the Church . . . it shall be no crown of their faith but a punishment of their perfidiousness: it will not be a glorious end of their religious virtue but a death of desperation," and so on, so that "therefore if any of their acts be committed to writing, it is not a report of their praises but a rehearsal of their iniquities."[145] The actual pneumatic force of (true) martyrdom, then, is necessarily transferred from the individual life and death itself and its specific contours to a more formal association of that life to certain institutional claims. As with miracle, martyrdom as a pneumatic event becomes clear only retrospectively, through the authoritative confirmation of institutional loyalty. Which, of course, renders the death itself a cipher amid the other failings of a failing world.

Protestant martyrdom fares no better in its retention of actual pneumatic character. Much has been written of late on the novel and specific character of Protestant martyrology, and there is clearly an attitude taken that peculiarly reflects the separative framework of the groups represented.[146] Just as the demonization of the persecutor by Catholics grew in proportion to the obscurement of the boundaries of Christian filiation, so too among the Protestants, the very nature of their witness as victims of the satanized Church required the deluding Devil to take center stage. Luther had, from the start of his major theological refocusing of the 1520s, been troubled by the phenomenon of martyrdom.[147] He recognized, among the Enthusiasts and Anabaptists (not to mention earlier Catholics, like Thomas à Becket), the presence of all the martyrial virtues, displayed on behalf of what he considered to be blatant heresy. This was, of course, the traditional problem Catholics had always faced with respect to "martyred" heretics. To distinguish real from false martyrs, he gave a traditional answer, that "the cause and not the suffering makes a martyr."[148] The Protestant tack of adjudicating any phenomenon according to the standard of pure doctrine was obviously applied

145. Southwell, pp. 213, 217f.

146. Recent useful discussions can be found in Catharine Randall Coats, *(Em)bodying the Word: Textual Resurrections in the Martyrological Narratives of Foxe, Crespin, de Bèze and d'Aubigné* (New York/Frankfurt am Main: Peter Land, 1992); Jean François Gilmont, "Les martyologies du XVIe siècle," in *Ketzerverfolgung im 16. und frühen 17. Jahrhundert* (*Wolfenbütteler Forschungen* 51, Wiesbaden: Otto Harrassowitz, 1992), pp. 175-92. See also the contributions of David Watson (on Crespin) and Andrew Pettegree (on van Haemstede) in Brice Gordon, ed., *Protestant History and Identity in Sixteenth-Century Europe* (Aldershot: The Scolar Press, 1996), vol. 2.

147. Cf. the discussion in David Baghi, "Luther and the problem of martyrdom," in Diana Wood, ed., *Martyrs and Martyrologies* (Oxford: Basil Blackwell, 1993), pp. 209-19.

148. Luther, "Lectures on I John," in *Works*, vol. 20, p. 239.

in this case. Those seeming martyrs that are not dying on behalf of the true Gospel are clearly "martyrs of the Devil." But Luther's ambivalence about applying this rule properly often led him to denigrate martyrdom as a whole, by whomever, in favor of the "hidden" life of holiness and patience demonstrated by the long-lived patriarchs. It is the case, at any rate, that among Lutherans, but for one notable and unsuccessful exception, martyrologies as a genre were never popular.[149]

Not so among the Reformed of France, England, and even the Netherlands, where several classic collections were made by Jean Crespin (with additions by Simon Goulart),[150] John Foxe,[151] and Adriaen van Haemstede[152] respectively. One of the most distinctive elements of these works was the massive gathering of documentation pertaining to the procedural aspects of the martyrdoms, especially the records of the inquisitions and responses. As scholars have pointed out, the Protestant martyrology was, more than anything else, a means of propagating, under the form of a heightened rhetorical genre, doctrinal teaching. Indeed, the individuals and the details of their lives and deaths, though often recounted with gruesome detail, serve as typical buttresses to sermonic explication, the Word in this case being disseminated through its accessible "embodiment" in a suffering witness. The pneumatic character of these episodes, as a result, becomes rather vague, since the doctrinal "testimony" of the witness — usually given in scholastic theological detail — is more or less independent of the events through which it is articulated; and the sanctifying element of the martyrdom is actually a dehistoricized catechism. Indeed, for all their emphasis upon virtues exemplified, the lives of the Protestant martyrs are necessarily devalued as pneumatic vehicles, in favor of the doctrine to which they point, arrayed in the set of historical dispensations that, as we have seen, mask an underlying uniformity of principle, realized temporally in the repetitive assault on the

149. The exception being Ludwig Rabus, whose multivolume *Account of God's Chosen Witnesses, Confessors, and Martyrs* (1554-58), including the proto-Protestant martyrs of the Middle Ages, is amply discussed in Kolb.

150. *Histoire des martyres persecutez et mis a mort pour la verite de l'evangile, depuis le temps des apotres iusques a present,* first ed. of 1554. The greatly expanded 1619 edition (again, one of many different ones), was re-edited in 1885 by Daniel Benoit (Toulouse: Société des Livres Religieux).

151. Begun in 1559, what became the *Actes and Monuments of These Latter and Perilous Dayes Touching Matters of the Church*. The history of the multiple editions, including the posthumous ones, is complex. The fullest version accessible is that reprinted by AMS Press (New York, 1965).

152. First edition, 1559, eventually under the title *Historien der Vromer Martelaren* (1633).

Truth by a church-inhering Satan.[153] Oriented in this fashion, the only character within Protestant martyrologies who has a palpable story is the Devil himself, along with his vassals, whose ever-novel modes of deception and torture, as they are recounted through the centuries, provide the discourses with a narrative vigor, and not a little admiration for his unrelenting ingenuity and almost heroic persistence and rage. We are well on the way to the Mephistophelean transformation of evil into mournful, tragic loss.[154]

Crespin, in the various prefaces of succeeding versions, is among the most explicit on this matter: the proper "use" of the accounts of martyrs is to "see them alive in their responses, letters, and disputes, remembering their constancy in order to be edified as appropriate."[155] This purpose, as served by the martyrology itself, constitutes the main weapon in the true Church's battle against Satan, whose greatest desire is silence. The Word, as it is spoken in the inquisitions, unmasks, in its very presentation, every act of the Antichrist that is Rome. There is, then, a logical necessity that the martyrology preserve, as an antiphon to the truth, a running account of "the cruelties of the adversary," not so much to found the courage of the martyr as to prove the truth of the

153. Charles Parker, in an interesting recent article, has examined the particular issue of the appeal made to Old Testament figuration as a descriptor of true martyrdom among Protestant martyrologies. He has found some significant differences among such martyrologies in the frequency of this kind of figural application, it being most fully used by the French Calvinists, in distinction from the English and the Dutch. It is a variable he cautiously links with the highly charged adversarial militancy of Huguenot witness, which found the violently confrontational narratives of Israel's relation with pagan peoples a congenial image for their own situation. From the standpoint of our own discussion of figurally described sanctity, we can note here how this kind of appeal perceived the Catholics in the role of pagan oppressors — Egyptians, Canaanites, Sodomites — and had little logical room for an exploration of the more appropriate *ecclesial* figures of the divided monarchy, for example, David versus Absalom, let alone the kingdoms of Judah and Israel (where, even if one depicted Jeroboam in the North as an apostate Roman Church — which Calvin was fond of doing — one had trouble, on purely scriptural grounds, interpreting "Protestant" Judah's travails in a martyrial fashion). See Parker's "French Calvinists as the Children of Israel: An Old Testament Self-Consciousness in Jean Crespin's *Histoire des Martyrs* before the Wars of Religion," in *Sixteenth Century Journal* 24, no. 2 (1993): pp. 227-48.

154. The most sustainedly thrilling version of this Protestant historical vision may be Théodore-Agrippa d'Aubigné's 1613 epic poem *Les Tragiques* (begun in 1574). *Haute*-demonization and extravagant malice color this verse account of the oppression of the just by the grotesque powers of the world, marked by detailed descriptions of torture and death. The final two books unveil the divine vengeance awaiting the persecutors, ordered around the story of the two churches of the anti-Christian Cain and of Abel, "the first martyr" (cf. book 6, vv. 155ff.).

155. Crespin, vol. 1, p. xli.

martyr's teaching.[156] In an odd transformation, it is the presence of Satan, the historical embodiment of evil, and not the explosion of holy light, that grounds the probative weight of the Gospel's truth. The pure "act" of martyrdom — as Luther, Southwell, and earlier Catholic teaching on heretical deaths also taught — proves nothing. In fact, Crespin emphasizes, Satan is eager to feign martyrdoms of all kinds just in order to seduce people into error: he mixes among the "wheat" the martyrdoms of the Anabaptists in Holland and the Jesuits in England, displaying real examples of "courage," "goodness," "holiness"; "but if they are outside Christ, and thus from the way, the truth, and the life, their faith is evil, their zeal without foundation, and their cross precluded of blessing."[157] True doctrine, not suffering, is what counts. And it is just this need to discriminate doctrinally among the confusing welter of competing martyrs that provides the observer the edifying task a good martyrology sustains.[158] The Holy Spirit, no longer adjudicator, is now divined through the historically penetrating application of theological principles, which alone stand above the otherwise undifferentiated morass of human cruelty. There is something plaintive about John Bale's hope to valorize an early victim of the Antichrist's perversion: did not the ancient pagans have their heroes? did not the men and women of the Scriptures celebrate their ancestors, fallen for the faith? and

> among the papists also (which are a most prodigious kind of men) are they most highly advanced by lying signs, false miracles, erroneous writings, shrines, relics, lights, tabernacles, altars, censings, songs, and holy days, which have been slain for the liberties, privileges, authority, honour, riches, and proud maintenance of their holy whorish church: . . . What is then to be thought of those godly and valiant warriors, which have not spared to bestow their most dear lives for the verity of Jesus Christ against the malignant muster of that execrable antichrist of Rome, the devil's own vicar?[159]

Everyone has a martyr, Bale seems to say; there is nothing to distinguish the otherwise monochromatic goodness of the nations outside the claims of the memorialist.

One of the few distinctively modern responses to this circumstance — distinctive in its attempt to maintain a traditional pre-Reformation conception

---

156. Cf. Crespin, p. xxxiv.
157. Crespin, p. xxxviii.
158. Crespin, p. xliii.
159. John Bale, *A Brief Chronicle Concerning the Examination and Death of the Blessed Martyr of Christ, Sir John Oldcastle, the Lord Cobham,* in *Select Works of John Bale,* pp. 5-6.

of the Church's incorruptibility while taking seriously the contemporary reality of the Church's pneumatic demise — was that of the eighteenth-century Jansenists. Persecuted for refusing to sign a national "constitution" affirming the Vatican's 1713 condemnation of Jansenist doctrine, the movement developed a prolific literature of confessional witness. But the persecutions were rarely "unto death" — at most they involved imprisonment, banishment, loss of livings, and excommunication — and this limitation on suffering was in large measure because the Jansenists refused to leave the Catholic Church or even to threaten the authority of its hierarchy. Filled with a Protestant-flavored defense of the assaulted "Truth" and of "true doctrine," Jansenist "necrologies," detailing the lives and deaths of holy defenders of the faith as they saw it, managed to contain their unappealing chauvinism within an uncompromising commitment to unity. But the result was, as it turned out, the veiling of martyrdom altogether.[160] Jansenists could not manage to get themselves killed for their faith, precisely because they had forsworn the Christian schism that might have demanded it under the circumstances of the time. In martyrdom's place, therefore, was a traditionalist espousal of the reality of holy virtue, generally of an ascetic kind, whose rejection by the ecclesial culture itself constituted a form of "death for the faith." In theory, holiness has a decisive immediacy that carries divine adjudicatory force:

> How glorious it is for the cause of Religion that one should observe the force of a great virtue! This living expression of Divinity is exactly what renders it sensible. Through the rich images of virtue, God seems to emerge from his secret. Carried, as it were, on this luminous cloud, God's radiance pierces to the depths of the soul, through the channel of the senses.[161]

But, in practice, such holiness is called forth in contrast to a "laxist" ecclesial reality that all but suffocates its brilliance.[162] In the end, the Jansenist vision of holiness is, in any case, one of obscured penitence, and martyrdom is given in a form of *self*-immolation into the hiddenness of "ignored sufferings."[163] And this end is presented quite explicitly as a demanded response to the separative logic of Protestantism: if we will not leave, then our painful witness on behalf of the truth must accept its own burial.[164]

160. Cf. [le P. Labelle], *Necrologe des appellans et opposans a la bulle "Unigenitus," De l'un & l'autre Sexe* (1755), 5 vols., one of a number of such works.
161. Ibid., vol. 1, p. lxxiv.
162. Ibid., pp. xlv-lxxii; lxxxix-cx.
163. Ibid., pp. cliv-clxxviii.
164. Ibid., pp. lxxix-lxxxviii. It is interesting to see, from the Protestant side, an appeal

Whether true martyrdoms take place today or not, even among denominational partisans they are less and less noticed, remembered, or certainly celebrated. That today's "martyrs," like Bishop Oscar Romero, tend to be political victims, whose pneumatic witness is therefore subject to as much dispute as were the victims of confessionalism, does not disconfirm this observation; the holiness that they embody, at least in the eyes of much of the world, pertains, as we have seen, to the universally recognized virtues of courage and conviction, which, devoid of a clearly accepted Christian impetus, is at best admired, but not evidently inspired. A newspaper may or may not record the death of this or that Christian somewhere in the world, for some reason or other. But in a world where the ordinary has been so demonized, dragged down into the shadows by the internally accusing logic of ecclesial division, it must appear inevitable that "good deaths" become appropriated to what is perceived as being the universally tortured confusion of the human condi-

---

to an accepted veiling of martyrdom on the part of Catholics, and by extension, all Christians involved in rooted intra-Christian conflict. John Donne's 1610 *Pseudomartyr, Wherein out of Certaine Propositions and Gradations, This Conclusion Is Evicted. That Those Which Are of the Romane Religion in This Kingdome, May and Ought to Take the Oath of Allegeance* is hardly read anymore, despite its author's continued scholarly popularity. In it, Donne argues that martyrdom suffered by those Roman Catholic missionaries and others refusing to take the oath of allegiance to the Protestant king (a refusal demanded by the Pope) could not constitute true martyrdom for the faith, since it was occasioned by a dispute over temporal jurisdictions, and not spiritual ones. The ex-Catholic and newly Anglican Donne was at the time jockeying for preferment from the king, and the treatise is widely seen as a cast for royal favor. But Donne was sincerely and deeply vexed over the reality of Christian division. And this particular Protestant work is notable in the way Donne carefully avoids characterizing Catholic *doctrine* as in any fundamental way heretical. Indeed, Donne goes so far as to insist that the differences between Catholics and Protestants are not over Christian fundamentals at all, and hence cannot occasion true martyrdom in the sense that it was suffered by early Christians or missionaries at the hands of pagans or even at the hands of gross heretics who denied, for example, the Trinity. This judgment cuts both ways, obviously: there can hardly be any Protestant martyrs at the hands of Catholics under these circumstances either. The attitude Donne commends to Catholics, then, is finally one of political subjection and painful endurance, but not resistance and death, which is tantamount to suicide. Where all of this leads ecclesiologically was problematic for a Protestant. In the *Pseudomartyr* Donne has recourse to arguments that are similar to Hooker's on the matter, but are just as hard to sustain in a larger historical framework that looks for ecclesial continuity and catholicity across time. The tensions are apparent, for instance, in Donne's rejection of the miraculous in Catholic spirituality, pneumatic phenomena whose at least provisional acceptance was logically necessary in order to found his commitment to ecclesial continuity in diversity. A fine modern edition, with a useful introduction and commentary by Anthony Raspa (including discussions of Protestant-Catholic martyrology) was published in 1993 by McGill-Queen's University Press (Montreal and Kingston).

tion.[165] Death, in the potential beauty of its embrace, no longer astonishes us any more than does the explosion of radiance once associated with the wonder-worker and the saint. What shall the Spirit show us, what shall we see, if the visible itself has been cursed by self-justifying retreat into separation? The world is given over, if not outright to Satan, at least to the anxiety of his constant presence, masquerading beneath the veneer, always the veneer, of Christian believing.

To apprehend, once again, the scripturally figural reality to which the Church, in this aspect of its pneumatic existence, may conform, one might recall the images through which Jesus himself describes the condition of Israel's leadership, images of deceptive visibility and contested deaths. The Pharisees who guide the people are compared to "white-washed tombs" with an "outward beauty" but an "inner iniquity," and their devotion to the prophets is belied by their genetic complicity in the prophets' martyrdoms (cf. Matt. 23:27-39). Jesus even refers to a hidden stream of righteous individuals who have constantly suffered through the historical course of God's people — "all the righteous blood shed on earth, from the blood of innocent Abel to the blood of Zechariah" (v. 35) — in a manner that will later become transformed into the "church of Abel" persecuted by the people of Cain (already in 1 John 3:12 and Jude 11). But the *hiddenness* of this stream of martyrs to which Jesus refers is what is striking in the context of our discussion. The murdered "Zechariah" to whom Jesus refers here, whether he is the prophet whose words are contained in the scriptural book bearing his name (as Matthew may indicate) or the son of the priest Jehoiada, killed by the princes of Judah during the time of the divided monarchy (cf. 2 Chron. 23–24), as is more likely, is in any case someone caught up in the political and religious struggles of a people torn asunder. The "killing of prophets and stoning of those sent" is an experience firmly planted within a history of reiterated confusions among the people over who is truly a holy messenger. They are confusions that include the divine "turning in foolishness" of wise "counsel" at the time of Absalom's rebellion (cf. 2 Sam. 15–17), the sending of "lying spirits" by God into the mouths of prophets at the time of Ahab (cf. 1 Kings 22:19ff.), and the whole battle

---

165. It is hard to know what one is to make of figures like those calculated by the respected "missiometrician" David Barrett, who claims that in 1996 there will be an estimated "average" of 159,000 Christian "martyrs," up from 35,000 in 1900, down from 230,000 in 1970, but predicted to rise to 300,000 by the year 2025 (*International Bulletin of Missionary Research* 20, no. 1 [January 1996]: p. 25). The figures form part of a table, a line item marked "average Christian martyrs per year," sharing space with other items like "ecclesiastical crime in $ per year," "total monthly listeners of Christian radio stations," and so on. The figures may well be accurate, but their epiphanic significance is hardly compelling within the context of their utterance and reception.

between Jeremiah and the "pseudo-prophets" of Judah's last days, where finally only the visible outcome of *events* — not the character or actions of the individuals in question — is left to distinguish openly the true from the false (cf. Jer. 28). Jesus himself appropriates this hidden history of the martyred righteous to the integral condition of Israel as a whole — "O Jerusalem, Jerusalem" — and he labels that history, however clear in the eyes of God, a worldly mass of contestation, whose end is "desolation."

Doubtless, Protestant and Catholic Christians have "died for the faith," for the pure Gospel at the hands of the pure Gospel's enemies. Doubtless, too, the lives of these and other Christian saints embody some real holiness. But to *see* this purity, to *see* this holiness, as the Spirit's life unveiled and resplendent in its "power" and "authority" is no longer something any one of us could dare affirm before the eyes of the Church, let alone the world. Such affirmations are defined today by their demand to be brushed aside. And perhaps this is the very character of their "proof." To "recognize" and to see the Spirit's forms is an act of divine love, of *charity,* much as the New Testament teaches. Pope John Paul II's appeal to the evidence of sanctity for the presence of the Spirit's unity makes sense only within the sphere of the actual operation of divine love for one another among separated Christians. And where such love is working may well be found only in some realm of pneumatic existence so deep as to escape denominational form — so deep, even, as to escape notice altogether. Is it any wonder — are we astonished — when we are told that the Catholic Church's only beatified "martyr to unity" was "hidden" in her "witness"? Maria Gabriella Sagghedu, a young Sardinian Trappist nun, who had never met a Protestant in her life, who did not know exactly what one was, and who accepted, in utter ignorance of the issues at stake, a call to make "reparative suffering" for the divisions of the Church, died in 1939 of tuberculosis. The Catholic Church has seen fit to style her death a "martyrdom." At whose hands, in this case? She dug in her garden and sewed clothes in an upper room. She prayed. If the traditional structures of pneumatic visibility assert themselves any longer, it seems, they will do so in a realm protected from the offenses against charity waged by the Church, a realm from which we receive only reports after dying, enigmatically, controversially, as from afar.[166]

---

166. Cf. Martha Driscoll, OCSO, *A Silent Herald of Unity: The Life of Maria Gabriella Sagheddu* (Kalamazoo: Cistercian Publications, 1990). In January 1983, Pope John Paul II presided at the ceremony by which Sister Maria Gabriella Sagheddu was officially beatified, that is, pronounced worthy of local veneration. The Pope called her a model of "spiritual ecumenism," someone to follow in her expiatory sacrifice of self on behalf of the Church's unity.

Chapter Three

The Veiling of Vocation:
Ministry in the Divided Church

Apostolicity and Holiness

It may be that the veiling of the Spirit's explosive clarity, and the rendering of its arresting charismata as things contestable is a lamentable, but hardly debilitating, circumstance for the Church. As with Israel, the Church will carry through the dry lands, deprived of graces of the marvelous, just because it is gifted with those of the more ordinary. It will plug away and plug along, because it is sustained by the gifts of pure functioning, the structures of daily living, through which God sustains, however distantly. If not prophets, then priests and scribes at least, whose insistent labors grind the time of the Church's weariness into meal still capable of imparting life, though lacking savor.

It is certainly an unexpected conclusion to be forced to grasp after, however: making the structural scaffolding of the Church bear the weight of its existence. For it is the Church's structures that have traditionally been allowed the freedom of fallibility, the right of secondary qualities to corrupt; while the soul of the Church, its holiness and life-blood, dwells and flows beneath the surfaces of these sociologically vulnerable institutions. In this regard, both Protestants and Catholics have often joined in pointing to the continuity of ecclesial integrity through the unbroken chain of the elect, saints visible and invisible, whose pneumatic purity alone was capable (in terms of historical embodiments) of sustaining a Mystical Body otherwise strained and burdened by its ostensive structures.[1]

That the pneumatic deprivation of the divided Church should render doubtful the location of such holiness has, then, ironically placed a greater responsibility for historical ecclesial integrity upon the representatives of those structures previously minimized, the official ministry of the churches. And questions of ministry, not of holiness, have assumed among the most prominent of places in the ecumenical dialogues of the last five decades. If miracles could not prove (at least in a persuasive fashion) the location of the true Church, and holiness could not ratify the integrity of the separated churches themselves, then where might we locate the concrete instances of each body's continuing health over time except in the structures of their social maintenance? The locus of disputed, and of potentially recovered, pneumatic character has, in fact, decisively shifted from supernatural confirmations to the realm of ordinary sustenance, that is, the authorized or ordained ministry.

However understandable, it is an odd evolution, in that it assumes that a disjunction between holiness and ministry could ever attain a practicable theological significance with respect to the identity of the Church — as if the order of ministry were somehow distinct from the pneumatic self-offering of the Church's figural holiness, and therefore immune from its troubling obscurement. The long-standing theological formulations surrounding sacramental efficacy associated with the Donatist schism have certainly been used to further this disjunction within the modern era; but in fact, they are peripheral to the issue of the pneumatic character of the historic ministry as it assumes the burden of the temporal continuity of the Church's integrity. Quite independent of the issue of ordination's nonrepeatable character (under certain conditions), the question specifically of the *holiness* of the authorized ministry's pursuit has, from the Christian Church's beginnings, been persistently linked to the historical validity, in the sense of pneumatic efficacy, of the larger Church's mission.[2]

---

1. A Roman Catholic like Congar — though he inverts the vocabulary here — finds it necessary to distinguish the grossly fallible institutional "functioning" of the Church from the "institution" (defined not sociologically in this case, but mystically, as the *sponsa Christi*) itself, in order to make a place for the "entrance of sin" into the concrete life of the Church. And he does this, building up a case upon the direction of the tradition on this matter, precisely by identifying ecclesial fallibility with the actual practice of the Church's quotidian "leadership." Cf. his *Vraie et Fausse Réforme dans l'Eglise* (Paris: Editions du Cerf, 1969), pp. 92ff.

2. Whether or not Donatist ordinations were subsequently "recognized" by the Catholic Church (and they were not so recognized universally), there was never any question but that the Donatist "church," so long as it remained in the "unholy sin" of schism, was not a church

The Christian ministry is a holy ministry. This was an original ecclesiological presupposition, along with its corollary, that an absence of holiness suffocates the ministry. Although the charism of the prophet was, in stricter scholastic terms, later seen as a gift independent of the recipient's character — *gratia gratis data* — yet the person called into the prophetic office fulfilled it effectively only to the degree that he or she conformed to the righteousness of the divine vocation so given. If the Old Testament prophets were "saints," as Christians had always affirmed, then their exemplary ministry was also defined by their saintliness. When, for instance, James writes of the work of prayer to be regularly performed by the "elders" of a church in the course of their pastoral duties with the sick, he speaks in terms of their "righteousness" and compares them to the prophet Elijah, in his capacity as miracle-worker (James 5:14-18). And if the Pastorals speak of the Church's authorized leadership in less figural terms, they nonetheless stress, above all, the character of "blamelessness" (cf. 1 Tim. 3:2, 10; Titus 1:7) such leaders must exhibit, which Paul explains, in Timothy's case, through the image of ritual "purity" (2 Tim. 2:20ff.; cf. Titus 1:15f.).

When modern ecumenical discussions speak about the "mutual recognition of ministries" among divided churches, however, the element of holiness within such ministries does not generally come up. There is a sense in which the "corruption" of the ministry, which formed a critical impetus to the Reformation division as well as to the intra-Catholic response to that division, has been largely resolved. Vatican II's *Decree on Ecumenism* (cc. 20-23) already acknowledged the divine "fruits" and "charity" present in non-Catholic churches, an acknowledgment reiterated and made more explicit in subsequent Vatican documents.[3] Protestants, for their part, have done the same.[4] Thrust to one side, ministerial holiness has given way in these discussions to the obstacle presented by the theological understanding of other defining characteristics, notably that of "apostolicity." "Mutual recognition [of ministries] presupposes acceptance of the apostolicity of each other's ministry," was the bald conclusion of the Anglican–Roman Catholic International Commission

---

at all, and thus that its ministers, to the extent that they were participants in this realm of ecclesial blasphemy constituted by the Donatist community, did not function as true ministers of the Gospel. The importance of this distinction — between recognizing that a valid ordination has taken place and recognizing a valid ministry — and the confusion to which an ignoring of this distinction has given rise in discussions of the "validity" of schismatic ordinations will be discussed below.

3. Cf. the discussion, in the previous chapter, of John Paul II's recent remarks in *Ut Unum Sint.*

4. Cf. the "Common Declaration" of John Paul II and Robert Runcie, of Oct. 2, 1989.

in 1979.[5] And what, after all, is involved in "recognizing" the "apostolicity" of another church's official ministry? At root, it is a recognition that differing structures of ministry can embody the same theological meaning of ministry; it involves the examination of the meaning of *structures,* not an evaluation of their particularized embodiment in individualized practice.

Behind the Anglican–Roman Catholic conclusion, shared by many other ecumenical groups, then, has been the methodological conviction that if certain theories of the theological meaning of the ministry can be shown to be compatible with specific structures of ministry within particular separated churches, then the common acceptance of that theology of ministry can lead these churches into a movement of *structural* adaptation to similarly (if not identically) ordered and recognized forms of ministry. And one could speak, therefore, of at least a conceptual division, within recent ecumenical discussion, between the historically manifested pneumatic character of ministry (holiness) and its structural integrity (apostolicity). This may be a crude way of describing the shape of the discussion, but it points to a real orientation of discourse.[6]

5. Par. 6 of its "Elucidations" on the 1973 joint statement on "Ministry and Ordination," contained in Anglican–Roman Catholic International Commission, *The Final Report, Windsor, September 1981* (London: SPCK/Catholic Truth Society, 1982).

6. In 1971, the Groupe des Dombes had proposed a method for the "recognition and reconciliation of ministries" among Protestants and Catholics that was founded on a mutual recognition of "apostolic succession" in each set of churches and a commitment to embodying, through such recognition, the "fullness" of such apostolicity. This proposal came as the conclusion to a mutually agreed upon description of the "apostolic ministry" and its "succession" in terms of a continuity in a particular form of, for example, "witness to the faith, fraternal communion, sacramental life, human service, dialogue with the world and the sharing of the Lord's gifts to each individual" (par. 12). It was then shown that the general *structures* of Protestant and Catholic ordained ministry each, more or less, embody this overall set of "apostolic" characteristics; since that was the case, each might "recognize" the integrity of the other's ministry. The concrete "reconciliation" of ministries proposed by the group was, therefore, of a structural kind: Catholics would grant "episcopal" laying-on-of-hands to Protestant ministries and would attempt to pay more attention to the "conciliar" character of ministerial authority, as well as take more seriously the practical dimensions of the "priesthood of all believers" (par. 40-42); while Protestants would submit to the formal structures of "episcopal" ministerial oversight and reexamine the use of nonordained persons for sacramental and homiletic ministries (par. 43-45). Finally, this proposed evolution in structures by each side would be aimed not at questioning the various churches' apostolic integrity ("succession"), but at providing each a "fuller" participation in that apostolicity which it already possesses (cf. par. 39). The group suggests a formal act of "mutual" laying-on-of hands as a way to ratify this reconciliation of ministry (par. 46). See Groupe des Dombes, "Pour une réconciliation des ministères," par. 8-13, 38-45, reprinted in *Pour la communion des Églises. L'apport du Groupe des Dombes 1937–1987* (Paris: Le Centurion, 1988). The WCC's Faith and Order agreed statement on *Baptism, Eucharist, and Ministry* (1982) follows a similar treatment of the ministry to that

In theory, to be sure, such a structurally ordered "apostolicity" is generally admitted to be essentially tied to other fundamental ecclesial characteristics, including "holiness," as in the credal formula concerning the "one, holy, catholic, and apostolic Church." But in practice, given the ecumenical aim of formal reconciliation, the structural question, located under the rubric of "apostolicity," is treated as an independent, and often overriding, issue.[7]

Yet however pragmatic the motives for the conceptual division of apostolicity and holiness in the ecumenical discussion of the ministry, it serves to obscure the more fundamental question raised by the existence of separated ministries within the Christian Church: how does such division "render" or "characterize" or, more bluntly, simply "affect" the enacted reality of ministry? Does the historical fact of a divided ministry not effect a basic alteration in the very *meaning* of ministry, such that the logical passage from a common theological understanding of the ministry to its (possibly varied) structural embodiments cannot be made in the face of an embedded practical contradiction? The reality of holiness, as we have seen, involves the actual evaluation of its historical manifestation; and this evaluation was subverted by the emer-

---

of the earlier Groupe des Dombes: the goal of the common statement on the theological meaning of ministry is the practical "mutual recognition of ministries" by separated churches; and this is founded on an acceptance of each church's "apostolic succession," possible through an "assurance that the intention of each [church is] to transmit the ministry of the Word and the sacraments in continuity with the apostolic era." The statement focuses the demonstration of this intention, however, in formal and structural elements of ordination and ministerial organization: the "invocation of the Holy Spirit and the laying-on-of-hands," the adoption of "episcopal" forms of oversight by those churches that do not have them, and the recognition, by episcopally ordered churches, of the valid "apostolic content" and "oversight" of nonepiscopal ministries. Cf. par. 51-53.

7. Cf. the Anglican–Roman Catholic International Commission's (ARCIC) more recent and widely applauded statement on "Church as Communion" (1991), where, in part III, "Communion" is described in terms of "Apostolicity, Catholicity, and Holiness" in a manner that seeks to make each aspect "inseparable" from the others and that is careful to acknowledge the relationship of ministry (in the shape of "oversight") to the "witness" and "fostering" of holiness within the Church (e.g., par. 39). As a whole, the statement is unusual among ecumenical documents in its synthetic treatment of these elements. However, the statement is also oriented by a governing conviction that Anglicans and Roman Catholics already share such a substantive degree of communion that the historically embodied relationship between the apostolicity and holiness of the ministry, for instance, is wholly ignored. The commission's serene insistence that the ecclesial "communion" ideally presented actually exists in significant measure, despite the glaring contradictions to the very elements of communion described, which are implied by the reality of division, places in question the seriousness with which these elements are themselves understood as being essentially linked. This evaluation of the document is informed by the entire discussion of apostolicity and holiness that follows in the present chapter.

gence, through the Reformation division, of separated communities of discernment. And if ecclesial division marks a general obscurement of such pneumatic manifestation, it can only undermine the historical identification of existing structures of ministry that might exhibit apostolic integrity. The ability to discover "structural compatibilities" of ministry with some common theological ground — the ability, in other words, to identify "succession," in contemporary ecumenical parlance — is made uncertain. Indeed, to the degree that ecclesial division stands in itself as an informing "sin," the holiness of a ministry subjected to that division is called into question from the first, and therefore its structural integrity becomes, at best, a second order concern, and, at worst, a matter without conceptual resolution.[8] That, at least, is a potential conclusion that needs to be examined.

Ministry and the Perfective Character of Love: The Classical Version of Thomas Aquinas

It is important to note in what way pre-Reformation conceptions of the ministry tended to present the latter's pneumatic character in the form of an integration of ecclesial qualities like holiness and apostolicity, from which questions regarding structure (including structures of ordination) were largely independent. The division of ecclesial communities alone provided the conditions of justifying self-consciousness that would make compelling the elevation of structural concerns in relation to the other aspects of pneumatic manifestation.

Thomas Aquinas, to take a classic example, discusses the ordained ministry solely in terms of practiced holiness — defined strictly in terms of charity — while leaving the issue of ordination itself, if not unaddressed, at least

---

8. "[Ecclesial communion is constituted by] a life of shared concern for one another in mutual forbearance, submission, gentleness and love; [by] the placing of the interests of others above the interests of self; in making room for each other in the body of Christ. . . . For the nurture and growth of this communion, Christ the Lord has provided a ministry of oversight, the fullness of which is entrusted to the episcopate, which has the responsibility of maintaining and expressing the unity of the churches" (ARCIC II, "Church As Communion," par. 45): on the basis of this kind of normative description of the Church, it is necessary to conclude, then, that either the division between Anglicans and Roman Catholics represents "a life of mutual forbearance, submission, making room for each other in the body of Christ," and so on or that the "ministry of oversight entrusted to the episcopate" has been critically abused, if not denied outright, in practice, in which case we must ask whether such a thing as the "episcopate" actually exists in historical terms. It is not clear what logical, let alone practical, middle ground between these two possibilities there might be.

hanging to the side as a species of another topic altogether. This last topic, sacramental efficacy, has a meaning that does not touch directly on the historical discernment and evaluation of the ordained person, except derivatively, and then still determined by the charity of the Church. The fullest account he offers of the ministry comes not in his systematic works, but in three *opuscula* that speak to more topical debates, concerning the propriety and character of entering and living in religious orders.[9]

Of the three, the treatise on *The Perfection of the Religious Life* states most coherently Aquinas's view of the ordained ministry's meaning. And the work's title presents the context of his thoughts straightforwardly: the religious life, to which the ordained ministry is related, represents a "state" committed to a life of "perfection." The nature of the ministry's relationship to this state is, in part, the focus of the argument; and very clear distinctions between the episcopacy and the priestly office are made in this regard, to which we shall return. At the base of his explication, however, Aquinas lays out the simple axiom (cc. 1-4) that all human life aims at a perfection of holiness that is embodied in perfect love — love for God and neighbor — and that the religious life is a particular and deliberately taken path to this goal of loving perfectly. While perfect love is a goal whose attainment is possible only in the state of "beatitude" among the saints in heaven (c. 4), all persons in this world are called, as a condition of their salvation, to certain actual and habitual actions by which we refer our deeds, thoughts, and affections to God alone (c. 5).

In between these two poles of divine love — the ordinary love of the ordinary *viator* and the truly perfect love of the *beati* — Aquinas locates a particular and voluntary "condition," in which a person may choose to "emulate," as far as possible and through concrete means, the "perfection of the blessed." This is done by consciously following the "counsels of perfection" given by Jesus, which provide concrete forms of life by which our attention to God is made less distracted. The counsels include the renunciation of possessions (cf. Matt. 19:21), the renunciation of "earthly ties" (cf. Luke 14:26), especially of matrimony (e.g. Matt. 19:12), and, finally, the renuncia-

---

9. *Contra impugnantes religionem, De Perfectione vitae spirituali,* and *Contra pestiferam doctrinam detrahentium pueros a religionis ingressu* (I, II, and III, of the *Opuscula* in the Parma edition). There is an English translation of *De Perfectione* by John Procter, under the title *The Religious State: The Episcopate and the Priestly Office* (Westminster [Md.]: The Newman Press, 1950), as well as a combined edition of the other two, also by Procter, entitled *An Apology for the Religious Orders* (London: Sands & Co., 1902). The debates eliciting these works, including William of Saint-Amour's attack on the regular clergy to which Aquinas responds, is given in Procter's introductions.

tion of our own will (cf. Matt. 16:24). Those who follow these counsels, through the taking of vows of poverty, chastity, and obedience, enter into a "state of perfection," which, although not in fact truly perfect, constitutes a fashion for approaching that perfection which is most adapted to the realities of the *viator*.

Finally, in addition to the three Counsels of Perfection, which are instrumental in freeing our love for God, Aquinas adds a fourth counsel, that of "perfect love of neighbor," perfect in its comprehensive aspect (even to enemies), in its intensity (even to self-sacrifice), and in its object (the spiritual welfare of others) (c. 14). Aquinas goes so far as to see the love of God embodied in following the first three counsels as, in a sense, included in the perfect realization of the fourth. That is, the giving of self in love of neighbor is, materially, the fullest love a person can offer within the temporal order.[10]

The "religious life," in the sense of the life of a monk or member of an order, obviously falls within the category of the "state of perfection." But what is important to note for our discussion is the way that Aquinas locates the episcopacy (and, in a very derivative and limited sense, the priesthood) within this category of perfected state as well, and the way he justifies this (cc. 16-17). A bishop may not make the same solemn vows to follow the Three Counsels as do members of religious orders, yet these vows are included, in a real sense, in the primary vow of service he makes at the time of his consecration. Indeed, Aquinas stresses, the "ordination" of the bishop constitutes the perpetually obligatory step that places him within the "state" for which the object of his life stands under the vow of perfection. This is a critical affirmation: episcopal ordination is itself voluntary entrance into the obligated life of charity.

Thus, the episcopal vow, unlike those of the religious, is defined in the most fundamental way in terms of the Fourth Counsel, that of "fraternal love," given in such a breadth of character as to comprehend and then surpass the perfection of the other three counsels alone: in caring for the Church and poor, the bishop "uses" material possessions completely for the sake of others; in teaching a "purity" of life to the Church, the bishop must embody it in his own person (including chastity); in acting as the chief minister of his flock

---

10. Two things are to be noted here. First, the counsels are given as means to love God perfectly, and their significance and outworking are defined by such love. Second, it is only by taking vows to keep them, that is, by putting oneself under the obligation to follow the counsels, that one enters into the "state of perfection." This is a matter both of the "merit" of the vow (c. 12), which represents a desired willingness (and hence augmented love) to follow a divine directive, and of verbal definition (a "state" is understood as a "condition" of existence, which, in the case of the counsels, can be given only through some form of "stability" and "perpetuity," that is, through a vow of obligation [cc. 15, 23]).

and within the Church at large, the bishop "subjects himself" to all people, in the most expansive form of obedience. The Three Counsels, then, are taken up by the fourth, which is described in terms of a complete and utter self-giving for the people of the Church, with respect both to their physical and to their spiritual needs, to the point even of death. The bishop, Aquinas concludes, must be deemed to be in a "greater state of perfection" than all others, a state comparable in its historical self-presentation to the pneumatic holiness of the saints (c. 18). And in this sense, a sense built solidly upon the obligatory character of their acts, bishops are truly "the successors of the Apostles." Apostolicity, to coin a term, is "caritative" in nature, in that it embodies ecclesially the historical reality of divine love.

The secular priest, it must be said, does not stand in the same position as the bishop in this regard, according to Aquinas. Indeed, Aquinas's remarks on the subjective significance of the priesthood, as opposed to the episcopacy, seem dissonant with the modern focus upon the centrality of the ordinary authorized pastors of the Church in discussions of ministry. As regards their "rank," in that they are both in "orders," priests and bishops share something. But the nature of their "state" differs significantly, in that priests do not take solemn "vows" to live according to any of the counsels. Unlike members of religious orders, priests can receive a dispensation to resign and can marry lawfully, a reality (among others) that, in Aquinas's mind, proves the gulf in obligatory power — and hence perfective status — between the simple priest and the religious or the bishop (cf. c. 25).

It is not the case, however, that the "office" of priest is unrelated to the life of perfection. Quite the opposite. All people are called to a perfection of love, and priests are called to a work — that of pastoring in the broad sense — that is specifically oriented toward the achievement of this universally ordered caritative goal. In doing this, they are called, like bishops, to acts, often extraordinary acts, of love on behalf of others; and these acts are, furthermore, directly tied to their office. In fact, in terms of effective *caritas,* the concrete life of love that joins us to God, simple parish priests may well be more "perfect" in virtue than many monks or bishops. But an "act" is not a "state"; and the very fact that priests are, in a manner, "free to fail" at such love in a way that the obligated bishop is not demonstrates their ministries as being in another "condition" (or "state) than that of the bishop. Priests are called to deeds of love, not to a state of love. If their ministry is joined to that of the bishop, as it is, it is because they are nonobligated "vicars" or "lieutenants" of the bishops, "helps" to the apostolic ministry of their superiors (c. 23).[11]

---

11. The question of the relation between the orders of episcopacy and priesthood (under-

But unlike the priest, the bishop is not "free to fail," because his consecratory vow obliges him to an extreme pursuit of charity, which his subordinates need not maintain and for which he is responsible before God. And, even more than with the religious, the failure of the bishop is of disastrous proportions, because the nature of his caritative ministry involves the lives of others, the neglect of which exposes one to the most extreme spiritual dangers. Hence, although the virtues of the episcopal office are the greatest, since they require the greatest love, they are also the least to be sought after, since their subversion requires the greatest punishment (c. 19).

It is possible, within this pre-Reformation scheme, to frame the character of the ministry in the following way: holiness (defined in terms of perfect love) informs the meaning of the ministry in particular, as it does the purpose of human life in general; all ministry is both ordered to divine love and ordered by it, through a hierarchy of perfections (Aquinas follows the Dionysian model of the Church here); the fullest embodiment of this ministry of love is that given by Christ to the apostles and enacted by the episcopacy, whose sole *raison d'être* is to manifest and further the manifestation of this love within the body of the Church. The priesthood represents an office of assistance to this apostolic purpose, which is given in a certain kind of life.

Notice how, according to this framework, the issue of structural meaning is wholly governed by the substance of the enacted apostolic ministry of love. Ordination itself has only an ancillary significance for Aquinas: it provides the priest with certain functional "powers" (the consecration of the Eucharist, primarily), but it does not define the shape of his life in any way — he is not "changed"; and, to that degree, it is not central to the apostolic ministry that the priest assists in (cf. c. 24). He treats the reality of priestly ordination, therefore, as a matter of functional arrangement — which is its place in the discussion of sacraments within, say, the *Summa*.[12] The consecration of the bishop, however — "episcopal ordination" — is of a wholly other order and represents just such a "change" of "state," in which the individual now stands before God and the Church's people in a new orientation of purpose, *because he has taken a vow to live a certain way,* which is the essence of the "apostolic" reality of the Church as

---

stood as the "presbyterate") was controverted, some arguing for a separate status of orders for each office, others that one or the other office was included within the other's order. Aquinas's position, that the presbyterate derives, in a subsidiary and dependent way, from the episcopacy (and hence maintains its apostolic validity only through its legitimate dependence upon the episcopacy) had strong (though not universal) patristic tradition behind it. It is retained intact in Roman Catholic teaching; cf. Vatican II's *Lumen Gentium* 21ff. and 28; also *Presbyterorum Ordinis* 2. Likewise, the new *Catechism of the Catholic Church* (the so-called *Universal Catechism*), 1555–1568.

12. See below.

a whole. Whereas there is a distinction between the "office" and the "character" of the priesthood — the former is variably controlled by the commission of the bishop toward particular acts of love, while the latter pertains solely to the power to consecrate the Eucharistic elements — for the bishop office and character are one and the same: "apostolicity" consists in the self-offering of love on behalf of the Church and its people (c. 24).

The distinction between bishops and priests on the matter of "character" in no way divorces the priesthood's meaning in particular from the caritative nature of apostolicity. The fact that the power conferred at ordination for the consecration of the Eucharist is not affected by the individual priest's holiness is seen rather as a way to safeguard the caritative end of the Church's communal life as a whole.[13] In defining the Eucharistic sacrifice, as well as the prayers of the priest "for the Church," as fully effected by Christ and only instrumentally by the priest, Aquinas is able to point out that the people of the Church are still oriented toward sanctification; and whatever the status in perfection of their priests, the Church as a whole is still able to grow in love. At the same time, however, priests who use their sacramental powers within a life oriented away from love — through hatred, heresy, or schism — withdraw themselves from the good effects of their work (i.e., their work, including the sacraments they administer, becomes an occasion of unholiness and sin for themselves). And, furthermore, those who receive such sacraments in a way that "consents" to the priest's own lack of love in these matters similarly cut themselves off from the divine fruit made possible through the priest's conferred "powers."[14] Finally, since the priest is a minister whose work partakes of the apostolic character only through temporal "commission" by a bishop, the full "effectiveness" of the priest's office is made dependent upon the episcopal will, and thus upon the integrity of the episcopal "character," which is ordered solely by the obligatory love of self-sacrifice for the Church.[15]

Caritative Apostolicity and the Divided Ministry

This final point is crucial in assessing the relationship of structure to holiness in the ministry in the context specifically of ecclesial division. The pneumatic effectiveness of all ministry is constituted by the enacted history of charity it embodies: this constitution, embodying the exemplary enactment of charity

---

13. Cf. *Summa Theologiae*, 3a 82,4-8.
14. Ibid., art. 6, 9, 10; and 2a2a. 39:3.
15. Ibid., 3a 82, 1, ad 4.

given in the life of Christ and figured in his first disciples, is what is meant by ministerial "apostolicity." In the case of the bishop, such enactment exhausts the significance of the ordination and office. In the case of a priest, his particular episcopal commission delimits the extent of that enactment with regard to its object, the Church, while his own response to that commission determines the subjective fruit he can receive from the enactment; the significance of his ordination is given in its objective instrumentality, through its commissioned agency for the Church or through its ancillary agency for the individual priest's pursuit of holiness. Thus, a bishop who fails to exhibit love is useless *qua* bishop; while a priest who fails in his ministry of charity is useless to himself *qua* individual Christian, although, if properly commissioned — that is, used in the service of the episcopally ordered apostolicity of the Church — he may still be useful to the Church *qua* priest. The whole set of controverted questions surrounding "validity" of orders or ministry within the Church, then, can be looked at in Aquinas's terms from two perspectives: either "validity" refers to the structures of "ordination," by which "powers" are conferred, or it refers to the historical practice of "commission," in which bishops and priests are both implicated and evaluated in terms of caritative enactment. Obviously, the first perspective refers to a subsidiary "validity" that has significance only to the degree that it is formed within valid apostolic life marked out by the second perspective. And the reality of a divided ministry must be evaluated within this latter realm of discernment.

While the category of "schism" is not necessarily the appropriate one in which to discuss post-Reformation divisions, it is the only one available within Aquinas's traditional schema in which to view the question of apostolicity as he has laid out its presuppositions in relation to such ministerial divisions. And, in the light of the distinction between structural and apostolic validity, his discussion of ministry in schism proves consistent on this topic.[16] Aquinas defines schism as, fundamentally, a sin against charity; not in a primary way, that is, by attacking the primary object of love, which is God, but in a secondary fashion, by attacking the *unitas ecclesiastica*, the unity formed by love among the Christian people of the Church, through which we participate in God's love. In this sense, "heresy," as a direct attack against the truth about God, is a "worse" sin than schism.[17] But as pertaining to the participated love of

---

16. Ibid., 2a2ae 39.

17. Ibid., art. 1 and art. 2, *sed contra*. As Aquinas points out, however, schism generally leads to heresy *(est via ad haeresim)* and may often in practice be a "worse sin" than heresy, insofar as the schismatic may be filled with a greater personal animosity toward God and the Church than the heretic, and may in fact wreak greater havoc.

neighbor, schism touches directly upon the sphere of caritative enactment that is embodied in the ministry; and the question of the significance — character and value — of a schismatic minister arises with a strict demand.

In answering the question as to whether a schismatic minister has any "power," Aquinas makes use of distinctions he has elsewhere drawn concerning bishops and priests.[18] Assuming someone is properly ordained in the manner of the Catholic Church *(catholice)*, a subsequent breach into schism redefines the character of that ministry in a particular way: the "spiritual power" of the ordained ministry being twofold, sacramental and jurisdictional, the subversion of charity that schism entails destroys the latter, though not the former. The *potestas sacramentalis* here corresponds to the "character" conferred upon the priest by ordination that allows him to consecrate the Eucharist, as well as perform other sacraments. This, as we saw, is a power unrelated to the caritative realm that constitutes the historical value of the ministry — its apostolicity — except insofar as it is properly "commissioned." Such commission corresponds, in the discussion of schism, to the *potestas jurisdictionalis,* and it is this power alone that is critically undermined by schism. The sacraments performed by a schismatic minister may be true sacraments, but they are not "licit"; and, to the degree that they are used in the commissioned ministry of the Church as a whole, they fail in their purpose.

It is for this reason that schismatic ministers are appropriately excommunicated: they have deliberately removed themselves from the temporal mission of the Church — they have denied their commission — and their own ministries thus no longer have any place within that mission. While they need not be reordained if they return to the Church (assuming an initially "Catholic" ordination), they require a new commission if they are to be "useful" once again in the service of love. As "separated" from the communion of the Church, their sacramental acts have an "efficacy" only if themselves accepted by the Church within its commissioned ministry (for instance, if those people receiving such schismatic sacraments were ignorant of their status, and required nourishment for their own legitimate Christian vocations). But *qua* ministerial acts, the sacramental works of schismatic ministers, as is the case with their ministries as a whole, are without fruit both for themselves and for those who participate in them by informed consent.[19]

Thus, while the ordaining structures that support a schismatic ministry may well be valid, the exercise of that ministry is not, because it has subverted

18. Ibid., art. 3.
19. Cf. ibid., art. 4. Also 3a 82, 7 and 9, which speaks of the "sin" of a schismatic Eucharist, both for the consecrater and for the participating people.

its own commission through separation. And although Aquinas speaks explicitly to the case of schismatic priests, it is clear that the same holds true, in an even more primary way, for a schismatic bishop, whose very "character," as we said, is identical with his "office," the temporal forms taken by his active ministry. Priests receive their *potestas jurisdictionalis,* that is, their particular commissioned ministries, variably from the bishop and independently of their ordination. But bishops, through their obligated consecration, are directly "commissioned" as Christ's active and apostolic "mediators"; and a temporal subversion of that commission, like schism, destroys at its root their ministry's usefulness and efficacy for the Church, however much their sacramental powers remain intact.[20] Schismatic ministry, then, is not an apostolic ministry, however much the ordaining structures undergirding schismatic bishops and priests may themselves be valid.

The question of the validity of schismatic ministries in their apostolic value — their caritative enactment — thus falls within the category of "commission": who has called such ministry forth, to what end, and within what context of service? Further, the category of "commission" is one of caritative integrity, that is, the holiness of love: the reality of a valid call is indicated by the enactment of love on the part of the one called. Apostolicity, then, describes a *temporal union of service in love* among the Church's ministers. If one speaks of the priority of holiness in this aspect, it is a holiness to be understood firmly in terms of concrete expressions of caritative enactment within and on behalf of the Body of the Church: the apostolic ministry is connected to the Church's life through the history of its service of love. And this description of orders, summarized by Aquinas, does little more than bring together two traditional ways of understanding apostolicity that had been inherited from the early Church and jointly formalized within something like the Dominican Order of Preachers, of which Aquinas was a member: (episcopal) commission and (perfective) vocation.

Background for the Classical View of Caritative Apostolicity

Two broad strands of usage for the word "apostolic," in Greek and Latin, have been identified from the early Church, the one dealing with "connection," the other with "resemblance" to the witness of the apostles.[21] Both of

20. Cf. ibid., 3a 82 1, ad 4.
21. The nomenclature for this distinction was given by P. L. M. Dewailly, O.P., in "Histoire de l'adjectif apostolique," *Mélanges de Science religieuse* 5, no. 11 (November 1948):

these strands are congruent with broad New Testament applications of the cognate terms, and therefore deserve a special and normative respect.[22] The notion that what was somehow and somewhat loosely "connected" to the apostles was properly "apostolic" was applied to a variety of Christian realities, including teaching, liturgical custom, moral example, and the official succession of the Church's leadership (especially bishops and the dioceses they

---

p. 147. For an overview on usage, see also Henri Holstein, S.J., "L'Évolution du mot 'apostolique' au cours de l'histoire de l'Église," in *L'Apostolat* (Paris: Éditions du Cerf, 1957), pp. 41-51.

22. Historical connection and spiritual resemblance are not inappropriate ways of designating New Testament usage, although perhaps less clear-cut than in the early Church subsequent to the writing of the canonical texts. The idea — emphasized anew in the modern age through a reappropriation of the term "apostolate" for all types of Christian vocation — that an "apostle" is someone "sent" by Jesus to do his work, is clearly present in the Gospel accounts and, obviously, forms the root meaning of the word itself: as Jesus was "sent," so he sent his followers. But other synonyms are used too (e.g., *pempein*), and the simple notion of "mission" proves a weak foundation for the bulk of the New Testament references to apostleship as a specified ministry. The Lucan writings, more than others, emphasize the special character of the historical figures who comprised "the Twelve," and their unique role in salvation history (cf. Luke 22:30). They are "chosen" by Jesus from among all others, they live a special kind of life in mutual communion, they have a specific "ministry," and they are designated "witnesses" to Christ's life, death, and resurrection (cf. Acts 1:2, 14, 17, 22). In addition, they guide the emerging Church and take full responsibility for its ministry, teaching, and expansion (cf. Acts 6:2-4, 6; 15 passim). The book of Revelation, for all of its distinctiveness, treats the apostles similarly, explicitly linking them to the Twelve, and giving them comparably foundational roles for the Christian Church (cf. Rev. 18:20; 21:14), using phrases surprisingly at one with Pauline texts like Ephesians (e.g., 2:20; 3:5). The underlying role given by all of these kinds of references to the present Church's historical connection, through various modes, with the outworking of Jesus' original salvific plan, is unmistakable. With Paul especially, the second strand of apostolic "resemblance" is given high relief. In the individual promotion of his contested authority, Paul, to be sure, makes use of the "connection" perspective, linking himself to other well-known apostles and witnesses (e.g., in 1 Cor. 15:8ff.; cf. 1 Tim. 1:12ff.). But he repeatedly stakes out his special claim to apostleship based on the formal witness given by the shape of his life to the figure of Christ's humiliated grace and love: the "signs" he gives appear in the form of "weaknesses" and "sufferings" that demonstrate the power of Christ Jesus' own self-given life to grant life to the dead and dying (cf. 1 Cor. 4:9; 2 Cor. 11:5, 13; 12:11-12; even 12:19–13:10). These themes, in fact, take up material from the Gospels themselves concerning the intimate communion of the apostles in Jesus' own Passion (cf. Matt. 19:28). Further, Paul (conformably with other New Testament writers) contrasts the shape of his apostleship with that of "false" apostles, precisely on the basis of the latter's failure to embody a certain kind of sacrificial life for the sake of the Christian community's well-being and unity (e.g., 2 Cor. 11:12ff.; cf. Rev. 2:2; Jude 17f.). The integration of most of these various elements is given in a text like 2 Timothy 2:1ff., which elevates "apostleship" to an ongoing, authoritatively commissioned, and imitative maintenance of the Church in a unified life of faithfulness and loving subjection. If "apostolicity" is to retain a coherent meaning, theologically, it will have to be congruent with this kind of summary.

oversaw).[23] With these variously drawn connections came authority of some kind, an authority only later defined in terms of specifically historical lineage, a development that lies behind the particular concepts of doctrinal or disciplinary "apostolic tradition" and "apostolic succession" as applied to the episcopacy (given in a person or a see).[24] These various elements of connection, including their formal and even canonical embodiments, lie behind the overarching description, made at Nicea, of the Christian Church as a whole (in the singular) being "apostolic."[25] To this authority of connection was attached the power to demarcate "true" from "false" Church, through the act of the Church's speaking from its consistent "identity": that is, the realm of "connection" informed the "apostolic" Church as that Body in personal identity, over time, with the Body of Christ given in the first Church of the apostles.[26]

This question of identity provides the logical bridge to the second aspect of the early Church's view of apostolicity. For besides the authority of connection, what was "apostolic" took the form, in a less historical fashion, of an imperative to apostolic resemblance, that is, a call to a life given in the very form of the apostles' existence. There is some direct evidence of this usage in writings from the early monastic movement, where the "apostolic authority" of, for instance, Paul is used to designate a form of communal existence, and not simply a command.[27] Indirectly, and especially when dealing with descriptions of the ordained ministry, the figure of the Apostle, either Peter or Paul, was frequently lifted up as the object of conformity for both bishop and priest.[28] In particular

23. While Irenaeus tends to characterize these elements as being "of the apostles," the use of the adjective "apostolic" was already adopted (e.g., Ignatius in the opening of his Epistle to the Trallians, and the *Martyrdom of Polycarp* 16:2), and, with Tertullian, was liberally followed (see the citations in Holstein, pp. 44f.).

24. Despite lacking any deliberate reflection upon "apostolicity," a compilation like the fourth-century (?) *Apostolic Constitutions* and *Canons,* with its sometimes elaborate partition of doctrinal and disciplinary instructions according to each of the twelve apostles, and given as a whole by the entire group, already points, in a rather profound way on the basis of its formal presuppositions, in this direction.

25. In, for example, the anathema at the end of the Creed.

26. The view that "apostolicity" refers, primarily, to the way that the church maintains its historical identity — in a manner analogous to a specific human personality — is a standard one. Cf. F. Vernet's definition, that "apostolicity is nothing else than the identity that the Church maintains with herself over time since Christ and the apostles" ("Apostolicité," in *Dictionnaire de la théologie catholique*, t. 1, col. 1618).

27. Cf. Cassian, *Conferences,* 24:12.

28. Cf. Gregory of Nazianzus, Oration II:54ff.; John Chrysostom, *On the Preisthood* III:5 and IV:6; Gregory the Great, *Pastoral Rule* II:5, 6.

Augustine's own monastic rule was fundamentally ordered around the notion of the "apostolic community" of the first chapters of Acts. By the tenth century, this rule formed the basis of a remarkably vital renewal of clerical practice, epitomized in the growth of the Canons Regular, according to which secular clergy committed themselves to a communal life of poverty, worship, and service, designated by the specific phrase *vita apostolica*.[29] This form of life was essentially determined by the absolute self-giving of love within the context of the temporal community, according to which the vows of poverty, chastity, and obedience were understood to uphold the "unity" of the *corpus caritatis*.[30]

From this "resemblance" understanding of apostolicity came the figurative basis of caritative holiness that proved so central to the early Church's conception of the ministry. Certainly, the evolving sacrificial character of the priestly role in the Eucharist carried with it explicit resonances of Old Testament Levitical purity.[31] But the sacrificial motif was subsidiary to the more weighty demands for sanctification made by the broader pastoral responsibili-

29. Cf. François Petit, O.Pream., *La Réforme des prêtres au moyen-âge. Pauvreté et vie commune* (Paris: Éditions du Cerf, 1968).

30. Cf. the opening of Augustine's Rule: "Before all else, *live together in harmony* (Ps. 67 [68]:7), *being of one mind and one heart* (Acts 4:32) on the way to God. For is it not precisely for this reason that you have come to live together?" (The translation is by Raymond Canning, OSA, in *The Rule of Saint Augustine: Masculine and Feminine Versions* [Garden City: Image/Doubleday, 1986], p. 11.)

31. Cf. Chrysostom, III:4: "The Paraclete himself . . . established this ministry, and . . . ordained that men abiding in the flesh should imitate the ministry of the angels. For that reason it behooves the bearer of the priesthood to be as pure as if he stood in the very heavens amidst those Powers. Fearful indeed, and most awe-inspiring, were those things which preceded the workings of grace. Such were the bells, the pomegranates, the stones on the base and on the mantle, the miter, the cincture, the robe reaching to the feet, the plate of gold, the Holy of Holies and the solemn stillness within . . . that which was spoken concerning the Old Law is true also of the New: *for though the former was made glorious; yet in this it is without glory, by reason of the overwhelming glory of the latter* [2 Cor. 3:10]. When you see the Lord immolated and lying upon the altar, and the priest bent over that sacrifice praying, and all the people empurpled by that precious blood, can you think that you are still among men and on earth?" (trans. W. A. Jurgens in *The Priesthood: A Translation of the Peri Hierosynes of St. John Chrysostom* [New York: The Macmillan Co., 1955], p. 31). Clement of Rome had very early on established the figurative parallel of the Jewish and Christian "priesthoods" (*Epistle to the Corinthians,* esp. chs. 42-44), a typology carried on consistently within the patristic corpus. Cf. the brief summary in Joseph Lécuyer, *Le Sacrement de l'ordination. Recherche historique et théologique* (Paris: Beauchesne, 1983), pp. 261-64, and the classic contributions by George H. Williams, "The Ministry of the Ante-Nicene Church (c. 125–315)" and "The Ministry in the Later Patristic Period (314–450)," in H. Richard Niebuhr and Daniel D. Williams, eds., *The Ministry in Historical Perspectives* (New York: Harper and Brothers, 1956), pp. 27-81, passim.

ties of the minister, according to which a particular kind of spiritual authority over the communal life of the Church required an appropriately shaped life in conformance with the importance of the salvation offered in Christ. The early tradition of granting the status of deacons or presbyters, without any ordination rite of laying on of hands, to those "confessors" who had suffered for their faith exemplifies the deeply held sense that the sanctification of life through self-giving for Christ formed the central core of the apostolic witness the ministry of the Church was meant to enact.[32] Gregory of Nazianzus's famous oration explicating the reasons for which he originally ran away from his ordained ministry relies on this sense that the responsibilities of the priest-hood to embody and further the redemptive fruit of God's work in Christ are so great as to overwhelm any person who may take them on.[33] Saint Paul, Gregory writes, demonstrated the extent of self-giving and suffering properly involved in such a ministry on behalf of the souls of men and women; and only those able to meet those standards, or at least approach them, can hope to fulfill their calling and escape the judgment that meets such a calling's frustration: "A man must himself be cleansed, before cleansing others: himself become wise, that he may make others wise; become light, and then give light; draw near to God, and so bring others near; be hallowed, then hallow them; be possessed of hands to lead others by the hand, of wisdom, to give advice."[34]

Such holiness derives, then, from the reality of a service that reflects the very condescension of God: "This is the aim of all his spiritual authority, in everything to neglect his own in comparison with the advantage of others."[35] The goal defines the Christian ministry as a whole, but it also determines the parameters of its success, of whether it be fruitfully or deficiently pursued. And so, Gregory the Great points out how those who respond positively and rigorously to the call to ministry as well as those who flee such a call out of fear of unworthiness both act out of "the same fountain of love," in that both groups take seriously the fact that the Church's life depends on their ability to

---

32. Cf. Hippolytus's *Apostolic Tradition*, c. 10 (in the Dix enumeration).

33. Cf. Gregory of Nazianzus, c. 22: "But the scope of our [the priest's] art is to provide the soul with wings, to rescue it from the world and give it to God, and to watch over that which is in His image, if it abides, to take it by the hand, if it is in danger, or restore it, if ruined, to make Christ to dwell in the heart by the Spirit: and, in short, to deify, and bestow heavenly bliss upon, one who belongs to the heavenly host" (trans. C. G. Browne and J. E. Swallow, in *Select Orations of Saint Gregory Nazianzen*, vol. 7 of *A Select Library of Nicene and Post-Nicene Fathers of the Christian Church*, Second Series (repr. Grand Rapids: Wm. B. Eerdmans, 1983), p. 209.

34. Gregory of Nazianzus, c. 71 (p. 219).

35. Gregory of Nazianzus, c. 54 (p. 216).

give fully of themselves in love.[36] Indeed, Gregory Nazianzus, John Chrysostom, and Gregory the Great all represent standard *exempla* of a tradition regarding the ordained ministry that honored its rejection on the part of one called out of a sober sense that the Church's integrity and the salvation of souls (including the potential minister's) radically depended upon the temporal exercise of love on behalf of the Body.[37]

The Dominican order itself represented a formal expression of these two strands of apostolic connection and resemblance: first, the Augustinian ideal of the *vita apostolica,* in common with much of the medieval reform movements, was taken as the basis of the order's spiritual mission, thereby retaining the traditional and central perfective character of the ministry; yet this ministry was rubrically tied to the temporal governance of the episcopal office, to which the Friars were directly responsible in an explicitly diaconal manner, thereby marking their ministry within the wider catholic oversight by which the Church's historical connectiveness and identity were maintained. Historical commission, given through such episcopal direction, was thereby seen as essentially tied to the perfective goal of the apostolic life-forms.[38]

Aquinas's description of the episcopal office as enacted within a "state of perfection," in which caritative service forms the essence of the office's character, represents a reflection of this apostolic center upon which his own order's ministry was constructed. For the bishop — and his vicars, whether priests or other missioners — a personal call to ministry emerged only from within the actual maintenance and furtherance of charity. Congruent with the patristic tradition on the matter, Aquinas taught that no one should "want" to be a bishop; rather, such an office should be avoided at all costs. Instead, the burden of a divine call to such work was apparent only through the sacrifice of self that proceeded from the reluctant pursuit but vigorous establishment of a history of love within the Church.[39] And the aspects of

36. Gregory the Great, I:7.

37. Cf. Gregory the Great, c. II:11, for Gregory's famous allegory of the Church as the Ark, whose unity is maintained only by the gold-plated poles, that is, by the priests, whose lives are adorned with holy virtue, held fast by the Word of God (the four rings).

38. Cf. H. Mandonnet, *Saint Dominique, l'idée, l'homme et l'oeuvre* (Paris: Desclée de Brouwer, 1938), t. II, pp. 171ff.

39. On Aquinas's teaching concerning the undesirability of the episcopacy, see the *De Perfectione,* in Procter, ch. 19, which includes several standard references to the patristic teaching on the matter. The question of "vocation" to the ministry is an interesting one within Aquinas's perspective. He actually devotes extensive remarks to the question of vocation in the *Contra pestiferam doctrinam retrahentium pueros a religionis ingressu* (esp. chs. 9, 10). Here he speaks of vocation under three aspects: an immediate audible call by Christ to certain men and women, that is, the apostles; a general call to all men and women, through the words of Scripture; and

commission and holiness, historical connection and perfective love, were given as inseparable elements of the unified identity — the apostolicity — of the Christian Church.

Post-Reformation Catholic Construals of Apostolicity: De Sales and Structural Jurisdiction

The continued pertinence of this complex category of commissioned love, as a context for the discussion of the validity of divided ministries, is demonstrated by the immediate deployment of its related and more technical concepts, "jurisdiction" and "vocation," within the post-Reformation debate over the ministry. The classic expressions of this debate were not framed until the churches of the Reformation were themselves sufficiently organized and socially entrenched as to present a continuously functioning ministry of their own. At this point, the confrontation between Roman and Reformed ministries became patently apparent, and some attempt at relating the character of authority vested in these two bodies became necessary. But the notion of "apostolicity" was not the obvious category in which to pursue this discussion, in large

---

finally, an "interior" call, given by the inwardly working voice of God. This latter is the form of vocation Aquinas sees as prevalent among religious; and he describes it in explicitly pneumatic terms, as an "interior unction of the Holy Spirit," an "impulse of grace" independent of human counsel, and so on. Indeed, he calls such interior vocation "preferable" to exterior calls, since it is, in a sense, more purely divine; and he advises that such calls be heeded "without hesitation" or "deliberation." If the Church provides external "tests" to interior vocations, it is only to demonstrate to others what the individual called "already knows." The issue of demonic vocational deception is ruled out by Aquinas, simply because the "state of perfection" to which interior vocations lead is an intrinsic good that could be offered only by God. Aquinas's reflections on vocation here have been used as a basis for many subsequent "pneumatic" construals of vocation in general, in the form of "inward" promptings. Such applications of his remarks are quite illegitimate, however, since the object of his discussion is quite explicitly limited to the case of "religious," that is, monks or members of religious orders. The case of the Church's pastoral ministers is clearly quite different: given the *un*desirability of the episcopacy and its charges, due to the burdens of caritative enactment its state of perfection demands, "vocation" in its regard will take a very dissimilar form from the monastic call. Instead of a clear interior call, the individual potentially called to the pastoral ministry engages in a difficult struggle with external realities, including the decisions of the Church's leaders and councils, the Church's historical condition, the temporal contexts in which ministry is to take place, and the sense and measurable reality of individual preparedness for such work. In this sense, vocation becomes visible only in the successful adaptation of historical commission: it is retrospectively proved through the work of an individual to maintain the historical realities of the Church's life of love.

measure because its compressed significance, as evidenced in descriptions like Aquinas's, was logically incapable of responding to the particular arguments that derived from a debate within division: a history of caritative enactment, within which the apostolic ministry had been traditionally seen as embodied, was simply contradicted by either the widely substantiated accusations of ministerial corruption made by the Protestants or the equally inescapable charges of deliberately schismatic contumacy leveled at the organizational independence, and its justifications, pursued by Reformed leaders. Instead, apostolicity's integral meaning was broken down into constituent parts, whose values were polemically wielded as separable defining terms for the ministry. Each side of the debate could appeal to something "apostolic" in its ministry, as was done, but only if the historically caritative bond of the expression was eliminated. Without such elimination, the apostolic validity of each church's ministries would be placed in question.

Hence, the Catholics seized upon the aspect of "commission," understood in a formally structural way. This tactic, following indicators given by Bellarmine in particular (who himself had taken up early Catholic responses to Luther's organizational efforts at reform), received crystalline expression in the widely circulated pamphlets of Francis de Sales at the end of the sixteenth century. In his effort to re-Catholicize the mostly Reformed region of Chabelais in eastern France, the young de Sales had issued a series of tracts arguing for the truth of the Roman church, later collected and issued as the *Controvèrses*.[40] He opened his sally with what became a famous attack on the Reformed ministers' pretension to a divine "mission." If the ordained ministry is understood, in some large fashion, as an "embassy of Christ," then the true Church's ministers must be properly "commissioned" of Christ. Can the Reformed Church demonstrate such commission?

For de Sales, a proper ministerial commission derives from Christ either "immediately" — by his direct command (e.g., to the apostles) — or "mediately," through some designated authority, as when St. Paul "commissioned" Timothy. The first five discourses of the *Controvèrses* aimed at refuting either form of commission for the Protestants. As for a mediated mission, de Sales argues that the people alone, or their secular princes, cannot commission their own ministers. He does this on scriptural grounds, using the examples of both the New Testament churches and Old Testament figures for the designation

---

40. In *Oeuvres complètes de Saint Frainçois de Sales* (Paris: Louis Vivès, 1859), vol. 8. A nineteenth-century English translation by H. B. Mackey, O.S.B., has been reissued as *The Catholic Controversy: St. Francis de Sales' Defense of the Faith* (Rockford [Ill.]: Tan Books and Publishers, 1989).

of priests within Israel.[41] More than this, de Sales notes that separation from the main body of the Church constitutes a *de facto* loss of authoritative power. If a people break communion — with Rome, of course — what Church is being represented by their chosen ministers?

> For this people was of the true Church or not: if it was of the true Church why did Luther take it therefrom? Would it really have called him in order to be taken out of its place and of the Church? . . . If they say this people was not Catholic, what was it then? It was not Lutheran; for we all know that when Luther began to preach in Germany there were no Lutherans, and it was he who was their origin. Since then such a people did not belong to the true Church, how could it give mission for true preaching?[42]

The question of mediated mission is reduced to the apostolic succession through the laying on hands within the episcopal order. And since neither Luther nor Calvin was a bishop, the ministers they ordained or otherwise chose cannot be said to have a valid commission.

In undermining a Protestant claim to immediate commission, through pneumatic imperative of some kind,[43] de Sales relies on a series of arguments that attempt to tie, historically and logically, the reality of any "extraordinary" mission to the "ordinary" structures of ecclesial authority. Thus, immediate commissions must be "confirmed by miracles" (which, of course, are themselves confirmed by the existing authorities of the Church); they must not place extraordinary ministers in conflict with the Church's ordinary leaders; and the ordinary life of the Church cannot be "destroyed" by the extraordinarily evoked labors of those immediately designated for ministry by God. Jesus' ministry was confirmed not only by his miracles, but by the mediating authority of the prophets; Paul's commission was ratified by the Jerusalem apostles (whether he liked it or not), and so on. Protestant ministers cannot point to any such mutual validation by extraordinary and ordinary authorities. Again, the very reality of a divided ministry belies any claim to extraordinary origin for one party.

In attacking both mediated and immediate ministerial commissions among the Protestants, de Sales ultimately relies on the formal structural elements of apostolicity, which he defines in terms of an ecclesially recognized

41. Mackey provides a note referring to a fragmentary comment de Sales wrote elsewhere, in which the figurative character of the divided Church is observed in Jeroboam's secular attempt to institute a new priesthood without ecclesial authority (Mackey, p. 16).

42. Discourses 3 and 4, in Mackey, p. 16.

43. Discourses 5 and 6.

instrument of conferral, or what he simply calls "jurisdiction": unless there is some formally concrete "connection" between the Reformed ministers and the structures of the Church from which they arose, their ministries are plainly "illegitimate"; they simply do not derive from Christ. And in the course of this argument, the category of "vocation" becomes subsumed within this jurisdictional model, according to which "mission" and "calling" are identical terms indicating the formalized place within the ordaining succession given through the episcopal imposition of hands.

The complex issue of priestly *potestas* (which in the Thomistic description of orders can be used by "illicit" ministers for the upbuilding of the Church precisely because proper "commission" refers to a certain kind of caritative *service* rather than solely to a formal set of instruments of conferral — although inclusive of such conferral) wholly disappears, for de Sales, into the form itself. And there is a logical demand for this kind of constriction, given the fact that the division of ministries to which de Sales speaks is one that has been mutually accepted, whether negatively or positively. For although the reality of "unity" informs the character of the ministry's apostolic integrity here, it no longer does so in a way that injects into the category of "vocation" any caritatively perfective quality. Indeed, de Sales shifts all discussion of the perfective vocation away from the ordained ministry altogether, and applies it to a much later examination of the *regula fidei* under the article of the "holy Church," in which he extols the Roman Church's maintenance of the obligated monastic existence under the Three Counsels of Perfection. Under this rubric, he can adroitly address Protestant charges of Catholic moral corruption because the occasion of demeaned monastic life does not threaten the integrity of the Church's authoritative structures, whose formal powers of conferral remain intact.[44] If the ministry were caritatively defined, then the absence of the demanded unity of its practice would form the standard of its apostolic evacuation.

That De Sales in fact emphasizes the jurisdictional element of valid ministry over against the Protestants, while ignoring what Aquinas called the *potestas sacramentalis,* or the power to consecrate and offer the Eucharistic sacrifice, may at first sight seem odd. Indeed, de Sales has little to say about the sacraments in the *Controvèrses* apart from some general remarks about ministerial "intention." Trent itself, by contrast, in its canons and through the catechism it sponsored and commended as a basis for popular instruction, had placed its stress, when discussing the ordained ministry, just here, on the priest's power to consecrate the elements of the Blessed Eucharist. The teaching of the Council concerning the Sacrament of Order is wholly predicated on this

44. Discourse 57, in Mackey, pp. 199ff.

fundamental character, which is explained in the opening chapter on the topic: "Sacrifice and priesthood are so joined by God's ordinance that they have existed together in every law. Since, then, in the New Covenant, the Catholic Church received the visible holy sacrifice of the Eucharist through the institution of the Lord, we must confess that in her [i.e., the Church] there is a new visible and external priesthood, into which the old has been translated."[45] The content of the four chapters revolves around maintaining this sacrificial *potestas* in the face of Protestant attacks upon it.[46] But this is done, in large measure, by defining the authoritative mechanisms by which the power is conferred and utilized, hierarchically, sacramentally, and, in the case of the

---

45. The Latin text of the Doctrine and Canons on Orders can be found in Denzinger, *Enchiridion Symbolorum Definitionum et Declarationum de Rebus Fidei et Morum*, 33rd ed. (Herder, 1965), no. 1764ff. The Tridentine emphasis quickly became exclusive. It forms the sole substantive basis for the late-nineteenth-century Roman rejection of Anglican orders (see below). Even Vatican II, which reverted in several critical respects to many pre-Reformation construals of the ordained ministry, still understands the significance of the priesthood as fundamentally lying in its valid sacrificial functions. Cf. the opening of *Presbyterorum Ordinis* (I:2), on "The Nature of the Priesthood," which, quoting directly from the Tridentine decree, defines the priesthood in terms of those who receive the "sacred power of Order" (*potestas ordinis* in the language of Trent), which is that "of offering sacrifice" (as well as forgiving sins); the rest of the section is an attempt to link such sacrificial function to the sacrificial character of the Church joined with Christ's own "paschal" self-offering. In the Anglican–Roman Catholic International Commission statements, the fundamentally sacrificial character of the priesthood is decidedly muted, although by no means forgotten (cf. ARCIC I on "Ministry and Ordination," 12-13). But in interpreting the Eucharistic sacrifice as a sacramental remembering *(anamnesis)* of reconciliation, the commission shifted the priestly character into one of being a focus and servant of "unity" (cf. par. 12; also the statement on "Eucharistic Doctrine," par. 5-6, and "Elucidation," par. 5-6). That a stress on ministry as embodying reconciled unity does not strike the commission as a historical contradiction to their claim to "agree" on the ministry and to call for "mutual recognition" of ministries can be explained only through the fact that they are still working with an implicit linkage of valid ministry to valid celebration of the Eucharist (whether termed "sacrifice" or not). This is suggested by the statement's final discussion of "vocation and ordination" in terms of proper instrumentalities of conferral for the exercise of their functions (episcopal laying on of hands), which is stated in actual terms: "every individual act of ordination is therefore an expression of the continuing apostolicity and catholicity of the whole Church." The historical fact that episcopal ordinations take place and that priests preside at the Eucharist — whether in the Anglican or the Roman Catholic Church — then, trumps the historical fact that such ministries are not actually pursued in a state of unity, but rather in a state of maintained division. Apostolicity, then, even when the language of the *potestas sacramentalis* is not made primary, is still given in the formal means of structural connection.

46. The *anathemas* in the Canons on Order aim at Protestant denials of a "visible priesthood" with the "power to consecrate" or the power of the keys (Denzinger no. 1771); but this is seen to rely on the process of hierarchical ordination, rightly instituted and authoritatively carried through by bishops — that is, jurisdiction (cf. Denzinger nos. 1772-1778).

catechism, ritually. And even though the latter devotes several sections to the "dispositions" required for ordination, including integrity of purpose, moral rectitude, and basic knowledge of the Scriptures, these qualifications are made to depend upon a "divine call" that coincides with the proper jurisdictional exercise of the conferral of powers: "they are called by God who are called by the lawful ministers of His Church."[47] The actual validity of the ministry relies on nothing other than this "lawfulness"; and holiness of purpose, only vaguely limned with the residue of the caritative tradition, is left as an adorning appendage. In the end, then, even when the sacramental purpose and character of the Catholic priesthood is pressed against the Protestants, it is done in a way that displays the significance of the ministry within a framework of a valid instrumentality of conferral, just like de Sales.

Reformed Construals of Apostolicity: The Jurisdiction of Right Doctrine

The logical attraction of the jurisdictional model of ministerial apostolicity for the divided churches is demonstrated by the fact that the Reformers themselves adopted it, albeit in a way that contradicted much of the Catholic functional content. But both sides understood that only by putting weight upon the structurally visible aspects of the ministry could one church justify its separation from another; for thereby each church could uphold a formal measure of validity that it alone could attain.

Quickly implicated in Luther's attack on the popular penitential system of the Church was the atoning efficacy of the Eucharistic sacrifice, a connection that made necessary, in the light of his developing views on justification, a complete rethinking of a priesthood tied to such a sacrificial office. A good summary of his line of reasoning is given in his 1523 Latin treatise *Concerning the Ministry,* which he sent to the Bohemian church, then struggling for over a century to maintain a legitimate ministry despite lacking a consecrating episcopal presence.[48] In the wake of the Hussite controversy over reception of Communion in two kinds by the laity, the "utraquist" Bohemians sent their ministerial candidates to northern Italy for ordination by Catholic bishops there; on their return they would renounce whatever vows they had made to withhold the cup from the people.

---

47. *Catechism of the Council of Trent for Parish Priests,* trans. John McHugh, O.P., and Charles J. Callan, O.P. (New York: Joseph F. Wagner, 1923), pp. 318f.

48. English translation by Conrad Bergendoff in *Luther's Works,* vol. 40 (Philadelphia: Fortress Press, 1958).

Luther's purpose in attempting to rally the Bohemians to the side of the Reform was to deny the need for, even the legitimacy of, papally sanctioned ordination.

The nub of Luther's critique of the Roman Catholic ministry lies in the purported perversion of the sacrificial Mass its priesthood serves. Better to do without the Eucharist at all, which is not so important a sacrament in any case, he urges the Bohemians, than to taint one's ministry with participation in a rite that obscures and even denies the sufficiency of Christ's singular sacrifice. "Now as if his unique sacrifice were not enough, or as if he had not obtained an eternal redemption, they [the Roman priests] daily offer body and blood in innumerable places throughout the world. . . . This abomination goes beyond all reason." Ministers who serve the Mass's pseudosacrifice are simply not true ministers at all: "We see then, what kind of priests are created by papal ordinations — not indeed priests of God, but priests of Satan, such as trample down Christ and destroy his sacrifice. So it is no longer a question of whether one should seek or receive holy orders from the Papists, but it is a definite conclusion that no one confers holy orders and makes priests less than those under the papal dominion."[49]

What then constitutes a true Christian minister, in Luther's view? Having laid as a foundation for his argument the unique sacrifice of Christ, he takes this "priestly" self-offering of the Son, in the image of Hebrews, as the basis, through participation, for establishing the only valid human priesthood in terms of the priesthood of all baptized persons. The bulk of the treatise treats each of several traditional ministerial functions — for example, preaching the Word, baptizing, consecrating the Eucharist, forgiving sins, offering up prayers and "spiritual sacrifices," adjudicating doctrine — and insists that each function represents evangelical labors given to the whole body of believers. Ordination of particular ministers, then, cannot confer any special powers of the Spirit or provide any distinct and "indelible character" to an individual that is not already common to all Christians. Special ministers of the Word and sacraments are but delegates of the people, chosen and confirmed solely on the basis of their considered human capabilities; and ritual ordinations serve only to mark their designation.[50]

The actual capabilities of such a designated minister are measured in accordance with Luther's reevaluation of the significance of the Eucharist: no longer viewed in sacrificial terms, it is seen as a divine affirmation of a "promise" or "covenant" of the forgiveness of sins offered in Christ's sacrifice, to be laid hold of by the faith of the individual participant (hence it can have no benefits for others not present in faith). The minister who presides at this sacrament does not

49. *Luther's Works*, pp. 14f.
50. *Luther's Works*, pp. 36ff.

consecrate in an operative fashion; rather, he is an instrument of proclamation, a preacher, who presents to the people a message whose faithful apprehension alone is subjectively operative. Indeed, Luther insists that the ordained ministry is, essentially and exhaustively, a preaching ministry of the Word: "The public ministry of the Word, I hold, by which the mysteries of God are made known, ought to be established by holy ordination as the highest and greatest of the functions of the church, on which the whole power of the church depends, since the church is nothing without the Word and everything in it exists by virtue of the Word alone."[51] The validity of a ministry, then, is marked by the conformance of its proclamatory practice with the Word of the Gospel.

To be sure, such validity is manifested within the public structures of call and consent; and Luther, as with his advice to the Bohemians, encouraged formal means of popularly delegated election of ministers.[52] But the standard for such election remained that of the proper adherence and expression of the Word, apart from which even officially sanctioned ordinations had no legitimacy before God. This is a crucial point, for it provided the Reformers with just the exclusive alternative to the Roman stress on episcopal jurisdiction that was needed to justify the denial of the other's ministry, and so uphold legitimate separation. Papal priests, Luther wrote, were not really priests, but ministers of Satan, because of their perverted commitment to a doctrine contrary to the Word of God, that is, the sacrificial nature of the Mass. Were a priest ordained in the Roman Church to hold a correct view of the Eucharist, founded on a proper understanding of God's Word, however, such a person's ordination would indeed be valid.[53] Similarly, the power of jurisdiction held by any priest, or especially by any bishop, was legitimate and valid only to the extent that it was exercised in accordance with the Word of God; otherwise it was nullified.[54]

51. *Luther's Works,* p. 11. On the connection between Luther's view of the Eucharist and his reformulation of the nature of the ordained ministry on that basis, see *The Babylonian Captivity of the Church,* culminating in the comment, "the sacrament of ordination cannot be other than the rite by which the church chooses its preacher" (cf. the English version in *Martin Luther: Selections from His Writings,* ed. John Dillenberger [Garden City: Doubleday and Sons, 1961], pp. 270ff. and 340ff.). Cf. also Melanchthon's *Apology of the Augsburg Confession,* art. 13, where exactly the same connection is made, adding the stress upon the Word as written scriptural authority, over and against the pneumatic illuminism of the Anabaptists.

52. Cf. *Augsburg Confession,* art. 14: "Our churches teach that nobody should preach publicly in the church or administer the sacraments unless he is regularly called *(rite vocatus)*" (in *The Book of Concord,* ed. T. G. Tappert [Philadelphia: Fortress Press, 1959], p. 36).

53. Cf. *Concerning the Ministry,* p. 14.

54. Cf. *Augsburg Confession,* art. 28, and the *Apology,* arts. 14 and 28. Calvin's teaching on the matter was wholly congruent with this perspective. For a compact exposition of his views, see his 1554 letter to Sigismund Augustus, the King of Poland (English translation by M. R.

While baptisms performed by papist priests may be considered valid in retrospect,[55] the deliberate seeking out of such ritual actions only "polluted" participants with the same sin as the priests embodied, a sin expressing the pretense of a ministry and church where the failure rightly to affirm the Word of God meant that no real church and ministry in fact existed.[56]

The question of invalid ministries among the Papists was logically linked, of course, to a reappraisal of the meaning of ecclesial separation, the shape of which brings into relief the shift in the significance of the ministry that resulted from a condition of intrinsic division among the churches. Whereas schism had, for Aquinas, essentially caritative implications — it was primarily a sin against the charity embodied in the *unitas ecclesiastica,* from which heretical deformities of the faith might only potentially and not necessarily arise — for the Reformers its significance was bound up rather with the issue of "faith": one separated oneself, rightly or wrongly, from other Christians on the basis of right or wrong teaching. From the Reformers' perspective, obviously, the division of the Church that their attempt at ecclesial correction had engendered was the product of their own commitment to right teaching. And on that basis alone such separation was justified. Indeed, the unity of the Church is defined for the Reformers by right doctrine, as we have seen;[57] and therefore one cannot

Gilchrist in *Letters of John Calvin,* ed. Jules Bonnet [repr., New York: Burt Franklin Reprints], pp. 99ff.), in which he tries to persuade the king to engage in a reformation of the ministry. Given that papal priests are "false," "apostate," "abhorrent," and "dead" — the sacrificial character of their service being one notable area of their fall — one should steadfastly separate oneself from their ministries. Calvin advises the king to set up a new ministry, although only gradually: first, he is to send out through the kingdom "teachers of the Gospel," who would "sow seed" of the truth and so prime the land for a change; at an appropriate time, "a more definite manner of ordaining pastors might be established," which would regularize them according to good "order" of election and testing. His more extended treatment of these matters is contained in the *Institutes* IV:cc. 3, 5-8, 19 (art. 22ff.).

55. Not all Protestants, in fact, accepted Roman Catholic baptisms (just as there was some initial dispute among Roman Catholics about Protestant baptisms), though in general the Augustinian position on the validity of baptisms administered by heretics and schismatics was retained. Cf. 1560 Scottish *First Book of Discipline*'s invalidation of all sacramental acts by "Papisticall Preastis" (found in *Works of John Knox,* ed. David Laing [Edinburgh: Wodrow Society, 1846], vol. 2, p. 255), and the 1565 Assembly's instruction that Catholic baptisms be "reiterated" (in the *Booke of the Universall Kirk of Scotland* [Edinburgh: Maitland Club, 1839], vol. 1, p. 75). The stated grounds for invalidating Roman sacraments lay, not surprisingly, in the fact that they were not accompanied by the proper preaching of the Word.

56. Cf. the Reformed "French Confession" of 1559, art. 28, which also, in art. 31, refers to the "extraordinary" mission of Reformed ministers under the "present" circumstances, due to the illegitimacy of Roman orders.

57. E.g., Calvin's "Reply to Sadoleto."

properly speak of a true, that is to say, evangelically harmful, "division" of the Church, when the positive issue is true doctrine: those who adhere to the true faith *are* the true Church, and those who do not — in this case the Roman Catholics — are not the Church at all.

On this basis, it is just as impossible to raise a serious discussion as to the validity of divided ministries, apart from the foregone conclusion that the Christian ministry of the doctrinally aberrant is nonexistent.[58] Just as the reality of the integrity of the Church's unity had been reviewed in a manner that left the impetus of divine charity to the side, so did the ministry of the Church emerge as a function primarily uninformed by an imperative toward charitable upbuilding. The demand to maintain the integrity of a newly separated Christian body also demanded, by definition, the obscurement of that service of self-giving for the sake of the other by which the ministry might be a labor of perfective love for the whole. As with the Roman Catholic response to division, the Protestant reformulation of the ministry seized upon jurisdiction, the jurisdiction provided by the historical expression of right doctrine, as the commissioning sanction to orders, over and against the complex demands of caritative enactment.[59]

58. Cf. Calvin's 1543 *Necessity of Reforming the Church,* in which the power to ordain, and hence the status of a valid ministry, is tied to a conception of the Church's unity that is synonymous with the maintenance of right teaching: "No one, therefore, can lay claim to the right of ordaining, who does not by the purity of doctrine preserve the unity of the Church," in *Calvin: Theological Treatises,* trans. and ed. J. K. S. Reid (Philadelphia: The Westminster Press, 1954), p. 209. Cf. also the *Second Helvetic Confession* of 1566, generally the work of Bullinger, ch. 17, which while acknowledging the preferability of visible unity, traces visible dissension back to the historical foundation of the Church apostolically and ultimately asserts that the true Church does not essentially reside under the sign of such visible unity. Rather, since the true Church is embodied in conformity to "the lawful and sincere preaching of the Word of God as it was delivered to us in the books of the prophets and the apostles," it is the case that the visible history of the ecclesial communities will take the form of continuous separations from error, and that, ostensibly, the actual identity of the true Church will be discerned temporally and geographically only with difficulty. The "repudiation" of "papal priesthood from the Church of Christ" (ch. 18) does not, therefore, indicate the "abolition of the ministry," only the occasion of a new discernment as to the historical shift in validity according to doctrinal purity within a given ecclesial grouping.

59. Only a few Protestants wrestled with the caritative dimensions of ecclesial separation, an issue that only became apparent as dissensions internal to the Reform began to threaten the clarity of division from popish apostasy. Within England especially, the politically peculiar motive of maintaining a national ecclesial unity required new considerations when, for instance, the dangers of Puritan nonconformity surfaced in the latter part of the sixteenth century. Hooker, not surprisingly, offers an unusually broad acceptance of the Roman Church's ecclesial integrity, despite its many "errors": Catholics are to be considered truly a part of the

And, in a mirror image of Catholic appeals to the legitimacy offered by the formal apostolic structures of episcopal ordination, an appeal that swallowed the elements of perfective vocation into the connective integrity of such

---

visible Church of Christ, and, since the actual membership of the invisible Mystical Body of the elect is quite hidden from our view, they are to be treated as Christian brethren, members of the "family of Jesus," holding to the general "Christian profession of faith" and deserving of our "fellowship" and prayers of love. He sharply castigates Calvin's admonition against receiving popish baptism, and engages in a careful reflection on the nature of the commingling of truth and error within the visible Body of Christ, after the figure of sinful Israel: however much the nation harbors sinners, the people as a whole, inclusive of its individual members, remains "beloved" of God. Hooker's insistence upon Rome's continued ecclesial integrity here, however, is necessitated by the main argument of his own work against the Puritans: Anglicans can recognize Rome as "Church" despite the particularities of the latter's infidelities, and so must Puritans recognize Anglicans as such: "as there are which make the Church of Rome utterly no Church at all, by reason of so many, so grievous errors in their doctrines; so we have them amongst us, who under pretence of imagined corruptions in our discipline do give even as hard a judgment of the Church of England herself" (*Laws of Ecclesiastical Polity* III:10; see also 8ff. and IV:9). An irenical divine like John Hales, from a more humanist impulse of tolerance, as well as from his personal observation of the Reformed battles in Holland, also maintained a caritative orientation in his reflection on ecclesial division, moving from the Thomistic definition of schism as a sin against charity, to a description of schism that includes within it any separation due to a "matter of opinion," to an almost ironic argument that therefore virtually all separations among Christians fall under the condemnation due such sin (he does not mention Rome, except to defend the rights of recusants, but the reality hovers behind the text), precisely because it is hard to imagine anyone adjudicating what constitutes a "matter of opinion" from a "matter of necessity," except on the basis of opinion itself. Disagreement, even tumultuous controversy, according to Hales, does not constitute schism until "one party swept an old cloyster, and by a pretty art suddenly made it a church, by putting a new pulpit in it, for the separating party there to meet." How the Church of England itself was not implicated in such a definition is not clear; Laud obviously saw the problem, and promptly attacked Hales. See *A Tract Concerning Schism and Schismatics: Wherein Is Briefly Discovered the Original Causes of All SCHISM,* and his *Letter of Archbishop Laud,* in *The Works of the Ever Memorable Mr. John Hales of Eaton* (Glasgow, 1765), vol. 1, pp. 114-44. A moderate like Richard Field, however, could still speak of schism only in terms of unity, which, independent of a caritative core, is easily maintained even in divisiveness, as long as it is identified with right doctrine: if Luther and the English Reformers emerged from a true Church, insofar as it still contained those who adhered to the truth, the post-Reformation Catholic Church cannot be so considered, since now it exists in overt distinction from the Reformed churches, and so embodies a visible contradiction to the truth. "The Church [of Rome] that now is consisteth of such only as pertinaciously resist against the clear manifestation of the truth . . . so that they that lived heretofore might in their simplicity be saved, and yet these that now are perish in their contradiction and wilful resistance against the truth." They are a "faction" of the Church that is in it, but not of it, and in this sense, not truly "Church." Cf. his *Of the Church* (Cambridge: Ecclesiastical History Society, 1852), appendix to book IV, vol. 4, p. 523, and book I:15 and book III:5 and 6.

legitimated successions, Protestants reduced ministerial apostolicity to the organizationally formal confirmations of doctrinal integrity. Those who are commissioned of Christ to serve his Church in continuity with the apostolic character of his historical Body are those who are duly ratified by ecclesial delegates as having met the standards of appropriate doctrinal conformity. Apostolicity resides in the expression of the right interpretation of Scripture; and ministerial vocation is expressed in the official certification by a consistory that such interpretation is held on the part of an individual. Those who are not thus certified are not true ministers of the Church; and their lack of jurisdictional powers embodies their failure to know, believe, or teach sound doctrine. Out of these convictions grew the set of formal ordination structures of the Reformed churches, which subsumed, as with the Catholics, the significance of ministerial validity.

First, "apostolicity," as a technical concept, was deliberately retained by Reformers in the description of their ministries, but it was decoupled from episcopal ordination and linked instead to doctrinal purity. Calvin acknowledged that a visibly ordered succession of ministers from apostolic times might be something "to be wished for"; but he asserted that such an organizational succession had been broken on many occasions, especially by the "apostasy" of Rome. However, since the Church has indeed existed continuously from the time of the apostles and since "purity of doctrine is the soul of a church," the locus of continuity must lie not in the organizational instruments of conferral, but in the historical existence of a continuous preaching of right doctrine.[60] If one is to speak of "apostolic succession," which most Reformers granted one could do, then it was to be a "succession of doctrine." This conviction was stated by, of all people, an Anglican bishop, John Jewel, in concluding from the sins of Roman prelates: "Succession you say is the chief way for any Christian man to avoid Antichrist. I grant you, if you mean Succession of Doctrine."[61] Even at their most "high church," when granting the "apostolic" character of the visible ministry through the ages, Reformed theologians insisted that this character was given through divinely protected succession of the ministerial remnant who indwelt the corrupt structures of the Latin church.[62] If Luther himself could ordain new "bishops," as he did,

60. Cf. Calvin's letter to the King of Poland in *Letters of John Calvin*, passim, esp. p. 107.

61. See the discussion in James L. Ainslie, *The Doctrines of Ministerial Order in the Reformed Churches of the 16th and 17th Centuries* (Edinburgh: T. & T. Clark, 1940), pp. 208ff.

62. This was the position of the 1654 London Assembly in their *Jus Divinum Ministerii Evangelici*.

it was because the power of succession lay in doctrinal conformance, and not in office.

The valid ordering of this apostolic ministry of pure doctrine lay in its public confirmation, which, as with the Catholics, enveloped the perfective elements of vocation within the structural scaffolding of organizational certification, albeit according to criteria of teaching rather than of right office. The term "vocation" was in fact raised into a new relief among Protestants, and we shall return to look at some of its significance shortly. For the moment, it is enough to note that, within the context of the professional ministry, the divine commissioning in which the category of ministerial vocation is located became identified in practice with the structures by which the apostolicity of doctrinal teaching could be assured with respect to a given candidate. The Second Helvetic Confession expresses this common compaction of meanings under the rubric that "Ministers Are to Be Called and Elected":

> No man ought to usurp the honor of the ecclesiastical ministry . . . but let the ministers of the Church be called and chosen by lawful and ecclesiastical election; that is to say, let them be carefully chosen by the Church or by those delegated from the Church. . . . Not any one may be elected, but capable men distinguished by sufficient consecrated learning, pious eloquence, simple wisdom.[63]

In practice, the "call" and "election" came down to the process of "examination," by which individuals were tested in the knowledge of Scripture and doctrine and in their ability to preach with integrity on the basis of such knowledge.[64] When Luther himself set about organizing for the ordination of ministers, he called the service of ordination itself the "call" given by the community to the individual; but the service only confirmed the process of a preceding "examination" and formed a public affirmation of the doctrinal basis of the ministry to which the person was entering. Much of the ordination service is given over to the public description of the office in terms of its duties in opposing "false doctrine" and the heretical "wolves" set on leading people astray.[65] In conformity with the conviction that wrong doctrine made of Roman orders no orders at all, Catholic priests who wished to become ministers in Reformed churches were obliged to give evidence of a new "call," which,

---

63. In *Reformed Confessions of the 16th Century,* ed. Arthur C. Cochrane (Philadelphia: Westminster Press, 1966), p. 271.

64. Cf. Ainslie, pp. 147ff., with many references to actual method.

65. Cf. Luther's order for "The Ordination of Ministers of the Word," introduction and notes by Ulrich Leupold, in *Luther's Works* (1965), vol. 53, pp. 122ff.

however, came down to submission to a strict and often lengthy process of doctrinal "examination," following which they would be "ordained" (for the first time, since their previous orders were only pretended).[66]

The distinction between the Reformed vision of ministerial calling, which is grounded on the ability to teach sound doctrine, and the perfective element of charity that had once been infused into the Church's understanding of apostolicity is given clear expression in someone like Jean Claude's description of the "two calls": the first "call" belongs to all Christians by virtue of their baptism, the second belongs only to the official ministers of the church. What is the defining character of these two vocations? That of the Christian in general is to "faith and charity." But the ministerial vocation is not essentially defined by these, but rather by the pastoral functions of preaching, discipline, and administration of the sacraments.[67] Indeed, most Reformed churches accepted

66. See Ainslie, pp. 210ff., for examples from French and Dutch Reformed disciplinary canons. The "Donatist" character of these rules may seem obvious; although, as we shall see, the traditional condemnation of "reordination" is founded on the question of right "intention," and this is an interpretively difficult reality to nail down. Strictly speaking, if Roman Catholic "ordinations" were viewed as intentionally perverted — and, in Protestant minds, a sacrificial priesthood was, by definition, just such a perversion — then they were not real ordinations in the first place; there can be no question of "reordination," but only of an initial and proper ordination, in admitting former Catholic priests into the Reformed ministry. The issue of intention, among Protestants, was clearly located in the realm of the right doctrine held by those taking part in an ordination. When, for instance, the question arose in the wake of the English Civil War and then of the Restoration, of ordination received at the hands of Anglican bishops, the same dynamic was at play. First, Independents and Presbyterians were at odds as to whether Church of England episcopal ordinations by "anti-Christian" bishops were valid: the most moderate view held that they were, to the degree that they were intended for the preaching of the Word of God "according to the mind of Christ," a matter, clearly, of doctrinal intent, if not actual knowledge. But many Independents simply refused to accept Anglican ordinations at all. At the Restoration, most nonepiscopally ordained ministers refused Anglican (re)ordination precisely because the doctrinally pure intent of their original ordinations during the Commonwealth rendered them wholly valid. Cf. Ainslie, pp. 195f.

67. Jean Claude, *A Historical Defence of the Reformation* (English trans., London, 1683), pt. IV, p. 49, cited in Ainslie, p. 142. It is clearly a vast oversimplification to describe "Protestant" views of the ministry in ways that exclude altogether, or even for the most part, the perfective qualities of holiness. But except for marginal movements, like those of the Anglican Non-Jurors, Protestant ministry was never seen as intrinsically founded on the embodiment of holiness. Furthermore, "holiness" as a generally ascetic orientation is not what is at stake in the issue of ministerial apostolicity, but rather the holiness of an enacted love for neighbor within the body of the Church. The explicitly caritative dimension of apostolicity simply cannot be affirmed within the context of division. Cf. E. C. Miller's discussion of the seventeenth-century Scottish Episcopalian James Sibbald's vision of priestly holiness, given in a funeral sermon entitled "Holinesse to the Lord": Sibbald's admittedly remarkable openness to the transfiguring character

the anti-Donatist position that the evil life of a presiding minister does not touch the efficacy of the sacraments and preaching, precisely because doctrine as determined according to formal examination, and *not* holiness of living, founds ministerial validity.

The division of the post-Reformation churches, then, required a contraction of the notion of ministerial validity into two alternative readings of structural integrity: authorized episcopal ordination and examined doctrinal purity. Through the application of such a contraction the ministry of the other could be excluded. But some of the same logical ecumenical difficulties attending the scriptural hermeneutics of division attach to this way of redefining ministerial validity: on the Catholic side, a noncompromising exclusion is built in on the basis of formal rites — Protestant ministries cannot hope to be accepted except they enter the Roman succession; and on the Protestant side, the criterion of doctrinal purity without an accepted adjudicator of its substance demands a continuously fluid relationship with validity that necessarily shifts the affirmation of other ministries into an ideal sphere.

---

upon the whole of creation of the Incarnation and Redemption of Christ derives rather from a vital Eucharistic doctrine of patristic antecedents (see above) than from a clear vision of ministerial service in caritative sacrifice (E. C. Miller, Jr., "James Sibbald's Doctrine of the Priesthood in Ecumenical Perspective," in his *Toward a Fuller Vision: Orthodoxy and the Anglican Experience* [Wilton: Morehouse Barlow Co., 1984]). As with the Tractarians of two centuries later, the commitment to a doctrine of ministerial sanctification was necessarily divorced from ecumenical penitence, precisely because the commitment itself was forged in part as a tool of exclusivist justification within a nation of divided ecclesial allegiances. The contemporary practice of uncovering convergences of theology and spirituality among separated traditions — in the case just mentioned, between Anglicans and Eastern Orthodox — while it is often illuminating of surprising individual parallels, cannot stand as an ultimately effective scholarly arm of ecumenical rapprochement; for convergences of outlook within division do not mean the same thing as convergences within unity. Indeed, what exactly they *do* mean is rarely clear. Another chapter in Miller's book, treating William Palmer's nineteenth-century effort to reconcile Anglican and Russian Orthodox doctrine on the basis of anthologized convergences, only notes in passing the ultimate and ironical outcome to this kind of method: Palmer, long an anti-Catholic philo-Orthodox theologian, discovered that the historical reality of division determined that parallel theological lines never meet and that neither Anglican nor Orthodox structures could recognize a real ecclesial confluence within similar doctrine when, in fact, the churches had not lived as one for centuries. Rebuffed by both, Palmer later became a Catholic. Division is constituted by the historically enacted refutation of charity; whatever holiness may mean within the context of ecclesial division, Protestant, Orthodox, or otherwise, it cannot comprehend such caritative enactment, and is therefore, at root, a different holiness from the apostolic holiness encouraged by the "old fathers."

Overcoming Criteria of Exclusivity?
Attempts at a Reconciliation of Ministries

Of course, attempts at a reconciliation of ministries among divided churches, such as those noted earlier, seek to deal with just these two different exclusionary alternatives: through "agreed statements" on the theological meaning of the ministry and its evangelical presuppositions (in a narrow sense, doctrine), Protestants satisfy themselves as to the doctrinal purity of the Catholic side; as part of these statements, the affirmation of episcopal ordination as a doctrinally acceptable and, more importantly, practically necessary element of a reformed ministry satisfies the Catholics as to the readiness of Protestant groups to reconcile. In other words, reconciliation of ministries is possible if the original exclusionary criteria are deemed to have been met by the other side.

The historical interpretation of this new satisfaction varies, and is decidedly easier for the Protestants to accomplish: they are able to explain the positive shift in Catholic doctrine simply on the basis of a new evolution of learning on Rome's part, a process that had originally informed, in a negative sense, the Catholic corruption of doctrine standing behind the Reformation division. Just as, in Field's phrase, the unreformed Roman Church was "not what she had been" before Luther's ministry brought the truth to light and so made her errors damnably "pertinacious," so now the Catholic Church is no longer what she had been, in her doctrinal commitments, at the time of Trent. A change in doctrine retrieves Roman validity.

The Catholic recognition of Protestant ministerial validity, within the context of a reacceptance of episcopal ordination, is more complicated: given the exclusionary nature of the practice, it would not seem possible to accept Protestant ministries *until* they reemerge from the renewal of episcopal succession; and this is a conviction that, however evident, is not a conducive reconciling attitude in which to hold dialogue. Therefore, Catholic theologians have attempted to articulate various ways in which some kind of ministerial validity might be affirmed among Protestants churches outside the episcopal succession. These have been based either on an appreciation of the perfective qualities of Protestant pastoral practice (their ostensive "fruits"),[68] or, in conjunction with an avowal of limited doctrinal integrity in the Protestant understanding of the sacraments (the Eucharist in particular), on a theory that the Catholic Church has the power to grant a certain apostolic fullness to these

---

68. Cf. the Groupe de Dombes, par. 40, referring to phrases in Vatican II's Decree on Ecumenism, *Unitatis redintegratio* III:20-23.

Protestant practices, such as to receive them as a kind of valid prior basis for episcopal reintegration.[69]

But however serious the motives for this contemporary strategy of reconciliation, simply acknowledging that each church has now finally met the other's criteria for ministerial validity cannot be a satisfactory response to the reality of divided ministries, precisely because the criteria were devised, in the first place, in order to maintain separation. And their potential "satisfaction" is therefore problematic on at least two scores. First, because the criteria, in their constricted and exclusionary significance, are logically tied to the practice of division, their satisfaction must remain intrinsically unstable. From the Protestant side, any significant deviance from doctrinal purity will impel toward a new separation; while from the Catholic side similarly, any newly identified deformity of the instruments of ministerial conferral will demand division. Even before reconciliation of ministries has taken place, we can observe the divisive outcome of this instability at work in inter- and intra-denominational debates over the ordination of sexually active homosexuals and

69. One of the classic arguments for this line of reasoning was given by Maurice Villain, S.M., in, for example, "Can There Be Apostolic Succession outside the Chain of Imposition of Hands?," in Hans Küng, ed., *Apostolic Succession: Rethinking a Barrier to Unity,* Concilium no. 34 (New York: Paulist Press, 1968). Villain makes use of a Catholic principle known as *Ecclesia supplet,* corresponding in some measure to Eastern Orthodox notions of the "economy" of the Church, by which the sacramental fullness that resides in the Church can be extended to circumstances outside its formal embrace, for example, in cases of sacramental defect (in, e.g., marriage), where the presence of right intention forms the foundation upon which the Church "supplies" the fullness of the sacramental effect. Applying this principle to Protestant ministries is, he admits, a novelty, and it would represent a kind of retrospective appreciation of the validity of Protestant ministries once some form of current agreement on sacramental theology and episcopal ordination could be achieved. One cannot help but feel, however, that there is something purely strategic, and thus reliant on a kind of subterfuge, to this approach. For the demand that Protestants agree with Catholics on sacramental theology and reenter the episcopal succession would seem to make unnecessary any retrospective validation of ministry: they have, in this case, simply agreed to take hold of the Catholic ministry once again, where in the past they rejected. Villain himself indicates an opposite belief: since they never really lost their validity, Protestant ministries that reenter the episcopal succession are really only adopting a visible structure of communion that was never, on a sacramental level, actually absent: while "Protestant communities would then have to accept this sign [i.e., the episcopal succession] in order to mend the schisms, . . . on that day *the internal bond that had always existed in Christ will be made manifest in the fullness of light*" [italics added] (Villain, p. 104). The phrasing of this hope seems to reflect a sense that the ministries of Protestants and Catholics only "appeared" to be divided, but were not in fact, in which case the need for agreement in sacramental doctrine and ordination practice is essentially superfluous. For a related discussion, see Jean-Marie Thillard, "Le 'votum ecclesiae'. L'eucharistie dans la rencontre des chrétiens," in *Miscellanea Litugica in onore di S.E. il Card. G. Lercaro* (Paris: Desclée, 1967), vol. 2, pp. 143ff.

of women. At root, any reconciliation that is based on the meeting of formal criteria cannot constitute unity at all, but only a contractual agreement, in which each side maintains the right to judge the other party's maintenance of accepted standards. It bears no resemblance to, for instance, the figural unity given in the joining into "one flesh" of the Christ and his Church (Eph. 5:32) or of divine Father and Son (John 17:23).

In addition to the instability of such criterial satisfaction, the reconciliation of ministries on this basis is historically inadequate. It cannot address the question of the nature of continuity between the "invalid" ministries of the post-Reformation past and the "valid" ones of the contemporary ecumenical present. One is left, as we saw analogously in the case of divided scriptural hermeneutics, either with pronouncing the division of ministries to have been always only fictive and apparent, though not real, or with maintaining the invalidity of the other church's past ministries, which, if held mutually, would constitute a contradiction upon which there would be little basis for dialogue. In both cases, the simultaneous historical realities of division and of the ecumenical imperative are theologically decoupled and thereby rendered ancillary. In effect, there can be no real "history" of ministerial division on the basis of these criteria, only of a truncated unity from each perspective, because the "other" ministry is excluded from the status of true ministry from the start. By contrast, an appreciation of the caritative core of the ministry would make of an assaulted unity a history of ministerial failure whose continuities would extend to all parties in an inclusive fashion. The challenge of such a history, of course, is that it subverts the pneumatic integrity of modern ministries altogether. It is the same subversion, with all of its exacting historical demands, that insinuates itself into a general reflection on the pneumatic condition of a Church professing its Savior's love through a practice of exclusive affections within a disintegrated Body.

Beyond the Criteria of Exclusivity: Vocational Obscurement and the Figural Meaning of Divided Ministries

The real historical shape lying behind their ministries was, to be sure, one with which post-Reformation theologians struggled, much as they did in reflecting on the scriptural models informing the ecclesial reality of the Protestant-Catholic split. And, just as the self-justifying need to maintain division pinched their reading of Israel's ecclesial figure and its pneumatic character, so too did the exclusionary criteria of their ministerial evaluations tally well with con-

171

stricted applications of the figures of Israel's pneumatic leaders. Still, the search for the providential meaning of separated meanings was grounded in the Israel-figure of the Church, and the significance of ministerial invalidity was understood as given in the history of the Church's formation in its Old Testament type, proffered in Christ Jesus. To see the direction of this figural constriction in the post-Reformation is also to see the basis upon which a fuller reading of validity and invalidity in divided ministries can take place.

There was, naturally, a crude level on which the scrutiny of invalidity was pursued: ministers from opposing churches were simply explicated as tools of error, and hence of Satan. This was Luther's and Calvin's and many Catholic polemicists' standard impulse of opprobrium. If there was scriptural inflection to these insults, it relied on easy metaphors of deceitful enmity, like the "ravening wolves" of Matthew 7:15, sent in to destroy the flock of Christ, or the "robbers" of John 10:10.[70] But the figural similitude went deeper, even if the impulse was not always different. Luther himself could call upon a wide variety of Old Testament texts alluding to "false prophets" or to sinful sacrificers and scribes to characterize the significance of papal "mass priests," turning, like Calvin, even to the figure of Israel's division to locate their emergence within the midst of the nation's single character: for lack of real ministers, he noted, Jeroboam was forced to draw from the least competent strata of society, a reality reasserted in the papal church.[71]

The figure of the "false prophet," especially, proved the most common scriptural referent by which the existence of a perverted Christian ministry was explained historically. Each side interpreted the "falsity" in question, however, in terms of the particular criterion of validity employed. De Sales, from the Catholic side, easily assimilated his unveiling of Protestant "pretenses" at ministerial commission with a fulfillment of Jeremiah's prophecy (ch. 23) against his false counterparts:

> Your first ministers then, gentlemen, are of the prophets whom God forbade to be heard, in Jeremias: *Hearken not to the words of the prophets that prophesy to you and deceive you: they speak a vision of their own heart and not out of the mouth of the Lord. . . . I did not send prophets, yet they ran: I have not spoken to them, yet they prophesied. . . .* Does it not seem to you that it is Zwingli and Luther, with their prophecies and visions?. . . At any rate they certainly possess this property of not having been sent; it is they who use their tongues, and say,

---

70. Cf. the section on ordination in Luther, *Babylonian Captivity of the Church*.

71. Cf. Luther, *Babylonian Captivity of the Church*: "they [i.e. the 'priests of the Hours and Missals'] are exactly the kind of priests whom Jeroboam ordained at Bethaven, and whom he had taken from the lowest dregs of the people, and not from the tribe of Levi" (in Dillenberger, p. 346).

The Lord saith it. For they can never prove any right to the office which they usurp; they can never produce any legitimate vocation.[72]

The problem with Protestant ministers, a problem prophetically framed in the scriptural record, is that they enter into the midst of God's people, claim to speak in his name, yet they are not truly sent.

Not surprisingly, the Protestants saw in the pseudoprophetic figure a sign of justification for separation from error, and the emphasis of their exegesis falls on the invalidation that false teaching in particular must place upon any alleged ministry and the duty of the people to distance themselves from it.[73] Protestant polemicists, perhaps in view of the Catholic use of the figural argument from illegitimate commission, tended to appeal, in their typology of doctrinal error, to Old Testament condemnations of falsity deriving from perverted members of the specifically sacerdotal order.[74] And, as time went on and the break with Rome required less evangelical support because already socially entrenched, the interpretive ground for separation provided by the Old Testament became less pertinent: the distinction between Reformed and Roman was less obviously one of true Israelite and false Israelite, within a single Body, but of Israelite and Canaanite, a confrontation no longer between a divided people, but between incompatibly dissimilar ethnicities.

Even at the outset of the Reformation divisions, however, it appeared impossible for the contending parties to keep hold of the larger figure of the Church-as-Israel within which to assess the presence of falsehood among its leaders: the logical pressure of the division was consistently exerted in the direction of ejecting the offending group from any essential connection with the nation, on the pretext, always, of their having themselves rejected the proper jurisdictional subjection to the nation's authorities. Division *derived* from illegitimate authority, it did not engender it. It is significant that schism itself was often explicated by the figure not of a corruption of legitimacy, but of a revolt against a prevailing (and continuous) jurisdiction of authority, a figure given in the episode of Korah and Dathan (Numbers 16 and Jude 11).[75] Catholics like de

---

72. De Sales, Discourse 6, p. 31.

73. Actually, this reality is more frequently addressed in terms of New Testament passages of warning on the topic. Cf. *Apology for the Augsburg Confession,* art. 7 and 8, in *Book of Concord,* p. 177.

74. Cf. *Apology for the Augsburg Confession,* art. 22, p. 238, on Ezekiel 7:26 ("The law perishes from the priest"), or Luther, *The Babylonian Captivity,* on Hosea 4:6 ("Because thou hast rejected knowledge, I will also reject thee, that thou shalt be no priest to me") (in Dillenberger, p. 246).

75. The episode is given as a figure for schism most prominently in the tradition in

Sales, then, speak of schism in terms of an improperly self-arrogated authority (always in the context of episcopal succession), after the figure of the rebels against Moses' leadership,[76] while Protestants took the same figure as an explication for schism, now in terms of an apostasy tied to the illegitimate scorning of authoritative direction, particularly the Scriptures.[77] In all of this, though, the figure of Israel beset by false leaders is never rendered whole, because falsity is excluded *a priori* from a description of the nation's, and thus the Church's, internal integrity. History cannot impinge on the ideal; nor can the ideal render history.

Calvin gives a splendid example of this tendency. He follows the general Protestant pattern of reading the Old Testament figures of the false prophets in terms of their doctrinal error and in connection (even identity) with the corrupted sacerdotal office of the sacrificing priesthood, fulfilled in the priesthood of the Roman Catholic Church.[78] The criterion of ministerial validity is consistently presented as the pure Word of God, given in the Scriptures of the Law, the Prophets, and the Gospel.[79] What then is the significance of ecclesial division? Calvin admits that people are confused when they see purportedly Christian groups engaged in controversy one with another, each claiming special divine authorization for their affirmations. How can anyone know who is speaking the truth? Is not the very concept of a true church contradicted by intra-Christian antagonisms? But the problem of division, Calvin assures his listeners, is only apparent: those who rely on the Word of the Scriptures can easily see who are the true and who are the false prophets. Indeed, an appeal to Scripture easily proves the lie to papal pretensions.[80] Those who worry about the epistemological quandary incited by Christian division are in fact those who have decided to ignore the direction God has given them, and have so proved their own implication in the lie of God's enemies. Ultimately, Calvin carries this reasoning to the point of demanding a temporal ratification for the denial of such divisional pretense, by arguing that the false prophets of the Old Testament represent those promulgators of error within the Church — "heretics" — who deserve physical eradication.[81] The form of the false prophet, then, serves as an instrument to contradict any capacity the Old Testament figure might have to refer to the Church as a whole.

Cyprian's *De Unitate* 18. The illustration there, however, decidedly points to the subversion of charity, not jurisdiction.

76. De Sales, Discourse 63, p. 215.

77. Cf. Calvin's long discussion of the incident in his *Harmony of the Books of Moses*. Cf. also Field, book III:5, p. 162.

78. Cf. Calvin, *Commentary* on Jeremiah, on 23:11.

79. Calvin, *Commentary* on Jeremiah, on vv. 16, 22.

80. Calvin, *Commentary* on Jeremiah, on v. 16.

81. Calvin, *Commentary* on Zechariah, on vv. 2 and 3.

The overwhelming power of this ostracistic premise for Calvin's exegesis appears when, in the course of a discussion on the false prophets and pastors fulfilled in the Roman Church, he comes upon a text traditionally understood as a messianic reference, like Zechariah 13:6, "and if one asks him [i.e., the rejected prophet], 'What are these wounds on your back?' he will say, 'The wounds I received in the house of my friends.'" The following verse (7: "'Awake, O sword, against my shepherd, against the man who stands next to me,' says the LORD of hosts. 'Strike the shepherd, that the sheep may be scattered; I will turn my hand against the little ones'") is partially quoted by Jesus in Matthew 26:31, at his Passion, as a fulfilled reference to his own disciples' abandonment of him. But if Zechariah is speaking pointedly to a nation — or Church — from whom heretical prophets and pastors must be excluded as being no prophets at all, and if it is this salutary process of exclusion that gives the historical appearance of ecclesial division, what is one to make of the traditional messianic interpretation of these verses? Calvin, in effect, dispenses with them altogether. He deems an application of verse 6 to Christ as "puerile," since, if the context is clearly about false prophets, there can be no joining of them to Christ. When he comes to verse 7, given its incontrovertible messianic application by Jesus himself, Calvin begins to stutter. It is "suitable" that the Christ be envisaged in this text, since "all the Prophets spoke by his Spirit," he writes, but what the significance of this application is he never says. Indeed, verse 7 is as illogically read in terms of Christ as verse 6, according to his reasoning. And to avoid this obstacle, he quickly lets drop this passing messianic potential in the text, and continues to hammer away at the fact that God appears to punish the Church when he removes from them those leaders who, through their error, are his enemies. The rest of Zechariah 13 simply falls into place according to this scheme, as Calvin uses the chapter to present a standard "remnant" theory about the Church and its reformation.[82]

The logic of exclusion, which upholds the practice of ministerial division, then, makes impossible a Christically figural reading of these kinds of Old Testament texts. In an exegete like Calvin, for whom the Old Testament's messianic *scopus* was a fundamental presupposition, the separatist disabling of this interpretive practice is especially glaring. Not, of course, that prophecies dealing with religious leadership, like Jeremiah's and Zechariah's, were especially clear-cut in their ecclesial significance in the pre-Reformation tradition. But, consistent with a pattern we have already seen at work, there is a marked shift in the Old Testament texts' figural capacity brought about by the ecclesial

82. Calvin, *Commentary* on Zechariah, on vv. 6 and 7.

division of the sixteenth century. Jerome's figuratively conservative reading of Jeremiah 23, for instance, still saw the whole Church as prophetically implicated in the condemnation of the false prophets and priests, and the ostracistic premise of the post-Reformation is absent in favor of a call to ministerial repentance.[83] Similarly, when Gregory Nazianzus looks at Zechariah 13, he presents a complex interweaving of warnings against the Christian priesthood, contrasted with these threats' removal in the sole just priest, who is Jesus. Gregory's mixture of perfective warnings and messianic fulfillments in his reading of the text demonstrates an unresolved interplay of referents that has as its point the promotion of a fearful acknowledgment of his own involvement in the sins of the Church's leadership.[84]

As a whole, the pattern of pre-Reformation exegesis saw the failure of ministry in the Old Testament as a figural reference to a Church whose continued corporate integrity demanded that all priests find their own ministries implicated in the warnings and condemnations. And if the exegetical context of ecclesial integrity meant that the "falsity" of the prophets depended on the falsity of the Christian reader's self whose ministry was confronted by the scriptural word, then a place for Christ's own figural role in the problem of defective ministry was necessarily given. For, as Gregory hinted, when the condition of the ministry is measured by the traditional perfective criteria of righteousness and holiness, then its corruption stands in the same relationship to God as the human condition in general: it requires not ostracism or separation, but redemption, in the form of the One who alone is righteous and holy. In terms of the prophecies of a Jeremiah or a Zechariah, the historical meaning of a corrupted ministry is therefore explicated in terms of its figural conformance to the suffering of the Christ. The false shepherds and the Good Shepherd cohere in the latter's punishment on their behalf.

Were the post-Reformation division of ministries to be read in this light, the exclusivist impulses upholding those divisions would no longer be tenable, and the divisions themselves would have to take their place within the general pattern of corruption by which the different parties ostensibly justified them. In this case, the figural shape of particular separated ministries, on all sides, would have to be gleaned from just those prophetic elements that controversialists had applied exclusively to their opponents alone. The interpretive framework for this kind of explication is, of course, that which supports the

---

83. E.g., in his *Commentary* on Jeremiah.

84. Gregory of Nazianzus, Oration 2, 62-63. In the wake of Jesus' use of the prophecy in Matthew 26, the text and its context received a consistent messianic application. Cf., e.g., the early prophetic *catena* in something like the *Epistle of Barnabas,* ch. 5.

judgment of pneumatic abandonment upon the divided Church as we have outlined it earlier; and it provides a prophetic resolution only through the form of the abandoned Christ. With respect to the question of the ministry specifically, the significance of its division is given in the character of denunciation uttered by the prophets against their own colleagues, now granted its Christian coherence through the integrating figure of, in the crucial text of Zechariah, the stricken Shepherd, in whom the failure of all other shepherds is gathered.

The question of the particular corruption instanced by a dividing of ministries can be left unanswered for the moment, as long as we see that the pneumatic effects of an inclusive judgment against the ministry of opposing Christian bodies will prove to be a species of the larger genus of ecclesial abandonment we have encountered earlier. Confining ourselves only to Jeremiah, we see these effects as both joined to and derivative of particular sins, including idolatry (32:32-34), misleading the people (23:14), and moral corruption (e.g., financial injustice, adultery — 6:13; 23:14). The culminating transgression of these prophets, however, lies in their unwillingness, and ultimate incapacity, to enunciate their own and the people's own inclusion in God's judgment, affirming the integrity of their ministry in conjunction with the people's condition in the famous refrain of "peace, peace" when there is none in fact (8:11, etc.). In the common pattern, more sinning is given as punishment to initial sinning, and the false pronouncement of peace gives rise to an actual inability to distinguish the truth. Thus, tied to these acts of unfaithfulness lies a further realm of "darkness, into which they shall be driven and fall" (23:12), which is formed by the emptying of the prophets' and priests' ostensive commission. Their words "fail" (4:9), they become "wind" (5:13), and their prophecies and prayers are made utterly ineffective (27:10-18).[85] All of this stands in parallel with the forms of pneumatic deprivation described elsewhere as afflicting the people as a whole.

In the case of the ministerial leadership of Israel, however, the category in which these effects of pneumatic abandonment is most frequently described is that of obscured, and indeed destroyed, "vocation." In an oft-cited verse in the post-Reformation polemic about the ministry, Jeremiah gives the Lord's judgment that "I did not send the prophets, yet they ran; I did not speak to them, yet they prophesied" (23:21; cf. v. 32). The point here is not simply that the "false" prophets are mere imposters, "usurpers" in the later language of the divided Church. Their sin, joined to that of the priests, is that they *are*

---

85. On this divinely ordered "ineffectiveness," see the discussion in Ronald Manahan, "A Theology of Pseudoprophets: A Study in Jeremiah," *Grace Theological Journal* 1, no. 1 (Spring 1980): pp. 92ff.

prophets and priests, who yet do not follow the true leading of God, and who thereby experience their commission as veiled and silenced. And in this, their loss of direction both mirrors and carries along with it the fall of the entire nation, as the persuasive character of their ignorance turns into an instrument of divine retribution.

Indeed, the loss of vocation comes to embody the descriptive center of what a prophet and priest have become in divided Israel: dedivinized ministers bereft of a godly commission and consigned to the self-motivated purposes of purely human discernment. Jeremiah himself is left to untangle and wonder at the actual direction of God's commands, at one point accusing God of deliberately misleading the people with prophetic promises of peace (4:10), and later, in his controversy with Hananiah, giving up any pretense to possessing a criterion of truth outside of its plain future confirmation, a temporal proof starkly shorn of any intrinsically divine figure. Far from evidencing Calvin's faith in the discriminating power of the right reading of Scripture to discern true from false ministers, or de Sales's appeal to the authorizing powers of the formal hierarchy, Jeremiah's picture of Israel's religious leadership is one in which only future outcomes can illuminate truth, and present ministries all fall into the shadows of groping and contested human powers. While the questions of commission and vocation determine the validity of leadership, it is a question that is deliberately — in the providential sense — left without a present answer.[86]

These specifically vocational effects of pneumatic abandonment of the ministry were already acknowledged by the Christian tradition, exclusively and antagonistically in the post-Reformation, as we have seen. They were also granted in a more general way in the pre-Reformation, in classic expositions like those of Gregory the Great.[87] But the specific *problem* of ministerial

---

86. For a concise sociohistorical version of this reading of Jeremiah, all the more compelling because it states so clearly as a literary-sociological problem what has always been figurally embedded in the text, see R. P. Carroll, "A Non-Cogent Argument in Jeremiah's Oracles against the Prophets," *Studia Theologica* 30 (1976): pp. 43-51. Carroll stresses how the argument between Jeremiah and the "pseudoprophets" he criticized could have no logical resolution given that God's own abandonment of his authorized leaders rendered obscure the appeal to legitimacy. Cf. his comment that "the idea of Yahweh misleading the prophets and stupefying them (cf. Is. 29:10) and causing the people to err (cf. Is. 63:17) made the prophetic mediation of the divine will a danger for any society" (p. 49), and "thus in the life and times of Jeremiah we see virtually the death throes of the type of prophetic stance typified by Amos and Isaiah" (p. 50).

87. Cf. the famous opening to his *Pastoral Rule*, I:1-2, in which the parallel verse in Hosea (8:4) is used as an organizing sentence: "they have reigned, and not by Me; they have been set up as princes, and I knew it not."

vocation as an unanswered and potentially unanswerable question, in the figural framework given by Jeremiah, did not emerge in an insistent fashion until the Reformation and post-Reformation, largely because the division of ministries constituted in itself for the first time an inescapably ecclesial counterpart to the confusion of legitimated leadership first typified in the demise of divided Israel. The critical character of the problem of vocation, however, was paradoxically demonstrated in the manner in which it was deliberately, if unconsciously, translated from the contested Old Testament figures of ecclesial corruption into the realm of ecclesiastical procedure.

The literature on Luther's and Calvin's important reflections on vocation is extended, and the critical role accorded this theme in their theologies need not concern us here.[88] What should be emphasized is simply the way that, however much the concept of vocation was elevated in Protestant thought within the sphere of the general Christian life, it was correspondingly constricted within the specifically ministerial sphere, precisely because the exclusivistic needs in justifying a divided ministry demanded a narrow appeal to structural apostolicity. Luther, for instance, had made much of rejecting the claim to a special monastic vocation insofar as it seemed to derive from the idolatrous desire to earn one's salvation on the basis of fulfilling a higher and more "perfect" calling. His concern had some foundation; and the distortions of the monastic vocation to perfection, a view of the religious life we have already noted in relation to Aquinas's understanding of the ministry, were ones that Luther understood on a personal and practical level. Perfection, Luther came to insist, was a calling common to all Christians, and also one that could be accomplished only through adhesion in faith to Christ's perfection. Any perfective element of the ministry, then, was shifted over to the general Christian vocation, and aspects peculiar to the ministry's enacted conformative character were denied or ignored. The specific "call" to ministry was reduced, practically, to the authorized certification of doctrinally articulate capacities, whose adjudication could maintain distinctions between true and false priesthoods. The same holds true for Calvin, whose consistent affirmation of a necessary "inner call" from God for the ministry was just as consistently subjugated to the discriminating powers of ecclesial examination.

---

88. With respect to the immediate subject, for Luther see his *De votis monasticis,* Church Postil on 1 Corinthians 7:20, and references and discussion in Karl Holl, "The History of the Vocation *(Beruf)*" (orig. 1924), Eng. translation in *Review and Expositor* 55 (1958): pp. 126ff., and in Gustaf Wingren, *Luther on Vocation,* trans. Carl C. Rasmussen (Philadelphia: Muhlenberg Press, 1957), pp. 1-14, esp. 171ff. On the rejection of monastic vows, see also art. 27 of the *Augsburg Confession,* and the *Apology.* On Calvin, see his *Institutes* III:6:2; 24:10-11; IV:3:10-16, and, in the context of the previous discussion, his *Commentary* on Jeremiah on 23:21.

Of course, Aquinas had distinguished the ordained ministry from the monastic vocation specifically on the basis of the former's caritative character. And it was the burdens of such demanded service in love that bishop or, derivatively, priest must enact that precluded the functioning of a "perfective call" in the sense that Luther rejected. One could never "desire" such an office, in human terms; hence, the discernment of its appropriateness could not be gauged on the basis of either human attraction — for example, for merit — or human will. The ministerial vocation, in Aquinas's traditional view, was only a retrospectively confirmed life of self-giving, whose validity was given in the recognized fruits of apostolic conformance. It is just because *this* notion of vocation could not be adapted to a situation where ecclesial separation demanded immediate and exclusivistic confirmation, in a form that antithesized the caritative function of subjection, that anything other than a purely structural view of calling was banished from an understanding of the ministry, on both Protestant and Catholic sides. There must be vocation if there is to be valid ministry; but in a context of contested validity, such vocation could only be located in the discriminating forms of organized ecclesial divisions, the hierarchy or the consistory.

Vocational Obscurement as a Post-Reformation Bequest

Were Christians to maintain the integrated figure of divided Israel's loss of prophetic commission, tied as it was to a general failure in holiness, clearly the problem of vocation would appear practically unresolvable, because divinely obscured. One of the few examples of this dynamic, intolerable to the sustenance of contested ministries, grew out of the rigoristic impulses of the post-Tridentine Catholic reform; and the deep ambivalences informing this instance serve as an indicator to the vocational turmoil at the heart of the divided Church. The reforming aims of Trent had included as a central element the revival of the priesthood and the elimination of abuses associated with it, long familiar from pre-Reformation critiques of the ministry[89] and their sharp crystallization among the Reformers themselves. The perfective elements of the priesthood were reaffirmed, including divine vocation, personal holiness, and Christian knowledge,[90] and numerous and serious efforts were made to apply these standards

---

89. Cf. the detail offered on the needs for and forms of clerical reform in the later Middle Ages, in Paul Adam, *La vie paroissiale in France au XIVe siècle* (Paris: Sirey, 1964), pp. 279-314.

90. See, for instance, the Council's *Catechism,* in the section on "Orders," which refers, familiarly, to the Jeremiah 23:21 text.

within dioceses of Italy, Spain, and especially France.[91] This approach could make sense, obviously, within a perspective that nullified the Protestant churches and that applied the scriptural figures of vocational obscurity in an exclusivist fashion. But when these same reformist aims took shape, as they did with someone like the abbé Saint-Cyran, within a perspective sustained anachronistically, to a large degree, by the integrated figural framework of the undivided Church, the perplexing status of divine vocation came to the fore.

The reform of the priesthood was at the center of Saint-Cyran's energetic vision for the renewal of the Church, a concern he shared with many of his contemporaries, from Jansenius to Bérulle to Vincent de Paul. And like them, he affirmed, unequivocally, that a renewed priesthood required its exclusive restoration on the foundation of genuine "vocations" from God.[92] Whatever Trent had advised fifty years earlier, the practice of entering orders for the sake of benefices, political ambition, or parental exigency was still widespread. But a priest is meant to be a "saint," according to the tradition Saint-Cyran shared, and without divine grace promised through God's actual call heeded, such sanctification is an impossibility.[93] The ordination of so many "uncalled" priests, lacking in the

91. For an overview that deals with synodical and diocesan efforts, described mainly in terms of the work of individual reformers and their writings, see Paul Broutin, S.J., *La Réforme pastorale en France au XVIIe siècle: Recherches sur la tradition pastorale après le Concile de Trente*, 2 vols. (Tournai: Desclée & Cie., 1956). Broutin usefully places these efforts within the context of the general post-Tridentine Reform. See, for a more sociohistorical summary, Philippe Loupès, *La vie religieuse en France au XVIIe siècle* (Paris: Sedes, 1993) pt. 2; cf. too Jean de Viguerie, *Le Catholicisme des français dans l'ancienne France* (Paris: Nouvelles Éditions Latines, 1988), chs. 5-8. On vocation specifically, see Jean de Viguerie, "La vocation religieuse et sacerdotale en France aux XVIIe et XVIIIe siècles. La théorie et la réalité," in *La vocation religieuse et sacerdotale en France. XVIIe-XIXe Siècles: Actes de la deuxième rencontre d'Histoire Religieuse à Fontevraud le 9 octobre, 1978* (Angers: Université d'Angers — Centre de Recherches d'Histoire Religieuse et d'Histoire des Idées, 1979).

92. On Saint-Cyran's views of the priesthood, see Jean Orcibal, *La Spiritualité de Saint-Cyran avec ses écrits de piété inédits* (Paris: J. Vrin, 1962), pp. 50ff. and 104ff. Pages 208ff. contain previously unedited primary source material on the topic. I shall be referring particularly to letters contained in the later posthumous collection of 1744 (Saint-Cyran, *Lettres chretiennes et spirituelles de Messire Jean Du Verger de Hauranne, Abbè de S. Cyran*, 2 vols.), which contains, among other things, correspondence on the priesthood with Arnauld and M. de Rebours and an important treatise on the priesthood addressed to A. M. Guillebert.

93. The priest's demanded sanctity has nothing to do with the merits accorded to his perfective state, as in the monastic model Luther condemned, but depends solely on the duties of service to the people of God which require holiness of life for their fulfillment. Cf. Saint-Cyran, vol. 1, p. 142: "as for the greatness and importance of the parish priest's work, there is nothing in the Church that can be compared to it. Even the bishop's work is no different, although, in its shared form, it is more eminent and superior to the priest's, upon which the latter depends. This

intention and divine supports for virtue, is the ruin of the Church — it under-
mines pastoral care (through priestly nonresidence), subverts baptism (through
the propagation of moral laxity, and therefore gross sin, before communion), and
destroys charity (through its permission of evangelical insouciance). While these
attitudes have become associated with the "Jansenism" of Saint-Cyran's followers,
they were, by and large, shared by the rigorist community of most post-Tridentine
reformers.[94] Further, most of the ascetical elements informing this conception of
priestly sanctity's expression were received from the consistent Patristic and
medieval commentary on the topic. What was novel, for all concerned, was the
special emphasis given to vocation itself.

In discussing the shape of priestly vocation in particular, Saint-Cyran's
general approach stuck to standard themes. Unlike the monastic call, an
authentic ministerial vocation was evidenced in an experienced struggle of
distaste and "repugnance" against entering the priesthood.[95] It was to be
discerned, really, only retrospectively in the agony of service to others.[96] And
finally, as such, authentic vocation could only be characterized as a complex
interplay of "interior" and "exterior" calls, whose actual resolution lay in the
historical enactment of submission to the demands of ecclesial *diakonia*, enunciated by the hierarchy.[97]

---

is why I have repeatedly said that the least parish priest can in no way fulfill his duty unless he
becomes holy, before men and before God." Cf. Saint-Cyran, p. 195. On the priesthood as a
consequent "reward for virtue," see Saint-Cyran, vol. 2, pp. 493ff.

94. Cf. Broutin. This view of priestly sanctity and vocation, in fact, entered the mainstream of literary description through the oratorical brilliance of many prominent non-Jansenists
like Vincent de Paul, or later, in the early eighteenth century, Massillon. Cf. especially the latter's
many earnest, yet rhetorically stunning, discourses to seminarians and priests of his diocese, for
example, "Discours sur l'Excellence du Sacerdoce," "Discours sur la vocation à l'Etat Ecclésiastique," "Discours à des Jeunes Gens, sur la vocation à l'Etat Ecclésiastique," "Retraite pour les
Curés," "Discours sur la Nécessité où sont les Ministres de se renouveler dans l'Esprit de leur
Vocation," all in *Oeuvres* (Paris: Dufour et Ce., 1825), vols. 10 and 11.

95. Saint-Cyran, *Lettres,* vol. 1, pp. 20, 24ff.; vol. 2, pp. 661ff.

96. Saint-Cyran, *Lettres,* vol. 2, pp. 577ff.

97. Saint-Cyran's emphasis on the general need to follow the "interior movement" of the
Holy Spirit has been pointed out as unusual, and the advice was an important part of his
description of priestly vocation. Yet this pneumatic (and allegedly "illuminist") element of his
thinking was not really so untraditional (cf. Aquinas's remarks on monastic vocation), and in
practice was, as with most Catholics, interpreted through the authoritative guidance offered by
the official Church. Saint-Cyran exemplified the developing confessional methods of his times
in that he placed great weight on the discerning role of the spiritual "director," and he expands
the self-scrutinizing meditative aspect of this relation by asserting the need for at least two years
of "retreat" before a decision about vocation be reached; but this was always linked to hierarchical
legitimation. Cf. Saint-Cyran, *Lettres,* vol. 1, pp. 8, 24ff., 51ff., 84ff.

But unlike many of his contemporaries, Saint-Cyran brought to this standard perspective at least two more peculiar convictions, both of which helped to define his contribution to later Jansenist views on the nature of the Church and the Christian life more broadly. They also cloud the ordered clarity, at least in its expression, of vocational discernment as the post-Tridentine rigorists presented it. The first conviction concerned a historical evaluation of the Church's condition. Saint-Cyran held to a radically pessimistic account of the Church's temporal development, which had much in common with Reformed judgments on the "decline" of ecclesial health since the time of the Fathers. Saint-Cyran differed profoundly from the Reformers, however, in viewing this decline in terms of the whole ecclesial body; he had no recourse to theories of a holy "remnant," as Protestants did, who pointed to the existence of invisible members of the Church of the Saints who, during the long period of corruption, maintained the continuity of the apostolic tradition. Rather, for Saint-Cyran, the history of the Church's decadence is a history of a general disease, analogous to Augustine's "aging world" now applied to the Christian body. The only way to make sense of such a "catholic" corruption was to view it in a figural perspective, according to which the continuity of the Church's apostolic life, however vitiated, was redemptively subsumed in the form of the Lord's life, whose Body in time the Church is. This figural perspective is just what Saint-Cyran's vision both demanded and sprang from. And an integral part of that figural vision was described by the history of the priesthood and the perfective vocation of the Church as a whole: the Christian people, instead of maintaining and growing in holiness, had slowly drifted from the divine call to be "perfect as your Father in heaven is perfect," a devolution supported and expressed by a weakening of penitential rigor and an increasing disdain for true priestly vocation.[98]

The second unusual (though hardly novel) conviction Saint-Cyran brought to his understanding of vocation was the more fundamental Augustinian priority given to the motive and act of love in the Christian life. Augustine's notion of the "two loves" — that all human action springs from either love of the flesh or love of God and that only actions directed in love toward God escape the condemnation of sin — had become problematic in the wake of its critical appropriation by the Reformers; and it was among the condemned propositions associated with Baius in 1567 and with the Jansenist Quesnel in 1713.[99] But the doctrine of the two loves held a determining place in Saint-Cyran's theology, which viewed the whole summary of the Christian under-

---

98. Saint-Cyran, *Lettres,* vol. 1, pp. 44ff., 55ff.
99. Cf. propositions 16, 34, and 38 of Baius, and propositions 44-47 of Quesnel.

standing of creation and redemption as the human creature's movement "in all things to God through love."[100] In the Augustinian scheme, such love was possible to the fallen creature only through the active energizing of the heart and will by the Holy Spirit, a personal presence in the soul identified with both grace and its divinely wrought embodiment, love itself.[101]

With respect to the priesthood, the theological key that this Augustinian conception of love provided gave access, in Saint-Cyran's teaching, to a focused restoration of the caritative character of ministerial apostolicity. This took the form not only of an underlining of the aspects of personal service on behalf of others in the Church, but also of an elevation of the ascetical elements of enacted contemplation, practices by which the priest could divest himself of distractions and adhere to God, and so draw others with him. The caritative unity of these two sides, service and asceticism, was never questioned, and the practices associated with each category are regarded as equivalent and connected expressions of the same love, for example, through the discipline of study, of generosity, of justice, of prayer, of poverty, of teaching, and so on.[102]

Taken together, Saint-Cyran's convictions concerning the figural decline of the Church and the salvific ground provided by a pure love tended in practice to eviscerate the possibility of discerning true vocations, as the rigorist program of reform demanded. For now, in the present state of the Church's life, the

100. Cf. the opening of Saint-Cyran's simple treatise on *Le Coeur Nouveau,* or the section ("lesson 9") on "charity" in his *Theologie familiere, ou Breve explication des principaux Mysteres de le Foy,* both found in *Theologie familiere, Avec divers autres petites traitez de devotion* (Paris, 1647). Again, this was neither novel nor heretical in itself, nor has this governing perspective simply lapsed; cf. the close to the prologue of the recent *Catechism of the Catholic Church* (25), which quotes from the *Catechism* of the Council of Trent ("all the works of perfect Christian virtue spring from love and have no other objective than to arrive at love"). The issue at stake in the censure of the Augustinian version of this principle was its exclusive formulation, which seemed to demand a rigorist denial of redemption to the Christianly fallible. Cf. Leszek Kolakowski, *God Owes Us Nothing: A Brief Remark on Pascal's Religion and on the Spirit of Jansenism* (Chicago: University of Chicago Press, 1995), pp. 86-110.

101. Cf. the advice he gives his young niece, recently entering the religious life, on the subject of how to pray: "after you have come before God at the blessed Sacrament, or in your room, or anywhere else you might be in profound humility, tell Him nothing else except this single word, 'love': He will hear the desire of your heart that asks for nothing else. I'm struck by the fact that God has led me to suggest this to you on this particular day, the Feast of St. Francis of Paula; for this good saint, who performed so many miracles, only did them while saying this single word: 'love'. God does no greater miracle than when He gives such love to someone, and places it in their heart" (Saint-Cyran, *Lettres,* letter 9).

102. Cf. the way these elements are approached negatively, in Saint-Cyran, *Lettres,* vol. 1, p. 49.

process of vocation was perceived as being necessarily entangled within the cascading corporate need for purification. The decline of the Church's perfective condition requires a greater penitence than in the first years of its life; its members are "sicker" now than before. Yet the sign and partial cause of its decline is the fact that the penitential life has been relaxed. And without the support of an *increasingly* rigorous repentance, by which the Holy Spirit's life is accepted as one's own, the love that ought to characterize the Christian life and the Church's leaders is made less and less accessible. Vocationally, Saint-Cyran calls the prospective and actually ordained priest to a life of discernment that cannot adequately resolve itself, because the times demand a depth and protraction of self-abnegation from which clarity cannot emerge, because to do so would be to defy the necessitated subjection to obscurity demanded by the ecclesial situation. The constant urgings toward withdrawal, solitude, and self-annihilation that Saint-Cyran commends as a portion of discernment, and within which the standards of the priesthood are unbridgeably contrasted with the historical condition of the individual and a Church that is so far gone as to set up "obstructions" rather than pathways to illumination, point not to the unveiling of a vocation. The pattern of the Church's figural fall and the perfective search it engenders rather obliterate vocation in favor of simple penance. If there is to be a love expressed in the Church, a love that informs the community's life before God, it will appear, paradoxically, only within the spaces of this interior withdrawal from the counterpressures of the Church's institutions.[103]

The hiddenness and inaccessibility of these vocations are presented by Saint-Cyran precisely as a faithful resolution to the battle over ministerial jurisdiction waged between the separated Protestants on the one hand and on the other the "lax" Catholics who have abandoned the perfective vocation altogether in their reliance upon purely hierarchical validation. Having described a history whereby the caritative rigors given in the sacraments of Penance, the Eucharist, and Orders have been gradually undermined over the course of centuries, by heretics, sinners, and schismatics, he makes the silence of penitential withdrawal the only place amongst the contesting parties where love can flourish, even though obscured:

103. Having insisted on an ecclesial history in which many, if not most, priests have actually been ordained without a true vocation from God, Saint-Cyran sees the Church's only hope to lie in a universal ministerial withdrawal into penance. An "inauthentic" priest has only one Christian duty: to resign and disappear in tears. And even so, most "uncalled" priests will fail to rectify the communal and individual disaster their "usurpation" has caused. Cf. Saint-Cyran, *Lettres*, vol. 1, pp. 72ff. on the question of whether such priests are "unconvertible."

THE END OF THE CHURCH

To live as a Christian in these times, to serve God in a pure way, and to worship Him in spirit and in truth, one must avoid two opposite extremes, with the heretics [i.e., the Reformers and their predecessors] on one side, and on the other, Catholics who are indifferent to the clear truth concerning the discipline of holy living. One must be careful not to complain, as the heretics do, about the decline that has taken place in the habits and discipline of Christians, especially of priests. Even less ought one to separate oneself from the Church and create schisms as they do. Rather, one must groan in one's heart, and lament . . . as did the Prophets over the fact that "the priest has become like the People." This interior groaning, like that of Samuel's mother Hannah, takes place in the heart and in the presence of God alone; it is a wonderful act of love. All the more wonderful, in fact, because it seems to come close to, without actually attaining, the ruinous extremity wherein the heretics rebelled and created that horrible separation by which the Church has been divided.

The Fathers always approved of a particular kind of separation, to which they exhorted true Christians, one that took place in the heart, by a secret disavowal and by the holiness of their lives and the example of their good habits. Only thus ought one to separate oneself from the habits, the attitudes, and the practices of other Christians who dwell within the Church while living wickedly and ignoring the true rules of the Church's discipline.[104]

Coming at the heart of a discussion of priestly vocation, it is a jarring admission: in a Church whose division represents an attack upon the holiness of God's love, a true minister will subject himself to his vocation's public silencing; it is *this* subjection that alone can constitute, albeit in a historically deformed though inevitable way, a caritative act of self-giving on behalf of the Church. If the Church takes upon itself the form of Christ's own abandonment, a figure already given in the nation of Israel, the Church's ministry, too, will subject itself not to a call from God, but to the chastened and chastening search for such a call.[105]

104. Saint-Cyran, *Lettres,* vol. 1, pp. 125f.

105. The explicit figural connection with the abandoned ministry of Israel is toyed with by the rigorist tradition (cf. Massillon's treatment of the theme, using texts from Isaiah and Micah, in his "Discours sur la Nécessité où sont les Ministres de se renouveler dans l'Esprit de leur Vocation," in *Oeuvres,* vol. 11, pp. 216ff.), but always as a warning. And however urgent, the warning presupposed the opportunity still to escape the pneumatic effects of abandonment. Saint-Cyran, however, assumed the full historical correlation of the prophetic fulfillment, even if he rarely turned to the Old Testament texts in question. Subsequent to Saint-Cyran, Jansenists of varying stripes continued to dwell on the question of vocation, often with the same historical and caritative emphases. See, among many examples, Duguet's "Lettre à un directeur de séminaire sur la vocation à l'état ecclésiastique," in his *Lettres sur divers sujets de morale et de piété* (Paris, 1726), vol. 2; Jean Girard de Ville-Thierry, *Traité de la vocation à l'état ecclésiastique* (Paris, 1695); [Jean Richard], *Règles de conduite pour les curés tirées de S. Jean Chrysostome* (Paris, 1684). On Jansenist

186

Denial of Charity and the Inefficacy of Divided Ministries

The discussion by Saint-Cyran on vocation, then, points to the contemporary dilemma faced by a set of Christian ministries whose enactment within the figure of Israel's disintegration dissolves into an unrequited search for divine commission. But before we can give a concluding assessment of the ecumenical significance of divided ministries, a final point needs to be made. And that is that, while the connection between vocational obscurement and ecclesial division is established through the figural framework of the Church as Israel, this very connection and logic are also firmly embedded in the traditional evaluation of the effect of schism upon ordination. We do not only need to adjust our thinking on the matter to a novel figuralist orientation; we can also observe how the discussion of ordination and schism has, from the time of Cyprian at least, pointed in the direction our own reflections have taken us.

We have already pointed out how schism was classically construed as a sin against charity, a position stressed by Cyprian. But it does not sufficiently clarify the character of ecclesially separated ministries to state this baldly and then to go on to admit that divided ministries must therefore, in some sense, lack a fullness of practiced love within the Body. No one interested in the unity of the Church could dispute this moderate admission of ministerial defect, not least those who have worked so hard in the past decades to further the reconciliation of ministries among separated denominations. The thrust of the present argument goes much further, in drawing out the historical connection between the ministry's character as caritative enactment and the suppression of that character through the practice of division, a view of ministerial defect that strikes at the root of attempts to "recognize" the apostolicity of any ordained service that takes its form within a context of mutual separation among Christians. The well-known anti-Donatist principles upholding the sacramentality of ordination have, unintentionally and unfortunately, distracted ecumenical discussion (and controversy) from confronting the effects of caritative diminishment and contradiction intrinsic to separated orders, effects that appear only as one traces the unresolved vocational crisis engendered by the Reformation divisions. For the *mutual* separation that defines these divisions above all impelled the parties involved, as we have seen, to appeal to structural criteria of exclusivity that, in turn, favored those aspects of the theological explanation of schism that did not treat of unity's basis in

---

pastoral practice and perspectives, related to these orientations, see René Taveneaux, *La vie quotidienne des Jansénistes aux XVIIe and XVIIIe siècles* (Paris: Hachette, 1973), pp. 103ff.

the diaconal subjection of love. And it is their concerns with structural apostolicity that have attracted ecumenical scrutiny as problems to be resolved. But vocational obscurement was, from the inception of the early Church's considered reflection on schism, a central aspect of division's effects, quite apart from the question of the sacramental efficacy of orders.

Attention has always been drawn to the fact that Cyprian's rejection of schismatic sacraments — baptism especially — was decisively, if not universally, denied by the Church at large, particularly through the efforts of Augustine to counter the perfective exclusivism of the Donatists. Less consistently noted has been the fact that the soteriological substance of Cyprian's rejection was always retained, not the least by Augustine himself, in the form of a clear judgment against the salutary *effects* of schismatic sacraments. And here the question at issue turns very deliberatively on the caritative foundation of the Church's ministry. Cyprian had identified that foundation in the unity of the Church's common life, of which the ministry was both the servant and the expressive enactment, and whose embodiment constituted the explicit "apostolicity" of the Church as a whole. More fundamental still was the fact that this apostolicity of unity in caritative service formed the very shape in which the being and love of God touch human life.[106] A separated church, which exists in division from the catholic Body of Christ, therefore denies the very basis upon which salvation is given in history, and so loses contact with the salvific matrix within which Christians receive and offer divine love. The underlying sacramental principle Cyprian establishes from all this is that outside the unity of the Church, there are "no rewards of Christ."[107] He expressed this by saying that schismatic baptisms did not bring with them salutary effects. The practical conclusion he drew was that Catholic baptisms were still required of those "baptized" schismatically (since there is but "one baptism," of course, there are no real schismatic baptisms, only empty gestures).[108] And while Augustine rejected the conclusion, claiming that schismatic sacraments were valid in that no further "Catholic" rites were required either to fulfill them or to replace them, he retained the principle that such sacraments were "ineffective" and without "fruit."[109]

106. These are all pervasive themes in Cyprian, *De ecclesiae catholicae unitate;* but see, e.g., chs. 4-6, 23-26. The unity of the Church figures the unity of Trinity, by whose life we are given divine life; this life is given historical expression in the temporal and physical unities of faith and ecclesial life, in service and government, the latter, especially, offered through the episcopal succession and college.

107. Cyprian, *De ecclesiae catholicae unitate,* ch. 6.

108. Cf. Cyprian, 70th Epistle to Quintus, Bishop of Mauritania.

109. Cf. Augustine, *Contra litteras Petiliani Donatistae Cortensis, Episcopi (In Answer to*

They were ineffective for the simple reason that they were performed and received without the "love" of Christ that informs the Christian life only as it is lived in mutual subjection and therefore in unity with other Christians. Augustine brings further theological clarity to Cyprian's initial caritative explanation by explicitly identifying the sacramental "effectiveness" with the grace of the Holy Spirit animating the Church, a divine presence who is Love itself and by whom the "fruit of the Spirit" is given to Christians even as they deepen their communion one with another.[110] There can be no true holiness in a separated Church, for such holiness derives from and instances the presence of pneumatic love, which is embodied in communion.

What exactly constitutes the nonrepeatable value of a sacrament administered in a schismatic church is not well described by Augustine — for example, in what way baptism is a washing away of sins and need not be repeated if, in fact, its schismatical character leaves a person still mired in sin. Whatever the case, however, it is clear that Augustine wishes to emphasize that it is the sin against charity (and hence the Holy Spirit) made in separation that foils sanctification, a sin for which schismatics are wholly responsible, not some defect intrinsic to the sacrament itself, which remains wholly Christ's. And the point is that, until unity is reestablished, the character of any sacrament is emptied of any practical divine effect, and turns into an instrument of increased defilement and alienation through the pneumatic abandonment given in the rejection of charity in unity. In a schismatic baptism, sins of an individual may indeed be remitted in the fundamental sense of their having been dealt with by Christ's sacrifice, but the individual is, as it were, simultaneously thrust into the corruption of postbaptismal sin through a loss of the Spirit: "so that the Holy Spirit has both been present with him at his baptism for the removal of his sins, and has also fled [Wisdom 1:5] before his perseverance in deceit. . . . For that sins which have been remitted do return upon a man, where there is no brotherly love, is most clearly taught by our Lord."[111] Similarly, when speaking of penitential absolution — a "repeatable" sacrament — attempted in ecclesial separation, Augustine stresses the aspect of the pneumatic inefficacy embodied in the contradiction of charity:

the Letters of Petilian), III:40: "For all the sacraments of Christ, if not combined with the love which belongs to the unity of Christ, are possessed not unto salvation, but unto judgment" (trans. J. R. King, in *A Select Library of the Nicene and Post-Nicene Fathers of the Christian Church* [repr. Grand Rapids: Wm. B. Eerdmans, 1983], pp. 615f.).

110. See Augustine, *De baptismo contra Donatistas (On Baptism, Against the Donatists)*, I, chs. 8-18; III, chs. 16-18.

111. Ibid., I:12 (in op. cit., pp. 419f.).

But when it is said that "the Holy Spirit is given by the imposition of hands in the Catholic Church only," I suppose that our ancestors meant that we should understand thereby what the apostle says, "Because the love of God is shed abroad in our hearts by the Holy Ghost which is given unto us [Rom. 5:5]." For this is the very love which is wanting in all who are cut off from the communion of the Catholic Church. . . . But those are wanting in God's love who do not care for the unity of the Church; and consequently we are right in understanding that the Holy Spirit may be said not to be received except in the Catholic Church. . . . Since, then, the sacrament is one thing, which even Simon Magus could have [Acts 8:13]; and the operation of the Spirit is another thing, which is even often found in wicked men, as Saul had the gift of prophecy; and that operation of the same Spirit is a third thing, which only the good can have, as "the end of the commandment is charity out of a pure heart, and of a good conscience, and of faith unfeigned [1 Tim. 1:5]": whatever, therefore, may be received by heretics and schismatics, the charity which covereth the multitude of sins is the especial gift of Catholic unity and peace.[112]

This goes for ministerial ordination as much as for baptism.[113] And it is critical to note that the texts used by, for example, Cyprian, to describe

112. Ibid., III:16 (p. 443).

113. Cf. Augustine, *Contra epistolam Parmeniani,* II:13:28, on the application of all these principles to the question of ordination and the ministry (a topic Augustine otherwise ignores): Donatist bishops who return to the Catholic Church are not reordained (although their office may be "suppressed"); however, as they are schismatic bishops, all their sacramental acts performed in disunity are done for their "ruin" (and, with consent, for the ruin of those who participate in them). Eastern Orthodox churches have maintained the same position, more or less, although stated in somewhat different language. Furthermore, they have been less clear on the distinction Augustine wished to maintain between the ontological status of a sacrament and its pneumatic fruit or efficacy, which is why rebaptisms of heretics and even schismatics were demanded in many more cases than in the West. To this day, Eastern churches understand the validity of sacraments to rest *essentially* in their enactment *within* the unity of the Church; and where, say, reordination may not be required of a schismatic Catholic priest who joins an Orthodox church, there is no implication made that that ordination had any "validity" *until* situated within the reconciled communion of the true Church. Further, the language used to describe the ministry of so-called priests within separated Christian communities *before* such reconciliation, is consistent in both East and West: such priests are equivalent to the "false" prophets spoken of by Jeremiah and elsewhere in the Old Testament: they are "blind," they are "confused," they are "ignorant," they are "cowardly," they are "avaricious"; in sum, they represent the purely human remains of a ministry that has been severed from divine direction. Cf. Charles-James N. Bailey, "Validity and Authenticity: The Difference Between Western and Orthodox Views on Orders," *Saint Vladimir's Seminary Quarterly* 8, no. 2 (1964): 86-92; and Jerome Cotsonis, "The Validity of the Anglican Orders According to the Canon Law of the Orthodox Church," *Greek Orthodox Theological Review* 3, no. 2 (1957): pp. 182-96, and 4, no. 1 (1958): pp. 44-65 (this last deals with issues discussed in part below).

schismatic ministers coincide with the Old Testament figures taken up by the controversial literature of the Reformation and post-Reformation, for example, Korah and Dathan and the "false prophets" of Jeremiah 23, among others.[114] Furthermore, the characteristics of the schismatic ministries' "unfruitfulness" also coincides with the elements of vocational obscurement increasingly identified with the predicament of the divided ministry by figuralist rigorists like Saint-Cyran: diluted holiness, confused teaching, cowardice in the face of injustice, ambition, and, at the root, the failure to love the Body and give oneself in love for it. They are blind leaders, gropingly guiding others who follow pointlessly by an isolated touch that can issue only in a chasm. They are the leaders Jeremiah pointed to as laboring independently, by themselves, abandoned of all divine commission.[115]

The fundamental relationship, therefore, between vocational obscurement and the assault upon caritative enactment that schism represents has been at the center of classical Western theological reflection upon ecclesial separation. As we saw earlier, it continued to inform standard presentations of the matter like Aquinas's. And it is easy to see why this fundamental relationship has been ignored in favor of structural issues of validity (through succession or examination), as separated churches have sought to justify their own ministries or, latterly, attempted to reconcile divided ministries: any acceptance of the caritative foundation in unity of the Christian ministry would demand an acknowledgment of universal vocational bewilderment and even absence.

One need offer but one example, the modern problem of the Catholic evaluation of the "validity of Anglican orders."[116] The limitation of the discussion on this matter to the question of structural apostolicity, in this

---

114. Cf. Cyprian, *De ecclesiae catholicae unitate* 11, 17, 18.

115. Cyprian, *De ecclesiae catholicae unitate* 11, 17, 18.

116. For some more recent, and divergent, discussions, see Francis Clark, S.J., *Anglican Orders and Defect of Intention* (London: Longmans, Green and Co., 1956), a defense of the Roman rejection of Anglican orders; John Jay Hughes, *Stewards of the Lord: A Reappraisal of Anglican Orders* (London: Sheed and Ward, 1970), a Roman Catholic argument against such rejection; George H. Tavard, *A Review of Anglican Orders: The Problem and the Solution* (Collegeville [Minn.]: Liturgical Press, 1990), a Roman Catholic survey, including an assessment (and generally a synthetic acceptance) of recent ecumenical dialogues and proposals. See also R. William Franklin and George H. Tavard, "Commentary on ARC/USA Statement on Anglican Orders," *Journal of Ecumenical Studies* 27, no. 2 (Spring 1990), which surveys historically recent ecumenical discussion on the issue. In all of these treatments, the categories of exclusivity define, negatively, the proposals for reconciliation, even when the latter are informed by contemporary reformulations of ecclesiology as, for example, communion: in Tavard's phrase, the validity of separated orders must be "presumed," a presumption that includes (and derives, in some cases, from) the efficacy of those orders.

case of an episcopal-succession type, has allowed one or the other (or perhaps both) sides to manipulate criteria of ministerial validity that will justify the separation of each, either in the past or even in the present. The Roman Catholic Church has pronounced, in Leo XIII's 1896 Bull *Apostolicae Curae*, Anglican ordinations invalid ("null and void") on two counts, that of "form" and that of "intention," both of which speak to the structural issue of episcopal succession.[117] In terms of "form," the Pope judged the verbal prayers made in Anglican ordination services insufficiently specific as to demonstrate that the ordination taking place was congruent with traditional Catholic episcopal conferral of orders. In terms of "intention," the Pope determined that the open rejection by the Anglican Reformers, often instanced in the revised liturgies of the Prayer Book and Ordinal, of a sacrificial Eucharist and sacrificing priesthood, made it clear that the priesthood envisaged by the Anglican ordination rite was not the same as that of the Catholic Church. The response of the Anglican bishops to these judgments was to offer counter-arguments in kind, not to reject the criteria themselves (however much they stressed the difficulty and temerity of applying them too stringently): if the question of form and intention could be resolved positively, then Anglican orders would be valid *whatever* response one gave to the further question of the Church of England's "schismatic" character. And however much each side claimed to have eventual ecclesial unity in mind — and the Bull itself grew out of the research spurred by such a desire in both churches — the reasoning of each was constricted by the historically inescapable demand to maintain as presuppositions the integrity of each church's *separated* ministry. The issue of sacramental effect, founded on the pneumatic dimension of caritative unity, was clearly a subversive perspective that would have rendered the whole discussion moot from the beginning.[118]

---

117. Latin and English texts of the Bull, as well as an official response given by the Archbishops of England in 1897, can be found in *Anglican Orders* (London: SPCK, 1954).

118. More contemporary views of the priesthood, from the Anglican and Roman Catholic side, have still not clearly faced this reality. The recent *Catechism of the Catholic Church* summarizes the ordained ministry in terms of the validity of proper conferral (1590–1600), identified with authentic vocation, which remains tied to the formal structures of ecclesial governance. By contrast, an ecumenically sensitive Anglican, Paul Avis, maintains that the ordained ministry is properly defined by its selection as a functional servant to the priestly life of the whole Church, a formulation that relies strongly on a Lutheran conception of baptism as the only distinctly pneumatic qualification for ministry and that construes the authenticity of ordained ministry in terms of its legitimate "election" through the Church (Paul Avis, *Christians in Communion* (Collegeville [Minn.]: Liturgical Press, 1990), pp. 86ff. In both cases, "apostolicity," with respect to the ordained ministry in particular, is reduced to a proper ecclesial validation of vocation, a reduction that sustains the integrity of divided ministries. In the case

The question of "intention" in ordination has always been poorly framed in any case, the concept used as a tool of judgment aimed at someone allegedly "outside" the Church, and thus ill-adapted for the self-reflexive reasoning of an ecumenical pursuit of unity.[119] The traditional principle has held that a

---

of Avis, this is an especially interesting fact, since his desire is to articulate a theological basis upon which to "recognize" the ordained ministries of other churches (if we can recognize the validity of baptisms in another denomination, then we must recognize their ministries, since such ministries are functional derivations from baptism — pp. 96f.): the reality that, whether or not we recognize another church's ministry, we can still carry on with our own denomination's baptismal functions in a state of at least recogniz*able* integrity does not strike him as problematic, precisely because his definition of ministry does not require unity; it only makes it a possibility dependent on ecclesial will. There need be, in any case, no contradiction in recognizing another church's baptism while rejecting their ministry: just as we accept the validity of the marriage vows made by two people, even though we may acknowledge their contradiction in a subsequent separation or divorce, just so may we acknowledge the validity of a baptism while acknowledging the subsequent (or even concomitant) contradiction to that baptism afforded by the divided ministry that represents it. If the apostolicity of unity resides in baptism — as indeed it does on a basic level, and not just in the ordained ministry — this does not mean that divided ministries must be "recognized" just as divided baptisms are; it means, rather, that ministries cannot "properly" reflect what baptism means, they cannot serve its figure, until they are remade within the figure of a penitential reconciliation in Christ Jesus. And surely, if we speak, as we do, of the pneumatic basis for such a penitential need, the same must be true for the baptized life in general — its vocation is obscured and rendered unrecognizable within a life divorced from the charity of Christian union. Avis, to be sure, realizes that communion somehow founds the apparition of its signs — in doctrinal agreement, for instance; but he seems to think that it is possible to "recognize" the fruit of unity in advance, as it were, and so frequently follows the logic not of pneumatic restoration that proceeds from mutual subjection, but of unveiling or affirming the already present gifts of the Spirit within division. Reliance on the logic of affirmation is understandable, of course; for what theologian or ecumenist could ever be motivated to study a unity of life in Christ whose shape is inaccessible to those who live apart from one another?

119. For an accessible survey of traditional concepts and major points of discussion, see Bernard Leeming, S.J., "Presumption of Intention," *Irish Theological Quarterly* 23 (1956): pp. 325ff. With respect to the stated example of Anglican orders, one can see how, in the debate on the matter, the notion of intention was applied with the same criteria of exclusivity that informed the embedded reality of the separated churches involved in the discussion, with the same inevitable results of incompatible interpretations. The "intention" of the Church of England, according to the archbishops' response to Leo XIII, was defined as being in accordance with the mind of the "Catholic Church," the traditional understanding of "right intention." But the archbishops, in continuity with Anglican reformed tradition, defined the "Catholic Church" as the "early" Church of the Fathers and the first four General Councils. On this basis, the explicitly Roman Catholic Church could not provide, in its peculiar practice, criteria of validity for the ministry. Therefore, to have ordained ministers with an intention that did *not* agree with the Roman Catholic Church's was no defect of "right" intention, for the Roman Church was *not* the embodiment of the Catholic Church in any fundamental way. This argument

sacrament is valid if (assuming a proper "form" and "matter" of administration) it is given with the "intent" to do "as the Church does," however wrongly one understands the Church's actual mind. On this basis, heretical and schismatic sacraments have been held as potentially "valid." In practice, since it is hard to know whether someone who deeply misunderstands the Church's own intent is actually intending to do what the Catholic Church does, judgments about intent either have been very liberal or have relied rather heavily on the power of "matter and form" to indicate hidden intent (this latter was the case with *Apostolicae Curae*). But how does the concept of "intention" apply to ordinations within divided denominations?

There can be no question at all that separated orders are given with the intent to maintain separation, even if there may also be the intent at some point in the future to remove obstacles to unity. No one can ordain ministers

---

concedes the point that the Anglican Church's "intention" is not the same as the Roman Church's, something that from the Roman side had always been argued, except from the presupposition that the Roman and the Catholic churches were one and the same. Indeed, the incompatibility of intentions had also always been argued by Anglicans, of a more Protestant stripe. On the early views of the initial Anglican reformers — very much at odds with nineteenth- and twentieth-century attempts to answer the Roman Catholics on their own ground of intention and structures of apostolicity — see the primary source material gathered by (the albeit partisan Congregationalist) John Brown, in his *Apostolical Succession in the Light of History and Fact* (London: Congregational Union of England and Wales, 1898), lectures 10 and 11. For a telling exposure, from a Protestant perspective, of the Anglican appeal to the "mind of the Church" with respect to the issue of apostolic succession in its own history — one can be either Protestant or Roman on this matter, not something in between, because the criteria of exclusivity uphold the very existence of the Church of England — see Charles Hodge, "The Church of England and Presbyterian Orders," in his *Discussions in Church Polity* (New York: Charles Scribner's Sons, 1878), pp. 134ff. Determining the "intention" of the early Anglican reformers and their various successors is probably a logical impossibility given the very nature of historical inquiry in general and the peculiar circumstances of shifting oppositions within the evolution of England's national church(es) in particular. What is one to make, for instance, of the "intention" regarding orders of Cranmer, whose public formulations on the matter were tied to an array of differing and specific political and ecclesiastical pressures? Cf. the "conceits" (in Gilbert Burnet's phrase) of his ruminations on the ministry given in a royal commission of inquiry, from the early 1540s, a combination of Erastian and radical Protestant theories that, if granted a serious role as signifiers of "intent," would surely scuttle attempts at ecumenical rapprochement with most historic churches (as edited in the volume of "Records and Original Papers" of Burnet's *The History of the Reformation of the Church of England*, I:21). The role that these kinds of documents can and ought to play in determining true "intent" within a public ecclesial practice is hardly obvious. The point here simply is that the concept of "intention" is not helpful unless it is applied from within a condition of unity; otherwise, it merges with other criteria of separation that are logically unresolvable apart from a return to the caritative dimension that must necessarily condemn both sides of the discussion.

in a separated church except with the intent to sustain, in some basic fashion, that separation. To the degree that ordination is the one sacrament that pertains in a primary way to the apostolicity of the Church, given in its unity in Christ's love, its administration in the context of deliberated disunity cannot but radically divest its outcome of its ostensive purpose. And therefore, however one construes the sacramental validity of such ordinations, their pneumatic efficacy must, at the least, be placed in doubt. Furthermore, in a situation of entrenched mutual division, the pneumatic consequences of such caritative contradiction must apply to all the parties that persist in maintaining the ministerial sustenance of such division.

The phenomenon of pneumatic deprivation as it is expressed in the figural life of the Church cannot be taken, as we have already stressed, in an absolute sense. It is a facet, not the foundation, of a historical process of conformance to the shape of Christ Jesus, and its ultimate significance is already revealed in him. But as a historical phenomenon, pneumatic deprivation cannot be experientially overleaped, anymore than can the various elements of Jesus' own life and death as they were both assumed in his flesh and subsequently received by his followers. The divided Church is still Christ's Body; and it is a Body for which the life of God is given and given with the promise of indelibility. But as a divided Church, it is a dead body, no less Christ's and no less taken up by a living God, but dead for all that. Of this body, the divided ministry is but an aspect.

A Ministry of Retreat

The ministerial criteria of structural apostolicity, unconsciously devised as exclusive arms of self-justification, cannot comprehend the ministry of such a body; for they are founded on the conviction that only *members* of this body ever die, never the whole, that only appendages fail, never the trunk, that there is always a living center (disguised perhaps as a margin) whose identity is known — and is one's own — which forms the standard of the other's potential revivification. Pneumatic deprivation cannot, in this perspective, offer anything but what lies in contrast to God; and how shall we agree to suffer such a condition without repugnance? Yet to consider a pneumatically deprived ministry as the sense by which we touch the habitation of God among us, the sphere in which the contours of the Church's life are known today, is not to nullify the Christian ministry historically, but only to see it whole in its own time. It is to name the motives of its current exercise, and then to note how little this nomenclature signifies the practice of a love now lost in the autonomous search for God's directive guidance.

195

Whether a strict phenomenological study would disclose, among the many denominational ministries pursued within the larger Church, clear marks of pneumatic abandonment is doubtful. As with the epiphanies of grace extraordinary holiness embodies, so in the divided ministry, the forms of apostolic love that figure Christ as given in the Church denote their obscurement mainly through contestation, not through admitted blindness on the part of those who look. The rigorist criteria of priestly holiness held by the post-Tridentine reformers failed in their certainty as surely as their efforts to discern the Spirit's prod to such criteria's fulfillment ended in a retreat from clear response. To recognize the caritative hole at the center of the divided ministry, the emptiness where traces of the Spirit may still alert the heart, is therefore not a premise for a program of renewed equipage in the arms of holiness. For we cannot hearken to a call whose voice is muffled or unheard. The vocation of the Christian ministry is something now we construct according to our own best devices and intentions — its goals and purposes, its methods and its inner meaning. On these, perhaps, individuals and churches, and churches among other churches, can find a common frame of mind and speech. There is no sin in such confluence, and we ought not to denigrate its search.

But such a common human understanding about the shape of ministry does not constitute a divine vocation, which alone can grant a real shape to the Church's service. The ecumenical challenge, then, turns less on agreement about the ideal meaning of the ministry, an ideal whose real substance must remain cloaked until the form of the Church's restored common life can give it body, than it does on the practical question of what might constitute the form of ministerial love in the midst of a present and sustained ecclesial division: what is the holiness of self-giving that the apostles of the Church's life in mutual subjection might enact? Surely not the construction of new structures of ecclesial justification, whether they be doctrinal or political, structures that, despite the motives of ecumenical convergence, remain tied to the dynamics of division itself. Pursued in the cloud of vocational obscurement, such constructive impulses require instead a strong inversion, such as that inadvertently discovered in the wake of Trent, an inversion into the forms of ministerial retreat: the letting go of the self's command of certain calling, the setting aside of ecclesially linked doctrinal resistance, the penitential acceptance of subjection to the other. The challenge of this kind of vocational retreat, tied to the related realms of life associated with the ministry, like that of education, mission, and liturgy, alone would seem to mark the willingness of leaders to assume the holiness of love their office requires. It is, finally, a challenge to find a form of life by which to give way, to step aside and disappear in favor of the men and women God has called when once the Church is pressed into the shape wherein his voice is clearly heard. How to become like Saul, prophet, king, erstwhile priest, chosen and rejected, faithful in the veiling of his call, the object of the Spirit's play of advent and flight, resorting in the end to a dead prophet who can reveal only the intractability of his own human course, while submitting at a distance to the one of "God's own choosing," who is being nurtured within the folds of the enemy? Here, in a figure only the post-Reformation could transform from merely disobedient into fully tragic,[120] is an outline of our inherited ministry, in whose withered place another reed can grow, be touched, be leaned upon.

120. The post-Reformation literary evolution of Saul — cf. Charles Jennens' libretto to Handel's well-known oratorio, Voltaire's production, as well as lesser poetic compositions by, for example, Joseph Trapp and William Southby — stands in sharp contrast to his traditional exegetical persona as a paragon of rebellion against God, as if some new sympathy had arisen to the inescapable predicament of his failed vocation and faithfulness. Even in the late sixteenth century, already, the tensions in Saul's status as both demonically manipulated and divinely established were explored in the context of discussions about diabolic deceptions, for example, by Bérulle (cf. our last chapter). The literary-historical question concerning the recovery of the "tragic" in Western narrative in the sixteenth century is an interesting one that still awaits a full investigation, one that would include the religious background to the reappropriation of classical outlooks.

Chapter Four

Vinegar and Gall:
Tasting the Eucharist
in the Divided Church

The Eucharistic Sign as Mark of the Separated Church:
Provisionality and Exclusivity

The flight of vocation into the wilderness could be suffered, perhaps, were there some sustenance forthcoming from God's hand in this desert, as by ravens to a hidden prophet. Or through manna from the heavens. From one perspective, modern theology, with liturgical and now ecumenical theology taking the practical lead in recent years, can be read as an attempt to affirm and to ground such feeding of the ministerially dispossessed as a preeminent pneumatic activity. In the face of institutional imperfections and ecclesial disappointments, in the face, that is, of the historical failures of communal Christian claims, divine life has slowly migrated to some realm beyond the landscapes of social apprehension, from which its intimate attractions are launched and its nourishment is scattered as it draws us to itself, or perhaps presses us from behind. What is curious about this modern orientation, in comparison with, say, medieval conceptions of the earthly "pilgrimage," is its urgent denial of the *significance* of the failures the Spirit's food now moves us on beyond. "Progress" and "evolution" are peculiarly modern conceptions, not in their assertion of the distance between present limitations and future fulfillments, nor in the sureness of the spanning bridge, but in their assiduous denial of an abiding life to those events that populate and litter the advancing and then retreating middle ground.[1] If Jesus has wounds, the modern church suggests, they are not permanent. Whatever the origins of the eventually flourishing interest in New Testament eschatology among late-nineteenth-century biblical scholars like Weiss and Bousset,[2] its evolved usefulness now, molded by interpreters who have tried to merge aspects of "futurist" and "realized," "other worldly" and "this worldly" conceptions of the Kingdom of God, seems to lie in the way it can explain how a perpetually disfigured Church of radically confused people can be offered certain salvific sustenance without disquiet. The "now and not yet" character of the "inbreaking Kingdom of God," which structures the popular versions of this already ingrained bit of scholarly wisdom about New Testament theology, has proven an adept instrument in assuring Christians of the unthreatening nature of ecclesial disintegration, as we have already noted in our first chapter. What is odd is how boldly this tool has been used to buttress a positive force in the actual labor on behalf of the reunion of the churches.

As much as anywhere, ecumenical reflection on the Eucharist has demonstrated this pattern. While it is possible, for instance, to maintain an ordered ministry even within a divided Church, a ministry that can be justified with at least a functional integrity, it is hard to make immediate sense of a continuing sacramental enactment whose traditionally understood caritative center is mocked by its currently rooted separative practice.[3] And however much that practice may be deplored by the servants of reunion, the

---

1. Cf. the second chapter of Christopher Lasch's *The True and Only Heaven* (New York: W. W. Norton, 1991), which succinctly surveys, and rejects, some recent theories about the compatibility of modern notions of "progress" with traditional Christian ideas of history. Lasch, borrowing from H. Richard Niebuhr, defines the Christian "prophetic tradition" as viewing the Kingdom of God "neither as the end of the world nor as an 'ideal for future society' but as a community of the faithful living under the judgment inherent in the evanescence of earthly affairs and more particularly in the 'doom of threatened societies'" (p. 47). Whether this characterization, even if inaccurate, is consistent with contemporary notions of the "eschatological" nature of the Church is, to my mind, doubtful.

2. Cf. Werner Georg Kümmel's description of this movement in his *The New Testament: The History of the Investigation of Its Problems* (Nashville: Abingdon Press, 1972), pp. 226-44 and 480-88. More theologically, cf. Brevard S. Childs, *Biblical Theology of the Old and New Testaments: Theological Reflections on the Christian Bible* (Minneapolis: Fortress Press, 1993), pp. 624-57.

3. Reference has already been made to Bruce Marshall's article, "The Disunity of the Church and the Credibility of the Gospel," in *Theology Today* 50 (April 1993). Part of the beauty of Marshall's concise argument is its obviousness, the clarity of which is not lessened by the fact that it is rarely acknowledged!

continuing sacramental enactment of the Eucharist by different churches has never been questioned. That questioning has been obscured by three elements in the logic of separation itself, still working their way through our common fund of theological apprehension, from which we draw even our weapons of unitive discourse. First, the "eschatological" character of divine presence, which has been applied to the Eucharist in particular, has permitted the sacrament to embody the essence of historical "provisionality," by which imperfections, while acknowledged, are made intractable and also relativized by the intangible presence of something more perfect. Second, a particular way of thinking about the Eucharist, namely, its significatory character (its "sign-function") has provided a certain conceptual framework in which to make the sacrament's essentially provisional blessing plausible. Finally, the root affirmation of pneumatic presence understood in its modern shape as a "dynamic" force, which underlies with increasing intensity so much contemporary ecclesiology, determines the application of this plausible reading of uninterrupted Eucharistic blessing. This in turn substantiates — and ironically, given the ecumenical purposes to which the arguments are directed — the continued distinction of the separated churches in which the sacrament is celebrated. "With reference to the Eucharist, it is in the missionary and eschatological context that we are enabled to see beyond the things which create divisions between and within our two communions," writes a well-known interdenominational dialogue commission, in an attempt to frame the sacrament as a present — and therefore in itself unproblematic — means for overcoming disunity.[4] The Eucharist is the nourishment by which Jesus "feeds his pilgrim people,"[5] as they move through the world toward greater faithfulness and missionary justice. It is "the presence of the Spirit" as "foretaste, pledge and first-fruits of God's coming Kingdom."[6] Finally, the Eucharist "constitutes" the Church, in an instrumental fashion.[7] And it can do all these things, despite the concerns of disunity and lack of charity, precisely because the Church itself is "provisional in relation to the Kingdom," is itself a "foretaste" of something greater, a missionary "sign," whose present dismemberment only points to the effectiveness of the sacramental act itself.[8]

4. *God's Reign and Our Unity: The Report of the Anglican-Reformed International Commission 1984* (London/Edinburgh: SPCK/The Saint Andrews Press, 1984), p. 39, par. 62.

5. *God's Reign and Our Unity*, p. 40, par. 63.

6. *God's Reign and Our Unity*, p. 43, par. 69.

7. *God's Reign and Our Unity*, p. 41, par. 64.

8. Cf. *God's Reign and Our Unity*, p. 11, par. 16.

Much of this kind of talk is so widespread today[9] that its ecumenical focus is generally lost altogether, even as the language is disseminated in contexts that have little interest in ecclesial unity and are more exclusively oriented toward issues of social and political action.[10] What needs to be

9. The classic treatment with respect to the Eucharist remains Geoffrey Wainwright's *Eucharist and Eschatology,* rev. ed. (New York: Oxford University Press, 1981), whose first chapter and appendix to the revision outline important works in biblical and systematic theology over the previous few decades that propagated the broad eschatological framework within which the Eucharist can be placed. Wainwright's ecumenical vision, judiciously supported by a wide swath of traditional (including Eastern Orthodox) material, is powerful and, in its own right, convincing. He sees the framework as itself "opening up" the range of historical experience in which the realities of sin and failure still corrupt the Church's life. But, as we shall note later, it is not clear that the weight given to eschatological "provisionality" actually serves to distinguish the real character of the Eucharist as it is currently enacted, a point he himself alludes to in passing. For a different kind of "eschatologizing" of the Eucharistic "signifier" from the Catholic side — also ecumenically aware — cf. E. Schillebeeckx's *The Eucharist* (New York: Sheed and Ward, 1968), esp. the second half of the book, from p. 76 on. For those who dig deeply in this literature, it is possible to become confused as to the actual practical distinctions being made by various "eschatological" viewpoints. Consider the impressively detailed and subtle comparative study of De Lubac and Zizioulas by Paul McPartlan, *The Eucharist Makes the Church: Henri de Lubac and John Zizioulas in dialogue* (Edingurgh: T. & T. Clark, 1993), esp. chs. 9 and 11. Two very different conceptions of history, ecclesiology, and pneumatology inform the sacramentologies of this Roman Catholic and Orthodox pairing; but it is not clear that in either case the ecclesial division inherent in Eucharistic practice as it is presently enacted can really touch the asserted significance of the experienced sacrament because, however carefully parsed according to such eschatological detail, the framework itself is essentially protective with respect to historical disease. (Cf. the brief n. 75 on p. 199 for an example of the timidity elicited by such a question. McPartlan cites Zizioulas, on the issue of Eucharists celebrated in "manifest" division, as saying, "I would even say that it ceases to be [the] Eucharist, but I know that that would provoke many objections." We shall see that this shunned alternative itself may be a way of avoiding the issue, since it is precisely a *real* Eucharist, in division — a Eucharist that has a history — that ought to make us tremble.)

10. The whole orientation of *Baptism, Eucharist, Ministry* (Faith and Order Commission of the WCC, 1982) on the topic of the Eucharist is suffused with this vision. The influential role of Eastern Orthodox contributions to ecumenical sacramentology and ecclesiology is important here, and beyond my expertise to describe. One might wonder, however, whether Orthodox notions of pneumatic "eschatology" are well understood by Western denominationalist theology or whether these notions themselves have not already been colored by a reverse influence, now sounding rather adjustable to the divisional character of so much Western discourse. Cf. Gennadio Limouris, ed., *Come, Holy Spirit, Renew the Whole Creation: An Orthodox Approach for the Seventh Assembly of the World Council of Churches, Canberra, Australia 6-21 February 1991* (Brookline [Mass.]: Holy Cross Orthodox Press, 1990), which, despite a deliberate attempt to offer a kind of "alternative" to other papers preparative to the assembly, actually offers much that is, to Western ears, perfectly congruent with a separatively justified reading of contemporary ecclesial life. See in that volume, for example, Emmanuel Clapsis's

stressed is the way that the Eucharist, within this conceptual framework, has been deliberately recast as a sacrament impervious to the history of its enactment, even in division. It is good "food" for the sinful; it is a "sign" of grace for those who need forgiveness; it is an "instrument" of missionary regeneration whose object, including the unity of the Church by which it is celebrated, lies still in the future; it is driven by and itself offers an "epiklesis," or invocation of the Spirit, whose open-ended power impels the Church away from its past and toward future arrangements and tasks whose shape is not yet revealed. It is at least one thing, one positive thing, that divided Christians can still do; and in doing it, the wounds of the past are at worst scarified, at best even healed. The possibility that the celebrated Eucharist itself engenders some new flow of blood is not raised. If the Eucharist is essentially a "sign," if that sign points away from the present, and if that pointing is itself a source of pneumatic fodder, ecclesial healing is given even as the body weakens.

The contemporary "eschatologizing" of the eucharistic "sign" is only a

---

"The Holy Spirit in the Church," which celebrates the pneumatic "transcending of all static institutions" (p. 168) that an eschatological ecclesiology allows. The way such a "critical" principle may popularly yield to a relativizing of institutional failure, on an ecumenical level, is manifest in the general acquiescence to division that contemporary missionary theology and practice has embodied. For by the time the Anglican-Reformed International Commission produced its report, there was already so much worry over the possible incompatibility of the search for Christian unity with the search for justice that a long section (cf. pars. 29-34) was deemed necessary to hold the two together, precisely by defining the Church in terms of its "provisionality" with respect to future perfections, the difference between which prods to a continual movement forward to "increased" structures of justice. In this section, the "sign" of the Church lies in the *partial* aspect of its eschatological fullness, its "foretasting" and "first-fruitfulness" in the Spirit, which grasps hold of the good (justice and unity), even while mired in the historical realities that contradict it. This kind of attempt to plead for unity in the midst of churches that no longer care about it, by arguing for the normative character of ecclesial sin, ought to be logically astonishing, but it is in fact rather common today. There is present a certain wistful hope that the Holy Spirit will prove a more adept escape artist than the Body it is purported to lead. The U.S. Lutheran-Episcopal Dialogue, Series III, *Implications of the Gospel* (1988), adopts so thoroughgoing and explicitly eschatological a perspective that the Church is baldly redefined as a community "called to wrestle with the implementation" of a particular "agenda against the powers of the 'old age'." Provisionality, which ought to enable the freedom for overcoming divisions, has here taken on a broader reach: "the New Testament documents are themselves evidence that the struggle of the 'new age' in Christ against slavery and economic oppression, against ethnic and racial oppression, against sexism and gender oppression has not always, perhaps not often, been successful. But it remains the agenda" (par. 60). The disclaimer of past success, of course, is what turns Christian unity into a progressive "struggle," in the analogy of political action, rather than leaving it an inescapable piece of historical debris to be cautiously and painstakingly climbed over, on hands and knees.

recent version of a more endemic modern — and separative — attempt to pry apart the Eucharistic act, as an ecclesial practice, from the significance of the sacrament itself. Our concern in this chapter is to bring into relief the way in which the significatory character of the Eucharist, as it has been increasingly focused upon, has evolved as itself a way of avoiding the specifically ecclesial question of a divided sacrament. To the degree that the Eucharist can be defined in terms of its sign-function, which points to something definably distinct from the historical practice of its own enactment, the sacrament can retain its positive power both to nourish and to indicate a body of Christians justifiably distinct from others. To the degree that the Eucharist is an instrumental tool — linguistically, semantically, semiotically, even substantively — its character has been spared from any history other than one of the Church's conceptual precision. The whole question of how *in fact* the Eucharist "tastes" in a *contemporaneously* divided church can be avoided in this framework, since its savor — "foretaste" — derives from something whose substance lies beyond the "bitter root" of the present. Speaking pneumatically, the Eucharist in this way has been bequeathed to an ahistorical Spirit, whose life, whose sensibilities, are granted immunity from the prophecies that touch the Church's form.

And this reconstruing of the Eucharist as a signifying instrument, capable of making present somehow (and however "realistically") what was historically absent — a function shared by contemporary eschatologizing sacramentologies — is logically tied in the West to the affirmation of ecclesial division in the sixteenth century. Let us take representatively a passing comment of John Calvin in his *Institutes,* made in the course of a discussion concerning the "grounds" upon which the Roman doctrine of transubstantiation might be (mis)laid. Calvin points to an "absurd" reading of Jeremiah 11:19 (according to the Vulgate) that the Papists have brought forward as one among many "proofs" for their interpretation of the Real Presence of Christ in the Eucharistic elements. The text of the prophet runs, "I was as a meek lamb that is carried to be a victim: and I knew not that they had devised counsels against me saying: *Let us put wood on his bread* and cut him off from the land of the living, and let his name be remembered no more" (Douay translation). This verse, applied figuratively to Christ Jesus by Catholic exegetes working in the tradition of the Fathers, had been used in the sixteenth-century Eucharistic controversy to demonstrate how this prophecy of the Cross also included a linguistic identification of "bread" with Christ's historical "body." For Calvin, this was a simple case of "twisting" the "true meaning" of the prophet: "the prophet complains that wood is put into his bread, signifying that by the enemies' cruelty his bread was infected with bitterness. So David by a similar figure of speech deplores that his bread was corrupted by gall and his drink with vinegar [Ps. 69:21]."[11]

The issue at stake here is whether the Eucharistic elements are or are not "substantively" the historical "body" of Christ. In this case, the import of scriptural language is brought to bear on the argument, in a manner familiar from our stock view of the Protestant-Catholic polemic over biblical exegesis. Calvin insists that the words be read "literally," as a first-order metaphor describing the prophet's own state of mind. "Bread mixed with wood," "bread mixed with gall," and "wine mixed with vinegar" are expressions denoting a feeling of "bitterness" on the part of the speaker.[12] The Papists read the text "allegorically," applying its meaning in a figurally prophetic manner not only to the person of Christ, but also to sacramental elements Jesus himself labeled as his "body." As with the Eucharistic controversy of the time in general, the debate turns on the question of "signification": first, what do the words of Scripture, including Jesus' words at the Last Supper, "this is my body," signify, and how; second, what do the Eucharistic elements themselves, as they are used by the Church, signify, and how? From both sides of the controversy, this search for the character of Eucharistic signification as a mode of communication, rooted to scriptural signification in general, subjected the Eucharist itself to an objectifying scrutiny, which separated it as an action from the actual phenomenal existence of the Church and transformed it into a text or an instrument that was conceptually independent of the communities in which it was celebrated. For Catholics, the figural import of the text from Jeremiah lay in the objective character of the Eucharistic elements themselves, as they embodied the sub-

11. Calvin, *Institutes*, IV:17:16, in *Institutes of the Christian Religion,* trans. F. L. Battles (Philadelphia: The Westminster Press, 1960), vol. 2, p. 1378. Calvin makes the same point in his *Commentary* on Jeremiah at this verse, although there he accepts that Jeremiah himself may well be a figure of Christ, even if no implications can be drawn from this. I have not been able to identify the Catholic exegetes to whom Calvin refers here — perhaps Thomas Aquinas. However, in the generation after Calvin, Cornelius à Lapide, the celebrated Flemish Jesuit, offered a careful defense of the "figural" reading of this text (in his much-reissued *Commentary* on Jeremiah [1621]), using Calvin specifically as a foil, and citing earlier Catholic Tridentine exegetes like Maldonatus. Many of the Fathers saw the verse as a whole as referring figurally to Christ; Tertullian especially went so far as to see in it a reference to the Eucharist in particular (cf. *Against Marcion*, 3:19), as did Lactantius, more obliquely (*Divine Institutes,* 4:18).

12. Calvin's insistence that the text from Psalm 69 also be read nonfigurally is odd, given the use of the verse in a figural sense applied to Christ on the Cross in the Gospels. But even in his *Commentary* on this psalm, Calvin only reluctantly accepts this application, and then only in a subordinate way.

stantive flesh and blood of Jesus; that is, the scriptural text "defined" the Eucharistic act in general. For Calvin, the Eucharistic act was properly defined, also generally, in a way that avoided scriptural figuralism altogether, but sought the application of principles of biblical signification to the particular question of this one doctrine. In each case, having properly explicated the significatory character of the Eucharist, ecclesial polemicists were able to trace the relationship between the objective nature of the Eucharist and any purported Christian community, and so determine the latter's integrity. Its signifying character having been objectified, the Eucharist itself was now capable of being made a "mark" of the true Church. The pattern here is congruent with the whole drift of divided hermeneutics and ecclesiology: the Church itself is carefully excluded from having any referential bearing in the figural meaning of Scripture, with a view to immunizing separated bodies from bearing the weight of Jesus' own historical form.

To illustrate this pattern from the start, we need to note how the controversy over the Eucharistic signification was itself a tool to support the claim of respective churches as to their purity or election. For Calvin, the nub of the problem lay in the alleged fact of Roman "idolatry," which doctrinal precision on the question only brought into relief.[13] To the degree that the Roman Mass was organized around Eucharistic elements that were falsely imbued with a "real corporeal presence," the Holy Supper had been transformed from a Christian sacrament into the "table of the devil," according to the locution of Paul in 1 Corinthians 10:21. False teaching was only a contributory factor here; the Roman Church's Eucharistic sin lay, most profoundly, in its false worship. As such, the Roman Church was to be *fled,* not simply corrected. Calvin brings his most robust polemical rhetoric to bear in those contexts wherein he attempts to persuade his co-religionists that virtually any participation in Catholic ritual is a form of blasphemy. A Mass informed by the doctrine of transubstantitive Real Presence he likens to Jeroboam's worship of "calves" at Bethel (1 Kings 12); and thereby the whole Roman Church becomes itself a schismatic body, inhabited by demons, and cut off from the remnant of Judah's Kingdom, from which the Messiah emerges. The only faithful Christian response to such a "body" is the complete repudiation of Communion and an utter separation of commerce. This whole argument forms the basis of Calvin's

13. Cf. John Calvin, "On Shunning the Unlawful Rites of the Ungodly and Preserving the Purity of the Christian Religion" (1537), in Calvin, *Tracts and Treatises in Defense of the Reformed Faith,* trans. Henry Beveridge (Grand Rapids: Wm. B. Eerdmans, 1958), esp. pp. 377-93, which treats specifically of the Mass.

attack on Protestant "Nicodemites," who feign participation in Catholic worship for the sake of concord.[14]

Here the Catholic Eucharist works as an illuminating negative marker to the false Church. The marker itself is explicated according to a right apprehension of the Eucharist's significatory character, which then becomes itself a positive marker for the True Church.[15] For Catholics, of course, the defense of the transubstantiation doctrine served a similarly transparent purpose from the opposite side: where that doctrine could be defended and upheld, so was upheld not so much the integrity of Papal teaching (although that too), but even more magnificently, the actual divinely elect character of the Roman Church, whose visible precincts were blessed by the condescended physical presence of Christ in the Eucharist. We can take, for an example, a sermon extract by the celebrated French controversial theologian Jacques Davy, the Cardinal Du Perron, who wrote in the late sixteenth and early seventeenth centuries and whose most famous works included several long treatises devoted to the Eucharist. Preaching on Easter, Du Perron uses the paschal imagery of the feast day to focus on the Eucharist itself, which he describes in the most extravagantly gustatory language ("angelic meat," "royal delicacies," divine "liquor" "ravishing and inebriating men," "voluptuous torrents" "flowing from the breasts of the Church," and so on), building on and transforming accounts of the pagan feasts of Roman emperors. But the beneficiaries of this banquet are defined by the ecclesial body that recognizes and accepts the food:

14. On this topic in general, see Carlos M. N. Eire, *War against the Idols: The Reformation of Worship from Erasmus to Calvin* (Cambridge: Cambridge University Press, 1986), ch. 7, "Calvin against the Nicodemites," pp. 234-75. We have noted, in our first chapter, the controversial use of the Jeroboam figure. It is interesting in this context to see that, while Calvin used the "schismatic" king as the basis for an argument about the necessity of breaking communion, later Protestants went so far as to use the episode as an argument for diversely separated but valid Christian denominations. The seventeenth-century French Reformed theologian Pierre Jurieu, for instance, argued that prophets of Jeroboam's separated kingdom in the North were as "elect" as those from the remnant kingdom to the south, even though they never participated in the Jerusalem cult. By contrast, some Catholics could use the larger story as an example of how communion must be maintained in situations of ecclesial fracture: surely, they argued, it is more likely that saints like Elijah in the North *did* stay in communion with the Temple worship in Jerusalem, despite the division of the two kingdoms. For the argument, which demonstrates again how ecclesial division was quickly either explained away or denied outright by each side, cf. Pierre Nicole, *De l'unité de l'église ou réfutation du nouveau système de M. Jurieu* (Luxembourg: 1727), pp. 282-89.

15. Cf. Calvin, "On Shunning the Unlawful Rites," pp. 384ff., where the whole significatory problem is broached.

Our Lord treats to his feast today not only the Roman people who live enclosed within the walls of Rome, but the whole Church, Catholic, Apostolic and Roman extended throughout the world. And He lays and furnishes not only twenty-two thousand tables [like a well-known Roman emperor of the past], but twenty-two million tables, that is, as many Catholic Altars as exist within the world.[16]

The true "Roman Church," the true "Roman feast," is marked by the Eucharistic presence, and Du Perron goes on to defend this demarcated body against the "harpies" of the Reformers, whose mission is to "infect" or "steal" away the heavenly food from unsuspecting Christians, leaving them to die hungry and abandoned.[17]

The Eucharist, then, in its significatory function, had become a mark of distinction between ecclesial bodies, a tool of separatist justification.[18] That the character of the Eucharistic presence should somehow be linked with the status of a church was not in itself, as we shall note, an untraditional notion. But that defining the Eucharistic presence should become an instru-

---

16. Du Perron, *Oeuvres Diverses*, 3rd ed. (1633; repr. Geneva: Slatkine Reprints, 1969), vol. 2, p. 678.

17. Du Perron, p. 681.

18. This role became so embedded in the post-Reformation construal of the sacrament that once even the doctrinal element of the rite became moot, as it did with time between many Protestant groups especially, the separative character of the Eucharist was maintained, as a superficial vestige of the much deeper logic that fueled sacramental piety. There is no space here to pursue this historical aspect, but the controversies in, for example, the Church of England over "occasional Communion" and within other denominations over the practice of "closed Communion" evidence this dynamic. On the former controversy, which touched on whether Dissenters ought "occasionally" to participate in the Anglican Eucharist as required if they wished to hold public office, the Calvinist rhetoric against the Nicodemites resurfaces, this time in the mouths of Anglicans concerned less with Eucharistic doctrine than with denominational exclusion. Cf. Henry Dodwell, *Occasional Communion Fundamentally Destructive of the Discipline of the Primite Catholick Church and Contrary to the Doctrine of the Latest Scriptures, Concerning Church-Communion* (London, 1705). More temperately, and with a certain appreciation of the dilemma faced by the existence of divided denominations that are not doctrinally separated with respect to the sacrament, William Sherlock, *A Resolution of Some Cases of Conscience Which Respect Church-Communion,* 2nd ed. (London, 1683). In Sherlock's case, as in Dodwell's, the existence of separate churches seems to demand separate Eucharistic communions; it makes no sense (versus modern ecumenical thought) to link ecclesial plurality with Eucharistic openness. The problem these theologians faced was how to justify toleration in this regard; and the tendency was to take hold again, in a grudgingly explicit manner, of the separative premise. On the controversies over "closed Communion" among Baptists especially, see the literature that followed the rigorist Isaac Marlow's *The Purity of Gospel-Communion* (London, 1694), a debate that continued well into the nineteenth century, in works by, for example, Robert Hall and J. G. Fuller.

ment for defining the Eucharistic community's status *as* Church indicated, in fact, a radically new task of theological and disciplinary discernment. For now, not simply a wedge, but a conceptual and realistic breakage between the thing called "Eucharist" and the thing called "Church" had occurred that made of each entity a logically distinct construct. The meaning of these two entities could be gleaned through independent avenues of analysis — one could ask what the Eucharist or the Church was without referring to the other *ab initio*. And their positive relationship one to another could now only be asserted as something existing between two discrete phenomena, separate signs that needed to be brought together through some externally imposed grammar if they were to make common sense. In the separative grammar of ecclesial division, the Eucharist was an *indicator* of the Church; but it was so in the manner of a "conventional" sign (to use Augustine's term),[19] an artificially designated "mark" whose meaning either Scripture or tradition had linked with the independent reality of "Church" already asserted oppositionally by each side.[20]

19. Cf. Augustine's *De Doctrina Christiana,* II:2-4. A "natural sign" is something that "signifies without intention or desire," because of its natural properties — for example, smoke "signifies" fire. A "conventional" sign is one that signifies through some human custom, for the purpose of communicating some reality that would otherwise not be publicly apparent. In the wake of Reformation debates, Roman Catholics were not, of course, content to call the Eucharistic elements merely "conventional" signs altogether, in the sense of being entities whose breadth of reference lay somehow "outside" their own being and whose signification of the Body and Blood of Christ was comprehensible only through some social convention. However, with respect to the *Church* as a referent in particular, even Roman Catholics ended by treating the Eucharist as significant in this way, the ecclesial meaning of the act being ancillary and contingently dependent upon the essential signification of Jesus' body and blood.

20. The Augsburg Confession's definition of the two "marks" of the Church, including the right administration of the sacraments, is well known (art. VII). Calvin, in the main, follows it (cf. the *Institutes* IV:1:9-10), as do later Protestant Confessions, with some elaboration. Curiously, the Roman Catholic literature on the *notae Ecclesiae,* which flourished in the wake of the Reformation, did not include the sacraments in any primary position. The Eucharist, for instance, tended to come up under the "note" of "apostolicity," as an example of a "doctrine" whose form was "perpetual" in its conformity with apostolic teaching. (Cf. Gustave Thils, *Les notes de l'église dans l'apologétique catholique depuis la réforme* [Gembloux: J. Duculot, 1937], pp. 260ff.) However, the particular topic of Eucharistic "teaching," especially on the real presence, quickly took on an independent life of its own in controversial literature, often eclipsing other polemical topics, and can hardly be called peripheral to the establishment of the true Church. (Cf. below.) De Sales, in a revealing move, can see the entire "apostolic rule of faith" in the Creed, which he defends against Protestant perversions, as summarized in the Eucharistic real presence itself, the sacramental reality affirming Catholic truth in its very enactment (cf. *Controvèrses,* Pt. II, ch. 3:2; Mackey translation, in *Library of St. Francis de Sales* [London: Burns and Oates, 1886], vol. 3, pp. 321ff.).

In the case of ecclesial separation, the Eucharist "indicated" the Church according to the public apprehension of its proper (though contested) signification as "body of Christ" or "blood of Christ," that is, as a certain kind of "sign" itelf. This was a necessary posture to take with respect to a central ecclesial practice that was now in dispute among opposing Christian groups, whose proper enactment needed to be claimed as a distinct possession of one group over against another. And so Protestants and Catholics, in their larger projects of self-justification, were pressed to locate the distinguishing indicative character of the Eucharist in each respective church's method for maintaining the practice's signifying mechanism: how did each group secure the integrity of the Communion's meaning? In doing this, however, the Eucharist's first order reality could no longer "refer" to the Church directly, or "naturally," as something whose essential being was, even prior to its theological articulation, of one substance with the Church. For such a direct reference offered no demarcating instrumentality to the Eucharist that could separate off the true from the false church. Only if the Eucharist referred to something other than the Church, through which the Church could be subsequently and derivatively affirmed in some way, could the practice prove suitable as a distinguishing ecclesial mark. Thus, we find Protestants defending a mode of Eucharistic signification that openly disengages the liturgy from *any* ecclesial reference at all (by locating the "true body of Christ," for instance, apart from the historical phenomena of the present); while Catholics asserted a mode of signification that pointed to something whose reality lies *within* the bounds of the true Church (the transubstantiated elements) but is not itself joined to it in a prior way. As a conventional indicator of the Church (cf. the Protestant predilection for describing it as a divinely artificial "ordinance"), and not an intrinsic aspect of the Church (and thus "naturally" signifying), the Eucharist lost its "figural" character, in the sense that we have been using the term. Its meaning and force could no longer be located within the formative shapes that historical reality, supremely the Church, assumed in coherence with the figure of Christ, worked by the Holy Spirit. Given such a disintegration of the Eucharistic figure, Christians found a way to insist that being a certain kind of church might not imply the suffering of a certain kind of "taste," for the sensibility of one entity was no longer linked to the sensitivity of the other. It is at least plausible in such circumstances that at some later time someone might recall the words of the prophet, "Ah you, who put bitter for sweet and sweet for bitter!" (Isa. 5:20).

Sign or Figure:
The Ecclesial "Body" of the Eucharist in Augustine

We can clearly perceive this devolution by examining the fate of the Augustin-ian description of Eucharistic signification that held a central place in Western sacramental reflections throughout the Middle Ages. With the sixteenth-century division of the Church, Protestants and Catholics each justified their mutual opposition over the issue of the Eucharist by appealing, in part, to Augustine's authority. What one sees in these appeals is the manner in which Augustine's sacramental explications have been reduced, on both sides, to the question of the *mechanism* of signification, to the blatant exclusion of his foundational figural understanding of the Eucharist's meaning. Protestants and Catholics, of course, had to deal with Augustine's teaching on the matter in different ways; but each did so in a manner — and was obliged to do so logically — that would leave aside the figural context in which Augustine developed his views about sacramental reference.

One of the most notorious texts in which Augustine speaks to the question of Eucharistic signification is in the treatise *On Christian Doctrine*. The book itself offers guidelines for teaching the truths of the Christian faith, but in fact focuses more narrowly in the first three of its four books, on the issues of discerning such truths and founding them in the Scriptures. This involves Augustine in an extended discussion of Scripture's "figurative" lan-guage and its interpretation (much of Book III). First, in III:13, Augustine describes the sacraments of baptism and the Eucharist as among that "small number" of divinely "instituted" signs that remained, after the fulfillment of the Old Testament figures, for the use of Christian edification. But just as spiritual "freedom" for the Old Testament saints lay in focusing not on the signs but on the referents to which they point, so too Christians must avoid a "servile" relationship to their own signs, and use them with an eye to their signification, neither confusing them with this signified reality nor emptying them of their use. More particularly, in III:24, Augustine turns to the text of John 6:54 — "Unless you eat the flesh of the Son of Man and unless you drink his blood, you will have no life in you" — as an example of a divine command that, on its face, must not be taken as the "reality" upon which Christians must focus. For Jesus' assertion, taken literally, seems to demand something "shameful" *(flagitium)* and "criminal" *(facinus)*, that is, cannibalism. In such a case, Augustine writes as a general rule, one must take the scriptural expression as a "figure" that points us to a (benign) truth to which it refers nonliterally. In this text, Jesus' words must be "a figure that prescribes our participation in the Passion of the Lord and our sweet and profitable guarding in remembrance of his flesh, crucified and wounded for our sake." This set of remarks, along with a few others scattered about Augustine's writings,[21] was early examined in discussions of the Eucharist[22] and became central in the Protestant-Catholic controversy. Its centrality derived from its apparent interest in defining the mode of Eucharistic signification, which might locate the "body" of Christ in some "place" useful to the indication of the true church. But how, in fact, did Augustine understand the character of figuration itself here? Later Roman Catholics wanted — properly — to stress that a "figure," for Augustine, might well signify something "present" and not merely something "absent" (as they claimed Zwinglian interpretations of the Eucharist demanded). Even so, this was to miss the point of Christian figuration as a divine phenomenon, in Augustine's eyes; for the very fact that things, or words, or images, whether in Scripture or in the Church's life, might be "useful" (or "effective") for the Christian vocation beyond their immediate or apparent sense lay, as he saw it, in the manner in which God had organized the historical forms of time on behalf of a larger destiny of salvation given in Christ Jesus — a destiny whose mode of accomplishment given in the Incarnation tends to blur any strict distinction between specifically Christian signs and their referents.[23]

21. Cf. Letter 98:9, to Boniface. These texts were much discussed in the sixteenth and seventeenth centuries. See, for instance, book I, ch. 7, of Bellarmine's *Controversarium de sacramento eucharistiae,* which provides a survey of the main debated texts; see also references below in Arnauld-Nicole's *Perpétuité de la foi.*

22. Ratramnus uses this text as his jumping-off point in the tradition for asserting a nonliteral mode of Eucharistic presence; cf. the *De corpore et sanguine Domini, 33;* and see below.

23. A useful and summary exposition of *De Doctrina Christiana*'s signification and hermeneutics (along with some bibliographical references to standard treatments of the theme by nineteenth- and early-twentieth-century scholars) is offered in the article-notes appended to the Latin-French version translated and edited by G. Combès and the Rev. Farges (*Oeuvres de Saint Augustin* [Paris: Desclée de Brouwer et Cie, 1949], vol. 11). For a recent discussion of Augustine's understanding of signification, see R. A. Markus, *Signs and Meanings: World and Text in Ancient Christianity* (Liverpool: Liverpool University Press, 1996), which includes good references on recent relevant secondary literature. Markus's book, containing chapters from several originally separate studies (chapter 4 is devoted explicitly to the *De Doctrina Christiana,* although chapters 1 and 3 also deal with this material), focuses on the more purely semiotic aspect of Augustine's understanding of signs, and to this degree represents a modern version of the tradition that has viewed Augustine's interest in this topic in terms of a theory of signification and its modes. Accurate as far is it goes, this kind of discussion does seem to ignore the figural context in which Augustine construes the specific character of Christian signification (see below), with the result that misleading distinctions are made between Augustine and late "Antique" Christian exegetes like, for example, Gregory the Great (ch. 2) on the issue of scriptural hermeneutics. Between Augustine and Gregory, according to Markus, lies a "huge change in Christian sensibility," a "watershed in the Christian imagination" (quoting Peter Brown), a "huge intellectual upheaval"

At the opening of his treatise, Augustine uses this distinction in what appears to be a fundamental way: there are "things" *(res)* and there are "signs" *(signa)* of things. While some things can also be signs of other things, it is important to keep clear the difference between the sign as "used" and the ultimate "thing" to which any kind of sign points, even a "translated" sign that is itself a certain kind of "thing." For there is also, in the realm of human destiny, another fundamental distinction with respect to "things," that between their "enjoyment" *(frui)* and their "use" *(uti)*.[24] We are created to enjoy those things that make us "happy" *(beati)* and to use all other things for the sake of that happiness. And the only "thing" that exclusively deserves our enjoyment is God, in the persons of the Trinity.[25] Now Augustine is most interested, in these first chapters that follow, to underline this exclusive character of the divine *res* given for our joy and to show that all the rest of the created order is properly granted only an instrumental status in helping us reach the goal of full knowledge and life with God. And in doing so, he brings into a kind of moral linkage that which is a "sign" and that which is "useful" for the sake of the goal: signs are not things; all things, except God, are to be enjoyed only insofar as they are used for the sake of God; "things" are not "*the* thing," the *res* that is God alone.

Taken only at the level of this basic set of distinctions, it would be possible to claim that Augustine viewed the basic phenomenon of Christian figuration

(pp. 67ff.), instanced in the way that figural readings of the Scriptures were now, with Gregory, unmediated by a complicated subjective process of significatory discrimination, marked ultimately by an interior process of conversion and illumination (Augustine): biblical texts, instead, signified "spiritual" meanings in a straightforward, communally regulated fashion, which made of figuration a nontypologically first-order grammar. Part of this simplification and normalizing of spiritual exegesis by Gregory's time, as Markus suggests, no doubt derived from the changed relation of church and "secular" society, a merging of forms that also elided levels of signification between worldly symbol and divine meaning. But the potential clarity of figurative signification was already embedded in Augustine's practice, in large measure because he locates Christian signification not within a general theory of semiotics, but in a limited and particular historical realm of divine creative initiative — the "dispensation" of the Incarnation — that tethers Christian "signs" directly to the ordered shape of the world and its history in a way that is as direct as Gregory's. The figural realm of Christian experience, including the experience of comprehending "meaning," was, for Augustine, materially moored in the phenomenal world being "conformed" to the shape of Christ's existence by God's grace. Gregory's monastic presuppositions and context certainly lightened the weight he placed on some initial cognitive transformation by which to grasp the *res* of scriptural signs, but the distance between creature and creator was not less appreciatively great in his mind; in his case, however, he dwells more on the ascetically practical aspects of its bridging than does Augustine in his larger theological perspective, and aimed at pastoral rather than monastic formation.

24. *De Doctrina Christiana*, I:2-3.
25. *De Doctrina Christiana*, I:3, 5, 37.

as an artificial mode of signification that linked a limited cipher with a ("naturally") alien referent, whether that referent be other created things or the *res* of the divine being and truth itself. Within this view, the Scriptures themselves are only a set of signs, even signs of things, whose "usefulness" lies in the written word's ability to lead us to the *res* of their referent and whose profitability is provisional with respect to the fullness of human contemplation of God. Augustine recognizes that, not only in paradise, but even now, there are Christians who "enjoy" God so deeply and directly that they have no need for the mediating instruments of the biblical writings, which only signify what is, in the case of some saints, already possessed.[26]

In the end, however, this is probably a reductive reading of Augustine's understanding of signs in their relation to their referents. For it is precisely because no "thing," no created entity, no image, no word or concept can properly refer to God's unsurpassable being, and because human persons cannot attain or apprehend the *res* to which their life points, that the economy of salvation given in the Son takes form.[27] The metaphysical distance between creature and Creator, not to mention the moral distance due to sin, demands that human beings be transformed in some fashion to be like the One they are to enjoy. They must learn to "love," their love must purify them, and they must have this love unite them exclusively to God.[28] This learning and this transformation are made possible solely by the Incarnation of the Son, wherein the inexpressible becomes expressed and the inaccessible *res* of the divine being takes its place among the things of the world, humiliating itself to the level of the transitory, that it might raise what is impermanent into the realm of eternity.

Augustine's appeal to this consistent patristic soteriology within the context of hermeneutics has the effect of refounding his basic attitudes toward Christian "signs," not only granting them providential validity, but tying them to the formative character of the Incarnation itself. On the one hand, the Scriptures are "provisional" in their usefulness when seen in relation to the state of blessed communion with God; but on the other, they form part of that great divine act in which God himself assumes an instrumental ("medicinal") form equal in kind — because their prototype and pneumatic source — to the provisional shapes of his other salvific tools. If the value of the Scriptures depends upon the benefit they supply, through their signifying function, in inculcating love, the presence of the

---

26. *De Doctrina Christiana*, I:43.
27. *De Doctrina Christiana*, I:6-12.
28. *De Doctrina Christiana*, I:10; 21ff. In most of these texts, Augustine uses the term *dilectio* and its cognates for the basic attitude of love, for God or creatures; but he also uses the term *caritas* as a synonym, especially where he is speaking in a more precise theological way (cf. I:42-44).

source of that love within the forms of time transforms such signifying function into a participatory, even if limited, vessel tied to the divine life itself. If we enjoy God by loving God, and if "love is the plenitude and end of the Law and of all the divine Scriptures" given by God for our formation in love according to his grace, this is because the "whole of the temporal dispensation has been created for our salvation by divine providence," so that we might, through its proper "use," "love" all these temporal things with a "love and a delight," albeit in an ultimately "transitory" fashion, that shares in the final love that is God's creative being.[29] And if Augustine goes so far as to say that even the forms of Jesus' incarnate and saving life are, in some sense, eventually to be "left behind" because of their temporality, this does not mitigate the fact that they are divinely and salvifically impregnated with the Word present. Rather, their "transitory" forms serve the purpose of engaging us in this temporal economy of love whose passage through history has a goal toward which we must move as participants in the forms of divine history, and not as immobilized spectators to the divine dispensation.[30]

Within the specific dispensation of the Incarnation, then, Augustine's seemingly fundamental distinction between the *res* of God and the *res* of its assumed historical forms is, at least experientially, elided. For these forms hold their providentially ordered formative powers through their participation in the single divine love from which they derive and to which they point. And to the degree that such historical *temporalia* signify, or "draw" us as "vehicles" to God in a formative sense, they do so because of such caritative participation.[31] The whole phenomenon of Christian signification is thereby given a special character, quite different from the rules of signification followed by signs in general: Christian signs, as providentially ordered by God within the realm of the Incarnation's history, cannot be posited as entities in essential isolation from their referent; they participate in the reality of the referent through the divine self-condescension of love that has given them birth in the first place.[32] In the case of the bare words of

---

29. *De Doctrina Christiana*, I:39.

30. *De Doctrina Christiana*, I:38.

31. Cf. *De Doctrina Christiana*, I:39.

32. Compare Augustine's earlier and constricted discussion of "signs" in the *De Magistro* to see how profoundly altered his mature notion of even verbal signification had become. In this short work, still infused with a strong Platonistic epistemology, signs in general are denigrated as a source of any real knowledge, because of their basic difference from their referent. Even Scripture, a discussion of which he defers to a later time, is relegated to a position of purely functional usefulness. Augustine's rapid assimilation of a scripturally based incarnational theology, however, and one centrally moored in the formative realm of the Church's common life, radically altered the way he would assess the significative character of material forms. Anyone who still wishes to describe patristic sacramentology in terms of a basic orientation given by

Scripture, for instance, Augustine describes their power in historical and metaphysical conjunction with the incarnation of "the Word" itself: the "communication" of God from his hidden inaccessibility takes place through the Word's appearance, as Son revealing the Father. It is not simply the case that we can think of the Son as Word in some kind of analogy with human words that express inner thoughts. For this revelation of the Word is extended through the scriptural law of the Old Testament before, and the preaching and writings of the apostles after, the actual temporal embodiment of the Word in Jesus of Nazareth. Scripture itself, through its signifying signs, is part of the divine self-expression that is the Word.[33] For this reason, the "rule" of Scripture's interpretation — that is, the character of its referential content and its apprehension — is identical to the character of the *res* whose being it communicates: *regnum caritatis,* the reign of love.[34] And the particular "signs" embedded in the scriptural language, whether they be interpreted literally or figuratively, are rightly understood when they give rise to an increased love in the reader. "Rightly understood," that is, because historically effective in accordance with their divine nature. A scriptural "figure" — or any Christian "sign" — is properly thus significative if it takes its place within the economy of salvation by which the incarnate God draws together the temporal elements of his creation into a participatory relation to his life.

As with the bare words of Scripture, even more so with other divinely ordained phenomena subject to the historical evolution of God's ordered destiny for the world. The forms of Christ's Incarnate life, as we saw, are both signs and the *res* to which these signs point. And these forms are given their temporally extended reach in the lives of their human objects through the form of the Church, continuous with its Lord. At the opening of his treatise, Augustine sets forth the basic structure of the Creed as the shape around which he describes the historical path through which the truth of God's being is given for the progress of creation to its term. And in this enumeration of elements that make up the incarnational dispensation that brings into expression the inexpressible God, the Church takes its place as the final historical *res,* following Jesus' resurrection and ascension, through which the *res* of the Trinity is given

---

Hellenistic metaphysics must come to terms with the genealogy of Augustine's evolution of thought on the topic, whose impetus is largely scriptural and whose outcome is broadly in line with a common core of sacramental and participatory realism.

33. Cf. *De Doctrina Christiana,* I:12 and II:4. Elsewhere, cf. *De Fide et Symbolo* 3-4; the *Confessions* IX:9f.; XIII:26ff. This linkage of Word and scriptural "words" as God's self-communicative design for salvation is not unfamiliar among the Fathers. Cf. Irenaeus, *Against Heresies,* IV:6; 20.

34. Cf. *De Doctrina Christiana,* I:39-42; cf. III:23; and 15-16, on the specific question of interpreting scriptural figures.

salvific form for humanity. First, the Church is mentioned, almost undeliberatively, as the outcome of the Holy Spirit's direction of the pilgrim's progress to God, the place where the pilgrimage through this world is pneumatically accomplished. With this almost passing observation, Augustine then pauses to define the Church more formally, as "in fact [Christ's] body, just as the apostolic teaching affirms [i.e., in Eph. 1:23]; indeed it is even called His spouse. And so He ties together His body, in which many members fulfill their various tasks, with the healing knot of unity and love."[35] The Church, at this point in the discussion, now forms the context in which the forgiveness of sins, the penitential life of self-purification, and the final resurrection of the body find their reality. And Augustine ends his credal exposition with an assertion of the final transformation of these historical enactments of the Christian life, useful instruments and vehicles for reaching the final *res* of God and given form within the ecclesial body, into the very goal itself, the condescended God, the "enjoyment" of whose presence in the temporal world is of a piece with eternal felicity: "therefore, among all these realities *(res)* which we have just noted, are those that are meant to be enjoyed, as being eternal and unchanging."[36]

So when Augustine much later (both in the time of composition and in the sequence of the treatise) concludes his particular discussion of scriptural interpretation with an exposition of the seven "rules" of Tychonius for parsing the figurative language of the Bible, he places as the first "rule" not a description of a linguistic trope, but a fundamental principle of the incarnational economy by means of which God takes a self-referring form in history. It is a principle whose supreme expression is given in the ecclesial reality of the Church as Christ's Body: " 'head' and 'body', that is, Christ and the Church, we know are grasped by us as a single person . . . and so let us not hesitate when one moves from [the word] 'head' to the 'body', or vice versa, even while we are speaking of one and the same person."[37] The ability of the scriptural text to speak meaningfully in this figurative way is founded, quite simply, in the fact that the referent, in this case, of the somatic terms is given in the *res* of the incarnate Lord's assumption of the forms of ecclesial life through which divine love molds and purifies us. The power of specifically Christian figuration, then, depends on the reality of a divine figural existence in time. And that "power" *(virtus)*, effective in the deployment of signs, both linguistic and otherwise, proceeds, as we have seen, from the human participation within that figural

---

35. *De Doctrina Christiana,* I:14-15.
36. *De Doctrina Christiana,* I:20: *in his igitur omnibus rebus illae tantum sunt quibus fruendum est, quas aeternas atque incommutabiles commemoravimus.*
37. *De Doctrina Christiana,* III:44.

formation whose shapes inculcate the love that binds us to God. Any discussion of the sacraments, or of sacramental reality, in Augustine's terms, cannot be divorced from this underlying conjunction of divine presence in love within the contours of a historical figure continuous with the life of the Church.

To describe an Augustinian understanding of the mode of Eucharistic signification, then, is to explicate a phenomenon much broader than the relationship between words and their referents, whether that relationship be understood as a narrow semiotic link or in terms of metaphysical presence. It is, rather, to specify the way the Eucharistic act itself participates in the larger figural reality of divine self-expression in the forms of ecclesial life and practice, wherein the "body" of Christ, his Church, and his sacrament intersignify according to the historical form of their mutual expression as ordered by God. It is possible to explore the meaning of the Eucharist on many levels apart from such a figural context; and the Reformation and post-Reformation discussions, carried on apart from this context, covered a full range of topics, from the Eucharistic presence, to its benefits, to its relation to (particular) ecclesial communion, to its pneumatic elements, even its eschatological character. In many cases these discussions contributed to profound and rich sacramental theologies on all sides, whose elements, when examined unpolemically as many ecumenical scholars have been doing for several decades, converge in striking and satisfying ways. But the central shape given to the Eucharist by Augustine's figural hermeneutic has remained steadily hidden from view during the modern period, even in these later pacific dialogues. For with the break of figural reference between "body" and "Church," there came the necessary obscurement of *caritas* as the *virtus* of sacrament. Both the disintegration of the figural linkage and the veiling of the caritative "virtue" are, of course, logically simultaneous changes in conception, even while their causal historical relation is probably the reverse. But whatever the case, the absence of Augustine's caritative explication of the eucharistic presence in the Reformation and post-Reformation debate over the Eucharist is, however inevitable, tangibly striking.[38]

---

38. Attempts, particularly "Augustinian" attempts, at retrieving aspects of this lost conceptual framework have been made recently. Cf. John Milbank's "The Name of Jesus: Incarnation, Atonement, Ecclesiology," *Modern Theology* 7, no. 4 (July 1991), which lays out some theological themes associated with the author's larger project. There is much in Milbank's scheme that has deliberate affinities with Augustine's caritative figuralism, especially its insistence on locating the historical specificity of Christ's efficacious "person" in the temporal outworkings of ecclesial existence, which somehow fill out the scriptural narratives and metaphors associated with Jesus in the Gospels. But there are some major divergences here that need to be noted if Augustine is not to be simply appropriated for a potentially alien postmodern political sacramentalism. Milbank has little discursive interest in the historical factuality of the Gospel narratives, however

For given the structure of Augustine's notion of incarnational significa-tion, in place even before the focusing of his ecclesiology in the course of the Donatist controversy, the figural manifestation of love that he saw as inherent in the very phenomenon of the Eucharistic act was a necessary foundation for his conception of the sacrament. Even in the controverted text from *De Doctrina Christiana* III:24, to which we referred at the beginning of our discussion, the signifying function of the words "unless you eat the flesh of the Son of Man" is explained by Augustine in terms of a command to "par-ticipate in" the Passion of the Lord *(passioni dominicae communicandum)*. The complex nuance of this explanation, narrowly interpreted in the divided Church according to opposing schemata of signifying function, is grasped only within the context of the larger figural history that joins eucharistic communi-cant, church, and Christ in the actual enactment of divine suffering love. Such a context refers the sacrament to a historical event to which the Eucharist is tied ecclesially in a way that surpasses the general ethical exhortation into which Augustine's phrase might otherwise be reduced (and/or defended). And if one were to explore further texts where Augustine treats of the Eucharist in a direct way, this underlying figural dynamic of *caritas,* by which the sacrament has any being at all, would be more than evident.

------

construed. Instead, he juxtaposes the "primary" narrative about Jesus — the bare shape of his deeds and words (to the degree that they can be described in what appears to be a historical-critical fashion) — with what he calls a "metanarrative," already embedded in the Gospel text itself. This "metanarrative," he claims, acts as a kind of built-in interpretive grid that grants significance to the bare narrative, by ascribing to Jesus words, forms of action, and scriptural/figural/metaphorical labels that somehow explain what is going on, by giving his otherwise vague historical life, as depicted, a formal religious content within the tradition. It is this "metanarrative" that grants the otherwise unknown Jesus some kind of sign-bearing function for the future; further, the referents for this future, embodied in the Church's common life, represent the "point" of Jesus in the first place. This is a move that Augustine, for one, had no interest in making. In fact, to make it at all would have struck him as undermining the efficaciousness of the whole signifying character of the Scriptures, let alone the ecclesial shapes that enact them. For Christian signs, according to Augustine, derive from the *historically primary* elements of the divine dispensation of the Incarnation, to which the Gospels refer directly. What appear as "metaphors" and "figures" in the narrative description do not provide a content to Jesus' life; they derive from that content, insofar as his life has given shape to the Scriptures and their imagistic language in a prior way, grounding them historically in his own experienced being. The fact that Milbank frequently chooses, perhaps despite himself, to redescribe the "metanarrative" of Jesus in terms that are conceptually and linguistically independent of the Gospel discourse itself is indicative of the way his higher "meaning" perhaps derives from a set of modern concerns extrinsic to the text (not just the narrative) as a whole. Cf. p. 319, where he claims: "the gospels narrate Jesus' utter refusal of selfish power, and relate this to a transformation which combines human words with power over violence and death in the suffering body itself. If the suffering body becomes an actively suffering body,

Take for instance his more substantively exegetical and homiletic discussion of the Eucharist in his twenty-sixth *Tractate* on John's Gospel (on 6:41-59). This work as well figured frequently in the Protestant-Catholic debate, because of Augustine's distinction here between the "visible sacrament" and the "virtue of the sacrament" (c. 11), which Protestants took to indicate a mode of sacramental signification that undermined the Catholic claim to a uniform (and historically real) Eucharistic presence, even while Catholics claimed the contrary. Augustine's own remarks, however, are not about signification at all: the distinction he makes between sacramental "visibility" and "virtue" is one he links instead with the distinction between "carnal" and "spiritual" as religious conditions that determine the "taste" of the Eucharist to the communicant. The issue here is tethered scripturally to 1 Corinthians 11:29, wherein Paul speaks of some Christians as "eating and drinking judgment" to themselves in the course of participating in the Eucharist. Those who do not receive the "virtue" of the sacrament are not described as those who do not properly

---

suffering for the sake of joy, and a greater joy for all, then it becomes the body that is united with other bodies. And united bodies are the resurrection [sic] — the making of words effective and life-giving, because no longer linked to selfish power, which means always the threat to kill, a power of death which in the long run spells the death of power." The (avowedly) "political" thrust of this kind of redescription is striking in the way that it semantically *divorces* ecclesial existence from the personalistic figures associated with Jesus (not to mention the Old Testament), not in the way it somehow brings them together; the latter (unfulfilled) linkage is Milbank's stated desire in locating "doctrine's" origin in the ecclesial history of the "community" of believers treating each other in a manner "founded" by Jesus and "repeated" discretely through time. And the wedge he has thereby placed between Gospel narrative and its "metanarrative" evidences a continued servitude to the purely modernist demand that the significance of Jesus be translated into some set of concepts — in this case political concepts of communal nonviolence — whose "attraction" offers an apology for the temporal extension and persistence of Christianity. It is instructive, in this light, that there is a total absence from Milbank's Gospel redescriptions of key Augustinian, and scriptural, "metaphors": God's ordering power, divine "grace," and (surprisingly, given Milbank's interest in the social practice of nonviolence) "love" itself. If nothing else, these are structural concepts upon which a figural understanding of divine and human history must minimally be grounded. This absence of descriptive terms for personal divine agency, human receptivity and humility, and pneumatic sensibility goes hand in hand with the abstracted character of Milbank's discussion of the Church's life as a whole, generally free from scriptural specificity (especially from the Old Testament) and from particular historical judgments about concrete events to which the Church contributes and subjects itself. (There is little room to speak of the Church's actual divisions in this framework; only of a "manifestly unredeemed world" [p. 329].) However one evaluates the ecclesially figural interpretation of Augustine suggested in the present work, its distance from modern and postmodern appeals to terminologically similar frameworks of understanding remains great, though perhaps not unbridgeable (cf. the way some of Milbank's proposals open up the possibility for at least a conceptual reappreciation of reparative love, as discussed in Chapter 5 below).

grasp the mode of the elements' significance — whether receiving super-stitiously and without faith, as Protestants interpreted the text, or receiving without apprehension of the real presence in Roman Catholic readings — as if the "visible sacrament" for Augustine meant the bare elements in their function *qua* signs.[39] Receiving the sacrament "visibly," or "unspiritually," or "carnally" meant simply refusing to participate in its figural reality as the historical enactment of God's love in Christ, into which we are grafted as members of Christ's Body, the Church; it meant to receive the sacrament without forgiveness of one's neighbors, without love. To those who received charitably, the Eucharist tasted of the "spirit" of Christ; to those who received uncharitably, the Eucharist was no less the "body and blood of Christ," but a body nonetheless that tasted of bitter wrath, because love rejected takes the form of justice. Judas received the "same" good "mouthful" from Jesus at the Last Supper as did the other apostles. Yet his own heart tasted nothing but the repugnance of the Word ensconced in enmity. But, Augustine points out, if you "approach in peace, it is bread, not poison."

The "virtue" of the sacrament, then, is the experienced sweetness of Christ's love, received as an effect of loving in return. But that virtue or outcome does not constitute the "reference" of the sacramental sign, which remains in place no matter the condition of the communicant. For the referent of the sign, in Augustine's figural sacramentology, persists as the actual body taken, given, and built up in Christ's incarnated self-offering, which has incorporated into its assaulted form, through their acceptance or rejection, the baptized individuals who partake of the consecrated elements within the Church. And because the Body of Christ, which includes the Church, stands as this primary reference, the integrity of its historical relation to its individual members is precisely what shapes the expression of the Eucharist's "virtue." Where love among members

---

39. The next chapter, 12, of this homily needs to be read carefully in this light. In it, Augustine brings into a rough equivalence the "sacrament" of communion among the Israelites mentioned by Paul in 1 Corinthians 10:1-4, in which the apostle speaks of the "same spiritual meat" and "same spiritual drink" received by the Hebrews in the exodus desert. Augustine can draw an equivalence here with the Eucharist because, as he writes, it is the "virtue" of the sacrament, received by an interior eating, that is the same, not the "visible" sacrament, which is only a "signifying form" for the "spiritual" reality that gives it virtue. This text seemed, obviously, of great value to the Protestant argument that wished to disassociate any essential connection between sacramental sign and its reference. But Augustine's point here has to do precisely with the reference — in this case, the crucified Son — held in common by both the Old and New Testament sacraments. He does not here discuss at all the mode of signification and whether or not there are differences or similarities in modes before or after Christ's Incarnation. Within this chapter's context, in fact, the question of signifying mode is answered through the larger discussion of caritative enactment through the Body.

does not exist, the Eucharist's force retreats into a "visible" symbology whose failure to touch the spiritual palate provides the harsh taste of a repudiated savor.

The Eucharist and the Figural History of Love

And so Augustine moves fluidly, in his discussion of "eating the flesh" of the Son, between remarks on signification, sacraments, worthy reception, while always circling around the topic of the Church's own unity in love. "Believers know the body of Christ, if they neglect not to be the body of Christ," he writes (c. 13), when trying to explain the nature of the Eucharistic presence of Christ as eaten "flesh," which is such a stumbling block to some. He quickly moves to 1 Corinthians 10:17, wherein St. Paul speaks of the "one bread" that we share because we are all "members of one body," and Augustine adds, "O mystery of piety! O sign of unity! O bond of charity! He that would live has where to live, has whence to live. Let him draw near, let him believe; let him be embodied, that he may be made to live. Let him not shrink from the compact of members." At the same time, he keeps this kind of extended signification tightly bound to the actual liturgical rite, which takes its physical shape as a central element in the drama of the ecclesial figure within which individuals live and die:

> The sacrament of this thing, namely, of the unity of the body and blood of Christ, is prepared on the Lord's table in some places daily, in some places at certain intervals of days, and from the Lord's table it is taken, by some to life, by some to destruction: but the thing itself [i.e., the *res* of the Church's unity in love embodied in Christ's Jesus], of which it is a sacrament, is for every man to life, for no man to destruction, whosoever shall have been a partaker thereof. (c. 15)

The issue of Eucharistic signification, then, Augustine subordinates to the historical manifestation of the Eucharist's referent in the life of the Church. To know the presence of the Christ in Eucharist, however that is ultimately defined, is possible primarily as one takes part in his figurated life in the Church's Body, which is governed by mutual love. One cannot "see" Jesus in the Eucharist, although he is truly present, until one perceives the unity of loving participation that the sacrament enacts.[40] One cannot perceive the

---

40. Cf. Augustine's discussion of the Emmaus encounter in the *Harmony of the Gospels*, III:72, where he uses the story of the disciples' ignorance of their companion's identity until their meal as a figure of the Eucharistic virtue in unity.

"conversion" of the elements of bread and wine to the Body and Blood of Jesus until one recognizes how the Eucharist itself has virtue in its figural manifestation of the "conversion" of hearts into a loving body within the Church. Especially in several of his later Easter sermons, which deal with the Eucharist the newly baptized are to receive, Augustine presses this aspect of figural participation in the sacramental referent to its limit: *quod accipitis, vos estis,* "you are that which you receive," he writes, if you receive with love for one another. Christ comes to the Church manifestly, as the Church embodies the love of his own self-offering among the Church's own members. And this manifestation is given for the sake of life within the Eucharist.[41]

It should be clear from all of this that the relationship between Eucharist, Church, and the sacramental presence of Christ is not, for Augustine, one whose primary explication can be conceived in terms of the workings of signs and their referents in a semantic fashion. Rather, they relate to one another as elements in a figural history, in which a variety of meanings are divinely given — that is, phenomenally enacted in some scriptural form — according to the shape that individual and corporate participation in this history has taken. When later denominational controversialists examined the example of Judas's participation in the Last Supper, it was done with an eye to distinguishing the conditions and parameters of the Eucharistic presence *per se* with respect to "worthy" and "unworthy" communion. With Augustine, the history of Judas stood instead as a figure of the sacramental efficacy as it took form in the history of the Church's embodiment of Christ's own love.[42] Judas joined in the same sacrament as the other apostles, received the same bread, but, as we have seen, received it for "poison" and not as a "sweet savor"; even more importantly, Augustine emphasizes the way that by his very presence in the Church, though he himself could not receive the blessings of the Church's life in communion with its Lord, Judas allowed the Church to enact its corporate figuration of Christ, by "bearing with him" as Jesus did, enduring him in love within its midst.[43] In this sense, the Eucharist

---

41. Cf. *Sermons* 227, 228B, and 229A. For the numbering, I am following the edition of the Augustinian Heritage Institute's translations of the *Works of Saint Augustine* (New Rochelle [N.Y.]: New City Press, n.d.), pt. III.

42. Augustine was not aberrant here. Alternative and more exclusivist readings of Judas's participation in the Last Supper were made by a few of the early Fathers, but they remained scattered and marginal within the tradition. Only at the time of the Reformation did they gain new currency. Cf. Kenneth Hein, *Eucharist and Excommunication: A Study in Early Christian Doctrine and Discipline* (Bern/Frankfurt: Herbert Lang/Peter Lang, 1973), pp. 38-49.

43. Cf. *Tractates* on John, 50:10-11. On Judas receiving the "true body and blood of the Lord" as was received by the apostles, see also *De Baptismo, contra Donatistas,* 5:9.

for Augustine had to be approached as a focal point of figural enactment; and just because of this, the questions surrounding the Eucharist tended, for him, to revolve almost exclusively around the historical question of the Church's caritative integrity.[44]

In his ninetieth Sermon, on Matthew 22:1-14 (the parable of the wedding guests), Augustine uses the occasion of a Eucharist in the cathedral of Carthage to speak of what it means to take Communion "worthily" (he refers to 1 Cor. 11:29) as the point of enactment for the final, eschatological feast of communion with God. That the sacrament here "figures" the eschatological banquet is a common patristic understanding. What is notable and characteristic in the sermon, however, is the way that Augustine not only merges the actual sacramental practice with the heavenly "feast" as its participating indicator, but establishes that signification through the practice of ecclesial charity in the present and future assemblings of the Church. The parable speaks of a banquet to which "the good and bad" are called together, after the initial guests had refused to come and been punished. But there is one man who has entered without a "wedding garment," and he himself is thrown out into the darkness. The Eucharist is the place where the whole of this narrative is enacted. But the Eucharist is not itself the point of the story, except in this regard of necessary temporal context. Nor, for that matter, is the "referent" of the story the heavenly banquet from which the inappropriately attired individual is thrust out and to which the Eucharist as sacrament points. It is the "garment" itself that bears the center of meaning here, and that garment refers neither to the sacrament nor to the eschatological referent of the sacrament's narrative symbology. The garment, as Augustine argues at great length, is "the goal of the commandment: love from a pure heart, and from a good conscience and from an unfeigned faith" (quoting 1 Tim. 1:5). "Love is the wedding garment."

Practiced love, which Augustine explores in concrete detail in this sermon, is the "point" of the parable; but it is also the point of the "sacrament," which enacts this story by figuring the marriage of a loving bridegroom with his church, gained through his crucifixion. The historical fulfillment of this love in its effects is given in the banquet of the redeemed in heaven, but only as a kind of expression of the love first given. It is true that each element of this discourse — the actual Eucharist in Carthage, the parabolic narrative of the Scripture, the Incarnation and Crucifixion, the future

---

44. For further references in Augustine's work, within the context of his historically rooted ecclesiology, see Émilien Lamirande, *La Situation ecclésiologique des Donatistes d'après saint Augustin. Contribution à l'histoire doctrinale de l'oecuménisme* (Ottawa: Éditions de l'Université d'Ottawa, 1972), esp. pp. 38-50.

enjoyment of the saints with God, the condition of this or that Christian in their relation to others — can be laid out as separate entities that are drawn together in a rhetorical line of semantic intersignification. One can make arguments about the "meaning" of the Eucharist in this regard (or the meaning of the parable, etc.). But Augustine wants further to ground all these realities in a single historical figure, within which the fate of actual loving assumes, through its transitory forms, a total coherence of divine meaning, clustered around God's own acts of self-giving. The Eucharist as a "bare sacrament" possesses no significance independent from this, just as its participants, whatever their dispositions, cannot be examined except as they maintain their place within the single story of the Wedding. But their relation to love, in a Eucharistic context as in life as a whole, determines the form of their roles within that story. The single story becomes their history, because the (ecclesial) body in which they live has been assumed by the Body of history's Lord. In this sense, the Eucharist has no "meaning" at all to which it refers, in whatever mode; it has no signifying function. Rather, the Eucharist has a *history*.

The Eucharistic history is at one with the history of divine love, given, refused, sullied, grasped after in whatever way among the people gathered for its reception in the body of love's labor. Augustine frequently turns to the Eucharist and its participants as temporal expositors of this history, which encompasses not just a sacramental relation, but the very character and shape of the Church as it evolves within the forms of a Scripture fulfilled in Christ. Commenting on verses of Psalm 69 applied in the Gospels to the Crucifixion — "they gave for My food gall, and in My thirst they gave Me vinegar to drink" (v. 22) — he refers this passional event to the Eucharist as it is enacted within a Church riven by heresies and scandals. "Unto this food so pleasant, so sweet, of the Unity of Christ" (1 Cor. 10:17), "they gave gall after so delectable meat," he writes, referring to those whose Eucharistic communion is linked with their divisiveness. But "if we did not suffer them neither at all should we taste [its bitterness along with the vinegar]; but because it is necessary to suffer them, we must needs taste," as Christ did on the Cross. The Body of the Church, although those who hate within it are not "truly" its members, tastes the poison of their enmity by enduring the presence of these antagonists and by enacting Eucharists characterized by disunity. The Eucharistic history, in whatever form it takes, necessarily conforms itself to the body of Jesus, because its form embodies his temporal existence. Again, speaking of the sacrifices of the Old Testament at one point in his homilies on the Psalms, Augustine writes that these were "signs" for a promise "not yet fulfilled." But now, the Substance that was promised is come. We are in this "Body". We are partakers of this "Body". We know that which we ourselves receive; and ye who know it not yet, will know it by and bye; and when ye come to know it, I pray ye may not receive it unto condemnation. "For he that eateth and drinketh unworthily, eateth and drinketh damnation unto himself" [1 Cor. 11:29]. "A body" hath been "perfected" for us; let us be made perfect in the Body.[45]

The passage of time itself, ordered by God's providential dispensations, which embrace individual histories, takes the Eucharist into itself and displays its "body" ecclesially as part of the unfolding character of its reach, contingent in its particulars, yet clearly bounded through their conformance to an overarching set of forms, which are Christ's own.

Signification and Body of Christ in the West, Prior to the Reformation

As a theoretician of the Eucharist's figural character, Augustine produced writings both idiosyncratic and unique in their focus. But they were not, for that reason, derivative of a fundamentally novel understanding of the sacrament. Quite the opposite. Augustine's achievement was to articulate what was in fact a common fund of attitudes and experiences with respect to the practice of the Eucharist that were dispersed throughout the Church of the first centuries and whose theological explication had been given by various writers only obliquely, although with a certain consistency, in the process of speaking to a variety of other concerns. This recognition confirms the ongoing value of those classic studies from the mid-twentieth century that surveyed the early Church's conception of the "Body of Christ," and that contributed to the exposition of that doctrine by Pius XII in his famous 1943 encyclical *Mystici Corporis*. The most famous of these studies, Émile Mersch's *Le Corps Mystique du Christ*,[46] can no longer be considered a particularly nuanced historical analysis of the theme.[47] But precisely in its somewhat inchoate and piecemeal collection of

---

45. *Enarrationes* on Psalms 69 and 40 (translation from A. Cleveland Coxe's version in *The Nicene and Post-Nicene Fathers of the Christian Church*, 1st Series (repr. Grand Rapids: Wm. B. Eerdmans, 1989), vol. 8, pp. 307 and 124.

46. Émile Mersch, *Le Corps Mystique du Christ. Études de théologie historique*, 3rd ed., 2 vols. (Paris: Desclée, de Brouwer & Cie, 1951).

47. Henri de Lubac later called his own *Corpus Mysticum. L'Eucharistie et l'Église au Moyen Age: Étude Historique* (Paris: Aubier, 1944) "naive" in its lack of historical rigor and context,

material on the basis of Mersch's rather expansive theological categories, the book's large survey of writings, when carefully examined, can reveal the existence of a number of underlying continuities out of which Augustine's own detailed reflections emerge logically.

First, the understanding of the Eucharist's basic character as being that of an ecclesial figure was one that Augustine shared with most of his immediate predecessors and contemporaries throughout the Church. This was sometimes expressed in the terms given by Paul in 1 Corinthians (on 10:16-17 or 11:29),[48] or in reflections about the Church as Christ's "body" to which the Eucharistic act was applied,[49] or in the sacramental extrapolations made from baptismal "incorporation,"[50] or in very explicit figural exegesis about the Church as Israel reenacted and fulfilled in the sacraments of the New Covenant.[51] Second, we find a consistent affirmation that the Eucharist is given as part of the incarnational history of God, both in terms of its signification and in terms of its divine construction as an ecclesial act that is providentially offered as an instrumental extension of God's self-offering.[52]

---

but also thought this very characteristic useful in allowing for the display of larger historical shifts of meaning (see below). A clear English summary of patristic material can be found in Walter J. Burghardt's "The Body of Christ: Patristic Insights," in Robert S. Pelton, ed., *The Church as the Body of Christ,* The Cardinal O'Hara Series. Studies and Research in Christian Theology at Notre Dame, vol. 1 (South Bend: University of Notre Dame Press, 1963), pp. 69-101. An important series of articles on the theme, in the wake of *Mystici Corporis,* was provided by D. C. Lialine, in his "Une Étape en écclesiologie: Réfléxions sur l'encyclique 'Mystici Corporis'," *Irenikon* 19 (1946): pp. 129-52 and 283-317, and 20 (1947): pp. 34-54.

48. Cf. Chrysostom's *Sermons* on 1 Corinthians, e.g., 27, 28; Cyril of Alexandria, *Against the Blasphemies of Nestorius* 4.

49. Cf. Chrysostom, *Sermons* on Ephesians 3, on Eph. 1:15-20; Cyril of Alexandria, *Commentary on John,* on 11:11.

50. Cf. Hilary, *On the Trinity,* 8:5-1; Theodore of Mopsuestia, *Commentary on the Eucharist and Liturgy,* cf. in *Woodbrooke Studies,* 6, ed. and trans. A. Mingana (Cambridge, 1933), pp. 110ff.

51. Cf. Athanasius, *Pascal Letter* 7.

52. Cf. Hilary and Theodore, above. Mersch's discussion of Gregory of Nazianzus's *Oration* 38, on the Nativity, is somewhat puzzling unless one locates it in this sacramental context, in which the figural conformations toward which Gregory exhorts his listeners are given efficacy not only in ascetic practice (as he indicates at the end of the sermon), but fundamentally through the means of sacramental participation, in baptism and the Eucharist (as he seems to assume after the opening of the sermon). Gregory's sermon is a stunning patristic example of what over a thousand years later would be carefully articulated by seventeenth-century French devotional writers in particular in terms of "participation in the mysteries of Christ," one of the few deliberate modern efforts, however pietistically limited, to reappropriate the figural grasp of Christian redemption.

Finally, we find a common practical presentation of the Eucharist, not in terms of its right apprehension as a meaning-bearing sign, but as a critical event within the history of God's ordered salvation for individuals through which the life of the Church is shaped. This is especially the case when we observe that, where the Eucharist is talked about in its own right, rather than as a theological example within some other argument, the question of right "reception" looms large and forms the natural outcome to a description of the Eucharist's very purpose.[53] Athanasius, for example, places the Eucharist in the context of "paschal feast" of the Exodus, as well as the divine feeding, through manna, in the desert. Both are commonly used types, and following Paul in 1 Corinthians 10, they provide a narrative framework in which to discuss the dispositions of participants within the Christian Church, as figures of the Israelites. But Athanasius's long elaboration of this theme, making use of a florid array of scriptural exempla and verbal *catenae,* slowly forms a picture of the Eucharistic event as a key within the vast outworking of the acts of God in Christ, through which humanity as a whole is judged and redeemed, molded in justice and mercy through the temporal streams of its individual fates. As with Augustine, the Eucharist becomes a historical pivot, providing the taste of sweetness or of bitterness, where a person joins with Judas or with the other apostles around a Jesus who remains present and unchanged while the world winds around him into its final form. It is a remarkably constant vision that ends by undergirding the long tradition of Eucharistic preparation so prominent in both Eastern and Western Christianity, and that, as we shall see, reasserts itself to a new purpose in the divided Church of early modernity.[54]

But if there is a constancy in this vision, identifiable at least in the fourth and fifth centuries, is it possible also to note its gradual dissolution in the course of subsequent centuries? The question is an important one to answer if we are to determine whether the fate of ecclesial life in division has any bearing on the meaning of Eucharistic practice as it is experienced and given theological articulation. De Lubac, for one, has suggested that the sixteenth-century division of the Western Church, as expressed in its concomitant Eucharistic controversies, instanced only an extreme evolution of a

53. Cf. the references to Athanasius, Chrysostom, and Theodore, above.
54. For a simple Eastern version of this common tradition, which reflects a widely diffused popular perspective, see Theodore the Studite, *Small Catecheses,* 8 and 107. (There is a recent French translation, by Anne-Marie Mohr, *Petites Catéchèses* [Paris: Migne/Brépols, 1993].) The semantic interdependence, based on an historical figuralism, between Eucharist, ecclesial body, and incarnational forms within the large "dispensation" or "economy" of Christ's mystery is ingenuously presented as assumed.

theological drift that had already long been underway from the early Middle Ages. De Lubac's *Corpus Mysticum* came to this conclusion through a very subtle tracing of linguistic usage in medieval sources, which attempted to register small displacements of vocabulary among the shared traditions utilized by theologians of the period. Crudely summarized, the historical shift he identified took the following form. Among the Fathers, de Lubac argued, the phrase "mystical body" *(corpus mysticum)* was generally attached to the sacramental body offered in the Eucharist, while the term "true body" *(verum corpus)* was easily attached to the body of the Church. In the wake of the debates over the Eucharistic presence that took place in the ninth century (e.g., between Paschasius Radbertus and Ratramnus) and the eleventh century (between especially Lanfranc and Berenger), this patristic usage was reversed. By stressing the "reality" of the corporal presence of the Eucharistic "body," *verum corpus* became an increasingly frequent Eucharistic term, while the phrase "mystical body" gradually came to be linked more exclusively with that of the Church's corporate existence. If the two "bodies" were still held together theologically in these early centuries of the Middle Ages, the distinction also took on a technical character that was to give rise to an eventual root distinction.[55]

For de Lubac, this reversal proved "fatal" to the evolution of ecclesiology in particular. For by the end of the thirteenth century, it became possible to speak of the Church as "mystical body" in a way that was wholly independent of the Eucharist itself. In contrast to the latter's "realistic" corporal substance, the Church's defining significance was more and more cut loose from religious realities altogether, creating a "vacuum" of tangible meaning into which rushed a host of potential frameworks for discussing the Church's "visible" character, most of them borrowed from the political structures of secular and papal states. Separated from the Eucharist, the notion of a "mystical body" applied to the Church became a "metaphor," applicable to all kinds of social bodies, whose own contours ended by subjecting the Church's actual theological form to their order. It is only in response to this gradual medieval development, wherein the Church as a mystical body became identified with the various shapes of temporal power, that the Reformers' own ecclesiology adopted an overt "spiritualizing" focus, and one that only further rigidified the Catholic drift itself in the opposite direction.[56]

The terminological evidence that de Lubac marshals for this thesis is compelling; but it remains terminological only, and seems to attribute to verbal

55. De Lubac, *Corpus Mysticum*, pp. 104ff.
56. Cf. de Lubac, *Corpus Mysticum*, pp. 131ff., 286ff.

reorientations a profound historical causality in the realm not only of conceptualities but of social practice, one that is, at the least, theoretically debatable. The question of why the *conceptual* "mysticizing" of the Church's corporality and its decoupling from the Eucharist could subsist for over six hundred years until the sixteenth century, buttressed by a fervent commitment to corporate catholicism, is not answerable on de Lubac's terms. Further, the question itself raises issues as to the significance of the terminological development. Particularly of late, there has grown an increased appreciation of the subordination of such conceptual divergences to social realities, which themselves embody theological commitments far more pointedly than does their verbal articulation. And these are realities that ecclesial division contradicts in a basic fashion, acting as a ground to theological development, and not merely as its receptor. In other words, it is possible that the contradiction of ecclesial love in the sixteenth century in and of itself altered the significance of a theological terminology that before that time, and despite verbal continuities, was bounded by a realm of meaning wholly divergent from its postdivisional articulation. If, in fact, the Eucharist's meaning is given in its history of practice — and this is its figural character as Augustine summarized it — then the terminological issue is properly interpreted only in light of the historical practice itself.

Let us take only the most famous example from among the medieval controversies, that between Paschasius Radbertus and Ratramnus.[57] There is no question but that these theologians assumed sharply divergent terminologies to express their understandings of the Eucharistic "presence." The former adopted expressions of heightened "realism" — the sacramental "body" being the "true body," identical with the historically incarnate body of Jesus — while the latter carefully laid out an explanation based on the application of "symbolic" and "mystical" terms to the sacramental "body." These differences were obvious enough to be grasped in the Protestant-Catholic polemic, and Ratramnus's work, after centuries of neglect, was dusted off, translated, and lifted up by Reformed apologists to demonstrate, within the context of the limited reading of Augustine utilized by Ratramnus, that a "realist" position like

---

57. Paschasius Radbertus, *De Corpore et Sanguine Domini,* ed. B. Paulus (Turnhout: Brepols, 1969); Paschasius reiterates his views later in his *Epistle to Fredugard* (included in the edition just cited), where he defends himself with more ample quotations from the Fathers. Ratramnus, *De Corpore et Sanguine Domini,* ed. J. N. Bakhuizen van den Brink (Amsterdam: North-Holland Publishing Co., 1954). An English translation of Ratramnus (as well as excerpts from the opening sections of Paschasius's treatise) can be found in George McCracken, ed., *Early Medieval Theology,* The Library of Christian Classics, vol. 9 (Philadelphia: The Westminster Press, n.d.).

Paschasius's was a Catholic "novelty."[58] But did these differences add up to the positing of divergent modes of Eucharistic presence, so that one might speak of divergently apprehended Eucharistic enactments?

Let us examine the conceptual question first of all.[59] Paschasius, whose treatise was apparently written for fellow monks before later being revised and submitted to King Charles the Bald, proposes to deepen our "knowledge" about the Eucharist by explaining what ought rightly to be perceived "by faith" in its reception (cf. II:1f.). To this end, he analyzes in what sense the Eucharistic elements convey the body and blood of Christ. Paschasius's "realism" in this regard lay in his insistence that this sacramental substance was identical to the historically incarnate body of Christ Jesus, conceived, born, crucified, and risen;[60] and this aspect of his argument became linked with his subsequent fame (or notoriety) as a precursor of the transubstantiation doctrine. But Paschasius, in all of this, did not see himself as an innovator. He was articulating, rather, the clear tradition as he had received it, and even his most brazen "realist" affirmations find their precedents among earlier Fathers.[61] Further, Paschasius framed his realism within a sacramentology that owed much to the broad theories of incarnational signification used by Augustine (cf. esp. III and IV). Adopting the term "character" (perhaps from Ambrose) to explain in what way the Eucharist is a "figure," he explains how the Incarnation acts as a kind of visible sign, analogous to written letters, which represent to the eyes the performative words and their meanings that express in time the divine reality: the flesh of Jesus was the "character" or "figure" of God (cf. Heb. 1:3), and so too the Eucharistic elements are the "character" or "figure" of the incarnate flesh of Christ. But this kind of "figure" is not merely artificial in its mode of

58. Cf. Bakhuizen van den Brink's introduction to Ratramnus, *De Corpore et Sanguine Domini*. For a separate discussion of Ratramnus's (misidentified) appropriation by sixteenth-century British Protestants like Ridley (via Peter Martyr especially), cf. J. N. Bakhuizen van den Brink, "Ratramn's Eucharistic Doctrine and Its Influence in Sixteenth-Century England," in *Studies in Church History*, vol. 2, ed. G. J. Cuming (London: Thomas Nelson and Sons, 1965), pp. 54-77. We shall see, in a moment, how Jean Claude, moving on from these early arguments, attempted in the seventeenth century to use Ratramnus as a significant pillar in the historical reconstruction he erected to refute Catholic claims to a continuous doctrine of transubstantiation within the Church (both Eastern and Western).

59. For two recent overviews, cf. Patricia McCormick Zirkel, "The Ninth-Century Eucharistic Controversy: A Context for the Beginnings of Eucharistic Doctrine in the West," *Worship* 68, no. 1 (January 1994): pp. 2-23; and Celia Chazelle, "Figure, Character, and the Glorified Body in the Carolingian Eucharistic Controversy," *Traditio* 47 (1992): 1-36.

60. Cf. I: "Haec, inquid, *caro mea est pro mundi vita*. Et ut mirabilius loquar, non alia plane, quam quae nata est de Maria et passa in cruce et resurrexit de sepulchro."

61. E.g., Ambrose, in *De Mysteriis* 53.

signification (it is not "false"), even as written letters, once constructed, do not simply refer to another word, but actually form that word visibly. The "figurative" nature of the flesh of Jesus, as of the Eucharist, does not stand in contrast to the "truth" of God's presence, since these visibilities are divinely assumed, in time, to draw people into greater and greater union with God.

Paschasius founds the very nature of all sacraments, including the Scriptures themselves, upon this providential ordering of historical form that is subsumed in the Incarnation above all: "The birth of Christ therefore, and all that dispensation of humanity, becomes, as it were, a great sacrament, because in the visible man the divine majesty inwardly for the sake of our consecration worked invisibly those things which came into being secretly by his power. Thus the mystery or sacrament, which is God made man, is rightly so called."[62]

Through all particular sacraments, the Holy Spirit works sovereignly to make God present within the temporal order. Sacramental referents are "true" to the degree that God — the ultimate *res* of their signification — gives himself historically to human beings within these things; they are "figures" to the degree that they are part of this historical dispensation by which God draws us to himself through a variegated set of phenomenal forms.

It is no surprise, within this fundamental Augustinian framework, to find Paschasius moving, often fluidly, within a figural ecclesiology that links the Eucharist to the history of the Church's embodiment of God's salvific love. The Eucharist emerges out of and leads toward "participation in Christ in the unity of his body" (I), which is the Church as it is constituted through baptism (cf. III). Indeed, the Eucharist as the "body of Christ" is an aspect of the Church as the "body of Christ," each seen from a different perspective (VII), an instrumentality by which the spousal union between redeemed humanity and its savior takes place through the incorporation of the sacramental flesh in the liturgy. In a remarkable chapter (IX), Paschasius draws together the Eucharist, the unity of the Church in Christ, and the unity of the Father and the Son through the Holy Spirit as poles in a historical dynamic that fulfills a number of scriptural figures that, taken as a whole, delineate the overarching ordering of humanity to God. Individuals enter into this ordering current or struggle against it, but the current's term is given in the very process of ecclesial life reflected in its doctrinal, political, and liturgical enactments. Paschasius deploys his technical terms — *figura, veritas, sacramentum, corpus mysticum,* etc. — only within this framework, which, like Augustine, he characterizes as a reflection of divine creative and historical omnipotence. And as with

---

62. Paschasius Radbertus, *De Corpore* III, in McCracken, p. 99.

Augustine, their use within a theory of signification is broadly subsumed by their subordination to a vision of divinely ordered temporal forms, given in the Incarnation, enacting the reality of *caritas*.[63]

The issue of "ignorance" and "knowledge" about the Eucharist was for Paschasius, in the end, not bound up with a right apprehension of its mode of signification, but with an acceptance of the Eucharist as an event by which the flesh of the Church was conformed to the flesh of God in Christ Jesus, within either the enactment of divine love's unifying self-offering or its human opposition. We shall have occasion, in the next chapter, to note how Paschasius's figural understanding of the Church was linked with a striking exegetical appropriation of the Old Testament as a revelation of the Christian "Israel's" refiguring of the Son in his Passion as well as redemption. With respect to the Eucharist, in particular, Paschasius's placement of the sacrament within the divine narrative of the Church's fate, often corrupted from within by false leaders and assaulted from without by heretics and schismatics, made of it a "sign" or descriptor of the Church's own conformation to its Lord, generally in the traditional mode of "deification," but also in the passional shape of figural conformance.[64] In all of this, we need to emphasize here how the "realism" of Paschasius's terminology was tethered not to the explanation of the "eucharistic presence" as a discrete phenomenon of liturgical practice, but to the assertion of the Church's figural concorporation in God's own historical self-giving. If the bread and wine offer the "same" body as the temporally incarnate Jesus possessed, it is because the union of divine love with human life has taken over, within the Church's historical existence, that which time once kept from God, and has made that ecclesial history fully the bearer of his life in the same form as Scripture reveals the Nazarene.

Ratramnus, by contrast, seems to have limited his concerns just to the liturgical phenomenon itself. His own treatise is clearly aimed at clarifying two controverted points, which may or may not have derived from Paschasius's teachings. But his questions *are* limited; and seeing their limitations, and the way they nonetheless fall back on common figural assumptions,

---

63. Cf. IX, where he quotes the argument of Hilary (in *De Trinitate* 8), taking over the traditional anti-Arian *topos* on John 17:20-21 ("that they all may be one as you Father are in me and I in you") and applying it quite explicitly to the question of ecclesial unity as the expression of the "body of Christ" both Eucharistically and corporately.

64. Cf., among many, his remarks in his Commentary on Lamentations (3:15), where he applies the drinking of vinegar and gall by Jesus on the Cross — words traditionally associated both with the Eucharistically reenacted Passion and with the conversion of Eucharistic savor into bitterness by communicating heretics — to the historical evolution of the Church as it moves to its consummation.

demonstrates the difficulty one has in holding Ratramnus up as a clear opponent of Paschasius's (and his tradition's) larger sacramentology. Ratramnus's treatise seems to have been a direct reply to questions posed by King Charles, though they may or may not have been occasioned by Paschasius's evidently earlier work on the Eucharist. The king apparently wanted Ratramnus's opinion on a terminological confusion — were the Eucharistic elements "mystically" or "truly" the body and blood of Christ — as well as on a referential confusion — was this "body" and "blood" identical to the "historical" flesh of Jesus, born, dead, risen, and ascended (c. 5). Answers to the two questions can obviously be related, as they are for Ratramnus, but in fact they need not be. For although Ratramnus attempts a more rigorous application of significatory vocabulary than Paschasius, and in doing so appears to contradict some of the latter's claims, his final affirmations on the matter are not so very different from Paschasius's. Clearly, Ratramnus is uncomfortable with the kind of elision between *figura* and *veritas* that Paschasius creates through his notion of divine "character"; and he is insistent that the two terms be held in contrast (cf. c. 9). *Veritas* refers to the empirically visible, *figura* to the "mystical" or "spiritual" realities of God (cf. cc. 11, 42). But his own description of the Eucharistic elements' "change" into Christ's body and blood is as realist as Paschasius's (cf. cc. 16-30), depending as it does on an insistence upon the divine omnipotence to effect historical change through and within material forms. He applies more consistently, though he still shares with Paschasius, a pneumatic understanding of this change, with the result that he can maintain the contrast between "visible truth" and "invisible figure" or "mystery" in a way that does not undercut the essential point regarding the *res* that is offered in the Eucharist. In this, as scholars have pointed out, Ratramnus is merely taking up, in a kind of exclusive way, the pneumatic sacramentology of Ambrose, whose "invisible" reality is grasped by the eyes of "faith" (a fact Paschasius himself insists upon repeatedly; cf. IV). But because he does not dispute the divine *res* present in the Eucharist, he is finally led to dissolve the careful linguistic distinction he has been maintaining all along, by admitting that, while "invisible," the "substance" of the Eucharistic elements is "truly Christ's body and blood" (c. 49). From *veritas* versus *figura,* Ratramnus ends with a far more limited, and clearly less controversial, distinction between *visibilis* and *invisibilis.*

With respect to the second question concerning the presence of the "historical body" of Jesus in the sacraments, Ratramnus's appeal to the visible/invisible distinction leads to a more obvious divergence from Paschasius. For if an essential aspect of temporal corporality is its visibility, then there can be no doubt but that the Eucharistic elements are not identical to the historical body of Jesus (cf. cc. 57, 72). Furthermore, if one of the characteristics of beatitude is the full vision of Christ, in his heavenly (but historical) body, and if this vision is not attainable while we are still *in via* on this earth, it is clear that the Eucharistic elements are the body of Christ only "mysteriously," as a "pledge" and "image" of something that is not yet wholly present (c. 86). This "eschatological" argument against a "literal" Eucharistic presence is interesting given its modern fate. In some of the modern versions of this argument, the "futuristic" and presently "incomplete" character of Christ's reality within the Eucharist is precisely what allows for the Church to enact Eucharists in a state of current *disunity*, though with a view to overcoming that division.[65] What is rarely perceived in Ratramnus's futurism, however, is that the argument against the literal presence of the "historical" body of Jesus in the Eucharist serves explicitly to buttress the claim that the Eucharistic "body" be understood in terms also of the "body" of the united Church!

It is, in large part, *because* the Church is Christ's "body" that the "mystical" or "spiritual" signification of the term is insisted upon consistently, even in the Eucharistic context (cf. cc. 73-74, 84) — perhaps even especially in the Eucharistic context. For Ratramnus ends his treatise (cc. 93-96) with a long quotation from Augustine's Sermon 272 — a sermon that reprises many of the themes and exact language of other paschal sermons we have noted, for

---

65. Cf. Wainwright, pp. 141-46. Wainwright's arguments, to repeat, are deployed in favor of immediate *intercommunion* among divided churches, and to this degree are aimed at the restoration of some form of undivided sacramental life. As with the issue of "recognizing" the ministries of divided churches, it remains unclear what is exactly the figural force of celebrating Eucharists "in common" among such churches. Our own line of reasoning suggests not that divided or multiple or shared Eucharists among separated churches are invalid or ineffective, only that they are somehow "bitter," even poisonous (however much they may be voluntarily, and properly so, accepted). This is a possibility Wainwright simply rejects out of hand (pp. 136f.), believing as he does that the Eucharist, however "expressive" of ecclesial unity, is also more effectively "creative" of such unity. This kind of distinction is designed to open up the practice of the Eucharist for a functionalist manipulation of the sacrament (i.e., even if the Eucharist today cannot signify unity achieved, it can at least, through its interdenominational practice, *bring about* such unity). While a figuralist construal of the Eucharist does not rule out this kind of "effectiveness," it does not promise it either (see below). The figural unity of the Church as the Body of Christ in both Paschasius's and Ratramnus's visions is given in the act of God's self-offering in the Incarnation, and whatever "instrumentality" the Eucharist possesses to effect this or that temporal transformation of ecclesial existence cannot be separated from the forms suffered by the Body that is Christ himself — hardly an ecumenical "strategy," even if ecumenically inevitable. Paschasius's rendering of this reality in terms of identities of "history" between forms of "flesh" is probably more clearly expressive of what is at stake here than is Ratramnus's; but they do not exclude one another.

example, 229 — which affirms the Eucharistic principle of *quod accipitis, vos estis* (you are what you receive) and which exhorts listeners to the practice of unity within the Church which is given in the very self-offering of God in love on the Cross passed on in the elements. If this "figure" is to have any reality for the Church in its present life as it moves toward a complete union with its "head," Ratramnus tells the king (cc. 97-98), then the figural character of the Eucharist as well must be maintained: "for it bears the figure of both bodies, that is, the one which suffered and rose again, and the body of the people reborn in Christ through Baptism and quickened from the dead." It is true, as de Lubac noted, that Ratramnus's assertion that the corporal figure of the Church as Christ's Body could only be sustained by divorcing it from the notion of Jesus' "historical flesh" had the effect, at least potentially, of linking the concept of the "mystical" to a mode of metaphoric signification. But this was clearly not Ratramnus's goal. Sharing, as he did, a figural ecclesiology and sacramentology with Paschasius, he was anxious to protect precisely the corporal term's temporal applicability by explaining its signifying force within the same framework as the Eucharist's. That he found the terminology of "visible appearance" confusing within this framework — and that his desire to banish it from its explication could be taken in new directions — does not alter the fundamental agreement in conceptual practice about the Eucharist he shared with his tradition and contemporaries.

And this agreement underscores the historical fact that the so-called ninth-century controversy over the Eucharist was neither conflictual nor divisive, if it was even controversial at all. As Patricia McCormick Zirkel has pointed out, while one might properly speak of a "theological debate" over the matter at the time, the debate itself does not indicate any true "doctrinal diversity" over the Eucharist, first, because there were not large numbers of either theologians or laypeople aligned with contrasting perspectives, and second, because it appears, in any case, that King Charles decided in favor of Paschasius's views (although without censuring Ratramnus), and thereby contributed to the solidifying of an official and uniform doctrine about the Eucharistic presence.[66] All of this was no doubt possible because of the accepted ecclesial framework of unity within which the discussion took place initially, and to which, as we have seen, it referred its conclusions as a criterion. The *history* of the Eucharist in the West, in this debate and until the sixteenth century, was, *in fact*, a history of a largely tacit commitment to this ecclesial framework, but a commitment nonetheless forceful, especially in view of the more rancorous debates that continued to occur through its

66. Zirkel, pp. 2-7, 21-23.

course.[67] However clearly someone like de Lubac may discern a progressive weakening of the conceptual linkage between ecclesial and Eucharistic bodies, gathering alarming steam in, say, Wycliffe during the late fourteenth century,[68] the conceptual weakening in some quarters cannot be said to have any

67. On the eleventh-century dispute over Berenger's rejection of Paschasian realism, see the magisterial study by Jean de Montclos, *Lanfranc et Bérenger. La controverse eucharistique du XIe siècle* (Louvain: Spicilegium Sacrum Lovaniense, 1971). Pages 448ff. provide a useful discussion of the way Lanfranc was able to reconcile Paschasius and Ratramnus (largely because they were never so far apart in the first place), thereby reappropriating the more technical aspects of Augustine's theory of signification for the realist position. On the other hand, de Montclos is also critical of Lanfranc for confusing this theoretical apparatus by insisting on a multiplication of referents for the Eucharist, including especially the Church in its unity (pp. 396-401, 457), a "confusion" that, we are arguing, was a continuously necessary support to the Eucharistic practice, especially as it now became subject to more numerous intellectual analyses, which did in fact limit the concerns more narrowly to the question of signification. One would find more representative discussions of the Eucharist in its historical reality, as we have been insisting it be understood, if one examined the devotional theology of this and subsequent periods. Among others, cf. the twelfth-century monk and later Archbishop of Canterbury, Baldwin of Ford, *De sacramento altaris* (Latin and French translation in de Ford, *Le sacrement de l'autel,* 2 vols., ed. J. Morson and E. de Solms, Sources chrétiennes, 93 [Paris: Éditions du Cerf, 1963]), esp. II:4, a long discussion of Pauline texts on the Eucharist, which combines treatments of ecclesial unity and love with an elaborate figural exegesis of the Eucharist's twin effects of "mercy" and "judgment" upon its participants, based on their historical relation to such unity, all held together by the order of Christ's own fulfillment, in his incarnate life, of the forms given to Israel in the Exodus. See below, in our discussion of the Eucharist's "taste." It is within this more representative outlook, surprisingly robust over the centuries, that one must look at the more theoretical discussions, and even the outright disputes over the character of the Eucharist.

68. Cf. de Lubac, *Corpus Mysticum,* p. 288. It is possible, however, to see even Wyclif's vigorous attack on transubstantiation as still lying within the figural framework of the ecclesially Eucharistic "body." His commitment to the visible unity of the Church is beyond question, despite his insistence upon defining the Church radically in terms of the elect, precisely because he located the outworking of election in a visible incorporation of love that was Eucharistically embodied, even while any human certainty of election is banished into a realm of complete ignorance in this world. On this issue, he had more in common with later Jansenists than with Calvinists, and his moral rigorism did not devolve into a Donatist posture just because the human uncertainty of electing grace coupled with the priority of that grace demanded a visible Church wrought through the structures of caritative regard, understood, at least historically even in elective ignorance, as a "body." Clearly, Wyclif's complete relativizing of the visible structures of the papacy calls into question how far he was ready to go on the matter of mutual subjugation; but his concerns about the visible structures of the Church, as well as the character of the Eucharist more particularly, always derived from a passionate regard for the historical enactments of *caritas* within the ministry and its ecclesial reach. Whatever one makes of his status as a "heretic" in the eyes of Rome, or of the influence of his ideas on schismatic "Lollardy," there is little to commend the later Protestant appropriation of his memory, if only because his

significant force until it is, in fact, put to practical use in order to justify, in the sixteenth century, a historical fissure within the ecclesial body that is experienced in the act of the Eucharist.

The Classic Sixteenth-Century Debate over a Non-Ecclesial Body

More than anything, this is what de Lubac's own survey demonstrates. If a "realist" Eucharistic theology and a "realist" ecclesiology "rely on each other," as he rightly observes, it is patently the case that with the sixteenth century neither side of the ecclesial divide could maintain this coherence. Through the general separative logic that maintained the integrity of their doctrinal commitments as a non-"Roman" Church, the Reformers let go of the realism of both aspects, sacramental and ecclesial.[69] Roman Catholics, for their part, did battle on the Eucharistic front by limiting themselves to the sacramental question of "presence," pressing the realism of this aspect to the point that its ecclesial figural import was no longer sustainable, and was thus necessarily forgotten.[70] Other scholars of the "mystical body" have had to face the fact that the notion in general went into eclipse in Roman Catholic theology by the seventeenth century; but de Lubac's evidence of its disappearance within the particular context of Eucharistic doctrine is

particular doctrinal and theoretical elaborations were fundamentally subordinate to his commitment to "Catholic" visibility (as can be seen by an examination of their course of development in connection with his reading of the Church's historical fate). This fact alone constitutes a reversal of Protestant principle. More indicative of the ecclesiologically conservative character of Wyclif's motivations, even to the point of being explicitly bounded by the figural nature of caritative form, are the attitudes expressed by a Langland, in his *Piers Plowman,* a work that springs from the general milieu of Wyclif's critical activity. For a convenient summary of Wyclif's late views on Church and Eucharist, see his English *The Church and Her Members,* in Herbert E. Winn, ed., *Wyclif: Select English Writings* (Oxford: Oxford University Press, 1929), pp. 118-39. See also his large Latin treatises, *De eucharistia* and *De ecclesia,* both edited by Johann Loserth for The Wyclif Society (London, 1892 and 1896 respectively). See also the useful anthology edited by Anthony Kenny, *Wyclif and His Times* (Oxford: Clarendon Press, 1986). A survey of Wyclif's reputation in the Reformation and post-Reformation debates can be found in Vaclav Mudroch's *The Wyclyf Tradition* (Athens: Ohio University Press, 1979), esp. chs. 1 and 2. The anachronistic labeling of someone like Wyclif as "proto-Protestant," even by contemporary nonconfessional scholars, simply ignores the *caesura* of division that so profoundly alters the very significance of the doctrinally terminological debate on matters like the Eucharist — a historical observation that strengthens the possibility that doctrines like those surrounding the sacraments cannot be sensibly discussed in a condition of ecclesial separation.

69. De Lubac, *Corpus Mysticum,* pp. 290f.
70. De Lubac, *Corpus Mysticum,* pp. 291ff.

sharply telling.[71] As he points out, Bellarmine is simply and strangely silent about the concept in his discussion of the Eucharist, as an examination of his long treatise on the sacrament in the *Controversaria* confirms. The almost three hundred pages of the first four books of this work deal so single-mindedly with the issue of the "real presence," properly understood in terms of transubstantiation, that the figural (not "figurative") significance of that presence is left wholly unmentioned. Again, as de Lubac has noticed, Bellarmine's recourse to Augustine (among many other patristic authorities) carefully avoids those many Eucharistic texts of his that link the sacrament with the ecclesial referent, let alone its incarnational history, in an explicit way. Paschasius, Berenger, Lanfranc, and others are all now used as interpreters of the Fathers, over and against the Protestant narrow reading of Augustine and others, on a topic numbingly and strictly limited to the *mode* of Eucharistic signification.[72] Where Augustine's ecclesial figuralism is noted by the post-Reformation Catholic apologists, as by Jacques Davy, the Cardinal Du Perron, it is dismissed, oddly, as a form of "allegorizing" speech (often given, as we saw, in the context of Easter sermons to the newly baptized or to those about to be baptized), designed to protect the realistic presence of Christ in the Eucharist from the uninstructed glare of the common listener or reader.[73]

Du Perron's argument is interesting insofar as it demonstrates the certain convergence of Protestant and Catholic understandings of Eucharistic figura-

---

71. This is not to say that de Lubac's argument does not admit of exceptions, and significant ones at that; cf. the example of Bérulle, and of the Oratorian tradition in general, which he founded. Hardly marginal, this perspective entered into diverse aspects of seventeenth- and eighteenth-century French devotional — though not dogmatic — theology, including Jansenist writing especially in the wake of Quesnel, whose commitment to an ecclesiology of the mystical body was profound and wide-ranging. For a brief comment on this, cf. Jean Orcibal's illuminating survey, "L'Idée d'Église aux XVI-XVIIème siècles," in *Relazioni del X Congresso Internazionale di Scienze Storiche,* vol. 4, Storia Moderna (Florence: G. C. Sansoni, 1955), pp. 117ff.

72. See Robert Bellarmine, *Opera Omnia,* ed. Justin Fevre (Paris, 1873; repr. Frankfurt: Minerva G.M.B.H., 1965), vol. 4.

73. I have not been able to examine de Lubac's references to Du Perron's exchange with James I, the *Réplique à la Response du Sereinissime Roy de la Grand Bretagne* (1620), pp. 879f., and to his major work on the Eucharist, the *Traité de l'Eucharistie* (1622), pp. 55f. But his use of Augustine is confirmed at length in his reply to Philippe Du Plessis-Mornay's 1598 treatise on the patristic doctrine of the Eucharist, *De l'institution, usage et doctrine du saint sacrement de l'eucharistie en l'Église ancienne, L'Examen du livre du sieur Du Plessis contre la Messe,* in his *Oeuvres diverses,* 3e édition, 2eme partie (Paris, 1633; repr. Geneva: Slatkine reprints, 1969), vol. 2, pp. 1094-1104.

tion, even while its ecclesial significance is interpreted differently. The fact that there are so few *unambiguous* references to the transubstantiated Body and Blood of Christ by the Fathers, Du Perron insists, is because so much of their extant discussion of the sacrament was public, and therefore could not deal directly with the greatest aspect of the Eucharistic mystery, the real presence. Du Perron uses Augustine in just this context, arguing that the latter's Sermons on the Gospel of John, for instance, which contain extended discussions of the Eucharist, concentrate on "figurative" and "metaphorical" explications because these were the only levels of signification that were accessible to the uninitiated. Thus, when Augustine speaks of the Eucharistic elements as refer- ring to the "unity of the Church," or to "the Holy Spirit," or to our "belief in Christ," he is saying something true, but grossly limited.

> Who does not recognize that all these propositions have a true and religious meaning? For other than real eating [*manducation*], which involves the perception of the substance of the body of our Lord, we demand a spiritual and metaphoric eating that consists in the contemplation and apprehension of the merits and effects of this same body, and consists also in the love of his Church.[74]

Du Perron describes this "spiritual eating" in distinctly Protestant terms of "faith in Christ," but then emphasizes, on the basis of 1 Corinthians 11:28, how such a meditation on Christ is only "preparatory" to the "true" eating of the Flesh of Christ:

> Every preparation is less excellent than the thing for which one prepares, just as every means is less excellent than its end. With respect to the eucharist, then, it is necessary that whatever eating we do of the body of Christ be different and more excellent than spiritual eating and eating by faith. That is to say, since preparing to eat the body of Christ consists in believing in him, the actual eating of the body of Christ must be something different than belief.[75]

Du Perron's cleavage of Augustine's figural understanding of the Eucharist is decisive, and is aimed very clearly at locating the real presence at the essential center of the Eucharist, even while identifying figural aspects as ancillary *and,* in their similarity with Protestant conceptions, as appropriate to the unini-

---

74. Du Perron, *De l'institution,* p. 1100.

75. Du Perron, *Bref traicté de l'eucharistie. Auquel par raisons et arguments infaillibles, pris de la Saincte Escriture, est prouvée la presence rëele du Corps de nostre Seigneur au Sainct Sacrement de l'Autel . . .* (1597), in *Oeuvres diverses,* pp. 853ff.

tiated, that is, to those still "outside" the Church. This method of, first, defining the figural as "figurative" and "metaphorical" and, second, segregating such meanings to the extra-ecclesial offered Protestant controversialists a contrastive tag by which to deal with the Eucharist in non-ecclesially-signifying terms (though not necessarily non-ecclesially-indicative), even while relativizing patristic authority on the matter as, in any case, hopelessly ambiguous, because (even as Catholics now claimed) constructed in self-consciously nondogmatic terms for the public at large.[76]

Du Perron, then, ends by granting a major Protestant claim with respect to the Eucharist's metaphoric character insofar as it involves anything *other* than the real presence. The notorious "symbolist" Zwingli, after all, had said no more than Du Perron, except that he also insisted that the real presence be excluded from the start. The Swiss Reformer had simply limited Eucharistic signification to what Du Perron would later describe as "spiritual manducation," using Augustine's ecclesial language about the Eucharist as a proof that the "metaphoric" meaning of the Eucharist was the only one acceptable. In a focused treatise like the 1526 *On the Lord's Supper,* Zwingli relies a good deal on citations from Augustine used in Catholic canon law, and drawn frequently from the saint's sermons on John, which suggest a "nonliteral" understanding of the Eucharistic elements' signification.[77] By the end of the work, however, Zwingli singles out in particular the Augustinian citations that deal with the concept of *quod accipitis, vos estis* (you are what you receive), explicated in conjunction with 1 Corinthians 10:16 (communion with the body and blood of Christ). The point here, in a manner reminiscent of Ratramnus's earlier argument, is that such a blatantly metaphorical reference for the eucharistic elements — that is, the Church — must rule out any "literal" corporalism.

Zwingli's use of this argument, however — and in contrast with Ratramnus's — is designed to appropriate the ecclesial metaphor of the Eucharist to his more basic construal of Eucharistic "faith" as being the sacrament's sole point. Those who participate in the Eucharist in the proper way receive the sacrament as a nourishment to their faith in Christ, its various narrative signs firing the spiritual inhalation of the Gospel's content. The full range of the incarnational figure embedded in the Eucharist is acknowledged by Zwingli, but now in strict terms of conventional signification, insofar as the performance of the rite calls to

---

76. Cf. de Lubac, *Corpus Mysticum,* pp. 292f.

77. An English translation of the work is available: *Zwingli and Bullinger,* trans. G. Bromiley, The Library of Christian Classics, vol. 24 (Philadelphia: The Westminster Press, 1953), pp. 185-245.

mind the various aspects of the redemptive history of Christ, which faith alone can receive in their spiritual impact. The ecclesial aspect of the Eucharistic reference specifically, in this framework, is this: those who come to the sacrament with such narrationally oriented faith and receive the sacrament with faith in the narrative's truth and personal significance are participants in a common faith; and it is this common faith whose uniform character marks them off as true Christians, in contrast to the "idolaters" of 1 Corinthians 10, as well as to idolaters of the present era (i.e., Papists and those who mistakenly support their view of the real presence, like the Lutherans).[78] Zwingli makes vigorous use of the ecclesial figure of the Body, even calling it the "mystical body," or the great "mystery," which somehow embraces the incarnational history. But he does so in a way that links the figure to the Eucharist only indirectly, so that both Church and sacrament gain their power of signification only through their independent reference to the act of faith. Faith, then, defines the Church; and the Eucharist is defined by faith so as to indicate that Church. And so St. Paul's words in 1 Corinthians 11:28-29, to "examine oneself" before eating and to "discern the body," according to this perspective, imply a confirmation that one's faith conforms to the same faith that identifies the Church: "For we ought to examine ourselves whether we have confessed and received Christ as the Son of God our Redeemer and Savior, so that we trust only in him as the infallible author and giver of salvation; and whether we rejoice in the fact that we are members of that Church of which Christ is the head."[79]

The Eucharist can refer to the Church only because it first refers to the true faith that indicates the Church. And Zwingli's emphasis on this ecclesial language is notable, as a result, just because it is used to buttress the Eucharist's *non*-figural — that is, non-Christic — ecclesial meaning, for the purpose of demarcating the true Church from the false. It is interesting to see that, while an "unfaithful" *participation* brings "judgment" to an individual, in Zwingli's eyes (and following St. Paul), the Eucharist itself has no role in that condemnation; as an act in its own right, it has become a degustified sign.

---

78. Cf. also Zwingli's 1531 *Exposition of the Faith* (publ. 1536), in Bromiley, pp. 259-65, which deals with the Eucharist's purpose and with the purpose of sacraments in general. Zwingli's conception of sacramental faith here includes both the "historical" aspect of the sacrament's informational reference to certain saving events and the "faith" held by the participant in these sacraments, which holds these past historical events to have saving significance for the individual. He calls this "spiritual eating" in the exact manner taken up by the Catholic Du Perron sixty years later (and not so different from Luther's early notion of receiving the sacrament as a "promise"): "to eat the body of Christ spiritually is equivalent to trusting with heart and soul upon the mercy and goodness of God through Christ" (p. 258).

79. Zwingli, *Exposition of the Faith,* in Bromiley, p. 260.

Zwingli, to be sure, became equated with the stock extremism of the Protestant side, and was repudiated by most Lutherans, in Luther's wake, from the first. But Luther's position came to be too conflicted within itself, as it adjusted to opposing polemical fronts, to achieve the status of a representative Protestant vision,[80] and this role was given over to Calvin's own views, views

80. Luther believed that the Catholic doctrine concerning the priestly "sacrifice" of the Mass constituted a Pelagian subversion of the grace conferred in the Eucharist, a grace whose very meaning was contradicted by the practice of "buying" Masses for the dead and so on. In response, Luther early stressed the way in which the Eucharist as a sacrament ought to be understood primarily in terms of its function as "proclamation" of a divine "promise" of forgiveness. Here he relied especially on the New Testament narratives of the Last Supper, where Jesus speaks of the wine as being his blood in terms of a "testament" for the remission of sins. In any promise, Luther writes in *The Pagan Servitude of the Church* (1520), God makes use of a "word" and a "sign." Luther identifies the "sacrament" with the "sign," which signifies, through the accompanying and explicating word, the full promise of forgiveness. The sign of the sacrament is a "memorial" that turns us to the significance of the word of promise. In laying it out this way, however, Luther explicitly wants to define the Eucharist in terms of its referent, which is the promise, and he clearly subordinates the sign-function of the elements to that referred content, which is grasped solely by faith. "Believe and you have eaten," he cites from Augustine, and then goes on to indicate a "spiritual eating and drinking" that, through contemplation of the promises alone, can strengthen faith without literal participation in the Mass at all. Luther, even here, is clear that he believes in the "real presence" of the glorified body and blood of Christ in the elements — the so-called doctrine of consubstantiation — and objects to the concept of transubstantiation only because it is nonscripturally speculative, intellectually confusing, and unnecessary in view of the simple requirement of faith in the miracle of divine presence. But the real presence of the Lord's body is itself, in the context of his argument against the Eucharistic sacrifice, only a "sign" of the promise of forgiveness, and does not seem to have a redemptive function apart from this referent to which it points, which exists independently of the sacramental presence itself. It is not hard to see how readers of Luther at this time could have taken his words in the direction of Zwingli. But Luther himself would have none of it. And when he turned his polemical sword against the Anabaptists, like Karlstadt, he did so on the basis of their attempt to "spiritualize" (and hence subjectivize) the promises of the Gospel, including their sacramental signs like the Eucharist. In works like *Against the Heavenly Prophets in the Matter of Images and Sacraments* (1525) and *Confession Concerning Christ's Supper* (1528), Luther lays out at great length a defense of the real presence, adopting language as palpable as Paschasius's. The corporeal realism in view here can plausibly be taken as a basis for a certain kind of historical ecclesiology, informed by an Augustinian understanding of incarnational signification, the *signum* of God's self-offering through condescension. Cf. Regin Prenter's treatment in *Spiritus Creator* (Philadelphia: Muhlenberg Press, 1953), pp. 254-302. But Luther's ecclesiology (including his views on the sacraments) is governed by a deep appreciation of its eschatological character, which is designed to maintain, in Prenter's words, a continual "hiatus" between divine and human practicalities, which can be bridged only from God's side by an historically unmalleable grace. If only in theory, then, Luther's Eucharistic realism does not conform to an Augustinian figuralism. And in practice, the theory cannot disallow the actual deployment of this Eucharistic realism for separative purposes, as the shape of his polemic against

that, because of the demarcative ecclesial sacramentology that underlay them, eventually and easily elided, within the Continental and British Reformed tradition, with Zwingli's decisive antirealism.[81] Calvin's use of Augustine, who

the "enthusiasts" demonstrates. One of the major thrusts of his argument in, for instance, *Against the Heavenly Prophets* is to emphasize how a realistic corporealism undergirds St. Paul's notion that "unworthy eating" of the sacrament brings condemnation. He makes use of Augustine's own repeated notation that Judas received the "same body" as the apostles, and hence that the "body of Christ" is located in the sacrament, not in the faith of the believer or the saint. However, the point of this is not, as in Augustine, to uncover the ecclesial referent of the sacrament as Christ's body suffering the unrighteous, but to identify the work of Satan, in Karlstadt as in Judas, with a failure to accept the realistic presence of Christ in the bread and the wine (cf. the English version in *Luther's Works,* ed. Conrad Bergendoff [Philadelphia: Muhlenberg Press, 1958], vol. 40, pp. 181-98). In this case, the demonization of his opponent cannot be limited to a rhetorical indulgence, but must be seen in the light of the Reformation and post-Reformation debate over the Eucharistic presence as an ecclesiological act of denominational self-justification. Against the Anabaptists, Luther slips into the same constricted logic as his Counter-Reformation foes (something he notes himself with a certain chagrin) by using the doctrine of the real presence, and its enactment, as an indicator of the true Church. Like his Papist opponents, Luther insists on interpreting the worthy eating that is linked with "discerning the body" in 1 Corinthians 11:29 as a right appreciation or apprehension of the elements' realistic mode of signification. Luther's reading of 1 Corinthians 10:17, to be sure, pressed for a visible (versus a "spiritual") ecclesial body as a referent for the text; but the aim of this explanation lay to the side of any Eucharistically figural notion of the Church. Rather, Luther used the verse analogically, to show in what way "bodies," whether of the Church or of the Eucharistic elements, must be understood as concrete "realities"; they are not, however, essentially connected realities (cf. *Confession concerning Christ's Supper,* in *Luther's Works,* vol. 37, pp. 354ff.). It is not so much that Luther's theology of the Eucharist was incoherent; instead, like many Anglicans after him, it was, in the context of the divided Church, *ecclesially* incoherent, in that it appealed to conflicting elements within the separation, not in a dynamic of resolution, but as a tool to an irresolvable conflict.

81. A useful, though out-of-print, overview of Reformed understandings of the Eucharist, as to the debate over presence, can be found in the essays by Harold Smith ("The Reform of Doctrine") and W. H. Mackean ("Anti-Roman Apologetics," pts. 1 and 2), in A. J. Macdonald, ed., *The Evangelical Doctrine of Holy Communion* (Cambridge: W. Heffer and Sons, 1933); more recently, Gordon E. Pruett, "A Protestant Doctrine of the Eucharistic Presence," *Calvin Theological Journal* 10, no. 2 (November 1975): pp. 142-74. On Calvin's Eucharistic teaching in particular, in the historical context of the intra-Protestant debate, see Joseph N. Tylanda, "The Ecumenical Intention of Calvin's Early Eucharistic Teaching," in B. A. Gerrish, ed., *Reformatio Perennis: Essays on Calvin and the Reformation in Honor of Ford Lewis Battles* (Pittsburgh: Pickwick Press, 1981), pp. 27-47. Still the most extensive survey of Eucharistic doctrine in the Reformation and post-Reformation, with unique attention to England and a coverage of Continental and later British Catholicism as well, is volume 2 of Darwell Stone's *A History of the Doctrine of the Holy Eucharist* (London: Longmans, Green, and Co., 1909). Stone's work is really an enormous compilation of primary text citations, with descriptive commentary, and is useful in this regard; but his almost exclusive focus on the question of Eucharistic presence as the center

stands at the center of his appeal to authority, is much more nuanced than Zwingli's.[82] But the interest remains one of significatory mode, maintaining the careful distinction between *signum* and its *res,* in the manner of a conventional sign, while also, however — in an attempt to counter what he supposes to be the potential "voiding" of the sign latent in the Zwinglian explanation — stressing that the sign carries with it a divine "effect."[83] Like the early Luther, Calvin founds the sacrament on its derivation from the proclamation of the divine "promise" of forgiveness,[84] a definition that could easily be taken in a Zwinglian direction. His understanding of the promise "received" and "believed," however, pushes his explanation of sacrament into the realm of effective grace, whereby the "word" is transformed into a living participation with Christ.

On the limited topic of the eucharistic "sign," in any case, Calvin's balance is impressive, as in IV:17:5-6 of the *Institutes,* where he carefully distinguishes the faith that must receive the gifts of Christ in the Supper from the gifts themselves, which embody a full and living participation in Christ's body. "I add that by faith we embrace Christ not as appearing from afar but as joining himself to us that he may be our head, we his members," a formulation he then elaborates upon in 17:9, in terms of the "mystery" of the "fleshly"

---

of Eucharistic theology — indicative of the whole outlook of the post-Reformation — makes the book's interest today much more limited, although in its reading no less numbing than the original works he presents. On sixteenth-century England, see also C. W. Dugmore, *The Mass and the English Reformers* (London: Macmillan & Co., 1958). The first four chapters of this volume provide a useful and clear discussion of patristic and medieval views of the Eucharist and give a compelling typology of "signifying modes" for the Eucharistic presence that lay behind the sixteenth-century debates. It is this kind of discussion, however, ultimately (and I believe anachronistically) using Augustine to explain the significatory problems with the Eucharist at the time of the Reformation, that I have been arguing obscures the deeper ecclesial concerns and meanings of the controversy.

82. Augustine's Sermons on John are a prominent resource for discussions of the Eucharist, as are a host of other scattered remarks about the sacraments in general, including discussions in the *De Doctrina Christiana.* Calvin's discussion of the Eucharist is systematically given in the *Institutes,* IV:17 (with a discussion of sacraments in general in IV:14); an English version of several more compact treatises on the topic (e.g., *Short Treatise on the Lord's Supper* [1541], *The Clear Explanation of Sound Doctrine Concerning the True Partaking of the Flesh and Blood of Christ in the Holy Supper* [1561]) can be found in J. K. S. Reid, ed. and trans., *Calvin: Theological Treatises,* Library of Christian Classics, vol. 22 (Philadelphia: Westminster Press, n.d.).

83. Calvin's wide-ranging foray into the theoretical issues of signification in the Eucharist are exemplified in the *Institutes,* IV:17:21-19.

84. Cf. Calvin, *Institutes,* IV:14:1: "it seems to me that a simple and proper definition would be to say that [a sacrament] is an outward sign by which the Lord seals on our consciences the promises of his good will toward us in order to sustain the weakness of our faith." Cf. 17:39.

union with Christ that is, in fact, an effect — a grace — of the Eucharist. Indeed, the "reality" and "efficacy" of the Eucharistic presence of Christ is repeatedly emphasized by Calvin, in a way that is perfectly conformable to the kind of limited Augustinianism that Ratramnus had earlier attempted to elucidate (and that made of the ninth-century monk a not unlikely precedent for Reformed apologists). His summary remarks in the appendix to *The Clear Explanation* ("The best method of obtaining concord") offer a delicate insistence on the "real communion" in the flesh and blood of Christ, "received in the Sacred Supper," and on the fact that the "figure" of the bread and the wine does not "exclude the reality," even while the two cannot be identified, nor divorced, in their efficacious signifying union, from the faith of the recipient. This faith is the means by which the Holy Spirit, in the sacrament, "draws us up" to heaven, where the true Body of Christ resides.[85]

But the issue of corporeal locality defines the scope of Calvin's Eucharistic doctrine ecclesially. He remained resolute in his opposition to Luther's "consubstantiative" notion of the real presence, seeing it as but a modified version of the root satanic evil at work in the Catholic doctrine of transubstantiation. This Romanist corruption of the Lord's Supper has several pernicious elements, according to Calvin. One is simply its nonscriptural absurdity, which Calvin considers dangerous insofar as its seems to subvert the useful application of other biblical metaphors, like the "simile" of the Church as "one loaf" used by Paul in 1 Corinthians 10:17. Such a metaphor, he argues, would be meaningless if taken literally (again, as with Luther, a correlation of the ecclesial with the Eucharistic figure, not an intersignification). More perverse still is transubstantiation's assertion that Christ's humanity is anywhere else except exclusively in heaven, a claim that confuses redemptive reality with the "corruptible elements of this world," which the faithful ought rather to flee as they rise "upward" through the Spirit to the exalted and ascended realm of incorruptibility. Whatever the implications this kind of reading of Christ's relation to the world may have for Calvinist devotion in general, its application to Eucharistic practice in the churches is plain. For the argument for delocalizing the "historical" presence of Christ that Calvin makes is directly applied to the delegitimating of the Roman Mass altogether. The direction of his logic is summarized in the *Short Treatise,* when, after enumerating the Catholic errors (including as well the notion of the Eucharistic "sacrifice," the use of Latin, and limitation of Communion to one kind) he writes:

85. On this notion of being "raised up to heaven," so important to Calvin's promotion of the nonlocal and nonhistorical presence of Christ in the Eucharist, cf. the *Institutes,* IV:17:31.

246

To come to an end, we comprehend under one article what could be considered separately. The article is that the devil introduced the manner of celebrating the Supper without any doctrine, and in place of the doctrine substituted ceremonies, partly unfitting and useless, and partly even dangerous, from which much ill has followed — to such an extent, that the mass, which takes the place of the Supper in the popish Church, when strictly defined, is nothing but pure apishness and buffoonery. I call it apishness, because the Supper of our Lord is there counterfeited without reason, just as an ape, capriciously and without discernment, follows what it sees done. This being so, the chief thing which our Lord recommends to us, is to celebrate this mystery with true intelligence. It follows then that the substance of it all consists in the doctrine. This taken away, it is no more than cold ceremony without efficacy . . . a manifest profanation of the Supper of Christ, rather than an observance of it. . . . I call it buffoonery, because the mimicry and gesture made there suit rather a farce than such a mystery as the Supper of the Lord.[86]

Here the Roman Church's obscurement of the "doctrine" — the promise of God's forgiveness in Christ — is tied to the web of satanic practices spun around the superstitious fascination with a false local presence of Christ, the sum of which transforms the Mass into a blasphemous parade.[87] Yet we are to note that the alleged blasphemy lies in the falseness of the Roman Mass's claim to be the Lord's Supper. It is not in fact that Supper, however, nor is there any danger of it being so, since the presence of Christ could never be so

---

86. *Short Treatise on the Lord's Supper*, in Reid, p. 161.

87. In the *Institutes*, IV:18, Calvin makes the popish doctrine of the "sacrifice" of the Mass, in particular, the "height of frightful abomination . . . when the devil raised up a sign by which [Christ's Sacred Supper] was not only to be obscured and perverted, but — being completely erased and annulled — to vanish and pass out of the human history" (18:1). Nowhere here, except perhaps in 18:8, where he talks of the origins of the sacrificial perversion in the early Church, does Calvin draw an explicit link between the doctrine of local presence and sacrifice, but certainly the structure and order of his discussion, even in the *Institutes*, implies this connection. In his *Commentary* on 1 Corinthians (on 11:27-30), Calvin covers much of the same ground in a short compass, although he doesn't directly mention transubstantiation at all in his list of popish errors concerning the Lord's Supper (v. 30), except in his lastly enumerated "abomination," where he speaks of the "idol" adored in the "room of Christ." However, the issue of locality is indirectly raised in the discussion of v. 27, when he defines the presence of Christ's body in the Eucharist in a way that is exclusively pneumatic: the unworthy do not receive the body of Christ in the Eucharist because, as they are devoid themselves of the Spirit, through their sin and lack of faith, there is no "body" that can reach them, however much they may come into contact with the physical sacrament (cf. *Institutes*, IV:17:32).

tied to a historical act in the first place. And it is this "nullity" of Christ's presence in the visible ecclesial gathering, taken in itself, that allows for the "annihilation" of the Supper in anything but a context of faithful reception. Calvin's entire discussion of "worthy" and "unworthy" communion, in the shadow of 1 Corinthians 11:27ff., relies on this presupposition. Leaning almost exclusively on texts from Augustine, while also acknowledging that there are other texts from the saint that somewhat confuse the picture presented, Calvin returns to the basic distinction between *signum,* which is an inert cipher, and the invisible *res* to which it points and which has no "virtue" or effect apart from the faith of the communicant. "Unbelievers," by definition, do not receive the body of Christ, but only bread, an empty sign. They are condemned in this, not because they have somehow made bad use of something good, crucified Christ anew, or the like, but because they have demonstrated a lack of faith and, in the process of coming to a sacrament whose participation "confesses" such faith, lied to God and to their neighbors.[88] "They do not receive what is offered" quite simply, and however much this rejection, though the bread enter the mouth, may fail to detract from the "efficacy" of the sacrament and the sacramental bread as it is shared within the Church as a whole, there is no "body" for the unbeliever.[89] The implication, in cases like the Roman Church where not only individuals, but whole communities, are engaged in unbelief, is clear: Christ is not present and the Eucharist is nonexistent. The true Body of Christ, just as the true sacrament of that body, however, is preserved elsewhere, in heaven and in a community of faith. And the Eucharist, thereby, is taken out of history altogether, in that, protected from the assaults of its failed participants, it shares no history with their world.

As with Zwingli, Calvin did not ignore the ecclesial figure associated with the Eucharist, and far more explicitly than Zwingli, he attempted to coordinate it with the Eucharist. He links the Lord's Supper with the Church

---

88. Calvin, *Institutes,* IV:17:34 and 40.

89. See the closing paragraph to *The Clear Explanation* (in Reid, p. 330). See also his *Commentary* on 1 Corinthians, on 11:29-30. The question of "unworthiness" in this discussion is more supple and perhaps interesting than in the *Institutes,* even if more compact, for Calvin faces openly the possibility of "degrees" of unworthiness, only the greatest of which — those tied to unbelief and idolatry — result in a full pneumatic abandonment of the individual. This last condemnation is clearly assumed for the Papists. Among those who had "returned from their captivity" to such impious deformations of the Lord's Supper, however, even the Protestants ought to consider their conduct at the Eucharist a cause of various "calamities" now besetting them — war, plague, famine. Here Calvin turns "unworthiness" into a question of moral and devotional purity, an area where divine judgment may come into play, but in which, apparently, the extreme forms of pneumatic abandonment do not intrude.

as Christ's body, both in making that community derive from the paradigmatic union of the believer with Christ that the Eucharist effects through faith[90] and in making worthy — that is, believing — reception of the sacrament depend, in part, on the maintenance of charity "with the brethren."[91] Further, in castigating the Roman practice of private Masses, Calvin notes how such usage subverts the Lord's Supper in its proper character as an "assembly," which images the "communion by which we all cleave to Christ."[92] But even while referring directly to Augustine's caritative figurating of the Eucharist in such contexts, Calvin sees mutual love within the Church as Christ's Body in terms of a set of dispositions coordinated with the Eucharist, not as something inherent to the color of its character. "Discord" is a matter of individual preparedness — worthiness or its lack — whose presence within the church, as with unworthiness and unbelief in general, cuts one off from the sacrament and its meaning, while the sacrament itself remains invulnerable to the scourges of its temporal location. "Assembly" and community," for Calvin, tend to refer to a common participation in Christ that individuals have received through faith, not to some basic aspect of redemption. Thus, the unity of Christians among themselves within the Church is itself finally a subordinate sign of the unity given by Christ between himself and the believer's soul, to which the Eucharist points primarily. Granted, there is richness and depth in Calvin's understanding of this primary referent, in terms of a truly "mystical union"; but it nonetheless plays the same role as Zwingli's referent of "faith" in defining the ecclesial figure of the Body only derivatively from such prior signification. Were the Body of Christ lived in the Church not intrinsically severed, in Calvin's thought, from the Body of Christ given in the Eucharist's incarnational figure, the beautiful and famous commentary Calvin wrote on Ephesians 4:1-14 — wherein he speaks of the Church as the mutual sustenance of its members in unity and self-subjugation to one another, capped by the assertion that "the church is the common mother of all the godly, which bears, nourishes, and brings up children to God, kings and peasants alike" — could not conclude its paean to ecclesial edification bound by the cord of love with the observation that "when the Papists avail themselves of the disguise of the church for burying doctrine, they give sufficient proof that they have a diabolical synagogue."[93]

90. Calvin, *Institutes,* IV:17:9.
91. Ibid., 17:38 and 40.
92. Calvin, *Institutes,* 18:7-8.
93. Calvin, *Commentary* on Ephesians 4:14, trans. William Pringle (Grand Rapids: Wm. B. Eerdmans, 1948), p. 285).

This judgment and the ecclesiological presuppositions of the sacramentology that surround it mutually support each other here.

The Seventeenth-Century Eucharist: A Body without a History

The direction taken in Reformed thinking about the Eucharist in Calvin's wake tended to pull away these presuppositions, and build on them apart from the realistic language still found in Calvin. The language itself became cause for a certain embarrassment within the broad evangelical and Puritan movements of the tradition; and among reactionaries, it also became the positive focus for much later nineteenth-century attempts to redirect what had became a turgid sacramental outlook within Reformed churches into a more vital appreciation of the Eucharist.[94] In general, though, it was left behind altogether, so that the Eucharist's role as an indicator of truth could remain free of historical ambiguities and the demands of difficult love they enforced, and thereby freed from the

94. Well into the early twentieth century, among mainstream (even more liberal) evangelicals, one finds remarks such as this one by the Scottish theologian Hugh Ross Mackintosh: "When Calvin goes beyond the objective reality of the presence of Christ's flesh and blood as something more, and more precious, we detect the traces of his age" (cited in Macdonald, p. 175). These denigrated "traces," however, also formed the partial basis for the revived sacramental and Reformed "catholicism" of, for instance, the Mercersberg school in the mid-nineteenth century, as exemplified in John Nevin's classic work on the Eucharist, *The Mystical Presence* (1846; repr. Hamden [Conn.]: Archon Books, 1963). Nevin's long attack on the "Puritan" and "rationalistic" deformations of Eucharistic doctrine on the part of evolved Protestantism is a useful illustration of where some of Calvin's basic orientations were taken. In Nevin's mind, however, the fault for this lay less in the Reformer's basic sacramental theology, let alone ecclesiology — both of which were fundamentally sound — than in the limited forms of expression Calvin's less evolved philosophical culture allowed him (which would have been mitigated had he shared the organic idealism of nineteenth-century German Romanticism!). Cf. Nevin, chs. 2 and 3, secs. 1 and 4. Still, Nevin was able to use Calvin as a buttress for a nascent, if halting, historical figuralism of the Church as Christ's Body, although he did not use this framework in anything other than an ancillary way in support of his Eucharistic doctrine (cf. ch. 4, sec. 5, e.g., p. 234, on the character of the liturgical calendar as ecclesial [and "objective"] participation in the historical life of Christ). As we have noted elsewhere, in relation to eighteenth- and nineteenth-century scriptural interpretation in Britain, the revival of figuralism as an exegetical hermeneutic is historically tied to concerns over the recovery of ecclesial unity. Despite the intrusion of an unpersuasive philosophical apparatus into the argument, and granting the protective separative framework Nevin still maintains for the elucidation of his Eucharistic doctrine, Nevin's work deserves continued study and regard as a notable milestone in the dismantling of just that framework on the basis of the Incarnation's historical assertion.

depredations of unbelievers in the mixed body of history's ecclesial masquerade. This can be seen in the paradigmatic Eucharistic debate of the mid-seventeenth century — perhaps the most extended and influential in defining the Protestant-Catholic opposition for the next few centuries — that took place between the French Reformed theologian Jean Claude and the Catholics Pierre Nicole and Antoine Arnauld, prominent Jansenists both, but in this case standard-bearers of a militant anti-Protestantism held in common with their co-religionists.

The controversy began in 1659, with the appearance in print of a large devotional collection of historical pieces, drawn mainly from the patristic period, designed to aid the nuns of Port-Royal in their Eucharistic adoration. The work was a collaborative effort of several Jansenist scholars, and shortly afterward was given a "Preface" from the hand of Nicole, which attempted to lay out a counterargument to then-circulating attacks by Protestants on the doctrine of the real presence. This preface, published separately in 1664, set the stage for an extensive controversy. Known as the *Petite Perpétuité*,[95] the preface brought several shorter refutations from Claude, which in turn gave rise to the truly monumental multivolume treatise, published under Arnauld's name but probably the work mostly of Nicole, known as the *Perpétuité de la foi de l'Eglise Catholique Touchant l'Eucharistie* ("The perpetuity of the Catholic Church's faith concerning the Eucharist"), three large volumes of which appeared between 1669 and 1674. (A fourth appeared in 1704, containing material written earlier, and two more volumes were added a decade later by another author.) Meanwhile, Claude had published a major attack on the first volume in 1670.[96] Taken as a whole, and given the provoking volume of patristic quotations, the controversy marked a notable development in the deployment of critical historical scholarship in the service of denominational polemic, even while strengthening the basis of historical theology as a discipline in its own right. These achievements have gained the notice of modern scholars. But their logical usefulness for maintaining a vision of the Eucharistic event severed from the historical figure of the Church is what interests us in particular. And in this case, Claude's arguments mark a streamlined Calvinism that stood in a logically bound symmetry to his Catholic opponents'.

95. The text of this work, along with a portion of the texts associated with the earlier devotional anthology and with an initial response to Claude, can be found in vol. 12 of Arnauld, *Oeuvres* (1777 ed.; repr. Brussels: Culture et Civilisation, 1967).

96. The whole of this background, as well as a rich discussion of the entire context of the debate (including earlier French Protestant-Catholic controversy on the Eucharist) as well as of its theological methodological content, can be found in Remi Snoeks, *L'Argument de tradition dans la controverse eucharistique entre catholiques et réformés français au XVIIe siècle* (Louvain/Gembloux: Publications Universitaires de Louvain/Éditions J. Duculot, 1951).

Few of Claude's perspectives were new; he expressed them, however, with a great eloquence, and, in the end, a more refined scholarship than most of his predecessors.[97] In sum, he argued for a general patristic consensus on the nature of the Eucharistic presence, defined anachronistically according to a broad Calvinism. This consensus, according to Claude, was broken by ninth-century innovation, spurred especially by Paschasius, which by the eleventh century had silently spread throughout the Western Church, to be officially foisted upon the faithful at large by the hierarchy.[98] The issue for Claude came down to locating, historically, the advent of a faulty grasp of Eucharistic signification. Augustine, among others, is used to establish what he views as the standard patristic perspective on this matter, which he summarizes in five aspects: first, the Eucharistic elements of bread and wine remain unchanged in their "nature"; second, as sacraments they are "images, figures, symbols, signs, types and antitypes of the Body and Blood of the Savior"; third, in their use they are called "the true body and the true blood of Jesus Christ," but "not because they are so actually, but because they contain and communicate the Mystery"; fourth, "eating the body" and "drinking the blood" of Christ means "communicating in his suffering through the soul's meditation" upon them; and fifth, the wicked do not receive the body and blood of Christ, but only their "sacrament," to great condemnation.[99]

Augustine in particular is cited to stress this general understanding; and Claude makes use of the famous text in *De Doctrina Christiana* III:16, as well as of texts drawn from the Sermons on John (e.g. 26 and 27), which were common elements in the Protestant arsenal.[100] Claude, however, has seized upon the more Zwinglian emphasis of faithful reception in his discussion of Eucharistic signification, in order to bring out the manner in which the Eucharistic "body" is immune to unfaithful participation, even while its whole purpose is to "nourish the faith" of believers and to "incite them to acts of piety" through their "meditation" upon the body of Jesus Christ, dead and

97. In particular, Edme Aubertin's several books on the Eucharist in the first part of the century proved a solid, and perhaps ultimately more judicious, critical source for Claude's writing.

98. Cf. the preface to Jean Claude, *Réponse aux deux traitez intitulez La Perpetuité de la foy de l'Eglise catholique touchant l'eucharistie* (Paris, 1665). This publication of his first two attacks on Arnauld and Nicole offers an accessible presentation of his argument, minus the long critical disquisitions on the Eastern Church and certain other matters that were part of his subsequent longer work. On Paschasius's role, and Ratramnus's exemplification of what Claude views as the "traditional" outlook, see pp. 38ff.

99. Claude, p. 23.

100. E.g., in Claude, pp. 158ff.

risen for them.[101] And within this meditative orientation, by which faith is inspired (via the Holy Spirit, of course) through its focus upon an image of a set of historical events and meanings, the Eucharist is recast into a carefully limited, though divinely directed, instrument of propositional signification. When Claude does in fact give his fullest presentation of Eucharistic "theology," it is delineated in terms of the character of Eucharistic "language" or "metaphor," in answer to the question, "what does it mean that the bread and the wine are 'referred' to as 'body' and 'blood'?"[102] The issue of "presence" has, in fact, disappeared altogether, even in the forms found in Calvin himself, as if the temporal encounter of the liturgical act itself — its history — had been peeled away in favor of the act's underlying content, accessible through translated idioms. Instead of the category of "presence," however defined, the Eucharist is explained as a metaphoric discourse, "reminding" us primarily of the life, death, resurrection, and ascension of Jesus, and subordinately (as "pledge") of our own future life with him. There is certainly a divine "effect" to this remembrance, which includes the dispositions of "peace and consolation," for example. But even when this "effect" is explicated in terms of a "communication" of the "Holy Spirit and his grace," this is mentioned in conjunction with the sacrament's role in "leading" us to receive the Spirit, in the way that a teacher prepares a pupil to receive knowledge.

The final purposeful element of the Eucharist as discourse, mentioned almost as an afterthought by Claude, is the sacrament's function as a "symbol of unity," bond of love and peace, according to the image of the one bread and many pieces in 1 Corinthians 10:17. Here, however, and with this reference in particular, he underlines his distance from any notion of an ecclesial "body of Christ" within the Eucharistic figure. Rather it is the bread alone, as bread, that functions as a diversified metaphor or "representation" of the "body of the faithful." Faced with Augustine's paschal sermons on the topic, he insists (again, in the tradition of Protestant apologists before him) that the reference to the Church as the "body of Christ" is as clearly a metaphoric reference to a "moral" reality as the fact that the Eucharistic elements are metaphors for an "absent" body of Jesus now located in heaven.[103] The "wicked" — the unfaithful — then, do not eat the "body of Christ," because the referents of the Eucharistic terms signify realities that do not admit of these two terms' semantic coherence.

101. This is all explained in the manner, again, of Augustine's brief remark in *De Doctrina Christiana* 3:16, interpreted in a strictly nonfigural and explicitly "moral" sense of "participation." Cf. Claude, pp. 238, 252.

102. Claude, pp. 318ff.

103. Claude, pp. 402ff.; cf. p. 245.

And if there is a historical dimension to the Eucharist that Claude's discussion uncovers, it is one that is confined to terminological usage, a history of misplaced and/or misunderstood metaphors that stands behind his entire project of apology and polemic.[104] If nothing else, the seventeenth-century debate gave full flower to what has become a staple of modern theological (and generally intellectual) self-understanding, no less controlling today, and not only among analytic philosophers, than three hundred years ago: if only we were able to reorder the signifying template of our ideas, the truth would become apparent. In this light, historical theology in particular is seen as the search for a cognitive correction, by which terms regain their proper referential bearing, and concepts thereby achieve their proper relation one to another, which, once restored, can be effectively marshaled for the needs of the present. The view of historical experience that undergirds this wide set of convictions is thoroughly Protestant in nature, based as it is on the search for a uniform and originally divine doctrine, independent of the vicissitudes of the Church's temporal existence. That Claude's peculiar reading of the history of the Eucharistic doctrine, assigning both a dubious uniformity of ideal understanding to the Fathers and an untenable deviation from this common articulation to Paschasius, may be flawed is not the most interesting feature of his thought. More pertinent for our argument is the way his defense of a Protestant ecclesiology of distinctive faithfulness deliberately and ahistorically redefined the Eucharist as a propositional text composed for those educated in the grammar of the Spirit, detached from the "bodies" of their historical ecclesial traditions. The "postmodernistic" linguistic and somatic terms that apply here simply underline a certain continuity with even contemporary habits of imagination.

On the opposite side of the debate, the actual outlook of the *Perpétuité* with which Claude took exception is itself not particularly surprising given the boundaries to Catholic apologetic erected by the ecclesial argument.[105] It shares the Protestant dehistoricization of the Eucharist as an event of the Church's

---

104. Granted that he is writing in response to the *Perpétuité*'s own history of metaphor, Claude's embrace of the method reflects the general Protestant and Catholic transformation of sacramentology into theories of signification.

105. I have consulted the 1781 edition of *La perpétuité de la foi de l'église catholique touchant l'eucharistie, défendue contre les livres du sieur Claude, Ministre de Charenton* (Paris, 1781). For a concise summary of Nicole's teaching on the Eucharistic presence, as well as on frequency of communion (see below), cf. his *Instructions théologiques et morales, sur les sacremens* (Paris, 1704), vol. 2, pp. 21-112. Taken as a whole, this last comprehensive statement does tend to give the impression that Nicole's sacramentology in this case was more or less in line with standard post-Tridentine rigorist devotion.

ongoing life, and even exaggerates it, in an effort to preserve the Roman Church's "unchanging" and "perpetual" link with the early Church, as the title of the book itself suggests. There is nothing in this work of the Jansenist conviction concerning the "declension" and "aging" of the Church, even on simply the level of "morals," which we see in Saint-Cyran or in the younger Arnauld. Instead, the thousands of pages of analysis, excerpts, and attacks amount to an unremitting assertion that the doctrine of the real presence, and of transubstantiation in its essence, has always been and still remains the unequivocal teaching of the Church Catholic, both in the West and in the East. Except for the occasional and limited outburst of this or that heretical contradiction, this teaching and its enactment have persisted solidly and integrally without alteration from the time of Jesus.

There is nothing ahistorical in the authors' appreciation of the Eucharist's and the Church's experiential practice, to be sure. In an effort to counter the Protestant charge both that the Christian laity could not have grasped the doctrine of the real presence on the basis of patristic teaching and that it was possible for Paschasius's novel doctrine to infiltrate the Church surreptitiously over several centuries, the *Perpétuité* provides one of the earliest extended attempts at a sociological analysis of religious behavior and understanding, detailing at length the ways in which lay populations may or may not have "understood" what was going on in the churches during the liturgies and trying to outline the relation between doctrinal articulation and popular devotion at certain historical periods.[106] Some of the most sensitive and fascinating discussion of this kind of "performative" understanding of the Eucharist's meaning as a liturgical act — how we "treat" the Eucharist demonstrates its meaning — is nonetheless tellingly given only in the context of an analysis of metaphorical signification. For the authors of the *Perpétuité*, such signification is judged incapable of ecclesiastical historical development because of the intrinsically unstable nature of its ambiguous referentiality. Only "natural" significations can make sense over time within the continuous life of a worshipping community; and hence, any realistic terminology used within the Eucharistic rite, especially with respect to the "body" and "blood" of Jesus, must be taken at face value, not only by the theologian, but by the historian of popular devotional perception.[107]

This kind of idiosyncratic sensitivity to social cognition aside, the *Perpétuité* has no distinctive Eucharistic theology, apart from reiterating its defense of Trent's teaching through the repeated citing of patristic, medieval, and scholastic texts.

---

106. This approach is used throughout the first volume.

107. The original argument was lucidly given in the *Petite Perpétuité*, in Arnauld, *Oeuvres*, pp. 129ff.

Where Claude reads Augustine in a narrow conventionalist significatory fashion, Nicole and Arnauld do so in a naturalistic or realistic mode. But they have no interest in his Eucharistic theology beyond this.[108] So that, as de Lubac noted, through its almost interminable exposition of primary material, the *Perpétuité* is virtually silent about the ecclesial referent of the Eucharist, and any kind of figuralist understanding of Augustine with respect to the topic is absent.[109] Given Jansenist predilections to such understandings in general, in Arnauld as much as in anyone, we might simply assign this absence to the primary authorship of the less exegetically imaginative Nicole. More likely, however, is the fact that the debate over the Eucharistic presence was at root an ecclesial debate about denominational integrity and the justification of separated Christian communities. Within this context, the Catholic position had little room for the self-questioning that a theology of the figural body of Christ, defined in terms of a history of Eucharistic sweetness and poison according to the seasoning of charity, afforded. Crucial to grasping this fundamental point is an understanding of the purpose given to the original devotional collection of historical "testimonies" to the real presence, the 1659 *Office du Saint-Sacrement,* to which the *Petite Perpétuité* was later written as a preface. This work, the not-so-innocent starting point to the whole ensuing controversy, was prepared for the nuns of Port-Royal to encourage them in their "perpetual adoration" of the sacrament, a devotion

108. On the *Perpétuité*'s reading of Augustine (including the text from *De Doctrina Christiana*), confined to the interest in signification, though from a realist perspective, see vol. 3, e.g., pp. 102ff. and 376ff., where the issue of "literal" versus "figurative" referentiality is addressed and an attempt is made to bring the two together in the manner of Paschasius. The authors do, however, admit to the difficulty of prying apart the signifying mechanism in Augustine's interpretation, and end by suggesting that the saint's texts on this issue not be given too much weight, because of their opaqueness. An odd caveat on the part of theologians for whom the Bishop of Hippo stood second only to Scripture in authority! But it is an admission that also points to the aridity of attempts at approaching the Eucharist, in Augustine's perspective, on the basis of a strict construal of signification. If the Eucharist's meaning was given in the posture of its caritative participation, as Augustine insisted, then the significatory reading of the rite is destined to be hopelessly misleading.

109. On the use the authors make of the ecclesial referent in patristic literature, cf. vol. 2, pp. 464f. Here, in a way that mirrors in reverse the Protestant use of, for example, 1 Corinthians 10:17 — and sounds a good bit like John Nevin in the nineteenth century in its positive assertions — the *Perpétuité* argues that the notion of the Church being "one body in Christ," in the image of "one bread," is sufficiently "physical and natural" (rather than "moral") that we must take the Eucharistic bread as being "Christ's body" in a "physical and natural sense," tying the two "incorporations" together through the "mystical" reality of Christ's own body. Just as, for the Protestants, the ecclesial body is a subordinate reality coordinated (not joined) to the Eucharistic "presence" via faith, so here, on the Catholic side, the ecclesial body is a subordinate reality coordinated, in a derivative sense, with the real presence of the Eucharistic transubstantiation.

pursued for the explicit purpose of *making reparation for the insults* borne by the Sacred Host from blaspheming Protestants. A short introduction to the work, perhaps written by Arnauld himself, details the kind of effect such prayer, made on behalf of a Church beset by the conflicts of heretics and schismatics, might have for the conversion of the unfaithful and their return to unity.[110] The *presence* of Christ in the Catholic Eucharist was that which brought into relief the distinction between the true Church and its enemies, and it was just that "indicating" presence that the entire debate, on the Catholic side, was designed to protect and promote. That Arnauld himself, however, could take a radically different approach to the Eucharist in the intra-Catholic debate on frequency of communion points to the constraints of this denominational logic, which managed to bind even Jansenists, in their dealings with Protestants and despite theological pulls in another direction, to a defiguralized, because self-justifying, Eucharistic understanding.

Eucharistic Repugnance and the Early Modern Disquiet with Communion

The great Protestant-Catholic question, "Where is Christ?" in the Eucharist, then, was a subordinate question to the more pressing query, "Where is the true Church"; and in answering that question, the Eucharist became a tool in the hands of self-maintaining ecclesial separatists. We need not review the development in later centuries of Eucharistic theologies on both sides of the divide on the matter of Christ's presence, because there was none,[111] nor could

---

110. Lengthy excerpts of Arnauld's introductory remarks to the *Office* are included in "Préface historique et critique" of his *Oeuvres,* vol. 12, pp. iii-1v. See also Snoeks, p. 185.

111. The history of sacramental theology, both Protestant and Catholic, after the seventeenth century is one of tiresome repetition, along the lines already denominationally established in the wake of the Reformation. One comes across distinctions made by scholars of this debate between the "receptionists," the "virtualists," and the "memorialists" among the Calvinist Protestants, not to mention more ambiguous descriptions of the belief in the real presence by certain English divines of the seventeenth century like Cosin or Thorndike. Among Roman Catholics there are also diversities of explanation concerning the "natural" versus the "sacramental" substantive presence of Christ in the elements, the exact character of the "adoration" to be given to the host, many of which have their roots in scholastic analysis dating back into the medieval period. The modern reader will rightly wonder at the exact force of the differences in these positions, many of which tend to a similar devotional posture, at least in theory. (Cf. the pragmatist philosopher Charles Pierce's notorious judgment that "it is foolish for Catholics and Protestants to fancy themselves in disagreement about the elements of the sacrament, if they agree in regard to all their sensible effects, here or hereafter," in "How To Make Our Ideas

there have been given the intractable reality that the Eucharist was being celebrated in an ecclesial condition that continuously bore the burden of its own referential contradiction or rejection. What is to be noted, instead, is the way that this burden managed to assert itself, even while the theologies of presence that were designed to obscure it maintained their separative disguise. And the most remarkable sign of this assertion was the prolonged struggle, on both Catholic and Protestant sides, with the question of how frequently the Christian ought to participate in the Eucharistic communion. The question itself was not new to the post-Reformation. But it erupted with such force and devotional disquietude in the wake of ecclesial division as to indicate a newly articulated and quite original problematic reality.

Most notorious in the discussion of frequent communion was Antoine Arnauld's 1643 volume *De La Fréquente Communion,* which rapidly went through many editions, despite the arid *longeurs* of its method, familiar from the period and perfected by the Jansenists, of collating, translating, and reviewing streams of primary source texts on a given topic.[112] As many have remarked, the book is less about "frequent" communion than about why such frequency ought to be avoided in favor of lengthy periods of penitential withdrawal from the sacrament. As such, it is aimed at the spiritual directors and their charges for whom the orchestration of confession, penance, absolution, and Communion were central devotional concerns. Arnauld's ultimate position, based on the rigorist discipline of a certain strand of Tridentine Catholic reform, advocated a "return" to strict penitential demands, threatened as he supposed by lax confes-

Clear," *Popular Science Monthly* 12 [January 1878].) The argument here, however is not that these differences are, for this reason, insignificant; rather it is that their theological significance lies primarily in their bond to a separated Eucharist, which in itself defines their logical status as descriptions of Christ's presence.

112. The work, over 600 pages long, is printed in vol. 27 of the *Oeuvres,* with a succeeding volume of 450 pages, providing even longer extracts *(La tradition de l'église sur le sujet de la pénitence et de la communion)* in vol. 28. The more discursive theological points can be found in each work's extensive preface, the former of which, though the authorship is disputed (some assigning it to Saint-Cyran's nephew, Martin de Barcos), I take to be Arnauld's own. The work itself, however, was written under the tutelage of (the then-imprisoned) Abbé de Saint-Cyran; and the overall outlook is properly reflective of the latter's distinctive historical vision. Accessible material on Saint-Cyran's views on the Eucharist and penance, which Arnauld promotes, can be found in the appropriate sections of Jean Orcibal, *La Spiritualité de Saint-Cyran avec ses écrits de piété inédits* (Paris: J. Vrin, 1962). For a general discussion of the context of this work, see Norman D. Kurland, "Antoine Arnauld's First Controversy; *De la Fréquente Communion,*" in Kenneth A. Strand, ed., *The Dawn of Modern Civilization: Studies in Renaissance, Reformation, and Other Topics Presented to Honor Albert Hyma,* 2nd ed. (Ann Arbor: Ann Arbor Publishing, 1964).

sors, which would severely curtail communion for most Christians, even those not in a state of "mortal sin," but simply "attached" to "venial sins." And while, it is true, penance looms as the greater focus here, Arnauld necessarily provides a theology of the Eucharist that reveals how, outside of denominational debate, a profound unease with the integral reception of the sacrament had surfaced in tandem with a sense of ecclesial disruption.

It is possible to schematize Arnauld's Eucharistic theology in the following way. First, there is the broad relationship of the Eucharist to baptism and to the Holy Spirit's work in this sacrament, understood in an abstract and individualized way. Baptism effects, through the gift of the Holy Spirit, a renewed and restored life in union with Christ Jesus. The baptized life is, in theory, a life lived in and through the Holy Spirit's presence.[113] It is this pneumatic presence that "impels" one to the Eucharist, which is given as the "perfecting food" to those who are already "healthy." Arnauld does not insist that those who receive the Eucharist somehow be in a state of perfect grace such as they would have fully in heaven; but he describes the incompleteness experienced by the pilgrim *in via* not as a state of sinfulness (or "sickness"), but of "hunger" for Jesus. While Jesus "invites" sinners to him, as Scripture repeatedly recounts, this is meant figurally of baptism, not of the Eucharist. Thus, the Holy Spirit "sends" us to the table, and must precede us at the meal. Postbaptismal sin, however, drives away this Spirit and — to the extent that the Spirit works in our life at all — impels us to penitence instead, as a way of restoring us to a pneumatic integrity necessary for Eucharistic communion. In Arnauld's rigorist theology, penitence is properly pursued through the process of offering "satis-factions" of suffering in love — alms, self-offering, intercession — that conform us to the suffering of Jesus, whose expiation for our sins is made effective postbaptismally only through this deliberate opening on our part to such conformance. Involved in this, of course, is withdrawal from Communion. Quoting the Fathers, penance is called a "laborious baptism" anew, and it is given scriptural figures in the wilderness wanderings of the Israelites, through which a new "hunger" is awakened and purified; or in the centurion, the woman with an issue of blood, or the prodigal son, all of whom, in a sense, stood "afar" from Jesus, out of humility, as they sought his aid.[114]

The unusual aspect of this rigorist theology, in addition to its prominent pneumatological basis, is the way it is explicated and applied, on a concrete

---

113. Arnauld, *Oeuvres,* pp. 556-61; cf. pp. 191f., 287, 603.

114. Arnauld, *Oeuvres,* pp. 87ff., 251, 350, 466f., 567-69, 589ff. On the matter of penitence through withdrawal from the Eucharist for venial, and not only mortal, sins, cf. pp. 289ff.

level, to the life of the Church as a whole. This marks the second major structuring element in Arnauld's Eucharistic theology, that is, its relation to the ecclesial figure of Christ. The early Church of the first few centuries, argues Arnauld, had a direct and forceful experience of pneumatic renewal, beginning at Pentecost. This afforded the first Christians a basis upon which to partake of the Eucharistic sacrament even daily, as it is stated in Acts. But the Church's historical life, following a unified but evolving course, gradually experienced a decline in moral virtue among its people, especially the clergy. The need for penance gradually increased, and became more continual, so that even venial sins took on a character that touched the basic "affections" of Christians more deeply than in the first years of the Church's life. Though frequent communion remained an end for every Christian, it became more and more difficult to attain, as the Church itself embroiled its members in careless and sinful living from which only increasingly demanding penance, including withdrawal from regular participation in the sacrament, could free them.

It is in this context that Arnauld construes the significance of various heretical movements in the Church, culminating in the Protestant divisions themselves, the last of which work as a whole to press the Church into an attitude of penance actually defined by a loss of Eucharistic communion as well as by an increased sin in communicating too frequently in response! Luther's attacks on penitential satisfactions themselves acted as God's scourge on the Church, weakening it further, even while demonstrating, through contrast, the potential source of its healing.[115]

Arnauld decisively goes beyond an individualist soteriology here when he wraps all of this up in an explicit historical figuralism, according to which the Church is being conformed to the mysteries of Jesus' own body as it suffered its temporal changes and fate. From its initial pneumatic fullness at Pentecost, the Church moves through periods of suffering and abandonment, the worst of which is to precede the final return, at the end times, of Elijah and Enoch, preaching a renewed penitence, in the manner of the Baptist *redivivus* sent to the Christian Body as a whole, before the return of Christ.[116] The explicitness of this figural vision is astonishing for the time, as is the starkness of its historical implications. Augustine himself, along with others of his era, had certainly never attempted to formalize a figural theory on this level of historical detail, attached

115. This historical argument is found explicated mostly in the preface, pp. 92-137; cf. also pp. 289ff. On the place of Protestantism in this, cf. pp. 103, 120, 130-40, 546, 554ff. Cf. Saint-Cyran's remarks on the Protestant Reformation as a necessary "recrucifixion" of Jesus, a historical and continuing penance for the Church as a whole, in Orcibal, p. 383.

116. Cf. Arnauld, *Oeuvres,* pp. 126ff. and 149f.

as it was to the fate not only of particular doctrinal and devotional concerns, but of broad social movements within ecclesiastical history. Yet in itself, Arnauld's treatise was nothing other than an attempt to write a "history of the Eucharist" more narrowly, not in terms of its various conceptions, but in terms of the critical place the sacrament has held in time, around which the shape of the Church forms itself historically. The "sufferings" of Eucharist and Church alike refer to each other, as together they refer and are referred by Christ's own life and self-giving. In this light, the whole theology of the "presence of Christ" in the Eucharist, while it informs the notion of "worthiness" in communion in a typical Tridentine fashion, is subsumed by the larger historical issue of what the Church has *done* in and with the Eucharist and how the Church is shaped in the course of that practice. With Augustine, this is parsed according to the measure of "love," the fullness of which alone determines the Eucharist's benign fulfillment, the wounding of which turns Communion into love's suffering self-sacrifice.[117] For Arnauld, separation from Communion, through infrequent participation both voluntary and historically enforced, marks an embraceable embodiment of this history, which through God's own Spirit "impels" the distancing of the Eucharistic savor, in favor of the bitterness of enforced hunger whose only alternative is the poison of intimacy with a flesh the Church evidently cannot abide. Applied to the Eucharist directly, the vision is congruent with Saint-Cyran's anguished attempt to move ministerial vocation from the order of pneumatic certainties into the realm of ascetic obscurity.

In this respect, the debate that came to swirl around Arnauld's book, and some of the Tridentine reform attitudes it attempted to represent (however accurately), was simply of a different order than were concerns over Eucharistic communion that evolved in the Middle Ages, when participation by the laity grew rare indeed and required official rulings on minimal attendance.[118] Churchmen at the time, as later, could refer to this last era as one in which "faith waxed cold" (cf. Matt. 24:12) in a vaguely charged reading of the end times,[119] but there was only a tacit awareness that the Eucharist itself and the Church to which it was bound as a body were implicated in this development. For Arnauld's own century, however, this awareness had broken out, almost despite itself, while laboring against the forces of ecclesial separation that would

---

117. On the central caritative dimension of Eucharistic preparation, pneumatically understood in a solid Augustinian sense, cf. the preface to *La Tradition de l'Église sur le sujet de la Pénitence et de la Communion,* in *Oeuvres,* pp. 152ff.

118. Descriptions of this history can be found in the major Catholic encyclopedias and textbooks, e.g., Jules Corblet, *Histoire dogmatique, liturgique et archéologique du sacrement de l'eucharistie* (Paris: Société Générale de Librairie Catholique, 1885), pp. 403ff.

119. Cf. Thomas Aquinas, *Summa Theologiae,* 3a 80:10 ad 5.

have denied the reality altogether. The scholarly argument, then, over whether or not Arnauld's views were representative of the Fathers, or of the Tridentine reformers or of his own era, or were entirely (and disastrously) novel, misses the point.[120] They hit an epochal nerve, when they were embraced and repudiated together, and the nerve remains raw to this day, in many cases.[121]

120. While it is probably true that the mind of the Council of Trent was less rigorist than subsequent Catholic reformers implied, it must be admitted that Trent's commendations were by no means unambiguous. A glance at the "Roman Catechism," which derived from the council, reveals that the practical directives regarding frequency of communion could be taken in several ways. While daily communion was encouraged ("desired"), it was not "commanded," and for a number of weighty reasons that revolve around "preparation." And while communion itself is seen as a means of relieving one of the weight of venial sin, the standards of preparation offered by the Catechism do not in fact rule out withdrawal from communion only for grave and mortal sins. It is fair to say that Arnauld and, say, the "frequentist" Fénelon were both speaking within the literal parameters of official policy (one reason, clearly, why Arnauld's book was never censured by the Vatican). See *Catechism of the Council of Trent for Parish Priests,* trans. John McHugh and Charles Callan (New York: Joseph F. Wagner, 1923), esp. pp. 243-51. For a scathing critique of Arnauld's book by a venerated contemporary, St. Vincent de Paul, cf. his long letter of September 10, 1648, to Jean De Horgny, which set the tone for subsequent attacks on Arnauld's sincerity and lays out the general bases, in the tradition, for the frequentist case. De Paul also raises the not impertinent question of how a man like Arnauld, who explicates such a high view of demanded Eucharistic purity, could at the same time admit to saying the Mass himself on a daily basis, an odd situation in which "his humility is as admirable as the charity and high opinion he demonstrates for so many wise directors, both priests and monks, and for so many devout and virtuous penitents, who together serve as the objects of his daily insults" (in Pierre Coste, ed., *Saint Vincent de Paul. Correspondance, entritiens, documents* [Paris: Gabalda, 1921], vol. 3, pp. 362-74).

121. In the present century, Henri Bremond (no real admirer of the Jansenists in general) made the case that Arnauld's strictures on unworthy reception, and the need for longer periods of penitential separation from the Eucharist, even after absolution, were well in accord with the standard "spiritual" recommendations of confessors of his time, including many Jesuits: frequent, even daily, communion was the goal; yet worthy reception demanded withdrawal for greater or lesser periods. Arnauld's book, in any case, was less concerned with the Eucharist than with the abuses of laxist confessors. Cf. his chapter on the subject in volume 9 of his *Histoire littéraire du sentiment religieux en France depuis la fin des guerres de religion jusqu'à nos jours* (Paris: Librairie Bloud et Gay, 1932), pp. 45-128. Bremond does see an evolution toward greater liberalism in this regard, but not one to alter profoundly the common perspective of the century, which took its tone from Francis de Sales's own cautious views on the matter (cf. ch. 21 in pt. II of the *Introduction to the Devout Life*). This assessment was contradicted by Paul Dudon in two heated articles the next year, which argued forcefully that Arnauld's position was indeed extreme, and deliberately framed to discourage frequent communion of any kind (cf. "Sur la 'Fréquente' d'Arnauld commentée par M. Bremond," *Revue d'Ascétique et de Mystique* 13, no. 52 [Oct. 1932] and 14, no. 53 [Jan. 1933]). Both pieces provide a good overview of the debate over frequent communion that took place in the late sixteenth and seventeenth centuries. Pure theory aside, there seems little doubt to me that Arnauld's (and Saint-Cyran's) teaching was *designed*

Within this historical realm, the later Jansenist stand in the *Perpétuité* against doctrinal malleability on the issue of the Eucharistic presence, asserted against Protestant questions on the matter, appears less a case of simply protecting the justified purity of the Roman Church than an appeal to respect the agony of Eucharistic unity in the present Body of Christ.

The actual relation between confession and Communion, in terms of the first being a divinely obligatory condition for the second in cases of grave sin, was argued over before, during, and after the Council of Trent had attempted to bring some order into a topic already confused by Protestant attacks on ritual penance and its significance for Eucharistic participation. But in and of itself, the discussion became tinctured with fury as it passed over from the denominational context into the realm of local ecclesial existence, in large measure because the issue of "worthiness" for the Eucharist was no longer resolvable even within this individualized sphere, wherein the peaceful conscience might remain intact. The debate itself could be traced just in terms of how 1 Corinthians 11:27 and 29 were read,[122] and here one sees an evolving need in this history of exegesis to come to terms with these verses in ways that can redefine the Church inclusive of the dislocations of division. The rigorists,

---

to provoke. Further, the historical and figural framework of the devotional recommendations was sufficiently idiosyncratic as to mark off Arnauld's fundamental motive from those of other writers on the topic. Neither Bremond nor Dudon, however, seems interested in what the phenomenon of the seventeenth-century debate really signified; and Dudon cannot really explain why it was that Arnauld's work (and sympathetic analogies) were in fact so popular and exercised such a "stranglehold" on Catholic devotion until the Revolution. It was not all mere subterfuge and pernicious politicking. It is interesting to note how, in contemporary times, the whole patristic notion of penitential "excommunication," whether self-inflicted or officially administered, and even in a relatively nonrigorist reading, has been seen as intrinsically problematic for the purposes of ecumenical progress: *if* separated "churches" are "truly Church" in some sense, then separated Eucharists make no sense; if separated Eucharists make no sense, then the very theology of Eucharistic exclusion, with its scriptural interests in "worthiness" and "judgment" and so on, upon which the sixteenth-century sacramental divisions were argued, appears to be essentially flawed. (Cf. Kenneth Hein, *Eucharist and Excommunication: A Study in Early Christian Doctrine and Discipline* [Frankfurt: Peter Lang, 1973], esp. pp. 439-49, for an example of this viewpoint.) The point of reviewing the phenomenon of deliberately "infrequent" communion in the modern era, however, is to emphasize how separation from communion is, in pneumatic historical terms, logically impelled, although not necessarily exclusively so, by the "poisonous" reality of ecclesial division. It is not a matter simply of asserting the need for "intercommunion" in the face of separations, as if the Eucharist were a creative or causative sign of unity, since such communions will retain their bitterness until some form of ecclesial penitence, "laborious" and "martyred" in the traditional sense, accompanies and sustains the communion itself.

122. Cf. the interesting study by L. Breackmans, S.J., *Confession et communion au moyen âge et au Concile de Trente* (Gembloux: Éditions J. Duculot, S.A., 1971).

with Arnauld as a creative theoretician, did so by making "unworthiness" an aspect of the moral life of the Church as a whole, whose penitential exigencies ineluctably flowed down into the lives of individual Christians. But those who resisted the rigorist view, and promoted instead a regular and frequent communion, were required to make "worthiness" and the "self-examination" it required something immune from the condition of the historical Church at large, even as the Church was immune from its unworthy communicants, a process of contortion that led to demands of individual devotion and fervor normal Christians were not likely to sustain.

Already in the early seventeenth century, Catholic exegetes like Estius had determined that the disorders in Corinth about which Paul speaks in 1 Corinthians 11 did not actually touch upon the Eucharist itself, but upon its preceding "love-feast." Confusing the Eucharist with such communal eating was part of the problem to be corrected.[123] This kind of exegesis, not in itself new, but now joined more determinedly to the topic of worthy eating, recast the question of preparation into a deliberately individualized context. Not that issues of mutual love were unimportant to right reception in such readings, but the condition of the Church itself, as Paul described it, was no longer relevant to the demanded consideration of personal integrity. By the time, a century later, Fénelon was writing his celebrated "Letter on Frequent Communion,"[124] he was addressing just this privatized space of reception carved out from the communal existence of the Church, wherein Eucharistic presence and individual conscience worked out a drama of need and redemption whose uniformity was projected onto history as a whole. Written explicitly against those who would "trouble" Christians with excessive scruples about worthiness, the letter revealingly finds it necessary to erect a highly artificial theory of historical impassibility for the Church, as if this were the only perspective from which individuals could now take Communion without the experience of fear. In this sense, it is a carefully constructed reversal of the whole of Arnauld's perspective.

Fénelon's positive assertions, backed by a judicious and succinct historical documentation, are firm and simple: daily communion was established by the first apostolic Church, and continued to be the stated goal of the Church consistently, except in officially determined cases of an individual's state in mortal sin; variations in practice (which are not traceable until after the first few centuries) never altered this fundamental teaching, restated by the Council

123. Cf. his commentary on 11:20ff., in his *In omnes D. Pauli epistolas, item in catholicas commentarii* (J. Holzammer ed. of 1858), vol. 1, pp. 606ff.

124. Found in Fénelon, *Oeuvres* (Paris: Firmin Didot, 1854), vol. 1, pp. 665-75.

of Trent. Theologically, the Eucharist can sustain such frequentation because it is primarily a medicinal sacrament, designed to heal the sick through its sacrificial powers. The Eucharistic sacrifice is at the center of Fénelon's perspective here and determines his insistence that "worthiness" for the Eucharist consists only in a "sincere desire" no longer to sin; frequent communion thus acts as a *necessary* "daily bread" (following the patristic connection between this petition of the Lord's Prayer and the Eucharist) that "strengthens" the weak still dragged down by venial sins.

To undergird this theology, Fénelon explicates a vision of ecclesial history that purposefully contradicts Arnauld's. "Behold the Church that is the same in all times; nothing can age her; nothing alters her purity; the same Spirit that moved her in the time of St. Justin and the other Fathers now has her speak in these last days: she invites all her children to a *frequent* communion."[125] Nothing has changed, he asserts. The Spirit works as before. There are no alterations. "Penitence," among the faithful, is a condition of the heart, rarely linked to historical particulars. Even the "saints" of the apostolic Church — though Fénelon is careful to preserve their prominence — have a holiness no different in kind from that of the average Christian who has, through simple choice, chosen God over the Devil.[126] It is a very modern-sounding affirmation of the Church's uniform integrity, strangely consonant with an evolved modern Protestantism as well, pressed to include even the diversities of popular sanctity, wherein the Everyman of faith cannot be separated from a general intimacy with God. Though a notion of the Christian's "right" to Communion may not be stated explicitly, Fénelon's combative tone is aimed at defending such guaranteed access.[127] In fact, if there is a difference between the modern Church and the early Church, according to Fénelon, it is due to the fact that the contemporary Church is at peace and that religion is less important to people. In the face of this creeping complacence (tinged with a threat of secularization), fed by the experience of unity — Fénelon writes after the revocation of the Edict of Nantes had more or less purged France of Protestant difference — what the Christian requires is increased devotional fervor, which frequent communion delivers in a way visible to the slackers and the atheists.[128] Here is a clear demonstration of the fact that the easy conscience of embraced Eucharistic participation often went hand in hand with the denial of ecclesial

---

125. Fénelon, p. 673.

126. Cf. Fénelon, p. 666.

127. He can only grudgingly acknowledge the "rare" times when separation from the Eucharist may be helpful to an individual (Fénelon, p. 674).

128. Fénelon, p. 674.

separations, indeed, with the interiorization and individualization of the Christian life altogether, against which the whole reality of ecclesial suffering held little relief.

In this regard, Fénelon's Eucharistic position embodies a paradigmatic development in modern devotion that cuts across Catholic and Protestant lines: frequency of communion presses to reflect either a real or a desired unity of Christian experience, which is achieved individualistically where it cannot be grasped communally. For such individualistic union itself becomes the means by which the pain of the Church's Eucharistic figural passion is simply denied — either through the basic Protestant distillation of divine history to the uniformity of atomistic faith or through a Catholic leveling of ecclesial experience in time, which ends itself by making such faith the only discernible distinctive, however universally accessible. We need not survey Protestant attitudes to the frequency of communion here to prove this point, except to emphasize how, in their theory, they ended up sounding themes consonant with this generalized ostinato of true faith's historical impassibility. Calvin's purified Church could rightly sustain the holy participation of a more-than-weekly communion, precisely because such a body was no longer temporally hindered by the drag of the past's corruptions.[129] By the late seventeenth century, as with Fénelon, the real historical challenge was seen as creeping "unbelief," not a history of Christian heresy or division, the problems of Catholic deviation with respect to the Eucharist having been definitively repudiated in most Protestant lands. Frequency of communion was, in such contexts, encouraged more for the purposes of social cohesion among disintegrating Reformed groups than for its referential figure of Christian unity, which, in ecclesial terms, had simply disappeared as a sacramental concern.[130]

129. Cf. his *Institutes*, IV: 45-46.

130. Cf. the Restoration Anglican Simon Patrick's *A Treatise of the Necessity and Frequency of Receiving the Holy Communion* (1684), in his *Works*, ed. A. Taylor (Oxford: Oxford University Press, 1858), vol. 2, pp. 11-91, a work whose author's alleged "latitudinarian" attitudes in no way detracts from its representative character as a description of a standard Reformed Eucharistic theology now seeking communion's justification in an established separative context. The purpose of communion, as with Fénelon, is medicinal, although effected not through the Eucharist's sacrificial function, but through its commemorative "nourishing" of faith via the soul's meditation on the Passion (cf. pp. 26ff.). The more frequently received, then, the better; further, because it is an individual's "faith" itself that is the object of the Holy Supper's repetition within the Church, frequent communion becomes a strong weapon against the dilution of faith within a society, as well as against that society's thereby weakened unity (cf. esp. "Discourse II"). Here is a specifically sacramental argument that lays at the feet of the (sacramentally disruptive) Puritans most of the social ills of England, using lines of attack not unfamiliar from Hooker. The argument, in addition, now links, again familiarly, Puritans (and their progeny, the "enthusiasts") and Catholics together

In their practice, however, both Catholic and Protestant exhortations to frequent communion often stumbled on the same lurking temporal rocks that, under a differently rendered surface, had made of early Jansenist theology a lament for the Church's love lost: individual faith came to bear the whole weight of the Body's communal figure, making Eucharistic participation an excruciating demand for subjective intensity. Despite the supposed conflicts between the two groups over the issue of the Eucharistic presence, both Protestant and Catholic *preparative devotion* for communion adopted inter-changeable burdens of individual fervency. Many people are perhaps still familiar, through its longevity, with the kind of Catholic Eucharistic piety associated with adorative devotion to the sacrament. Its apogee in an eigh-teenth-century figure like Alphonse Liguori demonstrates how a rejection of the rigorist notions of penitential separation from the Eucharist nonetheless reappropriated all the unmeetable demands of Arnauld's program into a project of individualized yearning. Liguori's famous *Visits to the Most Holy Sacrament,* often edited with other Eucharistic writings concerning frequent communion, dispositions for preparation and receiving of the sacrament, and so on, combine many of the post-Reformation strands of Eucharistic maintenance, couched in the language of desire so intense as to repel contemporary ears.[131] With most modern Protestants and Catholics, Liguori shared a historical evaluation of Communion that saw the Middle Ages as a period of pernicious decline in the frequency of the necessary and medicinal participation in the Eucharist. The sacrament is for the "weak," for the "sinful," to strengthen and renew them.[132] With post-Reformation Protestants and Catholics together, he sees

---

as explicitly "satanic" vessels of social disintegration, the former in their denigration of material sacraments altogether, the latter because of their earlier sacerdotal attempt to distance the people from communion for the sake of gain and through the "absurd" propagation of the transubstan-tiation doctrine. Simon would like "worthiness" to come down to a form of sincerity in motive, just because this kind of subjective orientation would most easily accommodate the formative reintegration of separated Christians into an educative, and socially enhancing, participation in the Supper. That he ends his treatise on a note that combines both an exhortation to English solidarity and an attack on Rome is but a logical flourish (pp. 89-91). Secularism as being generally the fault of other Christians' errors is a theme now well established to the present day. Simon's perspective, both theologically and devotionally, was widespread. Cf. the sequence of John Tillotson's Sermons, 24 and 26 ("A Persuasive to Frequent Communion" and "A Discourse against Transubstantiation"), in his *Works* (London, 1820), vol. 2, pp. 374-452; or William Sherlock's *A Practical Discourse of Religious Assemblies* (London, 1682).

131. I have in hand what appears to be a late nineteenth-century English edition, Alphonse Liguori, *Visits to the Most Holy Sacrament,* trans. N. Callan (Dublin: James Duffy and Co., n.d.).

132. Cf. "An Apologetic Reply on the Subject of Frequent Communion, to D. Cyprian Aristasio," in Liguori, pp. 160-82.

participation in the Eucharist as a means of countering the attacks of Satan through unbelief, although here he identifies such attacks with the Protestant denigration of the real presence.[133] And, in a kind of compensatory reaction, deliberately articulated in the forms of reparative devotion associated with the Sacred Heart spirituality of the era, he invests in the individual's accessible communion the integral claim of God's holiness on the human soul. Every meditation, "aspiration," prayer, adoration, and discussion of the Eucharist by Liguori is saturated with an appeal to the individual Christian spirit to expend itself "infinitely" with an "infinite love" to match the "infinite self-giving" of an "infinite" God. The following example, taken from an "Act of oblation after Communion," is typical and reiterated:

> I give Thee all my powers; I wish that they may be all Thine. I wish that my memory may serve only to remember Thy favours and Thy love; that my understanding may be employed only in thinking of Thee, whose thoughts are always fixed on my welfare; and that my will may be occupied only in loving Thee, my God and my all, and in wishing only what Thou dost wish. I consecrate, then, and sacrifice to Thee this morning, O my most sweet Saviour! all that I have and all that I am; my senses, my thoughts, my affections, my desires, my pleasures, my inclinations, and my liberty. In a word, I consign into Thy hands my entire body and soul. Accept, O infinite Majesty! the sacrifice of himself, presented to Thee by a sinner, who has been hitherto the most ungrateful on earth, but who now offers and gives himself entirely to Thee. Do with me, O Lord! and dispose of me as Thou pleasest. Come, O consuming fire, O divine love! and consume in me whatsoever is mine, and is not pleasing to Thy most pure eyes, and that I may fulfil not only Thy precepts and counsels, but also Thy holy desires, and whatever is most pleasing to Thee.[134]

Intensified to this level, as it included the whole act of Eucharistic participation — preparation, communion itself, postcommunion prayer, and adoration of the sacrament — it is little wonder that "frequent communion" was in fact little spurred by such piety, which, often for the most devout souls, was limited to acts of "spiritual communion" defined solely in terms of "desire."

133. Cf. the introduction to *Visits*, where he opens with a discussion of St. Marguerite Marie Alacoque's visionary devotion to the Sacred Heart as a divinely commanded response to Protestant "blasphemy" against the "host," as well as some of the individual meditations themselves (e.g., 1 and 24). In our next chapter, we shall examine how the post-Reformation Catholic devotion of "reparative love," including that of the Sacred Heart, was fed by an anti-Protestant separative motive.
134. In Liguori, pp. 101f.

As if the Eucharist, even at its most positive, had achieved its culminating caritative expression in a masked reformulation of Arnauld's "penitential hunger." Only the bravest or the most ignorant dared to broach the sacramental confines of an infinite abyss of unmet love.

That Protestants should have their own version of this retreat through fervor is not surprising, participating, as they did, in the same ecclesial and sacramental logic as the Catholics, even if their terminological commitments over the Eucharistic presence differed. Claude himself wrote a popular work, translated into English, devoted to preparation for communion that took hold of 1 Corinthians 11:28 and aimed the exhortation to "self-examination" toward an elaborated interior scrutiny already made notorious among Puritans in other contexts.[135] Although God's "presence" in the Eucharist is emphasized as being "spiritual," it is as august and holy as any Roman Catholic's version of the real presence; and it demands of each communicant a preceding and detailed accounting of his or her spiritual condition — enumerating sins, virtues, actions, circumstances, temptations, resistance, progress, obstacles, decline into "superstition," and so on. While Communion is offered to us as "unhappy Criminels," our reception of the sacrament includes the danger of condemnation so great as to impel a "continual" condition of stringent, and constricted, self-awareness. Far more popular still were works like *A Week's Preparation for the Lord's Supper,* an anonymous devotional volume first appearing in 1679 and going through more than fifty editions in eighty years. Here was a full variation on Catholic adorative literature, complete with its daily acts of prayer and meditation, equal in palpable fervor, and buttressed by the kind of self-controlled Protestant examination of conscience already well entrenched. "And oh! that my Soul could imitate my Saviour! Oh that my Heart might return the like Love, in giving myself, my whole self unto my Jesus."[136] This wildly successful work was designed to assist in weekly participation, but was branded already as "terrifying well-disposed minds with strange sorts of doubts and scruples," and led to an alternative, equally successful volume, *The New Week's Preparation,* which, while similarly focused on "worthy" reception, attempted to rein in language deemed too "popish" in its regard for the Eucharistic "presence."[137] That people like Simon and Tillotston, not

135. Jean Claude, *A Treatise of Self-Examination in Order to the Worthy Receiving of the Holy Communion Together with Suitable Prayers* (London, 1683).

136. *A Week's Preparation toward a Worthy Receiving of the Lord's Supper after the Warning of the Church for the Celebration of the Holy Communion . . . ,* 47th ed. (London, 1736), pp. 37f.

137. Cf. remarks in W. H. Mackean, "Anti-Roman Apologetics," in Macdonald, pp. 251f.

to mention the redoubtable liberal Hoadly, felt pushed to argue for "frequency" of communion on the basis of "good enough" preparation should not disguise the fact that their own fervent moralism could do little to make the Eucharist less imposing to a people increasingly alienated from the sacrament's meaning. Where, in the place of the Body of Christ, the virtue of individual faith, emotional ardor, and ethical rectitude came to inhabit the form of Christian religion, the Eucharist could only become unconsciously repugnant. Making its way through the disordered history of its own referent, its taste had turned, however much its food was cherished and celebrated.

Wine into Vinegar, Bread into Gall: The Suffered Taste of Divided Communion

This early modern disquiet with the Eucharist, itself a form of compensatory reordering of the perhaps only unconsciously perceived figural effects of division, has certainly lessened considerably in our own day. The eschatologizing of the Eucharistic sign, part of a wider displacement — a rendering "provisional" — of ecclesial integrity into a dehistoricized future, has provided a conceptual instrument for this reduction of sacramental stress. But the easing of conscience has perhaps itself been achieved, more fundamentally, through a progressive desensitization of the Body's own capacity to taste the bread it is in fact sharing in its fractured communities, the kind of numbing of the tongue that takes place through a long exposure to some acidic tincture of the mouth. This, at least, is what we might expect; and its logical unfolding can be traced, as we have tried to do in a loose fashion, in the figural dissolution of the sacrament along with the ecclesial Body with which it is historically joined in the person of Jesus Christ. The pneumatic event to which such dissolution testifies ought now to be familiar, and so too the epicletic character of the Eucharist itself ought to be apprehensible in this converted form of the Spirit's confounding mission.

It is instructive to see how the maintenance of this figural bond, in contrast, would explicate the actual nature of Eucharistic participation in our present era. The basic text of 1 Corinthians 11 remains the touchstone here, but now supplemented by the full panoply of scriptural forms that constellate around its topic, texts that, as with St. Paul, gather together from the history of Israel about the form of Christ. We have already remarked in passing on the Eucharistic treatise of the twelfth-century Archbishop of Canterbury, Baldwin of Ford. If we return to this treatise at this point, we can now engage the wide grasp of its net as it is cast about the Eucharistic history, which ought to include our own. In his book, Baldwin devotes a good deal of space to the Pauline text on "worthy" and "unworthy" eating.[138] Whatever medieval theoretical drift there may have been, as de Lubac insisted there had been, in decoupling the Eucharistic "body of Christ" from the "body of the Church," Baldwin's text offers clear testimony that, within the confines of exegetical meditation, the two remained tightly entwined, in large measure because the Church in which he lived was, in his experience, still an integral community. First, he explicates 1 Corinthians 10:14-21 in great detail, parsing its description of the Eucharist as the "perfection" and "consummation" of "true friendship" and "love," wherein God's love for us takes its form, through Christ's self-offering, in our love for one another. This text serves as the base upon which to understand 11:20-32, wherein the question of "worthiness" flows from the "unity" that the sacrament embodies. Aquinas's own remark regarding the overall point of Paul's discussion here was a common perspective, shared by Baldwin: *res sacramenti est caritas* ("the primary referent of the sacrament is love").[139] For Baldwin, as for other exegetes of his era, and in the tradition of Augustine, this underlying reality of the caritative figuration of Christ's life meant that the Eucharist itself does not stand apart somehow from its own mishandling, but suffers it in the same manner as Christ suffered Judas, and suffered *from* his actions in the process.[140] The "body," understood in its referent both to Christ and to the Church, as well as to the individual Christian, receives in the Eucharist the full range of response to its self-giving, remaining the Eucharist all the while, although expressing its form in a manner that is experientially indicative of its passion, a passion in the Church that is epitomized in disunity.

Baldwin lays out the character of this suffering Eucharist in great figural detail, as a way of describing what "unworthy" eating and drinking might mean, even as the sacrament becomes an object in the work of unworthiness while maintaining its "referent" as the "body of divine love." For this explication, Baldwin enters into an extended discussion of the scriptural meaning of "the Lord's cup" or "chalice," the various uses of which he ties to the Eucharistic chalice in a summary way.[141] The "cup of the Lord" is a "mixed wine," a drink

138. Baldwin of Ford, *De Sacramento Altaris* II:4, in Morson and de Solms, vol. 2, pp. 351-415.

139. Cf. his Lectio VII of his *Commentary* on 1 Corinthians 11.

140. Cf., among others, the remarks in Haimo of Halberstandt's *Expositio* of 1 Corinthians, in *Patrologia Latina,* vol. 117, col. 571.

141. Cf. Baldwin of Ford, in Morson and de Solms, pp. 343f., but especially pp. 383-401. The Old Testament citations, in particular, are drawn from a wide array of texts, including the Psalms, Isaiah, Jeremiah, Job, and others. Similarly, the New Testament citations — that is,

of wine and water together. By this we understand that in the divine chalice we receive, however purely it be the Lord's person, a "mixture of the sweet and the bitter, that is, of mercy and judgment," a unified character that only appears in this dual or mixed mode because of human sin's reception of divine love as somehow painful. The Eucharistic cup itself, then, becomes a place where "mercy and judgment" are manifested and received within the Church, drawing together in its action the whole range of God's self-giving form as it asserts itself temporally, in Israel's old and new covenants. And this is true not only for "unbelievers" who manage to participate, but for all Christians, and for the Church as a whole, which takes, in the "cup of Christ," the fullness of divine form given in the whole of Scripture's history, but fulfilled in Christ Jesus through the Cross's own assumption of that history's "mercy and judgment." "The 'cup of Christ' should be understood in three ways," Baldwin writes, "as the blood of Christ shed for us and which we drink at the altar; as the passion of Christ which we are obliged to suffer with Him; and finally as the imitation of the passion of Christ, by which we give back to Him who suffered for us a return, in our own measure, and an act of thanksgiving."[142] And thus, in any Eucharistic enactment, the forms of God's love given in Christ will be given to the Church in an array of figural layers, with the judgment upon "unworthy" eating — the contradiction of love — proffered in the unwilling suffering of conformity to the Son's Passion. Citing two Old Testament texts, Baldwin asserts that the cup is both a "shining" cup of "inebriating mercy" and one of "intoxicating torpor" given in divine anger.[143] In the same way, the Eucharistic cup can itself embody the drink of Jesus on the Cross, mixed with vinegar and gall — signs of human hatred at least "tasted" by Jesus, if not drunk outright — which is transformed into a "new wine" for Christians themselves to drink in the bond with his Passion, even while they submit, albeit in a new relation of saving effect, to the continued mortification of their own sinful desires.[144]

And so Baldwin poses the ultimate challenge of the Eucharistic history that he so studiously examines in its figural application: if the Eucharist forms

---

referring in some way to the "cup of the New Testament," in particular — are equally broad. Those interested in working through a piece of mature figural exegesis aimed at the theological clarification of a scriptural text for pastoral purposes could find no better place to start than in a text like Baldwin's here.

142. Baldwin of Ford, in Morson and de Solms, pp. 343f.

143. Baldwin of Ford, in Morson and de Solms, p. 395, citing, respectively, Psalm 23:5f. and Isaiah 51:17.

144. Baldwin of Ford, II:1, in Morson and de Solms, vol. 1, pp. 196ff. The use of Psalm 69:21 here is similar to Augustine's. See above.

a "life-giving" sacrament to the Christian, those who withdraw are deprived of life; yet if a sinner participates in this meal, then the cup of blessing is given in the liquor of wrath. "From both sides, the danger of death; for he is already in a state of death. What therefore will he do?"[145] Baldwin sees only one escape for life: "judge oneself" and "drink of the cup" together. This, he explains, means "bearing a punishment for Christ's sake, and suffering voluntarily and patiently the correction of the Lord," that is, in St. Paul's terms, "illness, weakness, and death" (1 Cor. 11:30).[146]

If the taste of the divided Eucharist is such as this — a "bitterness," a "bread and bowl of tears," a "wormwood," a "gall," and "poisoned wine"[147] — yet it is eaten and drunk with continued relish (as it is and as it must be), then it is because the taste itself has burned its way quite through the organs of the Church's palate. Baldwin's alternatives for the degraded Church remain ones that confront today's ecclesial bodies. Churches might properly respond to their own condition by avoiding the Eucharist altogether, knowing that "reconciliation" with one's brothers and sisters must precede and found any "offering of gifts" at the "altar" of God (Matt. 5:23f.).[148] But in this way lies the danger of death, a deprivation of the divine bread of Christ given even to the unworthy. Alternately, our churches might rush to communion alone, or with other denominations here and there, "intercommuning" while each community continues to go its own way, knowing that the Eucharist is a "medicine," a balm for sinners, a "causative," not merely an "expressive," sacrament (in Geoffrey Wainwright's terms).[149] But this way too is framed by a judgment that comes upon each enactment of a rite that speaks "love!," while love itself

---

145. Baldwin of Ford, in Morson and de Solms, pp. 154ff.

146. Baldwin of Ford, II:4, in Morson and de Solms, vol. 2, pp. 410-14.

147. The texts taken up, in part by Baldwin, are those found in the tradition from before Augustine: e.g., 2 Kings 2:19ff.; Jeremiah 8:14; 9:15; 23:15; 25:15, 17; 48:26; 49:12; 51:31; Lamentations 3:15, 19; Isaiah 24:9; 51:7; Psalm 69:21; 75:8; 80:5; Revelation 8:11; 14:10; 16:1.

148. Wainwright, p. 142, mentions this as a logical response to ecclesial disunity, and even cites (n. 473) a north Cameroonian people, the Kirdis, who take this injunction literally on the level of their own local community. But logic aside, with respect to the larger Church, "in fact, however, the disputing groups have always continued to celebrate a eucharist, in isolation from each other."

149. Cf. Wainwright, p. 142 and pp. 135-146 as a whole. The simple point our whole chapter had aimed at, however, is that "what the eucharist *makes of us*," its "causative" and "creative" power, is not in the first instance to be understood as experienced unity itself. Rather, it is to be understood as the fruit of disunity, the taste of its bitterness. Where a willing reception of such taste may lead us and how it will do so in the near term is hardly clear, however; nor is it necessarily benign.

remains scattered about the ecclesial fields of divided discipline, faith, and mission. Where then is the "life" of the sacrament? In the very savoring, in the tongue-washed taste of communions that bring so little solace beyond the pain of receiving from the Lord a flesh that repulses, but demands we do not turn away. It is the realization in oneself of the positive *fruit* of pneumatic abandonment freely borne, by which one takes into oneself the single bread of bitterness by which the world is saved.[150]

Such a fruit obviously does not include some clarifying of the "meaning" of the Eucharist or of its presence; and we certainly cannot attempt such constructive labor here. Indeed, that kind of particular theological grace about a central aspect of the Church's life is, as in other respects pertaining to the lasting fruit of Christian knowledge, something necessarily out of reach for ecclesial minds obscured. And apart from the certain pull such a willing manducation of the acrid would exert upon the direction of liturgical "revisions" in our day, it is hardly clear, of course, how such reflections are established. At the least they must involve the "judging" of the self that hurls one — churches as a whole — into the hands of God's own subjugating press. Penitence cannot take on only an ancillary role in such a course, particularly when this is assumed through suffering the condemnation we receive by sharing the Lord's body with those whom we still hate or reject for reasons we cannot,

---

150. Cf. the remarks on "unworthy" reception made by the Jansenist spiritual writer Jean Hamon, in his *Instructions chrétiennes et morales, sur les sacremens* (n.p., 1733), pp. 279-95. Hamon's open discussion of pneumatic abandonment was noted in our first chapter. Here he applies it directly to the Eucharistic sacrament, using the prophetic images of "blinding" and "hardening" as the specific outcomes to the pneumatic abandonment that results for those who participate unworthily, making use of the figural significance of Psalm 69:21ff., which Augustine and Baldwin used. In this context, Hamon provides a strong commendation of "separation" from the Eucharist, even for venial sins, in the manner of Arnauld. However, the Eucharistic paradox of his particularly Jansenist outlook, which tried to hold together utter depravity, *sola gratia,* and ascetic imperatives as a single devotional posture, is one he faces squarely: is one *ever* "worthy" of reception? His answer is intriguing: the major "fruit" of considering the topic raised by 1 Corinthians 11, he says, is the recognition that "we must judge ourselves unworthy to approach this sacrament" altogether, for no matter what preparation we offer, they are all "infinitely beneath those required by the holiness and excellence of this adorable Sacrament." What to do, then? In addition to suffering our willing separation from communion, we must "enter that interior disposition that accepts the most horrible torments and suffers the cruelest death" in the place of our deliberate transgression of the sacrament; this includes the interior pain caused by the very consciousness of our sinful communions (pp. 293f.). The figure of Judas is used here initially as a warning, that the torments of his damnation not be ours; at the same time, the terrors of his hell are positively transferred, by Hamon, to the interior life of the Eucharistic penitent in a way that elides the figure with the dilemma of the Christian's sacramental duty.

and perhaps must not, yet discard.[151] But penitence itself may well be far from our ken, as we shall explore in our next chapter. Intercommunion in itself is no salve, unless its hurt is acknowledged and its own wounds left uncovered. Here we must be content with living the given history of our sacramental thanksgivings: "Therefore thus says the LORD of hosts, the God of Israel: I am feeding this people with wormwood [or gall], and giving them poisonous water to drink" (Jer. 9:15). And we say in reply, "Why do we sit still? Gather together, let us go into the fortified cities and perish there; for the LORD our God has doomed us to perish, and has given us poisoned water to drink, because we have sinned against the LORD. We look for peace, but find no good, for a time of healing, but there is terror instead" (Jer. 8:15f.). But we might also further add — and this might stand as faithfulness — "Yet Lord, Your child knows that You are the Light. She asks You to forgive her unbelieving brethren; she will willingly eat the bread of sorrow for as long as You wish; she will, for love of You, sit at this table where the wretched sinners eat their bitter food and will not leave it until You give her the sign."[152]

151. This becomes a rather concrete challenge as denominations today realign themselves along conservative and liberal doctrinal grids, and so are faced with questions of "intercommunion" within their own bodies, often tinged with the same combative hostilities that usually accompany deliberative theological debates.

152. Thérèse of Lisieux, *The Autobiography of St. Thérèse of Lisieux: The Story of a Soul,* trans. John Beevers (Garden City: Doubleday & Co., 1957), p. 117. The role of "reparative suffering" as a form of penance — the attitude adopted here by Thérèse — will be discussed in the next chapter. Here we can note simply that, in this servant of Christ, the Eucharistic image itself has entered into the penitential realm.

Chapter Five

The Scent of Sacrifice
and the Loss of Repentance

Does Division Call for Repentance? A Sixteenth-Century Suggestion

We have touched at several points, in the course of these chapters, on the obvious impetus towards ecclesial repentance pressed upon the churches by their own division and its attendant pneumatic attenuations. But what kind of repentance might be suggested in this context? What would it mean for a denomination to "repent" of its condition as "denominated" church? For just as with the Gospel and its miracles of grace, just as with the groping after guidance and the taste of heavenly food, the substance of repentance in the midst of Christ's corporal fragmentation is given over to a gross obscurity.

Consider that the debilitation of the Body of Christ, the encroaching paralysis of its senses, is hardly a reality its members greet with comprehension, let alone with welcome. One might perhaps have thought a struggle would ensue against the torpor, a hard gasping after the remains of God's presence, a panting after the fragrance left by his passing, in the manner of the soul's own longing after a departed intimacy (cf. Song of Songs 1:3; 5). But even the Church's sense of smell has been confounded, and the sacrifices the Church thought pleasing were left unbreathed by God because of a foulness the Church could not detect (Lev. 26:31). Indeed, the most manifest mark of the divided Church appears to be its own insensibility to the symptoms of its condition. No stench reaches its nostrils; no shame cracks its heart. "They have healed the wound of my people lightly, saying, 'Peace, peace,' when there is no peace.

Were they ashamed when they committed abomination? No, they were not at all ashamed; they did not know how to blush" (Jer. 6:14f.).

The Church has ceased to repent. Such is the constriction given birth by a division that ceases to offend. Unrepentant, Christians wonder how division could be clothed in shame at all, and face even the suggestion of the Spirit's leave-taking as a folly. The search for reunion that guided the ecumenical movement from its vital inception, of course, was frequently promoted in specific penitential terms, as it still infrequently is. Yet we have seen how the drift of ecumenical effort and strategy has also been toward a dampening of denominational distress and a promotion of the churches' diverse integrities, a shift in emphasis that is in sharp rhetorical contrast to earlier attitudes toward the intrinsic fallenness of separated Christian bodies.[1] The valorization of "diversity" among Christians, used as a heuristic key for thinking ecumenically, then, can be seen as the most elaborated mask to this averted penitence.

For averted penitence on the basis of diversity is not only a contemporary attitude. The rejection of Christian unity as an essential mark of the Church is logically (and pneumatically) embedded in Western ecclesial disintegration itself. In the mid-sixteenth century, for instance, the Anglican John Jewel could affirm against the papists that "yet is not unity the sure and certain mark whereby to know the church of God," for were not the unfaithful Israelites in the desert "united" in their worship of the calf? Indeed, argues Jewel, it can be said that disunity itself, the deliberate separation of the godly remnant and chosen from the faithless crowd, is a sign of God's elect people. "We see no reason why Lot, Abraham, the Israelites, Christ, and Paul may not be accused of sects and sedition as well as others," he writes, in defending the "lawfulness"

---

1. To be sure, the initial impetus for an international "league of churches" that followed the First World War and lay in the background of the eventual founding of the World Council of Churches was a sense of opportunity for ecclesial strengthening amid assault upon Christianity, joined to an affirmation of existing unity in the manner of earlier pan-Protestant notions of the invisible Church. But outright "repentance" for division was also a major theme of these formative years in the ecumenical movement, especially as the hope mingled with concern that followed World War I began to face the disaster of the next international conflagration. Cf. W. A. Visser 't Hooft, *The Genesis and Formation of the World Council of Churches* (Geneva: World Council of Churches, 1982), chs. 1, 4, 19 with references. Even among those groups within the WCC still most committed to visible unity, repentance more recently has been cast in terms of "acceptance" of others and their integrity, rather than in terms of the recognition of the churches' general and common disease. Cf. "Towards a Confession of the Common Faith," sec. I (Faith and Order Document III.17 [1980]), in *Documentary History of Faith and Order, 1963–1993*, ed. Günther Gassman, Faith and Order Paper no. 159 (Geneva: WCC Publications), p. 171: "such repentance will be truly constructive of unity only if it leads it to offer to others its own characteristic goods and to receive from others what it lacks itself."

of schism in many circumstances.[2] Christ, the very type of schism! In this astonishing suggestion, Jewel stands close to the contemporary version of pneumatic diversity. For there has, he writes, always been division in the Church, that is, separations and distinctions of community between believers, from the time of Corinth to the present.[3] The Reformation did not need to wait for historical critics like the nineteenth-century F. C. Baur, with his imposition of Hegelian dialectic on the early Church's development, to suggest that the Church's aboriginal division into competing "sects" is perhaps itself a historical sign of its very divine nature.[4]

Yet how sincere was this new perception of the Church's character? The question must be asked, because the perception's novel insouciance to division was tied to an equally novel appeal to the historicality of the Church's essence. And both novelties were offered as justification for rejecting any call to conversion toward ecclesial reunion.[5] Jewel himself appealed to several "doctors" of the Church in order to demonstrate how the Catholic Church has always been penetrated by a host of errors, heresies, and hence divisions, such as almost to be no church at all. To "reform" such a church by separating from

2. John Jewel, *An Apology for the Church of England* (1564), ed. John Booty (Ithaca, N.Y.: Cornell University Press, 1963), pp. 46, 99. Jewel's scriptural exemplars are confused, however, since there is no parallel between the Israelites leaving Egypt and Jesus arguing against the Pharisees; in fact, maintaining the identity of Israel sinning (the Golden Calf, rejection of Christ) and Israel elect is just what gives the lie to Jewel's reformed commonplace.

3. Jewel, p. 44.

4. Baur's work on the Pastorals appeared in 1835. Twentieth-century works, like the classic *Orthodoxy and Heresy in Earliest Christianity* of Walter Bauer, carried on the tradition of gleaning Christian diversity, even division, from the essence of the primitive Church's life, a view now so traditional among contemporary historians of the early Church that it is rarely questioned, let alone investigated.

5. The claim to diversity as of the Church's essence, historically and theologically, has its roots in a formal practice of Reformation *polemic,* and has always, since then, served particular argumentative ends. Yet polemic need not be mendacious or blind. As with Jewel, Milton, for instance, erected a rhetorically brilliant defense of sectarian Christianity based on the notion that the Church *has always been* diverse, at odds with itself in various ways (and also corrupt). Cf. his *Of the Reformation in England,* pt. I. The argument was first voiced during the ascendancy of Congregationalism in Cromwell's England, and Milton at the time certainly saw no need to call on Puritans to back down, let alone "repent" of their hard-pressed "separations." When, later in life, during the Anglican restoration, Milton again treated of the intrinsic diversity — even schismaticism — of the Christian Church, in *Of True Religion, Heresy, Schism, and Toleration* (1673), he did so from a defensive posture, in which again, repentance was excluded as a viable ecclesial self-presentation in the face of establishment attacks on the nonconformists. Milton's sincerity in these works is not at issue; but it can be asked if the very relationship of separation on which his ecclesiology was founded had logical room within it for ecclesial penitence.

its egregious fallibles, as England has done, is therefore no theological error, because based on a consistent historical reality of mixture requiring sifting. And Jewel calls, for traditional support, on St. Bernard and Jean Gerson as earlier "Catholic reformers" who understood the evangelical motive within the true Church to drive out evils from within it, to press for separation of wheat and tares within its ranks.[6]

Jewel was hardly unaware, however, that Bernard's energetic attack on unworthy prelates and priests was joined to an equally vigorous attack on schism and separation (as well as an unyielding defense of submission to papal authority).[7] Likewise, Gerson's indefatigable work on behalf of the healing of breaches within the Western Church, as well as that between West and East, was well known.[8] In the former's case, the tendency toward and the fact of Christian divisiveness called for the Church's entrance into the prolonged act of self-humiliation; in the latter's case, separation among Christians ended by demanding "a founding hope in the aid of God" above all else, sought after through penitential "processions and public prayers throughout the Kingdom, joined to preaching aimed at leading all people everywhere to a reformation of behavior and a pleading for Heaven's help."[9] The acknowledgment of division among Jewel's "Catholic reformers" was tied thus to self-denial and penitential conversion.

That Jewel dared appeal to such examples of the tradition at all on behalf of his theory of diversity and division is a patent sign of the fact that the greatest casualty of the Church's disunity was repentance itself. In its place, Jewel, like others around him among both Protestants and Catholics, turned to what was left to behold spread out in time: the events and scattered evidences of a history, in its variety and its stutterings, without form, and hence amenable to purely rhetorical orchestration on behalf of an acceptable division. Jewel's 1567 and 1570 *Defence* of his *Apology* against Roman Catholic critics like Thomas Harding is an interminable dissection of historical and literary evi-

---

6. Jewel, pp. 68ff.

7. Cf. Bernard's statement that "the notorious and horrible death of those men whom, in the past, the earth swallowed up and sent down alive into hell because of the scourge of schism, plainly shows how great and evil in the Church is schism and how it should be avoided by every possible means" (Letter 219 [293 in the translated edition], in *The Letters of St. Bernard of Clairvaux,* trans. Bruno Scott James [Chicago: Henry Regnery Co., 1953], p. 359). Cf. also Letters 124 (127)ff.

8. Cf. Gerson's sermons, e.g., 365, 395, and 396, in the *Oeuvres Complètes,* ed. Mgr. Glorieux (Paris: Desclée & Cie, 1988) vol. 7, on "Peace and Union," "The Unity of the Church," and the famous "Discourse to the King on Reconciliation" respectively.

9. Gerson, Sermon 365, p. 774.

dences for his earlier and cruder portrait of "just separation," as if the meaning of an action could be overwhelmed with an even broader concatenation of temporal witnesses.

The Impossibility of Repentance

There is nothing to surprise in this flight from repentance into the embrace of a desiccated history of manipulable facts. The division of the Church, according to the scriptural figure of its future given in Israel, points to this outcome as being intrinsic to its pneumatic relationship with God. To lose God is to deny the loss, and so to deem a world as having substance that has none; to mourn the loss, by contrast, is to discover God's restoration with the cry.

The mark of Israel's return as one from exile was, both from the prophetic end and from the experienced burden, the voice of weeping. As Jeremiah recounts God's words, "in those days and in that time, says the LORD, the people of Israel and the people of Judah shall come together, weeping as they come" (50:4). A similar prophecy of reunion is recalled, given in 3:18, that is editorially placed in the context of the people's distressed admission of their guilt: "A voice on the bare heights is heard, the weeping and pleading of Israel's sons, because they have perverted their way, they have forgotten the LORD their God. . . . 'Let us lie down in our shame, and let our dishonor cover us; for we have sinned against the LORD our God'" (Jer. 3:21, 25).

When, after the exile, the beaten Israelites in fact return, pummeled into unity, their rediscovered identity as a single people is expressed through words of confession, like Ezra's: "O my God, I am ashamed and blush to lift my face to thee, my God, for our iniquities have risen higher than our heads, and our guilt has mounted up to the heavens" (Ezra 9:5). Such public penitence stands, in the accounts of the post-exilic community, as a formal witness to their restoration, as can be seen in the highly stylized confessions given not only in Ezra (9:5-15), but in Nehemiah (9:1-37), which return, in the flesh of a straitened blessing, what had only been an intimated illness in the prophetic verses built up around Deuteronomy 28 (e.g., vv. 47ff.).

Repentance was thus the posture of reunion for Israel. But its relief was given only as the outcome to the previous history of sin, of which the division of Israel had come to stand as a visible expression. "Faithless Israel" and "faithless Judah" are shown to hold their unity in disobedience long before they achieve it again in their return (cf. Jer. 3:11ff.). Repentance thus follows

281

division as an outcome to the history of pneumatic deprivation that is Israel's; yet its final articulation by the nation lies also as the outcome to the divine mercy, not as its condition. Indeed, repentance seems to stand wholly outside the experience of divided Israel, and to enter in only as a rupture provided by divine grace, a pity granted to God's judgment. Divided Israel cannot repent; it can only await repentance ignorantly.

"Thou has smitten them, but they felt no anguish; thou hast consumed them; but they refused to take correction. They have made their faces harder than rock; they have refused to repent" (Jer. 5:3). The mystery of Israel's history is bound up, in the minds of prophets and psalmists, with just this failure to understand the shape of their own history and to refer the nation's deeds to some system of unrelated happenings. Amos composes a song of incomprehension over the disappearance of remorse, even momentarily, when he repeats God's puzzlement:

> "I gave you cleanness of teeth in all your cities . . . yet you did not return to me. . . . I also withheld the rain from you . . . yet you did not return to me. . . . I smote you with blight and mildew . . . yet you did not return to me. . . . I sent among you a pestilence after the manner of Egypt . . . yet you did not return to me. . . . I overthrew some of you . . . yet you did not return to me, says the LORD." (Amos 4:6ff.)

As the nation's sin progresses, it drives from itself even the sense of sorrow. "No, they were not at all ashamed; they did not know how to blush" (Jer. 6:15).

This is perhaps the furthest distance into which pneumatic abandonment drifts. The collective dullness of heart about which Isaiah writes in 29:9ff. deadens even the apprehension of need, and the violence of pneumatic separation cuts off at the deepest root the mere groaning after repentance. It is repentance God promises when, through Zechariah, he announces the conversion to the crucified Christ given in the outpouring of the Holy Spirit (Zech. 12:10); and it is this embodiment of the Pentecostal gift that the first Christians celebrated in their description of the Church's establishment among the Gentiles: when the Holy Spirit came upon the non-Jews, it was clear that "to the Gentiles also God has granted repentance unto life" (Acts 11:18).

The pneumatic basis of repentance was, in any case, axiomatic in Israel (this is the backdrop of the famous prophecies of Ezek. 36:25ff.), and the Spirit's departure was therefore seen as fundamentally a paralysis of conversion: "Create in me a clean heart, O God . . . and take not thy holy Spirit from me" (Ps. 51:10f.). To the degree that pneumatic deprivation in the midst of division forms a very part of the Spirit's ordering toward life, that Israel's abandonment is providential even within the scope of salvation, the dullness of impenitence is stamped as an act of God: "Make the heart of this people fat, and their ears heavy, and shut their eyes; lest they see with their eyes and hear with their ears and understand with their heats, and turn and be healed" (Isa. 6:10). Repeated by Matthew with reference to unbelieving Israel faced with the Christ, the same prophecy is carried over into the new dispensation of the Church.

All of which raises the great and painful paradox of ecclesial divisions' implication in the Spirit's abandonment of the Church: deprived of the pneumatic gift indwelling its given unity, the Church cannot repent of its condition. Division itself precludes its own repair. When, then, Pope John Paul II, following Vatican II's lead, calls on Christians to pursue the ecumenical goal of visible reunion, and he does so on the basis of "repentance" empowered solely by the Holy Spirit, he states both a truth and that truth's own experiential contradiction.[10] For inasmuch as the power of repentance derives from the presence of the Spirit, and that Spirit expresses itself in the unity of the Body, repentance as an act depends upon a perception of wholeness now obscured. This is why Israel's conversion to sorrow was possible only after its return in unity. And it indicates how a sensitiveness to the Body of Christ itself, however threatened, is necessary for the groaning of remorse. St. Bernard's ecclesial Spouse, in his figural reading of the Song of Songs, could run out behind her departed Husband, dragged on by the perfumes of his train, only because she understood the unity of the one and the many in her midst and her own singular union with her Lord as a body whole.[11] To repent is to perceive the Body, which was just the point in Gerson that someone like Jewel was bound inevitably to miss.

---

10. Cf. the encyclical *Ut Unum Sint* of May 30, 1995 (as printed in *Origins* 25, no. 4 [June 8, 1995]: 15f., 21ff., 34f., and 82), which draws on a major theme of *Unitatis Redintegratio* of the council; for example, "even after the many sins which have contributed to our historical divisions, Christian unity is possible, provided that we are humbly conscious of having sinned against unity and are convinced of our need for conversion. Not only personal sins must be forgiven and left behind, but also social sins, which is to say the sinful 'structures' themselves which have contributed and can still contribute to division and to the reinforcing of division" (34), and this is done, primarily, through the "power of the Spirit" (82 and 83).

11. Cf. Bernard's beautiful exposition of the Church's dependence in travail upon Christ as her "image" in *Sermon XXI on the Song of Songs*, on the verse (3:1 in the Vulgate) *Trahe me, post te curremus in odorem unguentorum tuorum* ("draw me: we will run after thee to the odour of thy ointments").

The Form of Repentance

All this suggests that repentance, as a traditional Christian practice, is tied to a form of the Church's life, the form of the undivided Body, and that apart from this form, repentance devolves into something other than its true identity. To pursue this suggestion is to discover how the singular loss of repentance is a climaxing facet of the Church's demise, pointing further to a cluster of intransigent problems facing modern Christian attitudes, especially those regarding the character of historical experience.

Gerhart Ladner's 1959 volume *The Idea of Reform* was a pioneering study that first demonstrated the intimate historical relation between the practice of Christian repentance and the environing reality of the undivided Body of the Church.[12] Far from being an examination of ecclesiology or penitential theology, though, Ladner's research was ostensibly directed at an aspect of the Western history of ideas touching on religious anthropology, the permutations of the notion of the human creature as made in the "image of God." Ladner attempted to show that insofar as a patristic (especially Augustinian) paradigm of "reformation according to the Image of God" came to exert influence, it formed the conceptual basis especially for the concrete history of social renewal that was later carried through by monastic culture in the Latin West. In outlining, in particular, the Pauline parameters of this theme, Ladner exposed a central strand of Christian conviction that conceived the human person in terms of a continual "reformation," or "renewal," according to the image of Christ, to which the Christian was "bodily" joined (e.g., Col. 3:10: "you have put on a new nature, which is being renewed in knowledge after the image of its creator").

The details of this New Testament exposition were not newly perceived by Ladner, of course. They involve elements of incorporation and participation that have long been recognized in Paul's understanding of Christian anthropology.[13] The great virtue of Ladner's subsequent examination of patristic elaborations of these elements, however, was his demonstration that they formed the spring from which arose later specifically theological developments, detailing the relation of conversion, penitence, and sanctification. And that, conversely, these theologically and later canonically defined practices were intimately tied to a substantive conceptual framework that had as its unitive

12. Gerhart B. Ladner, *The Idea of Reform: Its Impact on Christian Thought and Action in the Age of the Fathers* (Cambridge: Harvard University Press, 1959).

13. Ladner, pp. 49-62. Ladner deals, for example, with Pauline texts like Romans 12:2; 2 Corinthians 3:18; 4:4; 6:16; 5:17; Ephesians 2:14ff.; 4:21ff.; Colossians 2:12; 3:9f.

purpose the historical conformance of men and women into the figure of Christ.[14]

Two important features of Christian repentance emerged from Ladner's research. The first is its historically prolonged nature. As a species of "renewal" and "reformation," repentance is at root tied to an extended life that goes beyond the punctiliar moments of conversion that came to characterize later devotional attitudes, particularly in the post-Reformation Western churches. As temporally extended, repentance is given reality to the degree that its supratemporal goal — conformance to the image of Christ — takes gradual shape within the larger shape of history itself. On a social scale, Augustine's conception of the City of God relies on just this process of historical conformance, wherein the collection of the *sancti,* those whose lives are continually renewed or converted into the image of Christ, grows to a fullness that ultimately finds itself outside of temporality itself.[15] Repentance, in other words, depends logically on the existence of a coherent set of larger historical shapes ordered to an end.

The second point Ladner brings into relief is intimately related to the first: repentance comes into being insofar as it represents an adhesion to the historical formation of the image of Christ among people, which is his Body historically given in the corporate Church. In a remarkable passage from *The City of God* (X:6), Augustine summarizes the constellation of concepts Ladner had identified in terms of continual reformation into the image of Christ (basing his remarks on Rom. 12:1-2) and crystallizes their meaning as an expression of "sacrifice" offered for the sake of Body, the Church, as a whole:

> A true sacrifice then is every work which is done in such a way that we may adhere to God in a holy society. . . . Our body . . . if we castigate it by temperance . . . is a sacrifice. . . . If then the body . . . is a sacrifice, how much more does the soul itself become a sacrifice, when it returns to God, so that, inflamed by fire of love for Him, it may lose the form of worldly concupiscence and, subject to His immutable form, may be reformed to

14. Cf. Ladner, pp. 303ff. and 341-77. In his early chapter on Paul, Ladner is even willing to point beyond the scope of his book to what he claims is the basic agreement between the Tridentine definition of penance and sanctification and this New Testament paradigm (cf. p. 61). Ladner does not use the language of "figure" beyond its "imagistic" sense, and curiously downplays the explicitly scriptural understanding of figure that lies behind exegetical practices like typology (cf. p. 53). Nonetheless, much of his analysis, in more exclusively theological terms, opens up just such a figuralist perspective, which is precisely what followers of Ladner like Morrison have studied. See below.

15. Cf. Ladner's detailed discussion of Augustine's choice of the "City of God" image and its meaning in Ladner, pp. 240-83.

Him and please Him because it has taken on something of His beauty. . . .
Since, therefore, true sacrifices are works of mercy toward ourselves or toward
our neighbors, which are referred to God . . . , it is actually brought about
that this whole redeemed city, that is to say, the congregation and society of
the saints, is offered to God as a universal sacrifice by the High Priest, who
also offered Himself in His passion for us according to the form of a servant,
so that we may be the body of such a head. . . . Thus, after the Apostle has
exhorted us that we present our bodies a living sacrifice . . . and that we be
not conformed to this world . . . , he says: . . . we being many are one body
in Christ and every one members of one another" (Rom. 12:5). . . . This is
the sacrifice of Christians: many are one body in Christ.[16]

That repentance as a "sacrificial" act was a given;[17] that such an act was
itself the instantiation of Christian unity within the single Body of Christ was a
surprisingly forceful explication of what had usually been left implicit in the
discourse on Christian renewal. Ladner persuasively explicated the way in which
it was just this "singleness" of the Body, maintained in deliberate opposition to
the Donatist descriptions of a "bipartite" Body — divided among the Lord and
Devil — that fueled Augustine's articulation of the Church as a continually
"renewable" people, a "mixed body" perhaps, of sinner and saint, but a unit whose
singular identity was precisely the object of divine conformance over time.[18]

The dependence of repentance upon some more basic perception of the
Body was a key insight Ladner's work offered. And it is an insight with larger
metahistorical ramifications, applicable in particular to a theology of the
church. The work of Karl Morrison, which built to some measure on Ladner's
research, proves useful here.[19] Morrison saw that the underlying conception

16. The translation is Ladner's, p. 280.
17. Cf. Ladner, p. 311 n. 32, in which the relation in Augustine's mind between the
Eucharistic sacrifice and the "medicine" by Christ offered through penance was drawn in parallel.
18. Cf. Ladner, pp. 259ff., on the probable role the Donatist Tyconius's work had on
the formulation of Augustine's ecclesiology, especially in *The City of God.* Augustine did not
wholly reject the "two-body" scheme, which has other patristic recommendations; but he
harnessed and limited the concept within the affirmed historical assertion of catholic unity. See
above, in Chapter 2.
19. Cf. Karl F. Morrison, *The Mimetic Tradition of Reform in the West* (Princeton: Princeton University Press, 1982). On Morrison's relation to Ladner, see his comments in the appendix,
esp. pp. 419f. Morrison's project goes far beyond the ecclesiological mark set by repentance
(although he has especial historical knowledge in this area), and attempts to trace the continuity
through the nineteenth century of a range of conceptual and cultural strategies for mediating
change and experiential "asymmetries" within consistent social realms in the West. But chapters
3–10 of the book (along with the following section on Luther and Calvin) act as a kind of
extension of Ladner's work through the sixteenth century, within this larger theme.

of continual reform according to the "image" of Christ could properly be described in terms of a "mimetic" dynamic of representation (taking up categories popularized by the critic Erich Auerbach). As applied to patristic and medieval Christian thought about "reform," these categories can be related to earlier Greek and Jewish Hellenistic modes of understanding the current of metaphysical conformance that underlies the natural and human worlds — for example, Platonic, Aristotelian, and Philonic theories of "form." Although these classical theories have different emphases in their depictions of how natural entities attain the fullness of their being, they are all joined by a common sense that such fullness lies in "becoming like" some more perfect archetype or intrinsic end.[20] By providing this conceptual context for the notion of Christian reform in particular, Morrison shifted the focus of Ladner's exposition of its character from a category of process to a suprahistorical referent, the Christ; he thereby also revealed how the historical process by which mimesis is achieved must be grounded in the particular embodiments of the referent, that is, in the historical figures by which Christ is given form to human persons. In particular, the "mimetic" context of repentance is allowed to be seen in its specific figural aspect.

Ladner had argued that until the later Middle Ages, Christian reform was always conceived on an individual basis: individuals repented and changed; the Church as a whole did not.[21] Morrison does not disagree with this distinction at root. But by stressing the Christically representational basis of such individual reform as he does, he essentially links individual repentance, through the figural transaction of Christ with His Body, to the Church's

---

20. It is significant that those chapters of Morrison's book dealing exclusively with the Christian mimetic tradition offer, as a piece of writing, by far the clearest exposition of his theme. The contrast in comprehensibility between these earlier sections on Christian "mimetic" traditions and those that follow after, on modern adaptations of more foundational "classical" conceptions of mimesis, points perhaps to their essential incongruities. Whatever appropriations theologians made of Platonic and Aristotelian mimetic categories, the controlling figure of Christ that drove their notions of "conformance" grounded their mimetic apparatus in a concrete historical realm — including particular practices and institutions, texts and individuals — completely foreign to the metaphysical abstractions Morrison must juggle in his description of (especially modern) non-Christian mimetic discourse. The grave logical flaw in Morrison's history-of-conceptual-traditions approach is to elevate the conceptual apparatus above its points of reference. When, in the Christian mimetic tradition, the referent of representation is the person of Christ Jesus, given in time and conformed to over time, the very nature of "mimesis" is defined incongruously with respect to any overarching mimetic program, and the attempt to locate such Christian mimesis as a set of moments within a larger Western "tradition" becomes semantically unsustainable.

21. Cf. Ladner, p. 277.

life much more explicitly. Thus, the meaning of Augustine's statement that Christian sacrifice is itself the fact that "the many are made one" in Christ's Body gains its sense through the recognition that repentance "takes its form," as it were, from the Church as a whole, that it derives its life and its purpose from the shape assumed by Christ in the historical existence of his people. Insofar as these shapes themselves figurally represent the life of Jesus, repentance is only possible to the degree that the individual lives a life bound to these ecclesial figures. Thus, if the Church as a whole does not repent, but only its members, yet it is also true that the Church's members can and do repent only because they are able to be appropriated to the image of Christ through the embodied figures of his life given in the Church, because they are joined, in their unity as Church, to the form of Christ, whose own life gave flesh to a profound penitence purely human representations could approach but distantly.

Let us take some typical examples from the pre-Reformation Church. Paschasius Radbertus and Hincmar of Rheims, two Carolingian monks and church leaders whose concerns with the character of history and figural participation have gained the recent attention not only of Morrison but of other students of ecclesiology like Congar, demonstrate the way in which a specifically mimetic reading of Christian reform explicates the fundamental theological reliance of repentance upon the figural construal of the Church as the single Body of Christ.[22] The writings of both testify to a fundamental conviction about the Church's existence as one of "edification," its growth through time, by which it draws to itself the fullness of the elect, until the final consummation. But such "upbuilding" takes place through the "conversion" of individuals, and thus the body of the Church is given a history through the extended transformation of men and women into the form of Christ. For each writer, this transformation takes place in the constant subjection of the old nature to the form of Christ — in short, in the ascetic practice of continual repentance. Yet just this individual life of self-denial and humiliation, by which the old is purged and the regenerate increasingly established, is given force through its participation in and contribution to the unified life of the One Body, through whom the means of penitential grace and the ultimate form of holiness are given. For Paschasius especially, the sacramental forms of Christ's own self-giving, and for Hincmar, the medicinal authority of the Church's orders, incorporated individuals into the movement of transformation that ultimately was Christ's alone, assumed in the Incarnation, Passion, and Resurrection. Apart from this reliance upon the expressed unity of the figure given

22. Morrison, pp. 121-61.

288

in the Church, individual repentance can neither see its end nor receive its power.[23]

Further, this very dependence of individual repentance upon the unitary figure of the Church makes possible the practical discernment of the Church's own need and ability to repent as a whole, *pace* Ladner. However one wishes to untangle pre-Reformation understandings of the indefectibility or holiness, and even infallibility, of the Church,[24] it was manifestly possible and even necessary for writers like Paschasius to call the Church to repentance simply because of their conviction that the very condition for individual repentance lay in the Church's own figural enactment of the types summed up in Christ: his fulfilling of those historical events related in Scripture around which the form of repentance was shaped — sin, admonishment, divine chastisement, and conversion, the very elements of experience bequeathed by Israel to the history of the New Testament. We have elsewhere noted how the liturgical retaining of the book of Lamentations in services of, say, Tenebrae, at least afforded the continued possibility among some post-Reformation Roman Catholics of confronting a figural construal of the Church as disintegrated, and therefore punished, Israel. That this possibility was only rarely seized, despite the cultural flourishing of the Tenebrae liturgy in Italy and France, is also a fact, and one that testifies to the intrinsic difficulty of the text's being heard within the denominational breakdown of the Church.[25] Yet the Lamen-

23. Hence the essentially ecclesial character of individual repentance, which was so powerfully obscured by the Reformation and post-Reformation argument over the location of the "true" Church: where the ground of the true Church is defended against rivals, it becomes necessary to assert its purity, and corporate penitence becomes strategically, perhaps even logically, incoherent.

24. Cf. the discussion, with the author's constructive proposals, by Yves M.-J. Congar, in his *Vraie et Fausse Réforme dans l'Église* (Paris: Éditions du Cerf, 1969), pp. 63-124.

25. In a telling irony, by the eighteenth century, in which some of the greatest musical settings of the Lamentations were being written (e.g., by Couperin and A. Scarlatti), the text was being prized for its ability to embody the passions of human *sensibilité* far more than the passion of Christ. Cf. Diderot's comment in describing one of the musical displays, made in a café, by Rameau's nephew: "While singing fragments of Jomelli's *Lamentations,* he reproduced with incredible precision, fidelity, and warmth the most beautiful passages of each scene. That magnificent recitative in which Jeremiah describes the desolation of Jerusalem, he drenched in tears which drew their like from every onlooker. His art was complete — delicacy of voice, expressive strength, true sorrow. He dwelt on the places where the musician had shown himself a master. If he left the vocal part, it was to take up the instrumental, which he abandoned suddenly to return to the voice, linking them so as to preserve the connection and unity of the whole, gripping our souls and keeping them suspended in the most singular state of being that I have ever experienced. Did I admire? Yes, I did admire. Was I moved to pity? I was moved" (translation by Jacques Barzun and Ralph H. Bowen, in Denis Diderot, *Rameau's Nephew and*

tations held an important place in the tradition of Western monastic exegesis, with individuals like Paschasius providing a directive example that laid out the essential figural relation between individual and corporate repentance.

Paschasius's commentary on Lamentations[26] remained open, in the manner of significant patristic exegesis, to the identification of the fallen city of Jerusalem with the Christian Church. Given the sheer intensity of the scriptural text's inhabitation of Jerusalem's misery at the hands of its conquerors as well as the unrelieved shadow of its guilt, the very suggestion of such an identity in the course of a full commentary is radically unsettling. But it is not ultimately destructive of ecclesial hope just because it derives from a clear apprehension of the Church's figural integrity as bound up wholly with Christ. For the foundation of the identification in Lamentations is the figural transposition that occurs between Israel and the Church through the person of Jesus Christ, a fact which keeps the particular explications of the Church's sins from devolving into hopeless castigations. Paschasius achieves this figural transposition by employing as a general interpretive framework the spousal symbolism of Solomon's Canticle. Just as the Song of Songs, he writes in his introduction, represents what is most truly melodic, through its embodiment of the joyful love given in Christ, so does Lamentations embody what is most truly sorrowful. For it marks the separation and distance that exists between us and our union with God in Christ; and more particularly, it embodies the historical experience of that separation through the Church's present pilgrimage *in via,* through which the self-giving of the Groom in love is obstructed by the Bride's own timidity and repulsion. In the figure of Israel, the Church suffers its own unworthiness and impenitence, but it also suffers them with the wounded pity of its Savior, whose sufferings for the impenitent the Church must itself absorb. The Church weeps for itself and weeps also for the damned, a figural tension whose disruption finds its resolution only in the fulfillment given it in the person of Christ.

Other Works [Indianapolis: Bobbs-Merrill Co., n.d.], p. 67). Such a revision of Jeremiah's usefulness from a Diderot is not surprising; but the whole musical set of forms that he extols, dating back to the sixteenth century already, had long ago, in their increasingly ornate attempts to embody a deliberately exclusive emotional resonance, banished from the scriptural texts any of the historically figural exposition they had once been prized as offering.

26. Paschasius Radbertus, *In Threnos sive Lamentationes Jeremiae* (PL 120:1059ff.). See the discussion in E. Ann Matter, "The Lamentations Commentaries of Hrabanus Maurus and Paschasius Radbertus," *Traditio* 38 (1982): pp. 137-63, for an overview of the exegetical history in which Paschasius and his contemporaries read Lamentations, as well as a sketch of the deteriorated social and ecclesial context, which may realistically have framed some of Paschasius's specific readings.

Within this vision, the application of particular verses of judgment within Lamentations to the Church can follow, without thereby overwhelming the blessing of ecclesial identity. Paschasius on many occasions points to the utter failure of the Church's leadership, its priests and monks, whose greed, lust, and worldliness have desecrated the sanctuary of the Church and scarred its beauty. Even its doctrine has been deformed, so that the help not only of virtue but of truth has been denied it. Many of the specific evils visited upon Judah and Jerusalem by God are made to stand against the Church as well: the ravages of its enemies, the destruction of its possessions, the suffering of its people, the sense of abandonment by its Lord. Paschasius goes so far as to see God threatening the very roots of the ecclesial tree with his axe because of the Church's unfruitfulness, in a manner reminiscent not only of those instruments of destruction wielded against the Temple in, for example, Psalm 74, but also, drawing on the literal image of John the Baptist in Matthew 3:10, or on the parallel of judgment between Jewish and Gentile Israel Paul constructs in Romans 11.[27]

But just to enter into this place of mourning for the vulnerable ugliness of the Church, given in complete identification with humiliated Israel though Christ, was, for Paschasius, to gain access through the same Christ to the promise of the Church's restoration in penitence, that is, in the further representation it could offer of his passion. As Morrison points out in this regard, both the recognition of failure and the ability to move beyond it depended for Paschasius on a vision of "wholeness" — *integritas* — as informing the end and the origin of the Church, a wholeness by which the Church could be "fully" offered the person of Christ in love and fully given over to it. The historical outcome to this fullness, the enactment of its shapes over time, was the "self-accusation, penitence, and weeping" by which the origin and end were themselves joined.[28] "The wholeness of the Church was enhanced by the 'happy desolation' and anguish that drove her to humility and led her through patience to hope. By grief and tears, her beauty was daily renewed."[29] Because of the figural dynamic at work in this perspective, it is truer to say that individual "reform" depends logically on ecclesial repentance than to affirm the reverse.

Repentance here, as in Augustine's formulation, is given in the very fact that the Body is "one," in the double sense of "one from many members" and "one with its head." The oneness in multiplicity that is the Church's unity is what gives rise to a human history of other-regarding failures and sorrows; these in turn bring into play the figural oneness with the Head, whose assump-

27. Cf. Paschasius Radbertus, 1119, 1221, and 1237ff.
28. Paschasius Radbertus, 1067, 1176.
29. Morrison, p. 134.

tion of the burden of this beleaguered Body provides the shape through which its threatened wholeness is given life, the suffering of sacrifice. Lamentations, perhaps more than any other scriptural text, discloses how a history of self-reflecting figural accusations, given in the particulars of the prophet's complaints, provides the form to repentance; and this repentance takes shape only through the apprehension of the single Body, in its historical subjection and adhesion to its Lord's own history.

The Historical Presuppositions of Repentance

A reading of Lamentations like Paschasius's was by no means universally followed.[30] But it formed part of a consistent line of interpretation, through Hugh of St.-Victor[31] to Bonaventure and beyond.[32] The latter is an especially

30. Many interpreters of the text limited the figural referents of Jerusalem either to the Jews alone (including their subsequent punishment for rejecting Jesus) or to the individual soul, in its fall from virtue. Cf. Rupert of Deutz, "In Jeremiam," a section of his large *De Trinitate et Operibus Ejus* (PL 167:1378ff.). Rupert, who also includes as a referent the fall of the human race as a whole in Adam, offers a succinct rule of thumb for apportioning figural meaning: all good elements in the texts (e.g., consolations, etc.) should be referred to Jesus Christ and his Church, while all bad elements (e.g., sufferings, punishments) should be referred to the Jews and to human sin in general (at 1379). Cf. also Guibert of Nogent, *Tropologiae in Lamentationes Jeremiae* (PL 156:451ff.), which interprets the book solely in terms of the Jews representing the Christian soul in its relation to God. Other exegetes combined these readings with the more pointed ecclesial referents of Paschasius. Cf. the latter's contemporary Rabanus Maurus, whose *Expositio super Jeremiam* (books 18–20 on the Lamentations; PL 111:1181ff.) singles out one level of meaning as referring to the Church *in vita tribulationis,* which he sees prophesied in Jesus' beatitude concerning "mourning" as well as in Psalm 125. Although this theme by no means predominates, Rabanus ends his commentary with a prayerful meditation on 5:21 (*"converte nos, Domine, ad te, et convertemur; innova dies nostros, sicut a principio"* — "turn us to you, O Lord, and we shall be turned; renew our days as from the beginning"), in which not only is the prophesied conversion of the Jews reiterated, but the fullness of the Church will be restored through the fruit of repentance and humiliation.

31. Hugh's commentary (PL 175:255ff.) stakes out the principal figure as referring the Church, especially with regard to the Church's sins. The low condition of the Church, given in the suffering of Jerusalem and Israel, is caused by its "bad" members, nominal Christians at best, who include especially the clergy. The "Church" itself includes, in its travails, not only individual Christians, but the race of Adam in its need. Thus, the "allegories" of the book, according to Hugh, break down according to their referents as sinful ecclesial leadership; the individual Christian *in via,* for whom the Church's disease is but part of the pains of pilgrimage; and the whole human race as it looks for redemption in Christ, and only in Him (the Church's weakness testifying, after a fashion, to this ultimate hope).

32. Bonaventure, *Expositio in Lamentationes Jeremiae Prophetae,* in his *Opera Omnia,* ed.

important example of the tradition because he demonstrates how the figuralist perspective undergirding the conception of repentance that was the common store of ecclesial exegetes was capable of an elaborated reflection on historical experience as a whole. Bonaventure's exegesis of the book is no different, in the main, from Paschasius's. Indeed, Bonaventure follows him closely, even in initially placing Jeremiah's lament as a complement to the Song of Songs. But he dwells yet more starkly than Paschasius on the Church's sins, repeatedly chastising the corruption of leaders through greed, the hoarding of wealth, and the abandonment of virtuous witness.[33] And even more directly than Paschasius, Bonaventure is willing to relate the divine abandonment of Jerusalem to God's "desertion" of the Church until his good pleasure to lead it again with some chosen saint, leaving it to the afflictions of schism, heresy, and other grave assaults.[34]

Many of these specific accusations, however, for all their precedent in the tradition, bear for Bonaventure a special meaning when understood as part of his larger understanding of the Church's history exposed through the advent of St. Francis. Drawing on the exegetical innovations of Joachim of Fiora as well as a previously developed historicizing of the Church's life by theologians like Rupert of Deutz and Anselm of Havelberg, Bonaventure had gradually constructed his own peculiar vision of the Church's temporal fate. This he arranged in its experience according to an unfolding series of "ages," capped by a culminating "seraphic" period of pneumatic fullness, inaugurated by Francis.[35] The turn of the present age was itself to be marked by the struggle over power and wealth, represented already in the celebrated and often vicious debate on poverty among the Friars, and finally effectuated through the penitential humility embodied by Francis. Bonaventure's concerns in explicating Lamentations, then, fall within this larger "Franciscan" vision. But the historicizing schema that Bonaventure adapted, in which seven (or six, or eight)

A. C. Peltier (Paris: Louis Vives, 1867), vol. 10. Mention has been made, in Chapter 1, of the fourteenth-century ecclesiologist Alvaro Pelayo, whose *De statu et planctu ecclesiae* opens its second book with a meditative application of Lamentations to the condition of the Christian Church. Pelayo's figural identification of Israel and the Church, rooted in an ecclesiology of the Mystical Body of Christ, is evidence of the power of this figural vision to found a self-critical "reforming" attitude that grows *out* of an apprehension of the Church's unity and does not relegate that unity to the process of mutilated penitence itself.

33. Cf. Bonaventure, *Expositio*, e.g., pp. 152f., 155, 160, 172, 176.

34. Bonaventure, *Expositio*, pp. 151, 153; or p. 176, in which Bonaventure describes the people, through their evil leaders, as being utterly deprived of God's consolation.

35. On Bonaventure's historical perspective, see Joseph Ratzinger, *The Theology of History in St. Bonaventure* (Chicago: Franciscan Herald Press, 1971).

293

successive ages correspond somehow to periods of the Old Testament history or the gifts of the Holy Spirit (e.g., Rupert) or the Seven Seals of the Apocalypse (Anselm) or the days of creation and the grades of the celestial hierarchy (Bonaventure) — all of these correspondences in fact emerge from the figuralist conception of historical experience in general.

Ratzinger has argued forcefully that people like Bonaventure were engaged in a re-eschatologizing of history, which looked once again for real "mutations" in the Church's life, for a *novus ordo* beyond the past and present. This was in contrast to an earlier, especially Augustinian, view, which saw in Christ the whole "end" of the ages and thus equated the eschaton in its fullness with the age of the Church as already given in Christ. This distinction tied to the contrast between intrahistorical millennialism, in which the "new age" will be established within temporal experience, and the amillennialism of Augustine, who saw the millennium as having been inaugurated in Jesus.[36] This kind of contrast, however, may well equate too readily the declension of "ages" with "development" in the modern sense of teleological change, and, at the same time, illegitimately regard the Augustinian limitation of such ages as a form of historical "stasis." As any attempt to give a precise match between Rupert's or even Anselm's "ages" with actual historical periods will show, the notion of strict temporal sequence in these schemes was never paramount. Rather, for these writers the identification of specific "ages" in history derives from the scriptural figures themselves, and not vice-versa; and these periods are subordinate in their temporal character to the relations between figures already given in the Scriptures. Ultimately, they are subordinate to the figurating center given in the person of Christ.

What did it mean for Bonaventure to call Christ the "fullness of time" or the "center" of time, yet also to look for the coming of a "new" time, as embodied in the life of Francis? Augustine himself expected historical "developments," which involved the elaborated work of the Antichrist and the events associated with the coming final judgment; he admits that these events could well be temporally extended.[37] Clearly, the resolution to these kinds of conceptual tensions lies elsewhere than in a purely sequentialist reading of history itself, such as Ratzinger imputes to theologians like Bonaventure. For Bonaventure, rather, as for the general tradition in which he worked, experienced temporality, for all of its sequentialist character, took its form from the person of Christ, a form expressed in the scriptural figures of Israel and transferred to the Church. These forms are not themselves sequentially limited, since they

36. Cf. esp. Ratzinger, ch. 3, pp. 95-118.
37. Cf. the *City of God,* XX:19ff.

are fulfilled in Christ; and in Christ, the whole of this experience is shared with the Body of the Church in the midst of its temporal journey. The hope for reform that Bonaventure held for the Church, while temporally instantiated for him in the witness of Francis, was possible only because it was already given and historically completed in the personal body of Christ, with whom the Church's historical experience was given only by participation. The *novum*, although given in time, is not bound by a limited time. Figural history, though it may have a temporal end, and hence can be provisionally arranged, is in fact tied to a form that, because of its typological malleability, is not sequentially limited.

Not only does historical hindsight upon the outcome of Franciscanism make this a necessary way of salvaging Bonaventure's scheme, but he himself worked within its parameters. The passing of the Church's existence from an age of corruption into a new order of humble dependence, the fury of which is revealed in Lamentations, is already fulfilled in the person of Jesus, to whom Bonaventure suddenly applies, figurally, the bulk of the third chapter of Jeremiah's song of mourning: "I am the man who has seen affliction under the rod of his wrath."[38] In a sense, the penitential character of the *novus ordo* Bonaventure apprehends in Francis, because of its immediate identification in the Passion of Jesus, which necessarily informs the whole of the Church's life, especially in her sinfulness and perpetual repentance, consigns the temporal parsing of the "new" to an iterated experience of humiliated discernment, for which Francis himself becomes but a moment. This is the logical outcome of treating, as Bonaventure does, true "revelation" as instanced in true "humility" (cf. Matt. 11:25, a favorite text of Bonaventure in relation to the meaning of Francis in the "Seraphic Age"):[39] historical events can only disclose or represent a form already given in the person of Jesus Christ, once embodied; they cannot initiate the form itself. Ultimately this kind of disclosure defines the very nature of figural history.

And the figural nature of history, once grasped, gives rise to the dynamic of repentance itself. This is what lies behind the entire conviction that the Christian's life in the Church is one of continual reform and renovation: the desire for conformance is experienced as a yearning for the disclosure in time of the promised configuration with Christ. Leaving aside the development of an organized system of sacramental penitential practice, which only in the post-Reformation era came to be fully identified with the meaning of "penance," positively by Catholics and negatively by Protestants, the tem-

38. Bonaventure, *Expositio*, pp. 183ff.
39. Cf. Ratzinger, p. 71.

porally extended and corporately embodied character of repentance tended rather to dominate within the figural universe of the Church, precisely in the form of an almost devotional reflection upon historical experience. In particular, this took the shape of "compunction," a spiritual virtue that, in the wake of Gregory the Great especially, defined repentance in terms of an individual's peculiarly Christian relation to history.[40]

Gregory made use of the monastic tradition he had been bequeathed in articulating the vocation (and thereby gift) Christians had to orient their spirits in a consistent posture of tautened penitential desire. Relying on the scriptural formulations from the Vulgate, taken from Acts 2:37 and especially from the Psalms (e.g., 4:4 and 109:16), Gregory elevated to a central place in his ascetical thinking the divine "bruising" or "pricking" of the heart that is implied in the phrase *compunctio cordis,* "compunction of the heart." Just as the listeners to Peter's sermon at Pentecost were "cut to the heart" by his words and moved to seek repentance, so Gregory exhorted this attitude as definitive of the regular Christian existence, always open to the intruding truths of Christ's being — usually extended in the hearing of Scripture — as they laid bare the soul and elicited its honest petition before God.

In particular, Gregory offered an oft-repeated description of this blessing in terms of a double character: genuine compunction of the heart arose from the legitimate fear of the divine punishment merited by one's sins; it arose also from a welling love for the liberty of God's children in heaven, now springing up from within a world still in travail.[41] This definition, in turn, provided the basis for Gregory's paradigmatic definition of the four sources of compunction: remembrance of one's past sins, fear of future judgment, consideration of present tribulation in the world, and desire for one's heavenly country with God. These were elucidated explicitly in terms of historical location: where one has been *(ubi fuit),* where one will end up *(ubi erit),* where one is now *(ubi est),* and where one is not yet *(ubi non est).*[42] Compunction consists, then, in apprehending the breadth of these locations as they stand in relation to God, that is, in applying to oneself the historical grid of scriptural description,

---

40. On the virtue of "compunction," see the article by Joseph de Guibert, S.J., "La Componction du Coeur," *Revue d'Ascétique et de Mystique* 15, no. 59 (July 1934): pp. 225-40. See also the overview and references in Joseph Pegon's treatment of the topic in *Dictionnaire de Spiritualité,* ed. M. Viller et al. (Paris, 1937ff.), vol. 2, col. 1312ff.

41. Gregory, *Dialogues,* III:34; see also the *Moralia,* XXIV:6:10 and *Homilies on Ezekiel,* II:10:20f.

42. Gregory, *Moralia,* XXIII:22:41. Both the twofold character and the fourfold source of compunction were given standard formulation for the subsequent centuries in Isidore of Seville's *Sentences,* II:12.

warning, and promise by which temporal experience is appropriated to the figures of Christ. By extension, furthermore, the very shape of repentance seen in the form of such compunction — one recent spiritual writer has defined it as "the habitual attitude of repentance"[43] — was its spiritual articulation of conformity to realities from the full canvas of historical experience, ranging from the past to the future, each detailing the soul's mimetic likeness to some facet of Christian truth as revealed in Scripture and inscribed in temporal existence: sinfulness, judgment, tribulation, and hope. And taken as an overriding orientation, this "habitual repentance" represented the driving energy of divine life as it pressed the Christian toward full conformity with Christ, justly engaging the individual's self-understanding with his or her participation in the historical configuration of the Church as a whole.[44]

The gift of tears, then, which was traditionally associated with compunction, became tied especially — as in the case of the widespread Augustinian exegesis of Lamentations we have examined, which used as one figural referent the City of God in pilgrimage — with mourning over the sins of the Body. One was moved by God to weep particularly over this Body still fixed within the earthly stream of its existence and beset by weakness or sorrow, embodying in its own life, through its incorporation in Christ, the suffering of God over the fate of the damned. The yearning of repentance inevitably caught up in its current the whole life of the Church, for its broadest object was the very history of Christian existence given first in Jesus, then showered on the Church,

43. Dom Marmion, *Le Christ idéal de moine* (Maredsous, 1922), p. 211, cited in de Guibert, p. 233.

44. We may note in passing here how in the latter Middle Ages, even though the term fell into disuse, compunction as an undergirding aspect of repentance maintained a vital and defining presence in the more elaborated penitential disciplines of the Church, though under the guise of a kind of "contritional mysticism" that gave theological and affective integrity to the otherwise purely formal structures of penance. This was true especially within certain nominalist circles like those associated with Gerson. Cf. Heiko A. Oberman, *The Harvest of Medieval Theology: Gabriel Biel and Late Medieval Nominalism* (Durham [N.C.]: Labyrinth Press, 1983), esp. pp. 331ff., on the penitential mysticism of the *viator*. The profound affective connection between the experience of the *viator* and a nominalist metaphysical framework ought to warn us against aligning nominalism with an ecclesial devolution for which the Reformation was a historically logical reaction (a standard myth), or seeing in the development of nominalist thinking the seeds of modern secularism's banishment of God from history. Nothing could be further from the truth, at least as regards the conceptual vigor of this kind of late-medieval Christian theology. The causal import of intellectual constructs, at least as they are assessed within the history that *conpunctio* embraces, lies in the use to which they are put by the yearning or repugnant heart, not in the ability of such constructs to create the shape of hearts themselves. The latter reality, despite the claims of intellectual historians, is better examined by the discerner of spirits than by the genealogists of ideas.

through which only finally the individual was granted a taste, and thus the *desideria,* or desire, of what was not yet.[45]

Paschasius's own work, reliant upon a vision of the City *in via,* was impregnated with just this informing sense of compunction, which drew the individual, through the Church, into a variegated mimetic similitude with the figure of Lord. The conceptual and existential condition to this kind of con-

---

45. One of fullest examples of this historical dynamic of repentance as compunction is to be found in the life and writings of Catherine of Siena. In book I of her *Dialogue,* she describes penance in terms of Gregory's *desideria,* the yearning of compunction, which she carefully joins, in an explicitly representational fashion, to the "desire" of the crucified Jesus for the salvation of the world from its sins. When, in book II, she outlines the various objects over which the accompanying blessing of "tears" that she has received is shed, she singles out especially the "tears of desire" she has been given for the Church in its disarray. God turns to her, and responds, "My sweetest daughter, thy tears constrain Me, because they are joined with My love, and fall for love of Me . . . ; but marvel, and see how My spouse has defiled her face, and become leprous, on account of her filthiness and self-love, and swollen with the pride and avarice of those who feed on their own sin. . . . Take therefore thy tears and thy sweat, drawn from the fountain of My divine love, and, with them, wash the face of my spouse . . ." (from the translation of Algar Thorold [Rockford: Tan Books and Publishers, 1974], pp. 65, 73). Later, in book III, Catherine gives a more systematic discussion of the nature of "tears," which she ties to different stages of the soul's journeying toward "unity" with God, moving from self-knowledge in penitence, through various loves and sorrows for others: though there is "progress" in knowledge and joy, at each point, the tears that are shed depend on a continued participation, through Christ's own divine love, in the sorrows of and over the Church and world, which are continually represented in the "truth" of Christ given in Scripture. The individual soul's "conversion" thus is given only in its continual participation in the "conversion" or repentance of the whole, joined in Christ. Catherine's own practical ministry on behalf of the Church of her time witnesses to the powerful breadth of this orientation. Catherine herself speaks to this reality of compunction without using the term in a prominent way. (On the relation of this attitude to the practical orientation of "reparative suffering," see below.) And by the seventeenth century, in any case, the whole Gregorian usage, which had so dominated the early Middle Ages, had been abandoned. But where it was retained, both literally and as an informing spirit for the conceptualization of repentance, as with Jansenists like Jean Hamon, it retained just the historically broad and ecclesially directed character found in its origins. Hamon, who speaks of a *componction continuelle* as a *pénitence enflammée,* a pneumatically "enflamed penitence," describes it in terms of a "unifying of the members with the sufferings of the Head" (cf. *Toute la Pénitence Abregée dans ce seul verset du Pseaume VI* and *Les Gémissements d'un coeur chrétien exprimés dans les Paroles du Pseaume CXVII* in *Divers Traités de Penitence* [Paris, 1737], pp. 574 and 291f. respectively). Such "penitence" itself, which is clearly distinguished from, though not in tension with, sacramental penances, stands as the existential means by which the Christian fastens him- or herself to the present "conformity between the passion of Jesus Christ and the final passion of his body, which is his Church," a conformity that, very much in the tradition of Radbertus or Bonaventure, is based in the "love of poverty and of the Cross" as it comes up against the opposing "abundance" of the Antichrist (Jean Hamon, *De La Solitude,* 2nd ed. [Amsterdam, 1735], pp. 331, 390).

formity, however, always remained an apprehension of the "integrity" of the figure itself, the way in which singular entities like Israel, Church, and Christ can be and are in fact consistently joined as One through the midst of historical variation. To repent was to behold one's connection, within the whole view of history's contingencies, with the constant reiteration of Christ's participated yet particular forms, bringing into a scripturally ordered figural identity the scattered elements of existence and eliciting from the heart the humbled sense of wonder, fear, and love this anticipated congruence would entail. Figural uniformity within temporal diversity, then, stood as the essential ground for the experience of repentance.[46]

Impenitence and the Invention of History

The pneumatic context of such a sense is immediately obvious. Repentance is a "gift," and it is tied to an apprehension of realities always understood as pneumatically informed. But it is not just the comprehension of Scripture,

---

46. A somewhat schematized, but just because of this, crystalline, version of this figurally grounded understanding of repentance is to be found in Oratorian developments of the incarnational devotions of Bérulle, for example, those of Quesnel. His small retreat manual, *Jésus-Christ Pénitent,* offers a remarkable example of a systematic elaboration of "penitence" as a deliberate conformance of the individual to the *Church's* figurated similitude, as the mystical body, to Christ's historical life (after the hints given in Col. 1:24). For Quesnel, following Bérulle, the Incarnation itself is an essentially "penitential" act — a self-emptying *(exinanito)* along the lines of Philippians 2. The glory of the Transfiguration demonstrates this by contrast, and the final mystery of Pentecost, whereby Christ's life is, as it were, "immolated" through the "fire" of the Spirit, provides the very source of the Church's existence in the world. The mystical body, then, is the fruit of and continuing historical witness to Christ's own self-sacrifice, and is thus "alive" only through its continued participation in a divine "penitence." Individual repentance takes place primarily through participation in the "lament of the dove," which is the Church, through whom both true sorrow takes form and true forgiveness, both established first in the historical body of Jesus. The retreat itself is organized according to a daily participatory meditation on one of the "penitential mysteries" of Jesus' life (e.g., his birth, his baptism, his temptation, his relationship with religious leaders, his betrayal, through to Pentecost, the sending in his stead of the Spirit), a vitally concrete way of describing individual repentance in terms of figural conformance. See Pasquier Quesnel, *Jésus-Christ Pénitent ou Exercice de Pieté Pour le tems du Carême, & pour une Retraitte de dix jours. . . . Par un Prêtre de l'Oratoire de JESUS* (Paris: Lambert Roulland, 1688), esp. preface (unpaged), introduction, pp. 39, 79, 98f., 201ff. Quesnel's identification with Jansenism points to the way in which the movement drew some of its later distinctive ecclesiology from devotional sources with profoundly traditional shapes and marks the official marginalization of that ecclesiology with its conscious connection to an ancient ecclesial situation no longer supported by historical experience.

with its figural referents now obscured, that is at issue in the divided Church's failure to repent. It is the nature of the referent itself, whose disintegrated character no longer supports the existential figural identification that fuels the heart's penitential longing.

Toward the beginning of the Council of Trent, Cardinal Pole addressed his fellow legates by reminding them — as others at the Council already had and were to continue to do — of the need they had, as representatives at this reforming council, to repent themselves:

> If we do not recognize all this, then it is in vain that we enter into council, it is in vain that we invoke the Holy Spirit, whose first entry into the human person comes through the condemnation of that person — 'to convict the world of sin' (John 16:8). To the degree that this Spirit has not condemned us to our face, we cannot yet say that he has come among us, and he will not if we refuse to attend to our own sins.[47]

Yet it was the very character of such a pneumatic penitence that the whole Church be apprehended as its motive and referent; and the Council itself, by whatever standards one uses, was shaped by the de facto exclusion of the Protestants. The subsequent demand, by the few Protestant attendees at the Council's later sessions, that earlier decisions made in their absence be tabled became the general argument from even the most irenic seekers of reunion among Lutheran ecumenicists. It was also a request whose resolute rejection became the touchstone of later Roman Catholic responses to such pacific overtures.[48] The Council of Trent embodied the Church in its fullness, according to the Roman Catholics, and those who were not represented and dispute its authority are therefore not a part of the Church for which the Council speaks.[49] If repentance touches the Body, it is thus a body that is limited by its own truncation. For the upholders of Trent, the Church did not include Protestants. But then, of what was there to repent? The very configuration of the event, taking as its object a Body lacking the *integritas* of full participation, gave a lie to Pole's salutary exhortation. From this point on, to whom would

---

47. Admonition to the legates at the Second Session (January 7, 1546), cited in Congar, p. 84.

48. Cf. Bossuet's discussion with Leibniz on this score, in his *Réflexions sur l'écrit de M. L'Abbé Molanus,* chs. 2 and 8, or in his letter to Mme. de Brinon (July 1691); for the correspondence between the two, see, e.g., Letters II, VII, VIII, XX, XXI, XXII, XXIII, XXVII, XXVIII, XXX, XXXV, XL, all in Bossuet, *Oeuvres Complètes,* ed. Guillaume (Paris: Berche et Tralin, 1887), IV:3.

49. Cf. Bossuet, Letter XL, p. 639.

a sorrowful conscience refer? While Pole's pneumatological reasoning was correct, its practical application proved impossible once the figural referents of its purpose had been obscured.

The intractable division of the sixteenth-century Church demanded instead that a vision of history be adjusted to the resulting confusion of objects, with a consequent pneumatic limitation on the very possibility of repentance. Is it possible that the "modern historical consciousness" that is touted as an outcome to the post-Reformation period is at root the inevitable cultural adaptation of a straitened Christian consciousness to the figural incapacitation rendered by a multiplied ecclesial referent? In a sense, historical sequentialism is the offspring of a divided Body, for it posits either the continuing rupture of entities in time or their incessant press toward order, or perhaps both at once. None of these perspectives provides a fruitful ground for repentance.

Consider Bishop Jewel's assertion, which we noted above, that the Church was intrinsically "schismatic," in that, from its inception, it grew out of a dynamic of separation — separation from Pharisaism, separation from Judaism, separation from this or that point of view, separations within itself even among geographical locales, and so on. Though Jewell has no desire to deny the reality of a true Church that is One — the Catholic Church — the criterion he seeks for it, its "mark," is something explicitly without historically embodied integrity: it is the "truth," simply. Congruent with the standard Protestant ecclesiological paradigm, Jewell identifies "catholicism" with a proper *sola scriptura* hermeneutic, wherever that might be.[50] The Church is not a Body, but a principle, variously enacted in time and evident only in a continual process among many individuals and groups of "leave-taking," of separation from error.[51]

Thus, to describe the Church historically, as Jewel does, is to describe a set and series of particular actions taken for the sake of purity, whose only continuity lies in their demonstration of this principle. Jewel can speak of the "Church" from the Old Testament through to the New, passing through Noah, the Kingdom and the prophets, and so to the New Covenant people; but the identity of these various moments lies not in their figural translation

---

50. Jewel, pp. 19ff. Jewel admits the authority of the "ancient bishops" and the "primitive church" and the "old catholic fathers" (p. 17), but he reduces the latter to a right submission to Scripture: "wherefore, if we be heretics, and they (as they would fain be called) be catholics, why do they not as they see the fathers, which were catholic men, have always done? Why do they not convince and master us by the divine Scriptures?" (p. 20).

51. Jewel, pp. 98ff.

through Christ, but in their evidence for a singular pursuit of the Christian truth.[52] In this way, the "church darkened and decayed" is not so much identified with as sloughed off. The Church of England, he insists, has "departed from that church whose errors were proved," not thereby losing continuity with the Church "itself" (which is defined by truth), but only with what was in fact not truly Church.[53] And in an extraordinary reversal of tradition, Jewel argues for the intrinsic fallibility of the Church as a *corpus mixtum,* not in order to maintain its figural and visible unity, but to justify separation. If there is such a thing as ecclesial repentance in Jewel's conceptual universe, it consists precisely in the act of disavowing the Body's integrity and in removing oneself from an identification with the fullness of its life, travails and all. And concomitant with this figurally deprived revisioning of repentance, the historical realm that forms the object of his consideration has been reduced to a world of temporal particulars, left only to their sequentialist order, as they are evaluated in accord with the abstract principle of "truth" and "error."

The constellation of these elements — the disposal of the figural Body and the consequent reduction of historical experience to a sequence of particulars judged according to some ahistorical principle — has determined the failure of penitence in the divided Church. Indeed, they are all three aspects of the same phenomenon, and together add to the definition of the shape of modern Christianity. And the evolution of "historical consciousness," then, that has buttressed both historical criticism in the churches as well as religious and political "historicism" (in Karl Popper's sense) manifests itself within the same constellation.[54] When Hans Frei detailed the "eclipse of biblical narrative" that took place in the scriptural hermeneutics of the early modern period in favor of imposed historical schemes of interpretation, he spoke to only one of

52. Jewel, pp. 68ff. Jewel's approach is jumbled here. He affirms the continuity of the Church in time from creation, according to a seemingly figuralist reality ("for even at those days was there the very same God that is now, the same Spirit, the same Christ, the same faith, the same doctrine, the same hope, the same inheritance, the same covenant," pp. 70f.). Yet his purpose is to show that this continuity "in Christ" lies not in the figures themselves Christ offers, but in the historical faithfulness individuals give to the "doctrine" of Christ offered continuously in "the same efficacy and virtue of God's word."

53. Jewel, p. 69.

54. On the development of this kind of "history" within the context of fifteenth- and sixteenth-century humanist "erudition" and jurisprudential scholarship — independent of the religious events of the Reformation — cf. George Huppert, *The Idea of Perfect History* (Champaign: University of Illinois, 1970), and Donald R. Kelley, *Foundations of Modern Historical Scholarship. Language, Law and History in the French Renaissance* (New York/London: Oxford University Press, 1970).

these elements; and it is important to see that the history of modern hermeneutics, including the marginalization of figuralist readings of Scripture, has been fundamentally bound to the historical obscurement of Scripture's corporal (Christic/ecclesial) referent, which makes possible a vital figural apprehension in the first place, and not to some independently formed set of critical habits developed in the seventeenth or eighteenth century.[55]

55. In Frei's work (*The Eclipse of Biblical Narrative: A Study in Eighteenth- and Nineteenth-Century Hermeneutics* [New Haven: Yale University Press, 1974]), especially the introduction and chapter 1, a puzzle is caused by his use of the category of "sequence" to define the figural narrative of Scripture as it was understood among "precritical" Christians. It is undeniable that Scripture, read as a whole, provides a sequential narrative that moves from Creation through to the initial life of the Christian Church; one can indeed speak of "a single world of one temporal sequence" with "one cumulative story to depict it" (p. 2). The issue Frei never satisfactorily clarified was the nature of a "figural" relationship between events within this sequence. (This is related to his silence about the large, and devotionally perhaps more important, category of nonnarrative Scripture, the Law, Wisdom, prophetic denunciation and imagery, and, of course, the New Testament Epistles, whose significance can be manifested in a figuralist understanding of history, but not in a purely sequentialist one.) In placing his emphasis on the "history-like" "realistic" quality of Scripture's narrative, the central figuralist hermeneutic he correctly identifies in precritical understanding of the Bible fades into a role of sequentialist support for a "literal"-realistic reading. But in fact figural understandings of Scripture are, in a basic sense, subversive of "sequentialist" experiences of history: they place, for instance, a pneumatically governed Christian Church within the moment of abandoned and destroyed Jewish Jerusalem, a temporal reversal that defies strictly sequentialist historical patterns. One could say that the discrete narrative "sequence" of Scripture founds or provides the figures by which historical experience is governed, but here one must then distinguish historical experience itself from some sequential character privy to the text. But even given the initial sequentialist primacy of how Scripture's narrative is primordially apprehended, the actual nature of how this "cumulative" story is appropriated in practice by listeners or readers is clouded. One rarely learns the story as a whole, but rather piece by piece, often in a nonsequential pattern (e.g., through the lectionary). And while at least the narrative of Jesus' life, even in the lectionary, is given some overall sequential pattern, it is provided this almost with the aim of its subsequent dispersal into continually reiterated figural pieces, which reveal themselves diversely in daily experience, reflection, and devotion. The fundamental inadequacy of thinking of Scripture in terms of sequence is tied, it seems, to the historical reality of Scripture's figural ongoing self-assertion, or rather the assertion of its figural referent given integrally as well as disjointedly in the person of Christ whom Scripture describes. The insight Victorinus first systematically elucidated in his commentary on the book of Revelation, that the prophecies were "recapitulative" in their figural representations and repeated similar temporal referents in the course of the book through a host of differing symbols, ought to be applied generally to the Christological figure itself in its historical referents. The latter is historically "recapitulative," in the standard patristic sense, insofar as it "sums up," in one personal form, a host of historical forms, which repeat their own reference to Christ in time, in overlapping and intersignificating ways. Scriptural narrative is indeed "historical," in that it describes real events, but the figural character of historical experience that conforms to it is decidedly unsequentialist. In fact, the insistence on sequence within historical experience

One need only glance at the necessary adjustments to the divided Church that were made by ecclesiastical historians in the wake of the Reformation, in order to observe the invention, in tandem, of a vision of history structurally defined by impenitence. Obviously, religious controversialists were motivated by blaming the other, and not by unmasking the self; that is a banal evaluation. More than this, the very project of uncovering a history in which events could be laid out so as to be evaluated in a morally adjudicated sequence — modern history — was the necessary result of distinguishing between "bodies" among Christians. A standard assessment has located the rise of a truly "historical" attitude toward the history of the Church only among eighteenth-century "critical" studies of dogma and change and has continued to lump Reformation and post-Reformation controversial history, from whatever side, in the same mold as Constantinian celebrations of the Church's uniformity and adhesion to an original apostolic purity.[56] As we have seen, neither side gave up the notion of a "true Church," defined by its purity. But the search to identify

---

is exactly the outcome of a nonfiguralist perspective, a perspective that, because of its incapacity to apprehend the shapes of history as figurally given, seeks history's meaning in the application of various exogenous schemes and principles, as the bulk of Frei's analysis of early modern hermeneutics demonstrates.

56. Cf. Robert Wilken, *The Myth of Christian Beginnings* (Notre Dame: University of Notre Dame Press, 1971), who idendifies a "Euseban construction" that, in different guises, still informs Christian attitudes toward an authoritative past all the way through Harnack. Only the advent of truly "critical studies" of texts, by people like Semler, initiated a current that has been able to resist and challenge the dominant Eusebianism and make a place for the positive identification and evaluation of change and development. Critical-historical studies demonstrate the elusiveness of discovering an "original" deposit, and Wilken promotes instead a "future-oriented" vision of Christian truth, in which change and diversity play essential roles over time in moving Christian faith and experience through a developing "penultimacy" toward this eschatological goal. In part, Wilken seeks a conception of ecclesial history that will take the church's experience over time more seriously. He uses as an example of the benefits of freeing oneself from a traditional historical reification of the Church — its purity, uniformity, and continuity — the new liberty with which Christians might confront the anti-Semitic attitudes, acts, and tendencies embedded in Christian experience (cf. pp. 196ff.). The curiousness of this proposal lies not only in how its positive vision depends on a recasting of Christian truth in a completely antihistorical fashion, applying to events a determinative principle of historical meaning — a mollified and critical Hegelianism — that is wholly extrinsic to the Christian understanding of their participants and unsupported by their interpreted experience. But even as a spur to some new "honesty" about the Church now released from the need to assert historical purity — an admission to anti-Semitism, for instance — it cannot deliver ecclesial repentance because it has given up continuous (and therefore figurally participated) identity. The constantly changing and diversifying Church critically located in the incoherent phenomena of history cannot carry the person, let alone the guilt, of a singularly shaped form that binds individuals to the character of the past and future.

that Church in a context of contested claims necessarily led to the historical description of diversity and contrast, in the manner of a theologian (not primarily an historian) like Jewel. And this involved a process of cataloguing a multiplication of phenomena, without any *a priori* figural integrity, awaiting evaluation through their critical ordering into a sequence of possessed virtue or repudiated shame, according to a number of self-justifying denominational schemes.[57]

The famous Magdeburg *Centuries,* directed by the Lutheran Matthias Flacius Illyricus, began to appear in 1559 and sought to record, "century" by century, the history of the Church's devolution in doctrine and morals from the first era of primitive purity, through the gradual rise in influence of the "Babylonian harlot" of the papacy, with a faithful remnant's continuous survival through this long night. With the Reformation, the primitive Christian truth, safeguarded by the few, was finally restored to an albeit embattled place of public vindication. This vision of decay, remnant, and restoration was shared by most Protestant historians, even those today judged to have sought a more critical basis to their work than had the "centuriators."[58] Roman Catholics, for their part, answered in kind, with varying degrees of critical acumen, by marshaling evidence for the "perpetuity" of Catholic thinking from primitive times to present on key topics like transubstantiation, papal primacy, and grace and merit. Whether among the true historians like Baronius or the theologians like the moderate Cassander and even Bellarmine, this sifting of primary sources for the manufacture of a historical structure that excluded by definition the purported "remnant" from the "origins" of the apostolic faith was a critical venture tied logically to a larger vision of the consistent and undifferentiated experience of the Church.[59]

57. In answer to a thesis like Wilken's, we must admit that it was possible to maintain a "Eusebian" view of the Church's identity throughout the Reformation debate. But the multiplication of ecclesial referents exploded any continuity this view still had with the early Church itself. In its place, one was given variously ordered histories, from which, because of their diversity, one was always capable of withdrawing oneself in the midst of discomfort.

58. E.g., Johannes Sleidan, whose 1555 *De statu religionis et reipublicae Carolo Quinto Caesare commentarii* ("Commentaries on Religion and the State in the Reign of Emperor Charles V") is judged by Dickens to be a major advance in critical-historical methodology, but whose metahistorical vision, following Melanchthon, posited a cycle of four "empires" (according to the prophecy in Daniel), whose final devolution coincided with the papacy's corruption and the rise of true religion. Similarly, Heinrich Bullinger's work on the history of the Swiss Reformation as well as his researches into the "origin" of Roman "errors" concerning, for example, the Eucharist, were based on a similar scheme of purity, fall, and restoration.

59. On the issue of ecclesial historiography in the Reformation debate, see especially Pontien Polman, *L'Élément Historique dans la Controverse religieuse du XVIe Siècle* (Gembloux:

It is important to grasp this relationship of critical history and uniform program in its contrast with the figural perspective of the undivided Body. The self-justifying motive of the separated parties led each to search for both an "original" and "primitive" base to their own positions and also a line of experiential continuity that tied it to the present while excluding the other party from its form. The search itself, however, was fundamentally "critical," in that it involved the dissection of documented evidence and the reconstruction of that evidence into a form whose coherence was to be justified by a persuasive analysis of cause and intent, but whose ultimate shape must lie outside the disparities of this amalgam of data. Indeed, the critical motive of this historiography logically demanded, if the work was to prove useful to a religious application, the imposition upon the material of some overarching order extrinsic to the discrete historical experiences that had been collected.[60]

J. Duculot, 1932); Wilken, chs. 5ff.; A. G. Dickens and John Tonkin, *The Reformation in Historical Thought* (Cambridge: Harvard University Press, 1985). The link between Reformation controversy, properly speaking, and the rise of critical historiography was not always direct. Humanist impulses prior to the Reformation, and reorientation of historical research in response to Tridentine reforms in areas quite remote from the experience of ecclesial division — for example, southern Italy — contributed to this historiographical evolution. Cf. Simon Ditchfield's *Liturgy, Sanctity, and History in Tridentine Italy: Pietro Maria Campi and the Preservation of the Particular* (Cambridge: Cambridge University Press, 1995), esp. chs. 11 and 12. Even so, the shadow of Baronius's project, as well as Trent's overarching contrastive character, loomed large even at this distance. Obviously, too, historical research was determined, to some extent, by varying interpretive views about not time itself, but the location within time of the contemporary Church. Thus, Luther's more apocalyptic reading of history provoked a different impulse toward reading the past than did Zwingli's or Calvin's, although, within the course of ecclesial controversy, many of these distinctions began to merge into a more generalized Protestant vision of history and purposes of historical scholarship. Cf. Bruce Gordan, "The Changing Face of Protestant History and Identity in the Sixteenth Century," in his edition of *Protestant History and Identity in Sixteenth-Century Europe* (Aldershot: Scolar Press, 1996), vol. 2, pp. 1-22. On Luther's distinctive eschatological parsing of the present, cf. Heiko Oberman, "Martin Luther: Forerunner of the Reformation" (a translated reprint of a 1982 essay), in his collection *The Reformation: Roots and Ramifications,* trans. Andrew Colin Gow (Grand Rapids: Wm. B. Eerdmans, 1994).

60. The refusal to apply such an extrinsic order led to a deliberately areligious historiography, such as that by Bodin and La Popelinière in the sixteenth century, representatives of a "rediscovered" ancestry for more contemporary secular histories. Yet, as in the case of Bodin in particular, there was an inescapable religious payoff even to these kinds of more exclusively critical practices, whose deliberate respect for the heterogeneity of events left a generally flattened uniformity to historical experience that called forth a kind of proto-Deism in its relativizing of diverse religious commitments. Cf. Bodin's *Heptaplomeres* (written late in the century though published only in 1857), a conversation among seven men of differing faiths and philosophical outlooks, which pleads a tolerance of the common denominator, or, more poignantly, of the impossibility of such commonality. Given the mess that is history's collection of disparate faiths

The compilers of the *Centuries,* like much later Lutheran and subsequent Protestant historiography, discerned their form according to the fortunes of the doctrine of justification by faith given in the Word of God, or, in the case of the Anglicans,[61] an originally apostolic liturgical and devotional simplicity; for the Roman Catholics, frequently, it was the acknowledgment of papal primacy or the Eucharistic sacrifice.[62] The critical scholarship of division, then, which dispersed evidence according to the multiplied referents of the Church, opened up a space that demanded the ahistorical principles of theology and polity as the orderer of historical experience.

Thus, despite the diversifying of historical fact that the critical enterprise of denominational justification encouraged, the necessary application of these larger ordering principles to the material involved discerning a certain uniformity to historical experience, analogous to the extraneous homogenizing schemes of meaning imposed on a previously figuralized Scripture, which Frei identified in modern hermeneutics and which we have discussed earlier in our chapter on miracles and holiness. Someone like the Swiss reformer Bullinger could retain as a central theological concept the unity of the Church from Adam to the present, just as did the Catholics. This unity, given under the second "covenant of grace," he also justified typologically in scriptural terms. But the referent of this continuous entity was no longer the Body of the Church given in the forms of Christ, but the consistent preaching and acceptance of Christ's Gospel, the "message" of salvation by grace. And the entire development of this reformed "covenantal theology," which made an ample appeal to scriptural figuration given in types and antitypes, did not, therefore, see history

---

and experiences, "concord" such as that envisaged by Psalm 134 is a unity of exhausted particularities, not of singular praise. For an anonymous early translation of the *Heptaplomeres,* see Jean Bodin, *Colloque Entre Sept Scavans qui sont de differens sentimens des secrets cachez des choses revelees,* ed. François Bemiot (Geneva: Librairie Drosz S.A., 1984).

61. The difference in critical sophistication between a Jewel or a Hooker and a historian like Gilbert Burnet, whose *History of the Reformation* (published 1679–1714) constituted a major advance in English historiography, lay in the materials they used and the manner of their collation; but the theory of original purity (even in division), remnancy, and restoration was shared by all.

62. The rise of "positive theology" — the establishment of dogma according to the historically documented congruence of tradition — is a phenomenon in Roman Catholic thought tied in large measure to the controversial needs of the divided post-Reformation Church. See Congar's remarks, in his *History of Theology* (New York: Doubleday, 1968), a translation of his major article "Théologie" in the *Dictionnaire de Théologie Catholique,* vol. 15. Cf. also his description of the central role of positive theology as "the summing up" of "the totality of what has been revealed about Christ over long ages," and thus "received and lived" (Congar, *Tradition and Traditions,* pt. II, pp. 268-70).

as a set of figural conformances, but rather as the temporal survival of a certain set of religious attitudes.[63] And although Roman Catholic historical reasoning eventually moved from the depiction of unchanging perpetuity to continuous "development" within the tradition, it was the common notion of historical uniformity that allowed for this evolution, seen finally in its pneumatic version of contemporary theologies of movement.[64] Where the Spirit becomes the single subject of the Church's historical life, the Church's experience, though it may appear variegated, is in reality determined by a uniform character. The celebrated phenomenon of "newness," even "innovation," when it is tied to a religious scheme of continuity, relies as much on a flattening of historical experience as does any contrasting phenomenon of "perpetuity" or "deposit." And within each of these realms ecclesial repentance is logically impossible: in the case of a history of original deposit, whether from the Protestant or the Catholic side, sin has been thrust out from the Body onto an object of separation; in the case of a pneumatically developing history, sin has been thrust onto a separated past.

It is instructive to note in contrast how, at least on a conceptual plane, a figurally integrated vision of the Church's history made ecclesial penitence a logical necessity. What would happen if the scheme of the Church's historical decadence from primitive purity — insisted upon by Protestants — were joined to a traditionally Catholic scheme of corporal continuity? Only the figuralist vision of history could sustain the conjunction; and as it did, repentance flourished as the figural character of historical experience as a whole. Marginal to the post-Reformation Church, this outlook had a few notable representatives among the Jansenists especially. We have already noted, in the

63. Cf. Aurelio A. Garcia Archilla, *The Theology of History and Apologetic Historiography in Heinrich Bullinger: Truth in History* (San Francisco: Mellen Research University Press, 1992), esp. chs. 1, 2, 5.

64. For an account of the shift from perpetuity to development, cf. Yves Congar, *Tradition and Traditions: An Historical and a Theological Essay* (London: Burns & Oates, 1966), esp. pp. 125ff. and 156-221; Georges Tavard, *La Tradition au XVIIe Siècle en France et en Angleterre* (Paris: Éditions Du Cerf, 1969). Congar offers his own constructive version of pneumatic development through the traditions of the Church — "the Holy Spirit, transcendent subject of tradition" — as they adhere to the deposit of Scripture; cf. Congar, *Tradition and Traditions*, pt. II, pp. 264ff. and 338ff. Parallel to this development was the crude reduction of Augustine's figural history to an abstract historicism of "Providence," a devolution only occasionally thwarted by the likes of Pascal and other Jansenists. Even Bossuet, who erected perhaps the most notable modern literary memorial to Augustinian historiography, was easily tempted to let go the scriptural figuralism of his master in favor of a more easily manipulated canvas of historical prediction and fulfillment. Cf. Gérard Ferreyrolles, "L'Influence de la conception augustinienne de l'histoire au XVIIe siècle," *XVIIe Siècle* 34, no. 2 (1982): pp. 216-41.

last chapter, how Antoine Arnauld caused a stir when, in 1643, he published *On Frequent Communion,* a long treatise about the need for rigorous penitential discipline (and the concomitant helpfulness of withholding absolution for a period after the sacrament of penance) before taking Communion.[65] The work is a typical example of the controversialist "positive theology" and, along with a sequel, inundates the reader with source evidence as to the "traditional" character of the rigorist penitential practice advocated. But the theological-historical framework Arnauld applies to this argument is ecclesiologically startling for the period; and although we touched upon it already, it deserves a second look.[66]

Arnauld, in fact, insists upon the same "decay" in the Church as did Protestant controversialists. He attributes to the early Church, through and in fact because of the persecutions, a fuller possession of the Holy Spirit. The result was that "frequent communion" was a spiritual possibility it can no longer be in the present. Christians today must be more rigoristic in their penitential disciplines prior to communion simply because they are less holy than the first Christians and thus less ready for a sacramental participation in the Body of the Lord. But Arnauld also insists that the pure Church of the martyrs and the decayed Church of the present are the same. They are the same insofar as they embody the same Christ. What holds these two truths together — historical degeneration and corporal continuity in the Church — is the figural reality that the Church in its integrity participates in the very forms of Christ's own life.

Arnauld approaches this figural reality from two angles. First, taken as a temporal whole, the Church's life conforms to the integrity of Jesus' own corporal history: much of its experience corresponds to the unknown and "hidden" life of Jesus from his childhood until his public ministry. Thus, in general, the Church "ages" in obscurity; and this figural aspect colors much of the Church's experience and, in contrast, marks it off from the singular spectacle of its "nativity" among the apostles and martyrs. But second, to the degree that the Incarnation is itself a divine form of humiliation — of "penitence" in the sense adumbrated by Quesnel in the wake of Bérulle — the time of the Church's "aging" will itself constitute a continual conformance to

65. The work can be found in Arnauld's *Oeuvres* (1775–1783; repr. Brussels: Culture et Civilisation, 1964–1967), vol. 28. Arnauld wrote the work as a defense of the confessional practices of his mentor Saint-Cyran, then in prison. Many of the ideas derive from Saint-Cyran's own teaching. On the traditional relationship of penance to communion, cf. L. Braeckmans, S.J., *Confession et Communion au Moyen Âge et au Concile de Trente* (Gembloux: J. Duculot, 1971).

66. See especially the preface of the work.

the pattern of Christ's unabated self-abnegation for the sake of sin. The only ultimate difference between the "hidden" years of Jesus' life and his final ministry and Passion was the latter's explicitness and publicly epiphanic visage. It is not simply the case that the Church's "corruption" is a figure of the "hidden" passion; rather, the continual impulse, in the midst of this corruption, to answer it through repentance provides an extended arena in which the Church's constricted and vulnerable struggle for faithfulness embodies repeated conformities to elements of Christ's life, both hidden and public. The very tension between purity and corruption, repentance and opposition, gives rise to the real "mark" of the Church: martyrdom in unity. Taking up a patristic and early medieval phrase, Arnauld speaks of the "continual reform" that is thus the innate penitential life of the single Church, whose integrity over time and within its corruption provided the only realm in which repentance could touch the Body as a whole, and hence have meaning for the individual.

The popularity of Arnauld's book — it went through at least fourteen editions in the next few decades — lay in the rigoristic arguments of its main text, not in its figural presuppositions, which were generally ignored or rejected outright.[67] And this lack of interest simply exemplified the reduction of repentance's reach and meaning in an antagonistically rendered Church. Without an ecclesial object for repentance, the divided Church was left to apprehend the penitential act as a set of individually subjective alterations within the uniform history of whatever denominational construct surrounded one. Drawing on the definitions given at the Council of Trent, the sacramental distinctions made in "penance" — contrition, confession, and satisfaction — were ever more intricately explored in their connection to subjective "virtues." The Council of Trent itself defined the fruit of penitence solely in terms of the relationship between the individual and God;[68] and the devotional tendency of this focus (given much theological exposition) was toward a multiplication

67. This was true as much for Jansenists as for non-Jansenists. Cf., for example, the pastorally promulgated version of Arnauld's argument by the Archdiocese of Tours, probably written by the Jansenist Pierre-Sébastien Gourlin, *Instruction pastorale de Monseigneur l'Archevêque de Tours, sur la justice chrétienne, Par rapport aux Sacremens de Penitence & d'Eucharistie* (Paris, 1749). Shorn of its historical and figural theology, Arnauld's "Augustinian" rigorism in this instance becomes a functionalist structure of moralistic discipline, the vision of whose end — union with divine love — remains evangelically enticing, but whose practical career has devolved into that caricature of Jansenist pessimistic striving bequeathed to post-Revolutionary Catholicism.

68. This fruit is "reconciliation with God, to which is usually joined the peace and tranquillity of the conscience along with a strong spiritual consolation" (Council of Trent, Session XIV, c.3 [Denzinger, n. 1674]).

310

of individual acts within the penitential whole, each of which would contribute to an increased measure of personal holiness.[69] Manuals and catechisms proliferated in this evolution, detailing "attitudes" and "dispositions" appropriate to this schooling in virtue; some of them demonstrated their ultimate degeneration into extrinsic functionalism by framing the whole penitential system in terms of an edifying bridle to be placed upon the otherwise unruly social behavior of the "people."[70] And while post–Vatican II discussions have restored a discussion of the "ecclesial character of penitence," this has meant in practice a focus on the individual's reconciliation to the Church's Body, rather than a participation within that Body's own continuing corruption and renewal.[71]

Present-day Catholic reflection on repentance, in any case, has tended in its novel developments to press more in the direction of already established Protestant conceptions, in which true repentance has been simplified (in Luther's forceful arguments) to the sinner's complete trust in the sole mercy of God given in Christ — no works, no satisfactions, no exercises or dispositions.[72] This

69. Thus, in addition to the three standard Tridentine divisions of penitence, one found encouraged formalized acts of "self-examination," "firm resolution," and so on.

70. In this regard, Jansenist "penitentialism" was simply co-opted by the general post-Tridentine mind-set, epitomized and propagated in the penitential *Instructions* (or *Manual for Confessors*) of Charles Borromeo, which became a touchstone in pastoral reform during the first part of the seventeenth century. Nicole, Arnauld's frequent collaborationist, applies the sacrament of penance, along with the other sacraments, to a system of individual moral formation *(Instructions Theologiques et Morales sur les Sacremens),* and the later Jansenist Jerôme Besoigne sharpens this into an ascetic ladder toward "perfect justice" *(Principes de la Pénitence et de la Conversion, ou Vie des Pénitens)* and almost complete repudiation of the figural understanding of "continual reform." Cf. the material discussed in Jean Delumeau, *Sin and Fear: The Emergence of a Western Guilt Culture. 13th-18th Centuries* (New York: St. Martin's Press, 1990).

71. The results of contemporary New Testament scholarship, wedded to Catholic notions of the Church, have given rise to a new appreciation of the "social nature of sin and reconciliation." The sin remains the individual's in connection with the world, while the reconciliation remains the Church's, now itself called the "sacrament of reconciliation," a division in attribution that derives from the preclusion of the Church's figural integrity. Cf. Bernard Häring, C.S.R., *Shalom: Peace. The Sacrament of Reconciliation,* rev. ed. (Garden City [N.Y.]: Doubleday & Co., 1969); Kenan B. Osborne, O.F.M., *Reconciliation and Justification: The Sacrament and Its Theology* (New York/Mahwah: Paulist Press, 1990), chs. 2, 9, 10.

72. Cf. George Tavard, *Justification: And Ecumenical Study* (New York/Mahwah: Paulist Press, 1983), esp. chs. 3 and 5. The Catholic Tavard, however, has taken up the doctrine (interpreted in his own way, to be sure) and urged its application in exactly the manner as the earlier Protestant historians: "The irony of Luther's situation is that he was right on the chief point of the Christian understanding of human life in its relationship to God, at a time when the Church's hierarchy . . . was blind to the point he was making. . . . But if justification by faith is not only a doctrine, but is also a central key to all Christian doctrine and life, then the entire edifice of Catholic thought since the sixteenth century stands in need of reconstruc-

intensely narrowed interest in justification by faith, in opposition to Catholic penitential practices (as well as much of their theological rationale) lay at the root of the Protestant distinction from Rome. Sinfulness is not so much a matter of individual actions, but of the basic nature of the person; and repentance is thus not a matter of dealing with specific sins but of turning the whole incapacitated self to the sole bearer of forgiveness, God. Repentance is located in the individual motion of faith in the promise of God, given in Christ's death on our behalf.[73] As in the Protestant exposition of ecclesial history, so for the shape of devotional practice, this revisioning of repentance subsumes the character of the individual Christian into a conformity with a principle, and not an embodied figure. When explicit scriptural figures of repentance are explained, such as Psalm 51, they pertain invariably to this individual instantiation of dependence; and despite the initial goal of the Reformers in freeing repentance from moralism, the practical application of this individual movement evinces an unexpected interpretive restriction to the morally exemplary.[74] If scriptural figures exemplify the principle

tion. . . . In its light the church must reform itself" (pp. 107, 110f.). Is this a plea for ecclesial repentance? Perhaps; but given Tavard's theology of pneumatic movement in the Church, he may also be thinking in terms of the Church's "leaving behind" of sin in her temporal advance. Cf. his *The Church, Community of Salvation: An Ecumenical Ecclesiology* (Collegeville [Minn.]: Liturgical Press, 1992), pp. 58f. and 243ff.

73. Cf. Luther's early *Confitendi Ratio* (Discussion of Confession, 1520), which was written before his break with Rome but which attempts to brush away penitential practices in favor of the simple act of "trusting in the Lord." Cf. also Calvin's 1543 *Necessity of Reforming the Church,* in which the discussion of justification by faith, along familiar lines, forms a prelude to an attack on the penitential "satisfactions" of the Catholics.

74. Both Luther's and Calvin's commentaries on this psalm fit this mode, with Calvin especially eschewing any figural extension of David's sin and repentance. When, in verse 18, Jerusalem is mentioned, Luther notes how the Church is properly built up by a doctrine of justification by faith, while Calvin ties the health of the city to individual righteousness and divine grace, a predictable mollifying of the Lutheran stance. With a psalm like 80, a lament over the destruction of Jerusalem, Calvin avoids the notion of repentance altogether, and interprets the prayer in terms of a petition by the "faithful remnant." (On Calvin's moralistic use of exegetical figures, cf. Barbara Pitkin, "Imitation of David: David as a Paradigm for Faith in Calvin's Exegesis of the Psalms," *Sixteenth Century Journal* 26, no. 4 [1993]: pp. 843-63.) Contrast this with the pre-Reformation penitential preaching of John Fisher earlier in the century. Fisher's focus on the absolute trust in God's mercy, given in His Son, that undergirds his notion of repentance, has been likened to Luther's, as a kind of Catholic version of an epochal concern over individual salvation for the troubled conscience. Cf. W. S. Stafford, "Repentance on the Eve of the Reformation: John Fisher's Sermons of 1508 and 1509," *Historical Magazine of the Protestant Episcopal Church* 54 (1985): pp. 297-338. But in fact, Fisher's undeniable interest and rhetorical facility with this theme is tethered to a much larger figural purpose, which demonstrates not so much the error of Protestant penitential concerns as their painfully pinched constriction. Fisher can, for instance, read David's individual search for forgiveness and pneu-

of individual trust, their meditation will logically entail the ordering of distinguished types of trust. Not surprisingly, then, Reformed theology ended by creating a practical system of repentance — understood as a species of the general principle of "conversion" — that was quite as elaborated and multiplied in its elements as the Roman Catholic penitential system.[75] Whatever figurated attitudes it upheld were well restricted to the moral similitudes instructive for personal righteousness and doctrinal conformity.

---

matic wholeness in the context of the Church's corporate eschatological history in a general way, as in Psalm 51; but, more pointedly, he is able to let the individualist devotionalism move in seamless counterpoint with this more foundational ecclesial framework in a full-blown figuralism that builds to a corporate reformational yearning remarkably consonant with traditional mimetic schemes of repentance built around the Christological form (cf. esp. his sermon on Psalm 102, pt. 2). Within this form, he can locate the aboriginal pride and divisiveness of the apostles and the early Church, and the contemporary corruptions of the clergy and leadership of the Church, touching not only upon moral failings, but on doctrinal rot as well. Yet, in the form of "Sion," given integrity in Jesus, these pneumatically repulsive failures are given residence within his mercy as to a single Body. It seemed obvious to Fisher that the sacrifice of Christ might subsume even the visible Church, and not merely the visible sinner. The distinction here from the Reformers could not be more striking. For an accessible version of Fisher's sermons on this topic, see his *Commentary on the Seven Penitential Psalms,* 2 vols., ed. J. S. Phillimore (St. Louis: B. Herder, and London: Manresa Press, 1915). On Fisher's theology of repentance, see Richard Rex, *The Theology of John Fisher* (Cambridge: Cambridge University Press, 1991), pp. 30-49, 110-28. See also Edward Surtz, S.J., *The Works and Days of John Fisher: An Introduction to the Position of St. John Fisher (1469–1535), Bishop of Rochester, in the English Renaissance and the Reformation* (Cambridge: Harvard University Press, 1967), esp. pp. 194ff.and 238ff.

75. Cf. Richard Baxter, "Treatise of Conversion" (vol. 7), and "Directions and Persuasions to a Sound Conversion" (vol. 8), in *The Practical Works of The Rev. Richard Baxter,* ed. W. Orme (London: James Duncan, 1830), which provide extravagant, though typical, examples of Puritan "dispositional" devotion around the topic of repentance (e.g., types, motives, manner, ends, mistakes of "consideration," "contrition," "humiliation," etc.). Where repentance of a more communal kind is aimed after — and such "public" orientations were common in Puritanism, in both England and America — it takes the form of a similarly constructed exhortation to a system of individual reformation designed in response to some calamity, threatened or real, or for its alleviation, and tied to the fate of the elect remnant, who are by no means identical with the visible body. Cf. Thomas Goodwin, "Two Sermons on Repentance" (based on Zeph. 2:1-3), in his *Works* (Edinburgh: James Nichol, 1863), vol. 7, where, not surprisingly, the remnant identified by individual repentance is defined in terms of its adhesion to the doctrine of justification by faith and grace alone. Not that this was always wooden; indeed, tied to a conviction of personal pneumatic experience, it could flower into quite supple, vibrant, and even sensual forms. Cf. Norman Pettit, *The Heart Prepared: Grace and Conversion in Puritan Spiritual Life* (New Haven: Yale University Press, 1966). Non-Puritan Anglican explorations of repentance fell back on the penitential overgrowth of Catholicism, which, however fertilized by acute psychological distinctions, followed a general pattern of individualization without ecclesial reference. Cf. Jeremy Taylor's various works for confessors and penitents, such as the famous *Ductor Dubitantium* (1658).

Ecclesial Repentance and the "History" of Redemption

And simply looking at the explicit penitential teaching of the post-Reformation churches gives only a limited, and often not that instructive, insight into the incapacity for grasping what repentance within the church might actually be in the wake of ecclesial division's dismantling of figuralist history. Redefining the character of the Church's experienced history went hand in hand with a great obscurement of how the Church in fact apprehends the very power of forgiveness and new life embodied not simply ecclesiastically, but in the very life of Jesus Christ. On this score, it is worth observing something of the post-Reformation disintegration of the broader perception of participatory suffering offered the penitent Church in the atonement, which was able to inform already with Augustine the equation of penitential sacrifice with the unity of the Church (see above). For within this larger devotional realm as well, the transformation of historical experience necessitated by denying a unitive temporal figure to the Church pressed Protestants into the principled uniformity of observed phenomena and Catholics into a self-referring moralism.

The particular theology of ecclesial participatory penance, under the rubric of "expiatory" or "reparative" suffering, is actually, in its articulated form, a product of the seventeenth-century Catholic reform. In particular, it derives from a spiritual evolution that began in the post-Reformation France of the early seventeenth century, when a reasserted theology of the Incarnation, associated with figures like Pierre de Bérulle and his French Oratory, was increasingly embodied in a devotion to the kenotic, self-emptying aspects of Jesus' oblation to the Father. A whole school of Christian piety began to flourish in that period that focused on the individual's joining, in prayer, in Jesus' sacrifice, a thrust that has been dubbed "victimal spirituality." One delimited form of this spirituality, associated with John Eudes, took as its special lens a vivid meditation on the Heart of Jesus, which was viewed figurally as the source of God's incarnated love for creation given in his Son's death. Devotion to the Sacred Heart of Jesus had a subdued following for much of the second part of the century. In keeping with the theological milieu out of which it grew, this early devotion to the Sacred Heart emphasized, in a thoroughly Augustinian way, the totality of God's grace in Christ, buttressed by a classical substitutionary view of his sacrifice. What was peculiar in the devotion to the Sacred Heart, however, was its complementary emphasis on the totality of human response this complete divine love called upon, a response that demanded the whole of one's life in return, that is, that demanded a "sacrifice" of one's limited self that could

314

instance the only possible human reply to an infinite self-sacrificing love on the part of God.[76]

In the early 1670s, the devotion to the Sacred Heart took a new turn with a series of visions received by a Visitandine nun, Marguerite-Marie Alacoque; out of these visions grew what would become an astoundingly popular spirituality that enveloped much of Europe and America, crowned in 1765 by papal approbation and sustained even in this century by two important encyclicals.[77] Marguerite-Marie's visions were essentially prophetic: they were given to her by Jesus himself, who advocated a special devotion to his Heart, given in a particularized form — crowned with thorns and riven by a cross — a devotion that was to be promoted for the special purpose of responding to what he called his "outraged love," the historical acts perpetrated against his loving sacrifice for sin. And the prophetic character of all this must be stressed: for if the exhorted devotion was to be "reparative," it was so in a historically specific sense, in that it would somehow act as a necessary form of repentance for sins against redemptive love that were concretely identified in the life of the Church as it lived in the shadow of the cross. Marguerite-Marie's visions — as well as the whole tenor of the subsequent spirituality that flowed from them — were aimed at organizing the Church's response to specific developments of religious pluralism and secularization: sins against the holiness of the Eucharistic sacrifice (by, e.g., Protestants and indifferent Catholics), sins of secular blasphemy and atheism, sins against the keeping of the Lord's day, and so on. And this attitude of prophetic concern and sacrifice for the assaulted historical life of the Church took particular force in the wake of the French Revolution.[78] The reparative aspects of Sacred Heart spirituality, in fact, came to color much of nineteenth- and early-twentieth-century Roman Catholic attitudes generally, including several religious orders, like the women Trappists, who were to produce some remarkable exemplars of self-oblation.

76. Cf. the English translation of the twelfth book of Eudes's masterwork, *The Admirable Heart of the Mother of God,* which treats of the Heart of Jesus, given in *The Sacred Heart of Jesus,* trans. Dom Richard Flower, OSB (New York: P. J. Kenedy & Sons, 1946), pp. 26, 29f., 35, 38, 55f., 102f., 105ff.

77. *Miserantissimus Redemptor* (Pius XI, 1928) and *Haurietis Aquas* (Pius XII, 1956). Background, historical and theological, to the devotion to the Sacred Heart can be found in Joseph Stierli, ed., *Heart of the Saviour: A Symposium on Devotion to the Sacred Heart* (New York: Herder and Herder, 1957).

78. The focus of the visions and later devotion on the Eucharistic sacrament of sacrifice has always been noted — the devotion itself was based on adoration of the sacrament and frequent communion; but the relation of this focus to the Church's contextual history has been less emphasized by scholars, even though it forms the scaffolding of the devotion's most recent apologies in the twentieth-century papal pronouncements.

Now the New Testament writings themselves offer many texts that touch on the notion of Christians offering their lives as sacrifices. While it is hardly clear in what way many of these texts actually define the character of such sacrifices, they are frequently drawn into some kind of representational relation with Jesus' own sacrifice. This includes, obviously, texts that may deal with the relation in terms of imitation (e.g., carrying one's "cross" or retracing his "steps" in following Jesus [cf. Mark 8:34 and 1 Peter 2:21]). But this representational outlook also includes texts that speak of a "sharing" of the sacrifice of Jesus itself, in the sense of participating in its occurrence somehow (e.g., Mark 10:39, "the cup that I drink you will drink; and with the baptism with which I am baptized, you will be baptized"). Particularly in Paul (e.g., 2 Cor. 1:5-7; 4:7-12, etc.), this kind of participation in Christ's sacrifice is given a certain kind of vicarious meaning, in that it is something borne by Paul "for the sake of" the Church, an implication given an emphasized (though debated) explicitness especially in Colossians 1:24, a verse whose echo is prominent in the visions of Marguerite-Marie Alacoque and which was frequently cited in explications of the reparative theology, "I rejoice in my sufferings for your sake, and in my flesh I complete what is lacking in Christ's afflictions for the sake of his body, that is, the church."

However adequate might be the exegesis on which is based such a view of the Christian's vicarious participation in the sacrifice of Jesus,[79] the view itself quickly entered the "apostolic" stream of the early Church, already informing, for instance, Ignatius of Antioch's interpretation of his own imminent martyrdom in the first century, which he repeatedly refers to as the "sacrifice" by which "I give my life for you." It is an attitude sustained by his deep conviction that the Church is defined by its essential "unity," through which each member is part of the other in Christ Jesus.[80] And by the time of Augustine, this participatory character of Christ's sacrifice was a central

---

79. See, most recently, the lengthy review of Colossians 1:24 in Markus Barth's *Colossians* (New York: Doubleday, 1994), pp. 251-58, 289-95. An English overview of the history of exegesis on this text, with special concern for its ecumenical import, can be found in John Reumann's "Colossians 1:24 ("What is Lacking in the Afflictions of Christ"): History of Exegesis and Ecumenical Advance," *Currents in Theology and Mission* 17, no. 6 (December 1990): pp. 454ff. (Reumann draws from, among others, Jacob Kremer's more extensive review of the material in his *Was an den Leiden Christi Noch Mangelt: Eine Interpretationsgeschichtliche une Exegetische Untersuchung zu Kol. 1,24b* [BBB 12; Bonn: Hanstein, 1956]. The historical exposition of this particular verse, however, must be placed in the context of the larger tradition concerning participatory reality; otherwise someone like Augustine (see below) will seem, inaccurately, innovative. (Cf. Kremer's and Reumann's treatment of the ambiguous views of Chrysostom regarding the ecclesial "body" of Christ.)

80. Cf. his Epistle to the Ephesians (21:1), to the Trallians (13:3), to Polycarp (6:1).

explicator of ecclesial and individual Christian existence. Taking Colossians 1:24 as his lens, for example, Augustine explains how the Body of Christ must be understood, historically, as an undivided whole that is inclusive of its "head" and its "members"; and thus, the concrete suffering of Christ's passion on behalf of the sinful world extends to and is properly incarnated in the historical existence of the Body's members, the Church in time, from Abel to the Parousia — the sacrifice is Christ Jesus', but its figural enactment encompasses the history of his Body, the Church.[81] In this sense, and in a way that is consistent with Augustine's view of the relation between sacrifice and penance in general, it is correct to speak of our sufferings as being sacrifices "on behalf" of others, in the same way as Jesus' are, for they are one and the same sacrifice of Jesus, and are "ours" only in a derivative sense, through our membership in his Body.

Two elements in this tradition of participatory suffering need to be emphasized in their relation to the atonement. The first is the way this tradition construes history. The sacrifice of Christ is a unique temporal event, which is neither supplemented nor replaced by the sufferings of his Body. But temporal history itself, in its outworking — the relation between past, present, and future within the created world — is somehow expressive of this unique event, it conforms to its shape, it embodies it spatially. The phenomenon of "reparative suffering," then, has no historical reality except insofar as it "refers" to the atonement of Christ, as a figure or natural sign does. Secondly, because participatory suffering is the expressive language of the atonement, it constitutes the way the atonement is known within history. It is an epistemological condition for the atonement's temporal — that is, experiential — apprehension.

The devotional payoff to this perspective was given in a defined recognition: that is, that the Body of Christ, the Church, is a suffering body, and suffers precisely to the degree that its conformance to Jesus is not yet realized historically. The Church does not suffer for the redemption of humankind; it suffers Jesus' redemption because, as Church, the Church itself still sins, concretely in time, even though it is also joined to his flesh. In other words, the Church suffers Jesus' suffering for the Church. The scholar Edouard Glotin has pointed to two areas of the Church's life in which this reality was early played out devotionally.[82] The first took form in the liturgical acts surrounding the Passion, particularly the Easter fast and the Good Friday liturgy (already in the fourth century). In these the Church became the figural actor through

---

81. Cf. on Psalm 61 (62) in the *Enarrationes*.
82. Cf. his review in the article "Réparation," in *Dictionnaire de la Spiritualité*, cols. 374ff.

the role assigned, scripturally, to the Jewish people. For example, in these liturgies, the Church takes its place as the ungrateful people for whom Christ gives his life; the Church is recipient of his prophetic calls to repent and to love in return for his love, as it stands to receive the great Good Friday "Reproaches," which Jesus hurls at the Church in the form of Old Testament texts from Micah, Deuteronomy (8:2-7), and the Psalms: for example, "*Populel meus, quid feci tibi* — O my people, what is it I have done unto thee? How have I grieved thee? Answer thou me" (Mic. 6:3-4). Far from embodying anti-Judaic sentiments, these liturgies, later expanded through new elements like the Tenebrae readings from Lamentations,[83] were an attempt to posture the Church as a sinner from whom Christ's suffering love called forth repentant love in return. And the theme itself migrated from the liturgy into a wide range of devotional expressions, from hymns and meditations to the plastic arts.[84] This became the classical notion of *redamatio* — "giving love back" to Jesus — which formed a basis of the later reparative prophecies of the Sacred Heart. John Eudes writes, typically, "O Creator, I owe Thee my body and soul, because Thou hast given me Thy body and soul, Thy life and Thy very self. . . . Let my tongue be torn from my mouth if I use it but to bless Thee; let my heart burst asunder rather than fail to love Thee."[85] And into the chasm dug by lack of *redamatio,* Eudes perceives the place where our own love can suffer on behalf of others: "O unhappy souls, why have you not loved Him who has loved you more than Himself, since He has given His very life and blood for your salvation? O Dearest Jesus, give me all the hearts of these unfortunate souls, that I may love and praise Thee for them eternally."[86] The point being that the Passion of Jesus was a living thing for the life of the Church — which includes us — who is paradoxically the lover and loved one, the harmed and the hurting at once, even today.

In addition to this continuing liturgical enactment of post-redemptive suffering, Glotin points to the developing aspect of monastic life that viewed one of its central vocations as that of "afflicting oneself and praying for the whole church and world" in its rejection of Jesus' loving oblation.[87] Repentance was viewed as a continual characteristic of the Church, because its perfection

83. See above.

84. Cf. examples of the "appeals of Christ" related to the Passion, in Frances M. M. Comper, ed., *Spiritual Songs from English Mss. of Fourteenth to Sixteenth Centuries* (London: SPCK, 1936).

85. Eudes, p. 56.

86. Eudes, p. 105.

87. See the discussion in Irénée Hausherr, S.J., *Penthos: The Doctrine of Compunction in the Christian East* (Kalamazoo: Cistercian Publications, 1982), chs. 5 and 6.

lies outside history, into which, through the temporal love of one another here and now, individual Christians were drawn on behalf of each other, very much according to the model of Colossians 1:24.

The conviction and practice of participatory suffering that was deemed somehow reparative, then, were based on a particular understanding of the historical relation between Christ and his Church. The two were seen to be joined as one body, and that relation of unity worked itself out historically, in time, through the Church's figural appropriation of a prophetically grounded identity with Israel. The Church lived Israel's vocation of repentant suffering, even as it lived Christ's vocation of redeeming love. These are the two sides of the Church's life in unity with the Lord, and thereby, in unity with itself.

Further, this figural understanding of the unity of the Church remained a consistent one throughout the Middle Ages, finding expression in a number of well-known spiritual writers like Mechtild of Magdeburg and her associates and, of course, Catherine of Siena, whose reparative vocation of "tears," joined to Jesus' passion, on behalf of the corrupted and disintegrating Church of her time defines her whole theology.[88] Even the classical theology of satisfaction explicated by Anselm — so discomfiting today — emerges more organically out of the experience of participatory and suffering *redamatio:* "In the Unity of the church, you are His very flesh; and in return I must love thee, I must love Thee, Lord . . . and carry after Thee the Cross Thy enemies have given Thee, now laid by You upon my shoulders."[89] Anselm's "Cur Deus Homo" — the famous treatise in which he outlines the pure theory of "satisfaction" that is now associated with his name and located behind more modern, post-Reformation penal substitution views of the atonement — is no more than a contemplative "wisdom" reflection that grows out of the experience of *redamatio,* a view of rational theology on the matter that sees "understanding" as arising out of loving Jesus in return, out of the participation in love's outworking in the Church.

The issue of the atonement's own contemporary obscurement as a coherent doctrine is properly tied to the fate of this classical sense of sacrificial *redamatio* bound to the figure of the unitary Church incorporated as Christ's

88. For Mechtild, see *The Revelations of Mechtild of Magdeburg,* trans. Lucy Menzies (London: Longmans, Green and Co, 1953), passim, esp. bk. 5:34 at pp. 159f. on the "three sheddings of blood" on behalf of the Church, inclusive of the saints'. On Catherine of Siena, see the opening chapters on her initial call by Christ; cf. also our brief discussion of Catherine above.

89. See his *Meditations,* esp. I and IX (cf. the anonymous English version of 1872 [London: Burns and Oates]).

Body.[90] On the most fundamental level, the theological substructure of participatory unity through the Church was undercut by its historical contradiction in the experience of the Reformation division of the Church; for in the case of passional self-giving, experience was the main window through which theological vision could move. In addition to any initiating role doctrinal concerns may have had, we must note the way in which the raw experience of division demanded a correlative devotional form that itself constricted doctrinal concern. Remember that participatory suffering, which had acted as the experiential appropriator of the atonement, had always been bound up with the experienced unity of the Church as Christ's Body, a unity that, as we saw, insisted on being inclusive even of the Church's sin. But the deliberate and condoned separation of Christians one from another on the basis of each other's alleged sins constituted an embodied denial of the traditional vision of that corporate unity of which participatory suffering was an essential element.

Lutherans, for instance, had raised serious questions about the integrity of certain practices like the selling of indulgences. But these objections included a whole range of devotional practices in fact tied to the reparative tradition of the Church — penance, intercessory prayer, and the like. Against them, and the scholastic theology of "merit" that had developed to explain them, the Reformers reverted to a single-minded assertion of the all-sufficiency of Christ's sacrifice for redemption, an assertion buttressed by an equally insistent emphasis upon the substitutionary payment for sin given by Christ. Documents like the Augsburg Confession and Luther's catechisms are driven by this dynamic. But what the Reformers never did was address the more basic theology of participatory unity that underlay the reparative tradition. And why was this? In large measure, because such a theology of participatory unity depended upon an ecclesiology that could not logically comprehend the separations and "schisms" embodied in the Reformation itself.

Roman Catholics like the Thomist Thomas de Vio Cajetan attempted to offer explications of "merit" that relied quite precisely on the Pauline theology of participation in the Body, including its passional aspects, without detriment to the *solus Christus* theology of redemption championed by the

---

90. Cf. John Milbank's article, discussed in the last chapter, "The Name of Jesus: Incarnation, Atonement, Ecclesiology," *Modern Theology* 7, no. 4 (1991): pp. 310-33, which places the comprehensibility of the doctrine squarely (and properly) within the historical enactment of participatory and even vicarious suffering (cf. p. 317). How much of Milbank's unusual (for the present) revalorization of such a notion derives from a peculiarly contemporary attempt to link traditional Christian doctrine with particular modern political concerns, rather than from a less constructive and more purely revelatory reading of Christian history, is open to debate. (Cf. our critical remarks above.)

Reformers. But such attempts were impossible to assimilate into Protestant arguments that had, as an essential experiential component, the need to justify their own separation.[91] Instead, something like the doctrine of justification by faith alone, with the single purpose of defending the *solo Christo* view of redemption, quickly became what can be called a "contrastive identifier" for the Christian faith as a whole: the justification-by-faith doctrine's "usefulness," along with its derivative elements like the penal substitution theory of the atonement (always held in common with Catholics), lay in the way its application or reception could "identify" true Christianity in "contrast" to false

---

91. In the 1530s, Thomas de Vio Cajetan had carefully articulated the reality of participatory sacrifice in responding, among others, to the Lutheran Augsburg Confession and Melanchthon's defense of it. We may rightly be said to "merit" eternal life, Cajetan insisted, insofar as we understand our meritorious actions of sacrificial love as "the action of Christ who is head in us and through us." "Holy Scripture teaches," he writes, "that the sufferings and deeds of Christ's living members are the sufferings and deeds of Christ the head. . . . [Paul said] in an all-embracing manner in Galatians 2[:20], 'I live, now not I, but Christ lives in me.' Hence I can most truly say, 'I merit, now not I, but Christ merits in me.' " Cajetan, *De fide et operibus contra Lutheranos,* 9, in Jared Wicks, S.J., ed. and trans., *Cajetan Responds: A Reader in Reformation Controversy* (Washington, D.C.: Catholic University of American Press, 1978), pp. 232f. Cajetan was responding to passages in Melanchthon's *Apology,* for example, in article 12, on Penitence, which dealt specifically with the question of "merit" and "satisfaction." The Catholic argument from participation was, of course, by no means unknown to Protestants, even if generally ignored; it was rather the case that the argument simply could not register within their logical framework. A typical example is provided by an Anglican anti-Catholic apologist, J. Gaskarth, whose discourses against the Roman doctrine of satisfaction became included in Bp. Gibson's hugely popular series, *A Preservative against Popery.* Gaskarth at one point dwells upon the key verse Colossians 1:24, as well as Ephesians 5:1f., describes the traditional participatory exegesis of the passage in terms of the mystical body, yet then simply dismisses the reading without argument as somehow being patent in its subversion of the *solo Christo* substitutionary view. Instead, like Calvin, he insists on the "edification" value of shared suffering, something deriving from Paul's "fellow-feeling" for his brethren (cf. J. Gaskarth, *The Popish Methods for the Pardon of Sin, Groundless; Upon the Head of Satisfactions,* in Edmund Gibson, ed., *A Preservative against Popery,* in *Select Discourses upon the Principal Heads of Controversy between Protestants and Papists: Being Written and Published by the Most Eminent Divines of the Church of England, Chiefly in the Reign of King James II,* rev. John Cumming (London: British Society for Promoting the Religious Principles of the Reformation, 1848), vol. 10, pp. 306ff. Cf. earlier Calvin (see below), and Thomas Cartwright's commentary on this verse, in his *Sermons on Colossians,* which follows Calvin's structure of argument. Most impressive, from a (somewhat) moderate, but constructive and deeply felt, anti-Catholic perspective is the long sermon (number 13) of Jean Daillé, in his *Sermons sur l'Epitre de l'Apotre Saint Paul aux Colossiens* (Geneva, 1662), pp. 429-71. The fact that the participatory argument of Cajetan was not itself consistently used by Catholics in their promotion of controverted topics like merits, satisfactions, and purgatory did not, furthermore, provide much encouragement for a discussion of this perspective.

Christianity. It is illuminating to see Luther using the doctrine of justification in just this way, to identify disassociatively the true Church in contrast to satanic Anabaptists and papists, in the very midst of a discussion about "love of the brethren" in 1 John![92] He cannot perceive the tension between the biblical text and the application of the doctrinal test. It is curious to note, too, that in Protestant devotion, a very rapid dilution of concern took place with respect to the Passion of Christ and its relation to his members.

Luther himself, whatever the still hotly debated status of his sacramental and mystical piety, took over traditional devotions to the Passion and pruned them into mainly moral or consoling observations about dependence upon God in suffering — justification by faith — after the example of Jesus, something subsequent pietist authors only slightly got beyond.[93] Reformed devotion, following confessional and catechetical formats, shifted away from any Incarnational focus altogether, except insofar as such a focus illustrated the conviction of divine agency over and against human passivity.[94] In all of this,

92. Cf. his Commentary on 1 John, e.g., 2:9ff.; or his Church Postil on 1 John 3:13-18 (Trinity 2), in which the Papists, in their theology of "merit," are simply disassociated from the Christian Body altogether, identified with the "Cain" of the "world," ranged against the "Abel" of the "little flock of the Church."

93. Cf. his popular "Meditation on Christ's Passion" (1519), in *Luther's Works* (Philadelphia: Fortress Press, 1969), vol. 42, and his 1530 sermon notes on "That a Christian Should Bear His Cross with Patience," in *Luther's Works* (1968), vol. 43. The contrast with Spener is minimal (cf. the latter's "Meditation on the Suffering of Christ," in Peter Erb, ed., *Pietists: Selected Writings* (New York: Paulist Press, 1983), pp. 76ff.

94. Whereas the Tridentine *Catechism* had elucidated the Passion in terms of its temporal representations, Protestant catechisms and confessions from the sixteenth century on described the Passion in extreme substitutionary and historically limited terms: Christ died *in our place.* There is no room in these descriptions for any further human representations, precisely because even any derivative human agency has been effaced. What Luther does with a verse like Galatians 2:20 ("I am crucified with Christ; nevertheless I live; yet not I, but Christ in me" — cf. the later Galatians *Commentary*) is well known: the participatory emphasis of his explication is profound, yet the purpose is surprisingly limited to the nonincorporative substitutionary elements of sin and righteousness, which simply bypasses the dynamic of someone like Cajetan's perspective. Article 2 of the *Augsburg Confession* orients the whole document's theological perspective clearly in this way: it concerns original sin and the extreme penalty due it; that is the foundation of the Gospel, that Christ died because we must die. When Calvin comes to commenting on Colossians 1:24, for instance, he struggles to explain the verse in a way that comes intriguingly close to one of the traditional participatory sacrifice; but then he stops short and accuses the Papists of *blasphèmes horribles* for suggesting such a reading. Only Christ redeems — *Christus solus,* he asserts, quoting Augustine. If Paul suffered "for the Church," it was in the sense that his sufferings derived from his commitment to it. On the Reformed side, then, we find that the demand to efface human embodiments of salvific agency leads to an extreme theory of the wholly subsuming character of divine agency over against human passivity. The Second

doctrinal integrity, which included an overarching emphasis on the atonement's accomplishment *solo Christo,* became a contrastive identifier that necessarily excluded the figural basis of the Church's unity that had made her participatory suffering with Christ comprehensible. Christ died because we must die, Protestants asserted; he died "in our place," as it were. And when pressed so exclusively, this spatial metaphor freed Christians from the demand for historical unity within the Church, because it ended by broadly effacing the historical connection between Head and Body. Other elements of contrast between Reformed and Catholic views of the atonement — the state of created human nature, the character of its corruption in the Fall, and so on — appear less decisive, historically, than this determining separative impetus undergirding the logic of theological formulation.[95]

On the Catholic side, we have just noted how a theologian like Cajetan could work out a theological rationale for the popular medieval merit devotions of the Church, one that was based on Pauline language of participation — "I live, not I, but Christ in me; I suffer, not I, but Christ suffers in me; I merit, not I, but Christ merits in me." And this rationale formed, to a great degree, the basis for the description of atonement promoted by the Council of Trent and given form in its catechism in the 1560s. Discussions of the Passion, baptism, penance, and satisfaction are all informed by the comprehensive participatory theology of the Body of Christ, through which Christ's own singular act of redemptive suffering is given historical embodiment and apprehension in the temporal life of the Church's historical suffering. We can suffer "for" each other because of this.[96] Indeed, we must enter such suffering, insofar

---

Helvetic Confession of 1566, for example, erects a vision of God's sole activating grace in which even the historical Jesus and his sacrifice plays only an exemplary role: the Confession lays out an ascending theological system that refers not to Christ, but to the fact that knowledge, the object of knowledge, and the means of knowledge are applied solely to God, and removed from any human participation. It is not until chapter 11 of this long confession that Incarnation is broached, and here only briefly. The sacrifice of Christ is an historical concretization of a more fundamental principle, that "glory belongs to God" and human beings are nothing before him, a principle more adequately expressed by the doctrine of justification by faith than by any representation of Jesus' own existence.

95. Cf. the unnuanced, but helpfully contrastive, discussion by Henry Oxenham, in his *The Catholic Doctrine of the Atonement: An Historical Review* (London: W. H. Allen & Co, 1881), pp. 219-300.

96. The *Catechism* uses the unity-in-participated-sacrifice perspective as a consistent means by which to draw into relation the Passion of Christ and its meaning for Christian existence. First, in the section of the Catechism dealing with the Creed, the Passion is explained in the full range of traditional atonement categories of "satisfaction," "sacrifice," "redemption," and "example." But the section is summarized in a closing "admonition" that exclaims, "would

as Christ's death is an enablement of our own with him: he dies in order that we might die.[97]

But the division of the Church worked its own constrictive logic on this peculiarly Roman Catholic theology as well. While Protestants were forced to exclude the figural unity of the Church through the articulation of doctrinal contrasting identifiers, the continued justification of division among Catholics meant that they, in their turn, could hold onto the experience of

---

to God that these mysteries were always present to our minds, and that *we learned to suffer, die, and be buried together with our Lord,*" to the end that we might also rise with him. The cognitive efficacy of the Passion's apprehension, then, lies intimately joined to our own existential representation of it. *Catechism of the Council of Trent for Parish Priests,* trans. J. A. McHugh, O.P., and C. J. Callan, O.P. (New York: Joseph F. Wagner, 1923), pp. 53-61.

This representation is later given specific form in the Catechism's discussion of baptism and penance. Baptism is, first of all, explained as a kind of "incorporation" into the Passion of Christ, and its effects for the individual are described in ways that mirror the effects earlier assigned more generally to the Passion itself. Special emphasis is laid on the fact that incorporation refers literally to a joining with the Body of Christ, and that this means finally that our historical existences are, through baptism, now to be shaped according to the experience of Jesus' Cross. (Cf. *Catechism of the Council of Trent,* pp. 168, 170, 182ff., esp. 186f.) Penance, finally, is explained as a reassertion, as it were, of Christ's Passion within our lives, in order to rescue those who have made "shipwreck" of their previously given baptismal innocence. All the atoning elements earlier identified in the historical Passion, and represented existentially in Baptism, are once again figured in an ongoing temporal fashion in the acts and sacrament of penance that a contrite Christian sinner performs — satisfaction, sacrifice, and so on, all of which are literal participations in the one sacrifice of Christ. Penance acts as a literal participation in "Christ and the merits of His Passion," "through which the force and efficacy of the . . . blood of Christ flows into our souls [and] washes away all the sins committed after Baptism," and thus it "leads us to recognize that it is to our Saviour alone we owe the blessing of reconciliation" (p. 266; cf. also p. 302: "For Christ our Lord continually infuses His grace into the devout soul united to Him by charity, as the head to the members, or as the vine through the branches. This grace always precedes, accompanies and follows our good works, and without it we can have no merit, nor can we at all satisfy God"). On this basis, participation in Christ's Passion and its merits, we may even, through our penitential sufferings, "satisfy" for the due penalties of another's sin, thereby "bearing each other's burdens" (pp. 303f.).

97. A clear exposition of this perspective, typically Catholic in contrast to Protestant attitudes, is found in Duguet's magisterial treatment of the Passion, *Explication du mystere de la passion de Notre-Seigneur Jesus-Christ suivant le Concorde. Jesus Crucifié* (Paris: Jacques Estienne, 1728), esp. pt. 2, ch. 8 (on 2 Cor. 5:14ff.). But Duguet also provides a good example of what a participatory theology of the Cross might look like that was somehow purged of any stress on the ecclesially unitive aspects that still lay, however constrictively, behind the reparative devotions of the eighteenth century: a tendency to moralism. As if perceiving the impossibility of applying consistently the figural outlook of the early Church to a contemporary Church of such incoherent embodiment, he translates the "outrages" to the love of God in almost exclusively moral, and hence individualized, terms associated with the tenor of "secularity" or "the world."

participatory suffering only insofar as the figural unity of the Church was opposed to the existence of Reformed Christian communities. In a general way, the theology of the Mystical Body, which had proved a compelling framework for sustaining the experience of participatory suffering, went into a certain eclipse,[98] threatened, in a sense, by the demands it might make upon a church prone to the anathematizing of its separated members.[99] Further, when promoted, reparative suffering then became a generally "oppositional" devotion, one whose object gradually shifted away from the sin of the Church as a whole and the vocation of ecclesial repentance — the Good Friday reproaches — and aimed more specifically at the sins of the "heretics" and "schismatics" — the "others," not the self. Reparative devotions tended to touch the Church only to the degree that the Church was wounded by the depredations of its opponents or lax in its hostility to them. Thus, the focus of the Sacred Heart devotions, as we mentioned, centered on the Eucharistic sacrifice — the Roman Catholic contrastive identifier par excellence; and the visions and reparative practices of Marguerite-Marie Alacoque and her supporters occurred during a time of increasing agitation against French Protestants, a movement that finally culminated in Louis XIV's revocation of the Edict of Nantes in 1685, withdrawing legal toleration of the Reformed churches within the kingdom. Shortly afterward, Marguerite-Marie received her final vision, which proclaimed, not coincidentally, a prophetic message to the king himself, that he promote a reparative devotion

98. See our discussion, following de Lubac, in Chapter 4 above.

99. Thus, the discussion of issues like penance and satisfaction on the part of post-Tridentine apologists (e.g., Bellarmine and, more eccentrically, Vazquez) tended to fall back on complex scholastic distinctions that did not grow out of central experiential affirmations determined by the figures of Scripture — distinctions, for instance, between the providential order of eternal guilt and temporal punishments, justice and friendship, and so on, by which Christ's atonement was logically divorced from the temporal suffering of the members of the Church. The result was a theological edifice that proved an easy target even for potentially sympathetic Protestant interlocutors. Cf. William Wake's series of commentaries on Bossuet's *Exposition of the Doctrine of the Catholic Church,* in his "The Doctrines in Dispute between the Church of England and the Church of Rome, Truly Represented" and his "Defence of the Exposition of the Doctrine of the Church of England," in Gibson, vol. 12, pp. 88-99, 182-89. Wake views Bossuet as an example of the "new Popery," a theological perspective as close to Protestantism as possible within the rhetorical framework allowed by Rome, but achieved only through a deliberate and insincere distorting of the "real" substance of Roman doctrine, represented by the "old Popery" of Bellarmine and others. That Bossuet's explication of merit and satisfaction does in fact draw on a rooted theology of participatory incorporation is little remarked by Wake, although he tends to judge such views approvingly, were they not (as he alleges) in fact disingenuous departures from actual Papist dogma! (Cf. Gibson, pp. 227ff.; and Wake's *A Second Defence of the Exposition,* in Gibson, pp. 287ff.).

to the Sacred Heart for the purification of the nation. And from the beginning of the devotion's promotion, doubts had been raised against it, not only on the basis of the devotion's supposed novelty, but also because its combination of concrete sentimentality and oppositional hostility was viewed as divisive, rather than unitive, within the Church.[100] If the flowering of reparative devotion in eighteenth-century Catholic Europe fed off what seemed a still vigorous figural view of history, it was in fact a deformed history, dependent upon deliberate and chauvinist propaganda more than on an attempt to embrace the wider experience of the Church into a single passional whole.[101] In a sense, the devotion reflected at a distance the strategies of an ideologically charged social reading of religious life that was being formulated more critically by political leaders closer to the ground. And it is not surprising that the devotion called forth, in its opposition, a round of historians, like the later Grégoire (not to mention the earlier Pope Benedict XIV), whose attempts to marginalize the significance of the Sacred Heart were grounded in critical methods of liturgical genealogy.

A Modern Bequest

The demise of ecclesial repentance, then, is matched by the ascendancy of "principled" theology — whether the principle be dogmatic, philosophical, or ethical — coupled with the methods of critical historiography. Nor was the coincidence of these developments fortuitous. One of the great merits of a massive piece of historical scholarship like François Laplanche's study of seventeenth-century French Protestant hermeneutics is precisely the way it demonstrates the ineluctable responsibility denominational controversialism held for the collapse of figuralist apprehensions of Scripture and the demand it concomitantly wielded for a critical history and a theologically principled —

100. Cf. the later comments of Grégoire, in his *Histoire des sectes religieuses,* I.3 (Paris: Baudouin Frères, 1828, t. 2), ch. 20, who also ties the whole outlook to what he perceives to be the antagonistic aspect of "victimal" devotion as a whole (ch. 5), an instance of his more rationalistic Jansenist leanings (as opposed to the "enthusiastic" Jansenism he here mocks), in the wake of Nicole.

101. The anti-Protestant fuel that fed modern Catholic reparative devotion can be seen already in someone like Teresa of Avila, who stresses, on more than one occasion, the way that a desire to suffer for the sake of damned "Lutheran" heretics in France and elsewhere played an important part in her sense of a vocation to sharpen the perfective (and mortifying) character of her monastic reforms. Cf. her *Autobiography,* ch. 32, and *The Way of Perfection,* chs. 1–3.

historically abstracted — program of interpretation.[102] Within the purely political realm, the fragmentation of the Body of the Church created a host of new pressures for the demonstration of social allegiance — among, for example, French Huguenots to a Catholic king or English Dissenters and Catholics to "conforming" Anglicanism — that both flourished in and were in part necessitated by the evacuation from history of common figural conformances. The controversy over origins in the divided Church required the application of criteria independent of any shared experience in Christ, with the result that the "origins" themselves became detached objects of varying modes of criticism, distant and unrelated witnesses called forward as needed to testify to the appropriateness of whoever's present. History was to be dissected, not crucified, then explained according to a rational generalization.[103]

102. François Laplanche, *L'Écriture, Le Sacré, Et L'Histoire. Érudits Et Politiques Protestants Devant La Bible En France Au XVIIe Siècle* (Amsterdam/Maarssen: Holland University Press, 1986). Laplanche's work focuses on the relatively "liberal" theological school of Saumur, and in particular the work of the exegete Louis Cappel and the theologian Moyse Amyraut. But he places their thought within the vast range of French and European Protestantism with a breadth of discussion and reference that has rarely been matched. Figuralism, in fact, stands as the great obstacle to the development of a proper "modern" historical consciousness, in Laplanche's eyes, and his own thesis about the evolution of such a "consciousness" and practice is advanced only to the degree that he is able show the paralysis to which figuralism was intrinsically consigned by the dynamic of confessional antagonism. And while he notes the contributing factors of nonreligious concerns, such as those detailed by Huppert and Kelley, he persuasively erects a case for the primacy of the religious motivation and for the effective logic behind the corresponding evolution of theological "principle" applied to a uniformly desacralized history. The notion of "repentance," to be sure, does not appear among Laplanche's concerns; but it lies hidden within the overwhelming influence of denominational strife he catalogues. Cf. the summary remarks on pp. 177ff., 364-78, 711-21. See also, on the relationship of a critical historical consciousness to developing modern apologetics for Christianity in general, as it evolved out of denominational controversy, the contributions to Maria-Cristina Pitassi, ed., *Apologétique 1680–1740. Sauvetage ou naufrage de la théologie?* (Geneva: Labor et Fides, 1991), especially those by A. McKenna, P. J. Morman, M.-C. Pitassi, and Laplanche himself.

103. Even the most nuanced and ecclesially aware theologians have carefully accepted and promoted versions of this perspective. Cf. Gerhard Ebeling, whose notion of the "unity" of the Church lying only and exclusively — in an historical sense — in the Church's "origin" who is Jesus, the Word, has managed both to dissolve the foundational impetus for reunion and at the same time to open up the serious practice of critical history as an ecclesial vocation: "church history" is nothing other than the necessary description of discrete episodes wherein the "origin" that is the Word is encountered in time by the Christian community. Ebeling's famous phrase that "church history is nothing other than the history of the interpretation of Scripture" is probably correct, although not in the sense he applied the tag: rather than history being the conglomeration of encounters with the original Word, given in Scripture, the Church's

Basic forces of logical — and in a religious sense, pneumatically rendered — continuity link the failure of Christian repentance as an apprehension of corporal disease and the justification of ecclesial division. One of the fullest discussions of ecclesial repentance to come out of the modern ecumenical movement, the Humanum Studies, is also one of the most astonishing embodiments of the constellation of perspectives we have been identifying in the wake of the loss of the figural referent of penitence. Noting its complete reversal of the original ecumenical agenda of unity, just as in the case of pneumatology but now centered around the theme of repentance, demonstrates the consistently encountered contradiction rooted in the center of ecclesial self-reflection.

On the recommendation of the WCC's 1968 Uppsala Assembly, a project was put into effect that was to study the "nature of man" for the benefit of the various working bodies of the council itself. The so-called Humanum Studies that appeared from 1969 to 1975,[104] mostly in the form of reports by the project's director, David Jenkins, fulfill his belief that the project itself stands as a kind of emblematic "case-study relating to human and organizational response to change." After some groping attempts to find a way to organize such a study of the "human," the project finally adopted a set of perspectives that are by now an almost proverbial exemplar of WCC platitudes regarding "indigenizing integrity" and "diversity." For our purposes, it is enough to point out how the spectacle of this project followed a predictable path.

In promoting the study of "man," the Uppsala Assembly had called for the "design and testing of new methods of ecumenical study, especially for experiments using inductive methods, and including the dimensions of biology, psychology, sociology," and so on — that is, the various "critical" disciplines.[105] But this directive was too vast and incoherent. Its initial pursuit led to a self-confessed confusion by the project participants, who then made the con-

---

history is the outworking of its conformity with the Word in his life, given in Scripture. The former makes penitence an epiphenomenon; the latter embodies it. See Ebeling, *The Problem of Historicity in the Church and Its Proclamation* (Philadelphia: Fortress Press, 1967), a translation of lectures originally given in 1954, esp. ch. 3. See also his "Church History Is the History of the Exposition of Scripture," in *The Word of God and Tradition: Historical Studies Interpreting the Divisions of Christianity* (Philadelphia: Fortress Press, 1964), which contains a number of other brilliantly stimulating essays bearing on our topic.

104. Cf. *The Humanum Studies 1969-1975: A Collection of Documents* (Geneva: World Council of Churches, 1975). Reference to the theme of "repentance" is made especially on pp. 65-68; cf. also pp. 77, 79, 81, 85, 91, 105, 107.

105. Cf. *The Humanum Studies*, p. 55.

scious decision to order this critically inchoate realm with certain theological "principles" that would, nevertheless, leave the diversity of the critical referents undisturbed.[106] The main principle applied was the notion of "the one new man in Jesus Christ," whose religious assertion represents a way of "transcendentally" authenticating human diversity, without giving anything up of its particularity. "Ecumenicity" becomes the practical imperative of this religious principle, defined in terms of finding "ways of holding together men and women who, in their particular situations and experiences, are bound to disagree, [and] will sometimes quarrel."[107]

By the end of their mandate, the Humanum group had come up with a set of rhetorically biting recommendations for the orienting of all the programs of the WCC that reflected the implications of principle and imperative in the fullest way possible: the Church is called to "repentance," but this is explained as a deliberate disavowal of the search for "consensus" regarding what "is of general value to Christians everywhere in their engagement with the problems and hopes of being human" and the disavowal of any "ecclesiastical body" that might speak to the "normative" within this realm.[108] "Humanization" (and hence true repentance) lies in the celebratory permission of division (not only ecclesial); "dehumanization" lies in the insistence on a nontranscendent corporal referent to the body of Christ, whose fate is history's, and not the reverse.

> The search for the truly ecumenical is the search for the immense riches which lie latent and often distorted in men and women who have been neglected or oppressed because of race, of culture, of poverty, of sex. It is also a search for a free exploration of possibilities unconstricted by methods of thought, procedure and practice . . . for opportunities where men and women are set free in their various particularities.[109]

That the particularity of Jesus the Christ and of his history bound to Israel, whom God has treated in a way unlike any other (and given in the particular and limited figures of Scripture) — that this particularity has disappeared from this discussion, in favor of another random history of unfigured particularities, bound together by shifting ethical or political abstractions — this is all a familiar criticism of contemporary WCC discourse. The point is this: even if Bishop Jewel could not have embraced the individual principles themselves, he could not fault the peremptory logic of this progression into

---

106. Cf. *The Humanum Studies,* pp. 24 and 41.
107. Cf. *The Humanum Studies,* pp. 37-40.
108. Cf. *The Humanum Studies,* p. 66; also pp. 70, 85.
109. *The Humanum Studies,* p. 111.

history, critical diversity, and its explicit ecumenical impenitence. He was limited by the same pneumatic insensibility.[110]

110. Even when most sensitive to baneful burdens of past exclusions, ecumenical discussion still seems unable to confront explicitly the reality of ecclesial sin's existence. The Joint Ecumenical Commission of Lutheran and Roman Catholic theologians who addressed the issue of whether the mutual condemnations between the two groups made during the sixteenth century still applied were fundamentally motivated by a sense of the impropriety of those earlier "anathemas" offered by one church toward the other. The group went so far as to state that "today both churches have cause to look back with shame to the history of mutual vilification"; and members of the discussion could openly raise the question of whether there ought to "be the admission of heavy guilt" (in Karl Lehmann and Wolfhart Pannenberg, eds., *The Condemnations of the Reformation Era: Do They Still Divide* (Minneapolis: Fortress Press, 1990), pp. 185, 20. Yet for all this acknowledgment of ecclesial failure, the questions of guilt and shame are left only as possibilities; such acknowledgments do not form the substance of an answer as to whether mutual condemnations between Christians still "stand," as if the theoretical possibility of such "vilifications" between Christians being legitimate must remain essentially open. And, as the response of some German Lutheran theologians to the report's publication demonstrated, Christian vilification is by no means a rejected ministry (cf. the discussion of this response in Wolfhart Pannenberg, "Must the Churches Continue to Condemn Each Other?" *Pro Ecclesia* 2, no. 4: pp. 404ff.). Furthermore, the Joint Commission's way of asserting the contemporary inapplicability of the sixteenth-century condemnations was, standard dialogical method, to argue for a misunderstood "commonality" between the two churches' theology from the beginning. The major difference between the sixteenth century and today is that today we have come to recognize that "it is apparently not uncommon for people to mean the same thing by different words" (Lehmann and Pannenberg, p. 17), an "insight" that has come as the fruit of a four-hundred-year intellectual evolution. Those who have been public in rejecting the commission's call for a retraction of the condemnations have at least noticed the astonishing banality of this purported historical paradigm shift. Granted that, in addition to such a new "insight," there have also been changes in the historical situation affecting the divided churches and that "new truths" have been learned in the last few centuries, the general impression left by the commission's work is not that repentance is called for, but that the churches are simply called to *ratify* a return to unity that has *already* taken place on an ideal plane. These comments are not designed, however, to question the radical, courageous, and even divinely demanded step the retraction of the condemnations represents, only to point out how, even in such a remarkable contemporary display of ecumenical risk, repentance itself remains obscured, and for reasons that lie beyond the integrity of the brave-hearted. In any case, ecumenical strategy is hardly the only reason for this kind of obscurement. In the realm of relations with non-Christians, no greater willingness to affirm corporate sin is apparent, as is evident in, for instance, the official teaching concerning anti-Semitism by the Roman Catholic Church — a vigorous condemnation of Christian anti-Judaism, glaringly bereft of any concrete admission of historical Christian sinfulness in the matter on the part of the Church in its official person. Of course, the ability to make such an admission depends on the grasp of the Christological figure whose integrity can maintain this fundamental accusation, an apprehension that the whole post-Reformation division renders logically problematic even when dealing with realities that go beyond intra-Christian claims: defectibility of such a monstrous kind must logically subvert any assertion of ecclesial integrity over and against

For Lack of Repentance

And peremptory the logic is. This is the burden of division's sin: it hides the Body, and in its place we grasp only the detritus of our own performances. If repentance is a continual conformance in time to another (historically embodied divine) image, then in impenitence, we are given over to the self-made figures of our own time; we are given over to our own history and made to wallow in it.

The inability to repent appears as a necessary aspect of the sin from which division emerges in the case of Israel. And it takes its place as a crowning insensibility ranged at the end of a host of other corporate incapacities linked to the Spirit's deprivation. The vacuum left by these withdrawals, however, is not left unfilled. Although Israel does not repent until restored in a chastened unity — until, in a sense, made the passive object of its Lord's intervention — it is nonetheless given a commission by God that precedes the recognition that will ground repentance when it comes. And that commission is to carry the burden of its history as if tendered by a present God, to give oneself over to the pneumatically derelict surfaces of time, in anticipation of their alteration, to think even a sterile history capable of patience.

Few commentators of Jeremiah 29 have perceived the constructive character of this chapter in relation to the figures of the Church's agony in Lamentations. The Fathers, like Jerome, and the medieval exegetes who followed them, had still not fully suffered the demise of Christian Israel as a body; and thus the tenor of this text was interpreted in an explicitly penitential manner congruent with their identifications of a chastised people cognizant of their condition. The Babylon in which the prophet urges the people to dwell retains, in the pre-Reformation exegesis, the figure of compunction's ordering, the "world" in which the Church moves as an alien traveler. By the time of the Reformation, this kind of coherent ecclesial self-reference no longer made sense, of course; and we find expositors like Calvin using the reference of Babylon either for moral instruction (Christians should be obedient to the state or accepting of divine punishment) or for anti-Catholic diatribes (the "false prophets" holding out hope for an easy and speedy restoration are akin to the papacy and its cohorts, offering cheap grace and perverted doctrine).

But Jeremiah's famous letter to the exiles casts a curious light when read within the shadows of fulfillment to the prophecies of Lamentations: "build

---

other denominational self-promotions. Cf. the comparison of recent documents on the matter assembled in Eugene J. Fisher and Leon Klenicki, eds., *In Our Time: The Flowering of Jewish-Catholic Dialogue* (New York/Mahwah: Paulist Press, 1990).

houses and live in them; plant gardens and eat their produce; take wives and have sons and daughters . . . multiply there, and do not decrease; but seek the welfare of the city where I have sent you into exile, and pray to the LORD on its behalf" (29:5-7). He counsels not a faithful acquiescence to a life *in via*, but an embracing of the very shape of divine abandonment embodied in their defeat. He does not advise tears; he does not suggest fasting; he does not urge a steeling of the heart against the onslaughts of a pagan master and his tribe. Israel is to suffer, like every other defeated and assimilated group, the practical forms of disaster and appeasement, open to the critical description of any sociologically sensitive observer. Hope and repentance will come later, Jeremiah insists, after the seventy years of, literally, marking time. Only "then you will call upon me and come and pray to me" (v. 12). Until "then," there is a formless existence of chronologically adjusted survival.

Is this to be read prophetically as a descriptive warning or as a figural imperative for the Church? Just as Jeremiah gave no devotional content to his letter, it is possible that the divided Church that is no Church is simply told of what the Church is, and not what the Church might make of it. Yet Jeremiah's letter is also a refutation of a set of lies about the nation (ch. 28), which prophets had tendered in an alluring but mendacious optimism concerning the brevity of Israel's captivity. In their face, he asserts that God will keep the present generations of Jews from enjoying the vision of return — seventy years, the span of a lifetime (Ps. 90:10). Only those born within the boundaries of Babylon would receive again the force of hope. Those born within divided Israel, however, must live and die as other men and women.

Yet other men and women hope falsely too, something that only Israel among the nations is divinely commanded to forsake. It so is here, in this small distinction that is made in history's otherwise uniformly dismantled cares — God's command to live in the brazen truth of disappointment — here alone is Israel's and the Church's continued touch with an alien form of graciousness. The Church cannot repent; yet it can die. The words "why have you forsaken me?" — once uttered and reiterated in the flesh of time — themselves restore the forms to time that God had given it from its foundation. "If we are faithless, he remains faithful — for he cannot deny himself" (2 Tim. 2:13). For lack of repentance, one can still assert the figure of our Lord, history can be disestablished in favor of God, simply by dying where one is and asking for no more than that God bless this dislodged place of standing.

Divided Israel actually dies. Here is the assertion of the Gospel, emblazoned with light. Though Israel will live, it will live only by seeing the literal death of its people born in division and the children born of its death. And only this figure supports "a future and a hope," in Jeremiah's words. What this might mean for a Church of churches that has come to an end, and whose accepted end is the assertion of Jesus Christ's own body, insensible in death, covered and wrapped for the sake of time's mastery — this is the subject of our concluding chapter.

Conclusion

Division and Abandonment: The Theological Sense of Ecclesial Penitence

"Jesus Christ came into the world for the sole reason of making penitents. . . . Jesus Christ came into the world for the sole reason of making people righteous."[1]

There is nothing normative for us about this particular Jansenist conviction. But it is worth noting how, at least for those Christians thus convicted, the salvation — the redemption and transformation of human life — wrought by God in Christ might embody a Church whose present times embrace a past God has already made his own. This, after all, is at the root of any positive evaluation of penitential history as God's history.

[Consider] the Babylonian captivity of seventy years, during which the promises made to Judah, that the scepter should never be taken away from her [Gen. 49:10] appeared contradicted; it is certainly possible that the defenders of the truth, who must always rule within the Church, should, with and within her, become like captives for a similar or even longer period. For in the end, what happened to the Jewish people was, according to the Apostle, the image of what would happen to us. *Haec omnia in figuris*

1. Anonymous, *Réflexions sur l'état présent de l'Église* (Amsterdam, 1731), pp. 7, 24.

335

contingebant illis, scripta sunt autem propter nos ["all these things happened to them in figure; and they are written on account of us" — 1 Cor. 10:11]. We should not be surprised, then, to see how good people within the Church are tested with respect to the promises, as were good people in Old Testament times. And one must behave in these times of testing as they behaved in their own trials. Those, for example, who are in exile, in chains, and oppressed, should console themselves as the pious Jewish captives in Babylon consoled themselves with the hope of one day seeing the rebuilding of Jerusalem and the Temple. And those who are too old to expect seeing the fulfillment of their present concerns, they should act like the elderly Tobias, who rejoiced in imagining how he would leave behind descendents who would one day see the glorious rebuilding of Jerusalem, which is nothing else than the image of that which we await in the triumph of the truth and of the Church. *Beatus ero si fuerint reliquiae seminis mei ad videndum claritatem Jerusalem* ["Happy shall I be if there shall remain of my seed, to see the glory of Jerusalem" — Tobias 13:20].[2]

These remarks, by an anonymous eighteenth-century French Jansenist Appellant, struggling to make devout sense of the movement's repudiation and marginalization by the Catholic Church's official hierarchy, demonstrate the experienced possibility of seeing the history of the Church in some measure as a penitential history; a penitential history, furthermore, whose moment achieves its form within the figure of a particularly shaped posture of repentance given providentially in the exile of Israel. And it may be worth spending a moment reflecting on the concrete conditions for such penitence from the vantage of this real, though limited, example before attempting to ground these conditions in a more general set of theological affirmations that might stand behind the "theory" of this volume as a whole.

The Appellant figural insight here, of course, was made in the midst of an ecclesial situation — the conflict over the Bull *Unigenitus* of 1713, which anathematized certain Jansenist propositions — that, on its own terms, had less to do with division than with the resistance to division of a group convinced, nonetheless, of the larger Church's doctrinal corruption. The penitence of the Jansenists was, in their own minds, quite deliberately different from the forms of *im*penitence bequeathed by the sixteenth-century divisions, but it was not self-consciously a response to those divisions. Still, even though the Appellant doctrinal concern was focused on the seemingly distinct Augustinian issues of grace and "dominating love," which Rome seemed to reject and which

2. *Réflexions sur l'état présent de l'Église*, p. 32.

spoke of penitence dogmatically, it was the movement's sensitivity to the impossibility of resolving these issues within the currents of denominational separation that went against the grain of modern Christian practice.[3] For the abandonment of the separative option among Appellants managed to fuse their dogmatic interests with an ecclesial practice that was quickly recognized as extending far beyond a particular situation to the definition of the Church's history as a whole. The Appellant (and generally Augustinian) assertion that prophecies, especially prophecies of ecclesial "ending," were ordered in Scripture toward a temporally "multiple" fulfillment in the history of the Church meant that the penitential subjugation and longing of the Christian community might be reestablished historically in diverse situations, penultimate to the affirmation of history's temporal "end."[4] In this sense, the Babylonian captivity was to be the Church's continual destiny, in time, insofar as "Jesus Christ came into the world for the sole purpose of making penitents," insofar as the Church was joined to Jesus as the penitent to its Savior and the Perfect Penitent to his beloved, insofar as the Church belongs to Jesus and Jesus is given over to the world in mastering it, and insofar as the Church's life springs from the wounded meeting of this world and its Master.

All such affirmations are logically embedded in the Appellant perspective, and are quite independent of any judgment one might make as to the actual status of the dogmatic controversies in which the perspective was embroiled. Appellancy, in any case, reluctantly acknowledged the character of the Church's penitential history in this mode of independence, to the degree that its adherents, as they often did, hesitantly admitted that the end of history — marked

---

3. Cf. *Réflexions sur l'état présent de l'Église*, p. 21. We have already noted this peculiar element in Jansenist ecclesiology, which one could argue alters fundamentally the otherwise similar Augustinian heritage shared with the Protestants. In a real way, the Jansenist inability to think of Church disputes *other* than unitively reorders the evident chauvinism and antagonistic character of Appellant ecclesial judgments, which otherwise seem so consonant, even in the language of demonization at times, with the eschatological distinctions informing the most anti-Catholic diatribes of the Reformers. Here is a case — that is, the Appellant repudiation of the separative option — where perhaps an act of communal will, simply and in itself, was able to rewrite theology. Of course, the price of this revision was an acquiescence to its own disappearance as an act of protest, an unsought humiliation whose fulfillment might have seemed to subvert the stated goals of the movement's cause, the "visible" maintenance of certain dogmatic truths. But such a case is perhaps also one wherein theology is handed back to the body of God, to be reordered in his own form.

4. Cf. *Réflexions sur l'état présent de l'Église*, pp. 27f. The notion of "multiple" prophetic fulfillments was pressed anew by Bossuet in his commentary on the book of Revelation, though its classic exposition goes back to Victorinus's own early discussion of that book in the late third century.

by Jesus' return and judgment — was not the same as the end of the Church, but that the history of the Church was the history of Christ's own ending given over to the time of the Church's conformation to him.[5] Division, apostasy, contest, and controversy — these are the end of the Church for which we do not need to wait, but into which we presently thrust ourselves by a violence comparable only to the humiliation that we discover there to be the very form of Christ Jesus given to us in time.

Which is to say, in brief, that the bereavement of Babylon is not therefore strangely apprehended by the Church. It is noted by those who will not flee and yet have ceased their fighting. Persons who wonder how a Christian can perceive the Church of Christ, can live within it and can serve it, can be nourished by its life and communion, when this Church is rendered in its historical character by the Spirit's very distance from the Church's forms — such persons as we should be consoled and led by those whose self-awareness was created by the discovery of a Temple whose very ruins could evoke a steady love. If Scripture speaks in ways we cannot hear, if holiness contracts into a form of continual argument or shrouded secret, if the shepherds lead only by groping and the body is nourished by distaste, and if the incense of the Christian life smokes fullest as the fires are allowed to burn away, all this can surely be observed and noted, not paradoxically or mystically, but simply by tying oneself to the Church as it suffers its own condition. There is grace in a dying that is merely and genuinely suffered. There is grace in living as the Church actually lives and in giving voice before God and humankind to the life this living forms. One can speak, in such a case, of the Spirit's life in the Church — divided as it is, experientially deprived of its pneumatic gifts as it is — one can speak of the "history" of the Spirit in the Church as the history of the Church's penitence, whereby withdrawal forms the temporal sphere of transformation and grace moves in a realm beyond the senses of those who are being saved, and so displays its creative nature by a retreat into its origin and ground within the hand of God.

It may seem as if *this* kind of penitence has more in common with the modern linguistic philosopher's vocation to leave the world just as it is, after seeing it more clearly, than with the restitutive activism of a convicted sinner.

---

5. Cf. *Réflexions sur l'état présent de l'Église,* pp. 25f. For Appellants like this author, the end of history was to be marked by the staggering conversion of the Jews to belief in Jesus as the Christ and by the universal and effective preaching of repentance through their instrumentality. Short of this final, and patently measurable, healing of the primitive division of Jew and Gentile only partially touched by the initial history of the Incarnation, all other divisions and controversies were evidently witnesses both to this future and to the means by which its fulfillment was guaranteed, that is, the Passion and the Cross.

And it is true that the exercise of this volume has not aimed at explicating such an activism. We have indeed merely tried to see, or at least state, and linger there where the Church lies. I do not doubt, however, that both the process of this lingering and the form discerned should have implications to which the student and practitioner of ecumenism, biblical exegesis, apologetics, evangelism, or mission ought to be attentive. But in any case, restitution lies beyond conviction, and this last is still unfolding for the Church, unless of course the loss of love be redeemed in the very act of losing self.

If then this is the divided Church, this abandoned Church left dangled at a distance from the Spirit, this Church at its end within the history of its endings, let us finally raise three questions that the theologian might pose before the face of such a history. First, can such a Church be the Church of Jesus Christ? Second, how shall we trust the Jesus whose Church this is (or conversely, trust that precisely *this* is the Church that is his)? And finally, how shall our trust in the Lord of our Church be given shape? The first is a theologically systematic question; the second is a question dealing with the scriptural hermeneutics of history; the third touches upon the ascetic impulse sprung at the heart of the Church itself.

The systemic issue — how the pneumatically deprived Church, that is, in this case, the divided Church, is in fact the Church of Jesus Christ — has been discussed obliquely in our first chapter and explored topically in the course of the chapters that followed. Drawing these observations together in a summary way, we can point to several elements that any systematic pneumatology of ecclesial division must attempt to make coherent: the theoretical derivation of the Church's phenomenal character from the actual historical character of Christ's own being as the incarnate Son; the relation, then, of this latter Christological reality to the actual shape of the Church's life as it has taken (divided) form in history and claims pneumatic ordering; and, finally, the general "end" toward which we can orient the reality of division in particular within the divine salvific will, that is, within the love of God who creates and redeems his works. The adumbrating of these elements, of course, presupposes the validity of the penitential impulse with respect to ecclesial division in the first place. And as a "theory," a penitential history of division was given over, in much of this book, to a process of testing: does the impulse itself makes sense; and are alternative reactions to division, many of them still controlling our ecclesial and theological practice, in any way compelling? Simply listing the elements of the systematic question as we have done expresses the answer to this test: Christian division gives necessary rise to penitence *because* the Church derives its form from Christ's incarnate body and remains bound to this body in time, and hence cannot escape, even in its sin, the controlling love of God.

In our first chapter, two parallel theological traditions emerged that might support a connection between a pneumatically abandoned Church and its Lord; both traditions depended upon a primacy given to the notion of Christ's "body" applied to the Church. One claim derived from the ascetical configuraion of the *mors mystica,* the ordered process by which the Christian soul is drawn into intimate union with God through its conformance to the incarnational and passional deprivations experienced by Christ Jesus. The second claim, founded more on exegetical practice and hermeneutical principle, affirmed the Church's phenomenal shape as borne in unity with Israel through their common form as Christ's "figural" body. We have seen how aspects of these two traditions reasserted themselves in various ways, both negatively and positively, in the face of the experience of ecclesial division: division contradicted the ecclesial virtues affirmed by these traditions, but also unleashed alternative theological outlooks that spawned logically unsuccessful circumventions of their basic commitments. Although contemporary ecumenical theories have attempted to recapture the original virtues of ecclesial unity, they have been hampered by a retention of the circumventing logic of division. One is left with the impression that the theological traditions explicating the phenomenal character of the Church in terms of the "body of Christ" deserve revisited scrutiny, especially as they are now applied to the actual form of the Church in division.

Such a systematic application of the ascetic and hermeneutic perspectives would yield a far more historically subtle ecclesiology of the Mystical Body than has heretofore generally been allowed. Take, for example, the general Thomistic principles governing the relationship of Christ with his Body, a relation of "subsisting" grace or holiness, by which our being is "justified" through our being joined to his Trinitarian "sonship."[6] If this Trinitarian unity of Father and Son devolves by grace, and through the incarnate human nature of the Son to the "members" of Christ — his Body, the Church — then it becomes possible to align phenomenally both the ascetic and the exegetically distinct elements of the Son's life with the life of the Church, precisely ordered around the character of "unity." The "unity" of Father and Son and the unity of the Church have always been seen in these terms, not only by Roman Catholics, but by Protestants like Calvin, who used the foundational text in John 17 in this context as an explicator, among other things, of his own version of Eucharistic "participation."[7] The historical relation of unity between Father and Son, however, has not always been construed in such a way as to admit within it any defining force for the passional experience of abandonment,

6. Cf. Thomas Aquinas, *Summa Theologiae* III, 23:4.
7. See above, Chapter 4.

whose details are given scripturally but whose systematic force has generally been taken up only within the ascetical traditions of individual contemplative deprivation, or more recently in the deliberately nonascetical theologies of historical theodicy, like the early Moltmann.

The exception to this tendency is found almost exclusively within aspects of the so-called French School of devotional theology in the seventeenth century. Bérulle, most famously, elaborated a Trinitarian theology of "annihilation," wherein the "love" of God made incarnate in the Son, yet immanent in the relations themselves, was properly understood in terms of a kind of "separation" and "humiliation" by the Son, through which love could be mutually rendered in the form of glorification. The humanly devotional implications of this Trinitarian vision are well known, giving rise to the revitalized "victim" spirituality of the seventeenth and later eighteenth centuries.

More acutely attuned to the systematic issues at stake was the stunning work of Louis Chardon, *The Cross of Jesus,* published in 1647, four years before his death. Chardon's volume — inexplicably no longer read today[8] — builds up a Trinitarian theology of the mystical life that is both bound to the careful Thomistic theological metaphysics regnant in the author's own Dominican order and creatively applied to the ascetic shape of spiritual (especially contemplative) justice. Chardon works from Thomistic notions of the Mystical Body subsisting, through grace, in the incarnate personhood of the Son and thereby moving into union with God; but he delves deeply into the significance of the historical aspects of the Incarnation itself as expressing the character of that divine grace. From this perspective, the infinite "liberality" of divine love, moving toward a "plenitude" of creaturely glorification, is seen as intrinsically informed by a "weight" towards the Cross, in that such infinite love achieves its fullest end only through the voluntary humiliation of its glory in assuming the curse and suffering of sin. If the historical experience of the Cross is thus seen as the paradoxical character of

---

8. A modern French edition of Louis Chardon, *The Cross of Jesus,* given by R. P. F. Florand, O.P., appeared in 1937 (Paris: Éditions du Cerf); and I am told that an English translation was made in America in the 1950s, although I have not been able to locate it. Chardon's work is, of course, known to specialists in seventeenth-century French spirituality. But as a genuine and original theological masterpiece, it deserves a far wider audience. Florand's edition contains a rich historical and theological introduction, summarizing scholarship he had marshaled in a number of earlier articles. There is much in Chardon's perspective that is consonant with Bérullian spirituality, but Florand makes a convincing argument that Chardon's sources and inspiration were far more narrowly found in the Dominican tradition of Thomistic exegesis and dogmatics — in the line of Cajetan, Jacobo Nacchiante, and Giovanni-Paulo Nazari — studied in conjunction with the broad contemplative tradition, Dionysian and Spanish, that was dominant in seventeenth-century French mystical theology.

divine grace, then the Trinitarian relations undergirding the Incarnation itself must be rearticulated so as both to express the unity-in-love of the Three Persons in a manner that includes the willed contradiction of "plenitude" and to delimit the historical shape of the Trinity's "indwelling," through sanctifying grace, in the souls of the "just members" of Christ's Body.[9]

The daring aspects of this kind of orientation appear especially in the pneumatological implications involved. While one may wish to continue to uphold traditional Trinitarian images of "communion" and mutuality among the persons, the fact that the divine "love" that describes the Trinitarian relations cannot be divorced from the willful release of such manifest mutual grounding with respect to the Son indicates a crucial disjunction of Son and Spirit, especially made evident just at the moment when the temporal phenomena of divine love are brought to their clearest expression in the Passion and death of Jesus. The perceived "abandonment" of the Son by the Father on the Cross is established as a full expression of the Trinitarian life only to the degree that the Crucifixion as a whole is understood as a *pneumatic* abandonment of the first order. Chardon explains this as the manner in which "love separates the Son from the Holy Spirit and from His own self," the Spirit's withdrawal itself revealing, as through a curtain drawn, the sacrifice of the Son in the face of the Father. As with others — for example, John Paul II — who have meditated on the pneumatological character of atonement, the basic text here is Hebrews 9:14, "Christ, who through the Spirit offered himself without blemish to God." The Spirit is, in a sense, the "crucifier," both as the "bond of love" (in the Augustinian sense) who joins Son to Father and also, because of that, as the dissolution of that bond within the life of the Triune God itself that allows for a costly, because saving, self-offering.

> As if it were not enough that you [i.e. the Spirit] made him languish upon this Cross of horror that holds him tightly to itself in a material way. Was it necessary that you work deeply within his soul an even more disastrous Cross, by withdrawing from Him those ravishing consolations that you owed Him as the only Son of God Almighty and as the most beautiful of His works? Without Him, you would lack, as would the Father and the Son, an uncreated end to your work of love. O Son without a Father! O God without God! And, yes, O Jesus without Jesus! for Jesus covered in insults is without the Jesus filled with glory. How Jesus now contradicts Jesus. How Jesus who rejoices has no mercy on Jesus who suffers. O Jesus, Cross of Jesus![10]

9. Cf. Chardon, I:5, 12, and 17.
10. Chardon, I:22; cf. I:20ff. for a fuller discussion of "separating love" in Trinitarian terms.

342

The "contradiction" noted here is hardly a theological novelty. A certain strand of contemplative negative theology had long explored it even before Luther made of it a centerpiece of his reforming "theology of the Cross." But that a specifically Christian pneumatology should be founded on this divine contradiction has rarely been asserted, even Luther preferring to make use of a certain functionalist attitude to the Spirit's "efficacious" operations in fructifying the work of Christ and faith, not so different from earlier medieval understandings of the pneumatic character of sanctification. But the realm of holiness, in the perspective we are outlining, will, in a sense, conform in its shape more generally, and irrespective of the specific divisional realities we have been studying, to the tendencies we in fact noted above in Chapter 2 as surrounding the very experience of division: obscurity and abandonment to the unordered notation of contested blessings. For this is the order of love too within the Mystical Body of the Son, the Church, whose life is impregnated with the very being of the Trinity's own projection of the Son into the isolated and lonely prominence of time. For Chardon, the apostolic life upon which the Church as Christ's Body is founded is given its propulsion by a resurrected Jesus — there is no danger here of relegating the Resurrection to an after-thought — whose demand for love (e.g, to Peter in John 21:17), a love given only in the indwelling to the "uncreated" love of the Spirit, can find no origin and continuance except in the repentance born of a sense of separation from the self-giving Lord.[11] The Spirit's presence in the Church presses always to the moment of perfect holiness and love when Jesus himself touched death alone.

It should be clear that pneumatic "abandonment," in this context, does not mean a deprivation of the spiritual gifts and "fruit" that form the basis of satisfaction for just persons. It is rather a question of the historical experience of this grace, which "appears" to rob the object of the Spirit's indwelling of an open apprehension of such presence, love forming itself, as it were, through its own consistent self-questioning. The appearance, however, is not an illusion in this case, because the Spirit's intimate work is accomplished — again, in figural conjunction with Jesus' own life — through the phenomenal assertion of its own distance. Applied to the Mystical Body of the Church, then, one would say that it is created and ordered by the same "separating" Trinitarian grace whose temporal manifestation lies in the suffering of this pneumatic withdrawal. And a pneumatically abandoned Church will be the Church of Jesus Christ insofar as it is the Body of the Son whom the Spirit abandons to the Father's sacrifice of love.

11. Chardon, I:23.

In a general way, it might be possible to accept this construal if, in fact, we hold rigorously to a simple Jesus-Church typology, whose intimacy would ground a certain New Testament exegetical figuralism with respect to the Church. Chardon can do this rather extensively with regard to the experiences of the "just" in the Church, understood in contemplative terms. The second half of his book, for instance, is given over to an examination of particular "consolations," "desolations," and "spiritual crosses" by which the Triune God "communicates" himself to the members of Christ's Body; the use of figurative exegesis that Chardon applies in these discussions is less exemplary, as in the style of much spiritual instruction, than it is properly figural, as can be seen in his broad use of the method in the more strictly systematic section of Part I (cf. I:7). Still, even on distinctive presuppositions like Chardon's, the pneumatic "abandonment" of the Church will always be provoked by the *positive* thrust toward ascetic purgation, toward the leaving behind of glory for the sake of love, toward the loosening of the world's grasp in favor of heaven's, and the like. While he ends his volume with a number of specifically Old Testament figures (e.g., Elijah, Jacob, Abraham, Benjamin), they have by this point devolved into figures of individual righteousness, through suffering, rather than standing as figures of the larger history of Israel, taken up in Christ. The idea of the Church "suffering" in the figure of Christ is, after all, fairly traditional and unexceptional if understood as limited by the Church's *integrity* — it patiently bears the ravages of heretics and persecutors, and does this out of the caritative core that is the Spirit leading the Church away from the Church's own self. But it is hardly clear that a reading such as this admits of the inclusion of willful sin from which division arises as the contradiction of the church's caritative core within the figure of love itself, which alone allows for the Trinitarian construal just suggested.

This brings us to the second of our questions, one which, in a sense, fills out the intent of the first: how shall we trust that *this* pneumatically deprived Church, which is specifically a sinfully divided Church, is the Church of Jesus Christ? And the realm in which this question is addressed is more hermeneutic than systematic, because it asks us to discern some kind of identity between a phenomenal entity and an ideal reference given, at its origin, in Scripture. It is important to be precise, and also consistent, in this matter. If Scripture speaks of Jesus as the Christ, and if it also speaks of the Church of Christ, it is not enough simply to draw the two together in a general figural fashion under the rubric of the "Body of Christ," because such a relation remains loose until it can clarify particular churches, or rather the Church at particular times, as being that Body in a way that is faithful to the relation as it is in fact expressed in Scripture. Modern ecclesiology of the Body of Christ has generally failed in such precision, perhaps in order to include the manifest failings of the Church in a way that can bypass their essential influence upon (separative) ecclesial practice itself, a pattern with which we are now familiar. If we let go of the particularities of scriptural reference in favor of other modern strategies of relating historical body to divine reality, we can easily set aside the foundationally penitential impetus of pneumatic abandonment for the sake of a more amenable figural relation.

Let us take but one example. The great Catholic theologian Karl Adam was able to promote a rich ecclesiology of the Body of Christ capable of incorporating the Church's historical failures into its fabric. But he did so only by forbidding the figural relation of Church and Christ to particularize itself on any scriptural level other than that of general principle.[12] Christ's *exinantio,* or self-emptying, he insisted, was to be apprehended as the Church's too, in its historical existence, and he was clear that this kenotic character of the Body, incarnationally shared between Savior and Redeemed, be expressed historically even in the sinful limitations experienced by the Christian community. These limitations were to be found in "structural," "cultural," and purely temporal variations and changes, each of which might well give rise even to the phenomena of heresy and division.[13] These kinds of ecclesial vicissitudes are viewed by Adam as "necessary" according to the figure of Christ's own "necessary sufferings" (e.g., in Matt. 16:21 and Luke 24:26); but it is interesting that Adam interprets this "necessity" in terms of a kind of historicist philosophy of time: to the degree that the Church is a temporal phenomenon, the various elements of historical existence — structural and cultural *change* — are built into its existence, and the Reformation divisions themselves are thereby explained as "inevitable" sociohistorical alterations, albeit negative ones, of an entity that could in any case never escape such burdens.[14] "Historical existence" in general, then, becomes the kenotic figure of the Incarnation, a principle that shifts the entire project of analyzing the Church's failures away from the particularities of scriptural discernment and toward more categorical ontological frameworks. And this is a shift, broadly speaking, that characterizes much modern discussion of the Church's seeming imperfections, apparent in the common argument, given sociohistorical grounding, that the Church has

---

12. Cf. Karl Adam, "The Mystery of Christ's Incarnation and of His Mystical Body," *Orate Fratres* 13 (1939).

13. "The self-abasement of the body of Christ will consist in this, that the 'visible sign' does not reveal its supernatural meaning and content but conceals it, and that for those of the faithful who are unable to penetrate its true nature, it becomes an occasion of fall rather than of resurrection" (Adam, p. 394).

14. Cf. Adam, pp. 399 and 437ff.

"always" been divided and that "division" and "diversity" represent aspects of the same set of historical constraints within which the Church takes form. Thus, Adam's final theological appeal to the Church's "eschatological" character, moving "by faith" *in statu viae,* as a pilgrim on an unfinished and imperfect journey, is an ecclesiological move already familiar to us as a post-Reformation adaptation to the failure of penitence.

It is doubtful, however, if this kind of transposition of ecclesial "sin" into ecclesial "weakness," determined by the fate of history, really addresses the central question of how to discern the Church's pneumatic deprivation in division as Christologically, that is, figurally, coherent. Since it is exactly this question that post-Reformation Western theology has deliberately sought to avoid, it is hardly surprising if its answer is not ready at hand in the various strands of our confessional traditions. Indeed, if our study has had any merit, it would be to indicate that the answer cannot be had by some kind of formulated principle at all, but only by tracing the existence of the Church in its particular choices and acts and by discerning the objects of its penitential response, in relation to the will of God for the Church's life and future. If, in a condition of obstructed hearing, the Church is thrown back upon the primordial practice of "searching the Scriptures" even to come to know the love and righteousness of Christ — as we stated in Chapter 1 — how much more so to perceive the Church's own form in relation to such righteousness and love! The actual relation between Christ and his Body, then, cannot be given in advance, through the application of a confessionally distinct framework or set of dogmatic principles, but must be teased out from the welter of stated relations with which God articulates his will. The Church cannot come to a realization of its being as Christ's Body — and thus, even a systematic exposition of the Church's nature like Chardon's must remain a conclusion and not a point of departure — until the Church has passed through the range of particular locations wherein God has expressed its form and then attempted a determination of its posture before his face, whose conjunction with Christ is then discerned. This must surely be true for a Church that apprehends, however dimly, its own pneumatic aimlessness: it must attempt, at least, to moor its image in the figures of Scripture through which it will discover its rootedness in Christ's own form.

This is not, as mentioned, a common discipline. But let us, once again, take as an example of the practice the eighteenth-century Appellant subgenre on "the promises to the Church," examples that are offered here in their "typical," rather than historically normative, character.[15] Those Catholics who

---

15. Here we refer to three typical examples of the genre: Nicholas LeGros, *Lettres à Monseigneur l'Evesque de Soissons sur les promesses faites a l'église,* 2nd ed. (Amsterdam, 1738);

opposed the teaching of Bull *Unigenitus* on the grounds that it seemed to outlaw sound and essential doctrine were faced with a difficult puzzle ecclesiologically: how could one stay bound to a Church whose leadership had apparently attacked basic truths of the Gospel? Such attacks, in the Jansenist ideology, were only the culminating expression of a corruption of moral and ecclesiastical discipline that had for some time been rotting out the core of the Church's integrity; but they were decisive in that they now were made with the power of severe sanctions (e.g., excommunication, imprisonment, banishment, etc.). The Protestant response to such a situation was that of separating from purported idolatry, and we have spent some time in examining this response from differing aspects. The Appellants, on the other hand, worked from an intuited sense of unbreakable solidarity with the Roman Church, and then attempted to ascertain how such a Church could still be Christ's Church in such a way as to demand continued allegiance.

The intuition of solidarity was not, to be sure, left unquestioned. Appellant theologians looked to the figure of Jesus and the Temple authorities, and also contested Christian communities, like Corinth, as examples of ecclesial "unbreakability" through "submission" and humility, even in relation to error.[16] If there is separation — as between the early Christians and the Jews after the destruction of the Temple — they determined that it can only come about by an "act of God" and must, in any case, remain relative (and so judged negatively) to a final restoration. The problem lay in the sense in which one could still speak of "Church" if the Church was riven by antievangelical error even of a doctrinal nature. The figure of Jesus "submitting" to Israel (in the form of its leaders), however, was clearly a precedent here, which thrust the Appellant scriptural student back into the biblical record of the Jewish nation as a whole.

If visible Israel remained Israel throughout the Old Testament, and remained the object and bearer of God's indefectible "promises" and covenant, then surely it was in terms of these Old Testament forms that the "promises of Jesus to the Church" — promises of similar indefectibility, perhaps even infallibility — needed to be viewed. The anti-Appellant and official position

---

Daniel-Charles-Gabriel de Postel de Lévis de Turières de Caylus, *Lettres de Monseigneur l'Evêque d'Auxerre à Monseigneur l'Éveque de Soissons, Au sujet des accusations intentées par M. l'Evêque de Soissons contre les Appellans* (n.p., 1723); Dominique-Marie Varlet, *Lettres d'un écclésiastique de Flanders. A M. l'Éveque de Soissons* (Utrecht, 1729). All these works were written in response to the arguments of the anti-Appellant bishop of Soissons, Jacques-Joseph Languet de Gergy, who had accused the Appellant demand for a General Council to decide the issue of the disputed doctrines condemned by *Unigenitus* of destroying the "promises" made to the Church, especially those of indefectibility and infallibility.

16. Cf. de Caylus, Letter I, pp. 62ff.

that these "promises" applied to the "whole Church at all times" faltered, Appellants argued, in the face of historical reality, which demonstrated clearly over time that there was *no* unanimity, no perfect righteousness, no consistent display of miracles and the like within the Church. And if the promises of the Church were not to be emptied through a process of increased abstraction from history, then the only recourse lay in exploring the figural relations between sinful, yet divinely beloved, Israel and the Church that bore that nation's continued identity.[17] This move, obviously, encouraged the kind of unitive figuralist reading of Scripture associated with Jansenism in general.

By and large, the conclusion was drawn that the Church remained the Church of Christ over time through the existence of a "remnant," whose presence within the larger body in doctrinal integrity and righteousness and love guaranteed the continuity of a sufficient object for the promises of God to his people. Though even the Pope be wrong, and the whole hierarchy with him, the fact that somewhere in the Church some small number of laypeople or priests — in the manner of Elijah and the several thousand who had not bent the knee to Baal — were still faithful marked the Catholic Church as yet the Church of Jesus.[18] This was a potentially chauvinist position, to be sure. And "remnant theology" had already seen itself put to use by Protestant separatists. But in fact Appellant ecclesiology did not atrophy into a series of repeated Puritan insistences — the application of the true/false grid of doctrine and discipline to locate the true/false churches of time according to a set series of typological denominators. Eighteenth-century Appellant theology of the Church instead evolved into a long and unsystematic exercise in the figural exegesis of the Old Testament, whose extent embraced a great diversity of variously pertinent devotional material.

Two commitments, one ecclesiological and the other hermeneutic, determined that this unsystematic figural exercise be maintained without an obvious closure by which separation itself could be upheld. (The end of the Church, to repeat, could not be equated with the end of history.) The first was the Jansenists' generally Catholic retention of the Augustinian assertion of the Church as a *corpus permixtum,* whose continuous existence in time as a single Body made up of both the elect and the (eventually) reprobate limited any discussion of the remnant to one of only presupposed presence, as opposed to precisely discerned identity.[19] The second, more hermeneutic, commitment focused on a refusal to identify the "final" apostasy of the Antichrist, as

17. Cf. LeGros, Letter 4, pp. 359ff.
18. Cf. LeGros, pp. 415ff.
19. Cf. LeGros, pp. 418ff.

described in Scripture, with any presently experienced historical corruption of the Church such as to demand a "final separation" from an ecclesially inherent demonism, because Scripture itself limited this ultimate distinction between the "faithful" and the "apostate" to the discretion of a divinely intervening judgment. Hence, on the basis of Scripture's own prophecies, it was impossible for the members of the Church ever to determine in history the "end of history" for which a willed ecclesial division could be justified.[20] And this self-conscious distinction in which Appellancy held itself from Protestantism engendered an intrinsic indeterminacy of certain figural applications to the Church. While one could be certain that a "faithful remnant" indwelt the Church and justified the promises made to the Church by Christ, one could not with certainty identify that remnant. Further, because of this tension, the ecclesial exegete was thrust back upon a mode of scriptural discernment that did not aim for the apprehension of directives that were specific to individual vocations within this mixed body, but instead grasped after the figural location of those virtues that the experience of the Church's inner struggle required as a whole.

This process itself was explained figurally, for example through an explication of Rebecca as the Church: within her womb fought the two "peoples" — Jacob and Esau, the Elect, or Remnant, and the Reprobate — whose perpetual and often bitter contest amongst themselves defined the historical experience of the Church in its integrity, but always a Church that, despite this *interior* conflict, remained at unity with itself, through its visible maintenance of communion between promise and warning, mercy and justice.[21] It was not possible to distinguish ostensibly the two peoples of the Church except to the degree that a *single* historical experience was given to each under different aspects: to the Elect, the warning emerged in the posture of penitence, and to the reprobate, the promises emerged in a posture of complacency, which taken together describe the shape of Israel. In typical Jansenist fashion, then, the conviction that only a "few" would be saved and that the remnant would be small did not give rise to locating a genealogy of the elect independent of the institutional Church.[22] Instead, the conviction issued in an awakening to the character by which the promises to the Church are actually fulfilled in their

20. Cf. Varlet, Letter 8 (unpag.).

21. Cf. LeGros, pp. 418ff.

22. A useful discussion of Jansenist ecclesiology as it works from the conviction of the "small number of the elect" can be found in Louis Cognet's "Note sur le P. Quesnel et sur l'ecclésiologie de Port-Royal," *Irenikon* 21 (1948): pp. 326-32 and 439-46. Cognet demonstrates the continuity of this outlook from the seventeenth-century Jansenists through at least the early-eighteenth-century Appellants, and also provides a fair, and on this topic rare, discussion of the unusual commitment to unity this Augustinian position engendered.

salvific guise: in penitence, in humility, and in suffering, which necessarily defines the unity of the Church in its historical continuity. The end of the Church, in both its goal and its term, is grasped in the willingly humiliated acceptance of the truth's contestation. The heart of the Church reflects a continual suffering of the rejection of God's love. In this sense, the sinfulness of the Church's ways joins it to the form of its being, that is, to the true body of Christ Jesus, whose flesh conjoined with the "curse of sin."[23]

Ecclesiology as figural exegesis, then, is the outcome of a perpetual struggle to apprehend the unity of the Church as the suffering of dispute, within which the figure of Jesus emerges and controls. It is this figure that alone is able to transform the otherwise potentially paralyzing reality of pneumatic withdrawal into a positive Christian mission. We have already argued that, from a providential perspective, the Jansenist promotion of a spirituality of suspended judgment about vocation and Eucharistic participation, for instance, is consonant with the general post-Reformation struggle with a novel skeptical intractability; it was a spirituality that, at least on a dogmatic level, was upheld by their stern notions of the veiled realities of predestination whose devotional character of "fearful hope," in turn, distinguished their Augustinian commitments from developed Reformed concerns with salvific "assurance." The Appellant conviction that unity with the visible Church was a necessary, if not sufficient, condition for Christian salvation was tied to this skepticism about individual futures whose status was intrinsically bound up with their continued participation in a caritative context.

For our purposes all we need to observe is how there can emerge from this particular area of devotional ferment an experiential affirmation that pneumatic obscurity, within the realm of the individual Christian's life, is itself bound to and conducive of a turn to the communion of the contested Church. The issue of the Church's sin is not thereby normalized so much as given over to the sacrificial power of the Lord, under whose looming figural sway the individual can only adjust him- or herself with a trembling, though desirous, expectation of transfigurative, but also purgative, conformation — that is, penitence. The judgmental aspects of pneumatic withdrawal, then, ought to be acknowledged as such and suffered as such; but they ought also to be seen as assumed by Christ Jesus as fully as all sin, and thus suffered by the Christian not only as a sentence, but as a sentence whose prior breadth of embrace by God's Son holds out a participatory invitation.

Pneumatic abandonment as a Trinitarian reality, then, does not somehow set in motion its own historical repetition in the Church, in the form of some

23. Cf. De Caylus, pp. 43ff.

fated "economic" self-expression; rather, it autonomously redeems the history of the Church's own rejection of its prior and foundational love. And the Church's figural conformity to such Trinitarian caritative "separation" is not its sin and pneumatically deprived condition, which it can justify according to some schema of process eschatology. Rather, the Church is "truly" the figure of Christ Jesus only in its acquiescence to the *justice* of this condition and in its own willingness to let abandonment be taken up into the transformation that love's separative impulse enacts. Enacts, but also, within time, proffers through "promises" the Scriptures themselves formally describe.

This brings us to our third concluding question, which touches upon the practical shape that the Christian and the churches of today's Christians embody within this history. It is the (in)sensible realities of pneumatic obscurement that thrust both the individual and individual churches back upon the figure of the Church as a whole, that is, upon the visible providential shapes that the Church as a single figural identity assumes. Each of our chapters on the loss of ecclesial spiritual capacity has pointed to this direction of movement. As the pneumatic senses of the Church, in its fragmented and torn existence, weaken or are numbed, confusion and contestation become the increasingly burdensome fruit of their own initial planting. The thickets of this harvest are not so much gathered to be tossed aside, as treaded and traversed, in search of the pattern to their sowing and the image there reflected of the self. The figural search for the Church in Israel is, in this sense, propelled by the Church's own pneumatic condition, both as a preservative in certain times and, in our own day, as an outcome to the Church's present disposition. It was, after all, the rejections and redemption of a people by which God's form in Christ was historically indicated; and the Church's indicative clarity as his Body is established in the same historical locutions, as St. Paul describes it in Romans 9–11. The relation between natural and unnatural branches to the one root as Paul explains it, is, in the end, the same, except that the "promises" that underlie their common history stand toward experience as a gracious embrace that does not preclude the particular conjunctions of justice and mercy that each will suffer in its own way. To find oneself as a Christian in this context takes place only as one finds the whole people of God — including the Jews — in its relation to this single, though variegated, scriptural figure; to find the life of a particular church takes place only as one finds the life of the whole Church in the same relation.

In each case, though, such finding is not constructed upon the ground that every Christian or every Christian community *is* the Church in its *integrity* — a peculiarly modern conceit in its separative logic, as if churches and individuals were free to renew themselves, to forge new strategies for construction and accomplishment according to resources independent of the whole's figural constraint.[24] The history of *this* penitence excludes the effective discernment of such strategies and their promotion. To say that individual churches are each the Church is only to say that each becomes the Church through suffering the condition of the whole as it cries out for and is given over to the redemptive and abandoned body of our Lord. Affirming, enacting, and protecting this identity, which itself manifests the person of Christ Jesus as a savior, because the person of his own Body, is to voice God's promise to the Church. This is also to say that penitence, as it is ecclesially moored and expressed, stands as a historically necessary aspect of love. Let no church or Christian think that the love of God given in Jesus Christ takes some form, in this day, unrooted in the soil, deep and dark, of penitence.

Many denominational boundaries in our day are crumbling, but not to the onslaught of ecclesial reconciliation. They are, rather, weakened by new divisions, drawn along reconstituted maps of theological and ideological commitment and further etched by the advanced and skeptical narcissism of cultural consumerism. No doubt God is working his purposes out. But there is hardly any reason for a Christian to suppose that in this divine labor today some new gateway has been opened to an escape from the captivity of division's exile, as if discernment in our era demanded that we wager on the bits of the Church that will survive this present set of social realignments, bets that involve our ecclesial participations. This cannot be what penitence will mean. It must mean, instead, some profound kind of staying put even while the place in which we stand is beaten down and reconfigured from its bottom up into a new household.

For we have already argued that the penitence of the pneumatically deprived Church is maddeningly antiprogrammatic, since it is enforced rather than constructed, discovered rather than orchestrated. It involves a willing continuance in the very arenas in which incapacity first surfaced — in reading Scripture, in viewing the holy, in leading and serving, in sharing the Lord's body and blood in their constricted offer — yet now with an eye to their unordered functions and unrealized instrumentalities, as frustration slowly transfigures itself into patience, and patience bears the clanging of the word's loud gong, the crashing of the mountains faith has destroyed together, the blur

24. For an unintentionally clear example of this relation between conceit and logic, wherein conservative separatism is buttressed, ironically, by the principles of the liberal ecclesial affirmationism that has its roots in the same separatist logic, cf. Alvin F. Kimel, Jr., "Being Church: Theological Theses on Parish and Diocese," *Sewanee Theological Review* 31, no. 1 (1994): pp. 54-69.

of mystery's infinite unveiling, and the cold of spoliated wealth, that in bearing this quieting of every boast, the Church might find beyond these stilled pretensions that love endures in a body only God can finally own (1 Cor. 13). Let no Christian church or individual think that the penitence arising from a true consideration of the Church's history, its history under God, takes some form in this day unoriented toward the wholly self-subjecting love for separated or even "lost" Christian sisters and brothers.

A paradigmatic debate of early modern ecclesial reformation would then find a certain de facto catholic resolution. The debate between the Jansenist Saint-Cyran and St. Vincent de Paul — and more proverbial than real — centered on just this question of repentance.[25] Saint-Cyran is said to have pronounced the following judgment in the hearing of St. Vincent de Paul: "God is finally wearied of the sins of all these regions [of the Church]; He is filled with wrath and has resolved to take away our faith, of which we are unworthy. It would be the height of temerity to oppose the designs of God and decide to defend the Church, which He has decided to let go of. For my part, I wish to work for this [divine] plan to destroy it." It should be said that Saint-Cyran was speaking only metaphorically here — he believed in the indefectibility and perpetuity of the Catholic Church as Christ's own Body. But he did seem to feel that the Church's visible disintegration in his day might indeed be according to the will of God. And to join oneself to this will would be to enter more fully into the life of the crucified Son whose Body the Church in fact is. If this was indeed Saint-Cyran's view, he gave it form through a method less of external troublemaking (a false charge of his enemies) than of interior subversion, by which he taught and pressed his notions of the Church's orthodox bequest through the conversation of his fasting and his prayers, a window onto which he left open for the scrutiny of his friends. As if to say, Let them know that I die *with* the Church, by suffering her own rejection of my sense of truth! His was an ecclesial communion perceived and stretched

25. The events behind this exchange are recorded in a conversation of 1650 by Vincent de Paul, included in Louis Abelly's seventeenth-century biography of the saint. There is doubt about the authenticity of the episode. However, it is probably true that Saint-Cyran did speak of God's plan to "destroy the Church" in some fashion, using the verse from Ecclesiastes 3:3. Cf. S. Vincent de Paul, *Correspondance, Entretiens, Documents,* ed. Pierre Coste (1923), vol. 8, p. 335; Saint-Cyran obliquely admitted to the phrase, although he hedged on its meaning, during a later official interrogation (cf. de Paul, vol. 13, p. 125). Pierre Coste discusses the relation between the two men in vol. 3 of his 1932 biography of de Paul, *Grand Saint du Grand Siècle.* Also, see Jean Orciban, *Jean Duvergier de Hauranne, Abbé de Saint-Cyran et son temps (1581–1638)* (Paris: J. Vrin, 1947), pp. 576-81 and appendix (1948), pp. 28-33, for detailed references.

across a chasm of conviction, which deprived him, quite deliberately, of any purchase on the Church's future, so that at least he might share the Church's present fate.

Ranged against Saint-Cyran's reading of the Church's time as the *tempus destruendi* — the time of tearing down in Ecclesiastes 3:3 — St. Vincent de Paul offered a response to his erstwhile friend's remark:

> Alas, gentlemen; perhaps he is right in asserting that God wishes to take the Church away from us on account of our sins. . . . But this author of heresy is a liar when he says that it is the height of temerity to oppose God in this plan and to spend oneself in preserving the Church or defending it. For God asks us to do this, and we must do it. There is no temerity in fasting, in mortifying oneself, in praying in order to pacify the wrath of God or in fighting to the very end to sustain the Church and to defend her in every place that she is found.

Perhaps it *is* God's will to bring the Church to its end. But in this case, it is not the Church that must die, but we ourselves, in giving ourselves over to its fictive welfare.

In the penitential figure of the Church, such attitudes as these — contrasting in their mode of activism perhaps — seem rather to embrace: the Church dies, as if I might live with her; I die, as if the Church might live with me. O Church without the Church! O Jesus without Jesus! O love without our love. . . .

There is no doubt that forms of such a penitential activism will *not* leave the churches alone, but will trouble and excite. How could the actual shape of ecumenical labor, missionary outreach and evangelism, apologetics, not to mention the voicing and the settling of disputes, be left untouched by such a patience? But patience, by definition, cannot manipulate the facts of history. The mystery of the Holy Spirit is that these facts, embodied by the Church, have been let loose for Christ alone to order as he in fact has ordered. O Church of Jesus! Your servants love her very rubble and are moved to pity even for her dust (Ps. 102:14)!

Index of Names and Subjects

Only the names of those writers contributing to the
main argument of the book are included here.

Index of Scripture References